C6

Also by Mike Davis

City of Quartz

Prisoners of the American Dream

ECOLOGY OF FEAR

ECOLOGY

OF FEAR

LOS ANGELES
AND THE
IMAGINATION
OF DISASTER

**MIKE
DAVIS**

METROPOLITAN BOOKS
HENRY HOLT AND COMPANY
NEW YORK

Metropolitan Books
Henry Holt and Company, Inc.
Publishers since 1866
115 West 18th Street
New York, New York 10011

Metropolitan Books™ is an imprint of
Henry Holt and Company, Inc.

Published in Canada by Fitzhenry & Whiteside Ltd.
195 Allstate Parkway, Markham, Ontario L3R 4T8

Library of Congress Cataloging-in-Publication Data
Davis, Mike, 1946–
Ecology of fear : Los Angeles and the imagination
of disaster / Mike Davis. — 1st ed.
p.   cm.
Includes bibliographical references and index.
ISBN 0-8050-5106-6 (hb : alk. paper)
1. Social problems—California—Los Angeles. 2. Disasters—
California—Los Angeles. 3. Los Angeles (Calif.)—Social
conditions. 4. Los Angeles (Calif.)—Environmental conditions.
I. Title.
HN80.L7D37   1998
303.48'5'0979494—dc21   98-2645
                                                   CIP

Henry Holt books are available for special promotions
and premiums. For details contact: Director, Special Markets.

First Edition 1998

Designed by Victoria Hartman

Printed in the United States of America
All first editions are printed on acid-free paper. ∞

10   9   8   7   6   5   4   3   2

for my kids, Jack and Roisin

"No place on Earth offers greater security
to life and greater freedom from natural disasters
than Southern California."

Los Angeles Times, 1934

CONTENTS

ECOLOGY OF FEAR

1

THE DIALECTIC OF ORDINARY DISASTER

Once or twice each decade, Hawaii sends Los Angeles a big, wet kiss. Sweeping far south of its usual path, the westerly jet stream hijacks warm water-laden air from the Hawaiian archipelago and hurls it toward the Southern California coast. This "Kona" storm system—dubbed the "Pineapple Express" by television weather reporters—often carries several cubic kilometers of water, or the equivalent of half of Los Angeles's annual precipitation. And when the billowing, dark turbulence of the storm front collides with the high mountain wall surrounding the Los Angeles Basin, it sometimes produces rainfall of a ferocity unrivaled anywhere on earth, even in the tropical monsoon belts.[1]

The two-week-long Kona storm of January 1995 differed little from the classic pattern, except perhaps in the unusual intensity of rainfall in the South Bay area—forcing the evacuation of low-lying neighborhoods in Long Beach, Carson, Torrance, and Hawaiian Gardens—and in Santa Barbara County where 10 inches of rain fell in 24 hours. Otherwise, the scenes were those of ordinary, familiar disaster: Power was cut off to tens of thousands of homes. Sinkholes mysteriously appeared in front yards. Waterspouts danced across Santa Monica Bay. Several children and pet animals were sucked into the deadly vortices of the flood channels. Reckless motorists were drowned at flooded intersections. Lifeguards had to rescue shoppers in downtown Laguna Beach. Million-dollar homes tobogganed off their hill-slope perches or were buried under giant landslides.[2]

January 1995 storm (Long Beach)

1. APOCALYPSE THEME PARK

[Southern California], often to its own surprise, has developed a style of urbanization that not only amplifies natural hazards but reactivates dormant hazards and creates hazards where none existed.

Wesley Marx, Acts of God,
Acts of Man *(1977)*

What was exceptional was not the storm itself (a "20-year event," according to meteorologists), but the way in which it was instantly assimilated to other recent disasters as a malevolent omen. As a *Los Angeles Times* columnist put it, "There's no question that [we are] caught in the middle of something strange . . . maybe God, as the biblical sorts preach, is mad at us for making all those dirty movies."[3] Divine wrath or not, there is widespread popular apprehension that the former Land of Sunshine is "reinventing" itself, to use a fashionable gerund, as a Book of the Apocalypse theme park. First the natives rioted, then nature. In fewer than three years, the megalopolis endured three of the ten most costly national disasters since the Civil War.[4]

The destructive February 1992, January 1993, and January 1995 floods ($500 million in damage) were mere brackets around the April 1992 insurrection ($1 billion), the October–November 1993 firestorms ($1 billion), and the January 1994 earthquake ($42 billion). When damage accounting was finally completed in 1997, the Northridge earthquake emerged as the costliest natural disaster in American history, more destructive, according to a Federal Emergency Management Agency (FEMA) spokesperson, "than the combined impacts of the Midwest floods, Hurricane Andrew, the Loma Prieta earthquake and South Carolina's Hurricane Hugo."[5]

From Ventura to Laguna, nearly two million Southern Californians were directly touched by disaster-related death, injury, or damage to their homes and businesses. The Northridge earthquake alone, according to the California Seismic Safety Commission, "affected the lives of more people than any previous natural disaster in the United States."[6] Cataclysm has become virtually routine. As Peter King, the *Los Angeles Times*'s analyst of California trends, wryly noted after the 1995 storms, "A sort of disaster fatigue has set in. Politicians have run out of fresh, Churchillian sound bites for the rubble walkthroughs. . . . Even victims sometimes seem to be going through the motions, dutifully struggling to reduce the sum of their misery to a pithy sentence or two."[7]

For some unlucky souls, disaster has been a relentless, Job-like ordeal. Los Angeles firefighter Scott Miller, for example, was shot in the face during the 1992 riots while riding in his fire truck. He spent months in the hospital and was dismissed from the fire department due to disability. Two years later, his Granada Hills home was wrecked in the Northridge earthquake. Then, in early 1996, his new four-bedroom home in the Ventura County suburb of Newberry Park was destroyed by fire.[8]

This virtually biblical conjugation of disaster, which coincided with the worst regional recession in 50 years, is unique in American history, and it has purchased thousands of one-way tickets to Seattle, Portland, and Santa Fe. After a century of population influx, 529,000 residents, mostly middle-class, fled the Los Angeles metropolitan region in the years 1993 and 1994 alone. Partly as a result of this exodus, the median household income in Los Angeles County fell by an astonishing 20 percent (from $36,000 to $29,000) between 1989 and 1995.[9] Middle-class apprehensions about the angry, abandoned underclasses are now only exceeded by anxieties about blind thrust faults and hundred-year floods. Meanwhile, Caltech seismologists warn that the Pacific Rim is only beginning its long overdue rock and roll: the Kobe catastrophe may be a 3-D preview of Los Angeles 2000. And waiting in the wings are the plague squirrels and killer bees.

BIBLICAL DISASTERS?

Date	Disaster	Dead	Damage (millions)
1992 February	Storm/flood	8	$ 150
1992 April	Riot	54	$ 1,000
1992 June	Earthquake	1	$ 50
1993 January	Storm/flood	9	$ 150
1993 October	Firestorm	3	$ 1,000
1994 January	Earthquake	72	$42,000
1995 January	Storm/flood	4	$ 200

Source: Figures from the *Los Angeles Times.*

It is still unclear, moreover, whether this vicious circle of disaster is coincidental or eschatological. Could this be merely what statisticians wave away as the "Joseph effect" of fractal geometry: "the common clustering of catastrophe"?[10] Could these be the Last Days, as prefigured so often in the genre of Los Angeles disaster fiction and film (from *Day of the Locust* to *Volcano*)? Or is nature in Southern California simply waking up after a long nap? Whatever the case, millions of Angelenos have become genuinely terrified of their environment.

The $42 billion earthquake

Paranoia about nature, of course, distracts attention from the obvious fact that Los Angeles has deliberately put itself in harm's way. For generations, market-driven urbanization has transgressed environmental common sense. Historic wildfire corridors have been turned into view-lot suburbs, wetland liquefaction zones into marinas, and floodplains into industrial districts and housing tracts. Monolithic public works have been substituted for regional planning and a responsible land ethic. As a result, Southern California has reaped flood, fire, and earthquake tragedies that were as avoidable, as unnatural, as the beating of Rodney King and the ensuing explosion in the streets. In failing to conserve natural ecosystems it has also squandered much of its charm and beauty.

But the social construction of "natural" disaster is largely hidden from view by a way of thinking that simultaneously imposes false expectations on the environment and then explains the inevitable disappointments as proof of a malign and hostile nature. Pseudoscience, in the service of rampant greed, has warped perceptions of the regional landscape. Southern California, in the most profound sense, is suffering a crisis of identity.

2. DEEP MEDITERRANEANEITY

This is a landscape of desire. . . . More than in almost any other major population concentration, people came to [Southern California] to consume the environment rather than to produce from it.

Geographer Homer Aschmann (1959)

No belief is more deeply rooted in the Southern Californian mind than the self-serving conviction that Los Angeles would be Death Valley except for the three great aqueducts that transfer the stolen snowmelt of the Sierra and Rockies to its lawns and pools. The city is advertised as the triumph of superengineers like William Mulholland who built rivers in the desert. A corollary of this promethean claim is the idea that beneath the artificial landscape is something sinister and barren, incapable on its own of sustaining even a tiny fraction of the current multitudes. As Boyle Workman, one of Los Angeles's pioneer real estate developers, put it, "Every tree, every lawn, every blade of grass in this section as it exists today, is a forced growth, made possible by man's ingenuity in bringing water to what otherwise would be a treeless waste."[11]

Although catastrophic drought has episodically posed a threat to human culture in Southern California, Los Angeles, for most of the Holocene (the past 11,000 years) at least, has been no more a "treeless waste" than Valencia or the Côte d'Azur (which have the same annual rainfall). In fact, the earliest written descriptions of the region, the eighteenth-century diaries of the Franciscan padres, eulogized its waterscapes and natural fertility.

"All the soil is black and loamy, and is capable of producing every kind of grain and fruit which may be planted," Father Juan Crespi wrote in 1769. "We went west, continually over good land well covered with grass. . . . All the land we saw this morning seemed admirable to us." The diaries of Fathers Francisco Palou and Pedro Font also extolled the "abundant springs (*cienegas*)," "beautiful rivers," and the valleys "green and flower-strewn." After crossing the true deserts of Sonora and Antigua California, these Mediterranean men (mainly from Majorca) were delighted to come upon familiar oak savannas and "the infinity of wild rosebushes in full bloom." From their cultural perspective, it was land "well-watered."[12]

However, three-quarters of a century later, Anglo-American conquistadors were riven by confusion and ambivalence. Boosterism coexisted with an irrational fear of aridity, and from the 1850s into the 1870s, there were great debates about whether California as a whole was Eden or worthless desolation.[13] Yankee morale tended to wax and wane with changes in the cycle of wet and dry years. The new settlers found it almost impossible to form a consistent picture of the capricious climate or protean landscape. As for other frontier ecologies of the New World, description veered between images of garden and desert, fertility and sterility.[14]

In the most fundamental sense, language and cultural inheritance failed the newcomers. English terminology, specific to a humid climate, proved incapable of accurately capturing the dialectic of water and drought that shapes Mediterranean environments. By no stretch of the imagination, for example, is an arroyo merely a "glen" or "hollow"— they are the results of radically different hydrological processes.* The Anglos often had little choice but to preserve the more befitting Spanish terms although they failed to grasp their larger environmental context.

It was not until the discovery of great artesian basins—millions of acre-feet of subterranean water—during the 1870s, and the subsequent growth of the citrus industry, that it became possible for an Edenic vision of Southern California to bloom uncontested. Even then, it was initially advertised as a "subtropical" paradise: which to nervous eastern imaginations evoked nightmares of malarial swamps with green tree snakes coiled in mossy tree branches.[15]

Ultimately, the railroad publicists and the chamber of commerce

---

* Arroyos, to be exact, are carved by episodic great storms and studied via "cusp catastrophe" models, while temperate glens and hollows are produced by more regular rainfall patterns and analyzed via traditional stream channel models.

promoters repackaged the Los Angeles region as "Our Mediterranean! Our Italy!"[16] For more than a century, this Mediterranean metaphor has been sprinkled like a cheap perfume over hundreds of instant subdivisions, creating a faux landscape celebrating a fictional history from which original Indian and Mexican ancestors have been expunged. The nadir of this specious historicism is probably southern Orange County, where the endlessly regimented rows of identical red-tiled townhouses (an affluent version of architectural Stalinism) are located on cul-de-sacs with names like "Avenida Sevilla" or "Via Capri."

This "Mediterranean" facade, moreover, has made it all the more difficult for Southern Californians to appreciate the profound ecological kinship between their regional landscape and the other mid-latitude regions of hot, dry summers and mild, wet winters (the classical Mediterranean, central Chile, and the coastal zones of South Africa's Cape Province and West and South Australia). Comprising but 3 to 5 percent of the earth's land surface, these Mediterranean littorals are the rarest of major environmental systems. Although the late-nineteenth-century pioneer of plant geography Andreas Schimper had marveled that all such regions "repeat in their [flora] essential ecological features of the Mediterranean vegetation," serious research on their similarities had to await the launching of the International Biological Program (IBP) financed by the National Science Foundation in the late 1960s.[17] Thirty years of collaborative research, involving hundreds of scientists from more than a dozen nations, has illuminated what historian J. R. McNeill calls the "deep history of Mediterranean landscapes."[18] This comparative perspective, in turn, has made it possible to decode the environmental specificity of Southern California, previously the subject of real estate hyperbole and apocalyptic cant, in a richly meaningful way.[19]

We now know that there has been a spectacular convergence of plant evolution in each Mediterranean region, as entirely unrelated species have adopted identical strategies, especially sclerophylly (the development of small, tough evergreen leaves), as a defense against drought.[20] Research has also revealed the far-reaching ways in which aboriginal human societies used fire to cultivate and modify each

Desert or garden? (Pasadena 1880)

Mediterranean ecosystem.[21] And, at least in the cases of California, Chile, and the Mediterranean Basin, similar climates acting upon comparable tectonics have produced distinctive torrential landforms and erosion patterns, as well as equivalent frequencies of floods, land-slides, and earthquakes.[22]

The Franciscans and their Spanish military escorts, of course, were intimately familiar with the dramatic landscape metabolism of the Mediterranean region and so were not shocked to discover similar "cataclysmic cycles" at work in Alta California. They recognized abundant evidence of recent great floods, and Governor Portola experienced such a violent earthquake that he named the stream he was crossing at the time Santa Ana de Los Temblores. Fathers Crespi and Palou both recorded their own memorable encounters with native seismicity while camped on the banks of the lovely Rio Porciuncula, as the Los Angeles River was originally called. With the example of southern Italy in mind, and noting the local abundance of asphaltum (*brea*), Palou speculated matter-of-factly that there were probably volcanoes nearby as well.[23]*

3. WALDEN POND ON LSD

If savannas are fuses, the Mediterranean landscapes are the explosives.

Fire historian Stephen Pyne (1991)

But the hucksters of the 1880s who franchised "Mediterranean California" were selling sunshine, not earthquakes and deluges. Immigrants from the humid states, moreover, brought with them deeply ingrained prejudices about climate and landscape shaped by their experiences in the environmental continuum of northwestern Europe and the eastern United States.[25] As the famous Berkeley geographer Carl Sauer once pointed out, the ecology of the original New England and Middle Atlantic colonies was simply a "lustier" version of that of England or Holland.

---

* Despite the portrait of Los Angeles as postmodern Pompeii in the 1997 film *Volcano,* there has been no volcanicity in the Los Angeles Basin since the mid-Miocene, 12 million years ago. On the other hand, Los Angeles's principal ski resort and the source of much of its drinking water, the Mammoth Lakes area in eastern California, sits in the giant Long Valley Caldera, which has erupted at least 20 times over the last five thousand years. An earthquake in 1979, followed in the next decade by crustal swelling and the emission of toxic gases, announced the renewal of magmatic unrest beneath the caldera. In December 1997, after thousands of small earthquakes had rattled the nerves of Mammoth Lakes residents, the *Los Angeles Times* reported that the Department of Water and Power was racing to create a contingency plan in case an eruption damaged or destroyed the aqueduct that supplies two-thirds of Los Angeles's water. Other officials openly worried how they would evacuate 50,000 visitors and residents from the mountain resort if an eruption occurred at the height of ski season.[24]

In most cases, the colonists were at no loss to identify the native plants and animals they found on the western side of the Atlantic. It would be impossible, indeed, to cross an ocean anywhere else and find as little that is unfamiliar in nature on the opposite side. In all the lands of earliest colonization, from Massachusetts Bay south to Virginia, flora and fauna were closely related to those in the European homeland and indicated to the settlers that they were still under familiar skies and seasons.[26]

In these temperate and forested lands, energy flows through the environment in a seasonal pattern that varies little from year to year. Geology is generally quiescent, and it's easy to perceive natural powers as orderly and incremental, rarely catastrophic. Frequent rainfall of low and moderate intensity is the principal geomorphic agency, and the landscape seems generally in equilibrium with the vector of the forces acting upon it.[27] Indeed, the canonical evocations of the English and New England countrysides—the Reverend Gilbert White's *Natural History of Selborne* (1788) and Henry David Thoreau's *Walden* (1854)—were microcosmic celebrations of nature's gentle balance (even as Thoreau sounded the tocsin against the potentially catastrophic environmental threat of the industrial revolution).

This geographically specific view of natural process—resonant with what American naturalist John Burroughs called "the pastoral quiet and sweetness and harmony of the English landscape"[28]—was transformed by Darwin's mentor, Sir Charles Lyell, into one of the great dogmas of Victorian science. Lyell's famous principle of "uniformitarianism," as Stephen Jay Gould has shown, conflated the constancy of natural laws with uniformities of rate and state. He believed that large-scale surface features—mountain ranges, islands, continental shields, even ocean basins—were the result "of insensible changes added through vast times" and that the earth was a conservative, steady state system without historical directionality. The moderate Whig Lyell, moreover, waged ceaseless philosophical warfare against the conceptions of abrupt "Earth Revolutions" favored by geologists in barricade-ridden France and Germany. Catastrophism of any sort, biblical or Jacobin, he branded as nothing more than prescientific superstition.[29]

A doggedly uniformitarian mindset—which might also be called the "humid fallacy"—still conditions most environmental expectations in Southern California. Imaginary "norms" and "averages" are constantly invoked, while the weather is ceaselessly berated for its perversity, as in "We have had an unusually dry/wet season" or "The weather isn't like it used to be." Despite daily reminders that "we live in earthquake country," every high-intensity natural event—temblor, flood, fire, windstorm, or landslide—produces shock and consternation. As a dazed survivor of the Northridge earthquake told a television crew: "I feel like Nature let us down."

Yet Southern California at least by Lyellian standards is a revolutionary, not a reformist landscape. It is Walden Pond on LSD. As in other Mediterranean and dryland environments, the "average" is merely an abstraction. Indeed, nothing is less likely to occur than "average rainfall." At Los Angeles City Hall, where the annual precipitation is pegged at 15.3 inches, that mark has been hit only a few times in the 127-year history of measured rainfall. Indeed, only 17 percent of years approach within 25 percent of the historical average. The actual norm turns out to be seven- to twelve-year swings between dry and wet spells. The graph of historical rainfall oscillates over the decades like a seismograph recording the successive shocks of a major earthquake. Sometimes the annual average rainfall is delivered during a single week-long Kona storm, as happened in 1938 and 1969; or even, incredibly, in a single 12-hour deluge, as in Bel Air on New Year's Day 1934. During droughts, on the other hand, it may take two or even three years to achieve the mean.[30]

In tranquil New Hampshire or Massachusetts, rivers swell to flood with a mere doubling of their normal flow. In Southern California, the Los Angeles River—growing from a sluggish stream to a storm-fed torrent equivalent in volume to the undammed Col-

An angry Los Angeles River (March 1938)

orado—has been known to increase its flow three-thousand-fold in a single 24-hour period. Local erosion and sedimentation rates also accelerate explosively. Fluvial environments in the Mediterranean Basin behave in the same way. In both regions, environmental fluctuations tend toward the exponential, which is why geomorphologists working in Israel and California have so eagerly adopted catastrophe theory as a framework for understanding landscape processes.[31]

Indeed, nothing so distinguishes Southern California from classical Anglo-American environments as the contrasting roles extreme events play in each. Research has generally supported the Lyellian stereotype that in humid, temperate environments the landscape slowly evolves through the action of low-intensity, high-frequency events, while the very opposite is the case in Mediterranean and desert regions.[32] There, high-intensity, low-frequency events ("disasters") are the ordinary agents of landscape and ecological change.*

For researchers in Southern California, the 1969 Kona storm (a 50-year or 100-year occurrence, according to different authorities) is the typical event "under the current regional climatic regime that accomplishes the most geomorphic work."[34] Quantitative studies of erosion—which use its product, sedimentation, as an index of geomorphic work—support this benchmark. "The bulk of the total sediment" discharged into coastal basins of Southern California from 1930 to 1980, as measured by stream gauges, "was delivered in a *few days*" during the great floods of 1938 and 1969.[35]

These episodic bursts of natural energy produce their most dramatic effects in what Andreas Schimper characterized as Mediterranean "basal zone" ecologies: the alluvial fans, floodplains, and intermontane basins at the foot of rugged mountain ranges like the San Gabriels, the Andes, the Pindus, and the Rif. These are areas of "rapid transition for virtually all aspects of habitat—geology and soils, moisture supply, topography, likelihood of inundation, climate, vegetation, and so forth." Consequently, they are at risk from multiple, interlinked disaster. "Southern California," writes one geographer, "is the epitome of this phenomenon."[36]

The extreme events that shape the Southern California environment tend to be organized in surprising and powerfully coupled causal chains. Drought, for example, dries fuel for wildfires which, in turn, remove ground cover and make soils impermeable to rain. This increases the risk of flooding in areas where earthquakes may have already exposed new surfaces to erosion and increased stream power by raising land elevation. In such conditions, storms are more likely to produce sheet flooding, landslides, and debris flows that result in dramatic erosion and landform change.[37] Vast volumes of sediment

---

* For the earth as a whole, the National Research Council recently reported, "it is not known whether the relocation of materials on the surface of the Earth is dominated by the slower but continuous fluxes operating all of the time or by the spectacular large fluxes that operate during short-lived cataclysmic events."[33]

rapidly realign river channels, and before the advent of twentieth-century flood-control engineering, even switched river courses between alternate deltas. Sedimentation can also create sandbars that temporarily cut off tidal flows to coastal marshes—initiating a 50- to 75-year-long cycle of ecological readjustment.

This is not random disorder, but a hugely complicated system of feedback loops that channels powerful pulses of climatic or tectonic energy (disasters) into environmental work. The Southern California landscape epitomizes the principle of *nonlinearity* where small changes in driving variables or inputs—magnified by feedback—can produce disproportionate, or even discontinuous, outcomes. As a result, the landscape incorporates a decisive quotient of surprise: it packs an eco-punch seldom easy to predict simply by extrapolating from existing trends.[38] In regions like Southern California, geomorphologists point out, "landscapes may take hundreds or thousands of years, or more, to recover from the effects of a single large-magnitude event." At the alluvial foot of the San Gabriels, for example, it is extremely difficult to distinguish between the debris of Recent or Holocene great floods and Pleistocene events.[39]

Mediterranean regions like Los Angeles tend to have greater topographical complexity than humid regions because they have more "information" in the form of catastrophic environmental history embedded in them.[40] This "complex physical geography," as fire historian Stephen Pyne points out, "makes possible, in turn, a complex geography of life, the mosaic of microclimates sustaining a mosaic of microbiotas."[41] The biodiversity of Mediterranean regions is, in fact, only second to that of tropical rainforests. California alone has more than seven thousand native plants, nearly a third more than Texas, the next most species-rich state.[42] Finally, landscape and biome have coevolved to meet conditions of periodic convulsion. Chaparral and oak savannas, for example, depend on wildfire to recycle nitrogen and ensure seed germination, and at least before dam building, floods periodically redistributed niches for aboriginal grasslands and riparian forests.[43]

Some researchers, it should be added, are trying to use complexity theory to model the behavior of high-energy Mediterranean environments in terms of "deterministic chaos" and "dissipative structures." But if Ilya Prigogine and the Santa Fe Institute provide an intriguing framework for thinking about the chaotic natural dynamics of Southern California, then so does the Old Testament. There is an interesting irony in the mismatch of the Lyellian paradigm with the region. The uniformitarians fought biblical literalism in the name of deistic rationalism. Yet the Bible, as three eminent seismologists recently pointed out, is superb environmental literature. It contains rich, encyclopedic descriptions of eastern Mediterranean landscape ecology that are far more appropriate to Southern California than the arcadian idylls of *Walden* or *Selborne*. In particular, the Book of Amos and the prophecies of Zechariah offer compelling accounts of the role of catastrophe in Mediterranean history.[44]

4. BAD NEWS FROM THE MIDDLE AGES

We're kidding ourselves to think that, in the long term, climate will continue to support California's huge urban and agricultural systems. The paleoclimatic record for just the past millennium indicates that it will not.

Paleoclimatologist Scott Stine (1994)

June 1996: Cartago, California. In his quest to learn more about a catastrophe of truly biblical proportions over much of California, Scott Stine is fishing for lightning in a dead sea. More precisely, he is searching the desiccated floor of Owens Lake (250 miles north of Los Angeles) for "fulgurites": sand fused into strangely shaped glass rods by bolts of lightning. The 112-mile-square Owens Lake was once the southern terminus of the Owens River, which drains the eastern watershed of the Sierra Nevada. At the turn of the century, an 85-foot steamboat, the *Bessie Brady,* carried silver ore from the Cerro Gordo mine on one shore to the railroad dock at Cartago on the other. Then, in 1910, Los Angeles built its famous aqueduct and cut off the lake's supply of freshwater. In the late 1920s, after at least one million years of existence, the lake completely disappeared and summer lightning began to leave glassy fingerprints in its dry bed.

Using a sophisticated technique—thermoluminescence analysis—which counts trapped electrons in glass and ceramics, and is commonly employed by archaeologists to date pottery fragments, Stine hopes to date Owens Lake fulgurites. Although most will be less than 60 years old, he suspects some may be 800 to 1,000 years old—proof that the lake bed was dry at least once before. Indeed, Stine has already found dramatic evidence, including ancient native American tool sites and tufa-encrusted shrub stumps in the middle of the lake bed, that Owens Lake dried up long ago, for entirely natural reasons. The stumps have been radiocarbon-dated to the twelfth century. "We now have compelling proof," says Stine, "that Owens Lake desiccated into a desert playa in the early medieval period. This has ominous implications for the future security of Los Angeles' water supply." To say the least.[45]

Stine, a paleoclimatologist at California State University, Hayward, caused a sensation in 1994 when he published research indicating that California had endured two epic droughts during the Middle Ages, one of about 220 years (from approximately 890 to 1100) and the other of about 140 years (from approximately 1210 to 1350). By contrast, the most severe modern drought—which created an unprecedented statewide water emergency—lasted only six years, from 1987 to 1992. Stine's primary evidence, now generally accepted by other researchers, consists of tree stumps exposed to view during the late 1980s when drought and Los Angeles's greed reduced water levels by more than 50 feet in Mono Lake (the northernmost catchment of the Los Angeles Aqueduct) and other Sierran lakes and streams.[46]

The rooted stumps of ancient cottonwoods and Jeffrey pines—representing two different generations that grew about one century apart—are eloquent proof that lake stands were once much lower and that the trees drowned when water levels rose during humid spells. By radiocarbon-dating the outermost tree layers, then counting the annual growth rings, Stine has been able to construct a remarkably accurate chronology of the two droughts as well as the interval of extraordinary wetness that separated them. "The medieval period in California," he wrote in *Nature,* "was thus marked not only by severe and prolonged drought, but by abrupt and extreme hydroclimatic shifts—from inordinate dryness, to inordinate wetness, and back to dryness."[47]

Stine estimates that snow-fed runoff from the Sierra (the source of two-thirds of California's present surface water supply) plummeted to less than 25 percent of the modern average during the most arid phases of the long droughts. (By contrast, during the 1987–92 drought, runoff averaged 65 percent of the mean.) His findings dovetail with work by dendroclimatologist Lisa Graumlich of the University of Arizona and geologist Lynn Ingram of U.C. Berkeley. In her study of tree rings in foxtail pines and western junipers along the eastern flank of the Sierra, Graumlich discovered evidence of a catastrophic decline in rainfall—up to 11.7 inches per year—during Stine's dry centuries. Ingram, meanwhile, analyzed drill cores taken from the bottom of San Francisco Bay to show that sediment deposition abruptly ceased while salinity soared during the Middle Ages—evidence that freshwater inflow to the bay was reduced to a trickle.[48]

Similar research, involving a 1,600-year tree ring record from forests near Santa Barbara, pollen cores from an Orange County marsh, and pack rat middens from the Mojave Desert (an archive of plant remains), unequivocally substantiated Stine's drought chronology in other parts of Southern California. More recently, an analysis of ancient pollen in Long Beach marsh sediments suggests that the Los Angeles coastal plain, normally a grassland, was covered by a semiarid sagebrush steppe during the age of the Crusades.[49]

Archaeologists have been quick to embrace Stine's megadroughts as an explanation for a major discontinuity that has long troubled them in the prehistoric forensic record. Human remains from all over coastal California show a radical increase in frequencies of malnutrition and violent death, as indicated by bone lesions and a decline in stature, dating from roughly the beginning of the European Middle Ages. Whereas early prehistoric cemeteries in the Santa Monica Mountains do not reveal "a single clear-cut instance of a projectile wound," fully 10 percent of the burials at the medieval Chumash cemetery at Calleguas Creek in Ventura County show arrow wounds.[50] As Mark Raab, an archaeologist at California State University, Northridge, explains: "Osteological data show that people buried in the Calleguas Creek cemetery struggled with malnutrition, disease and violence to an unprecedented degree." Raab and others now believe that as the desert encroached upon coastal Southern California during epic drought periods, native cultures may have battled fiercely over dwindling water and food supplies.[51]

This likely explosion of hunger and violence in medieval California can be suggestively linked to comparable drought-induced crises in the Great Plains (soaring warfare), Central America (the collapse of classical Maya), the Andes (the decline of Tiwanaku), eastern China (widespread desiccation of lakes), and perhaps Cambodia (desertion of Angkor Wat). (In Europe, conversely, the so-called Medieval Climate Anomaly, with its warm, reliable summers, saw a great expansion of productive forces, symbolized by the spread of vineyards in central England and the Norse settlement of Greenland.)[52] Stine himself has done recent fieldwork in the Patagonian Andes, where he discovered drowned stumps of southern beech trees in three lake basins whose radiocarbon dates correspond with remarkable fidelity to his Sierran samples. His findings suggest a simultaneous reorganization of climate patterns in both hemispheres. "The crisis in mediaeval California was undoubtedly part of a global pattern. Although Europe prospered from a warmer climate, there was a mass collapse of hydraulic civilization throughout much of the world."[53]

Could epic drought return to Southern California in the near future? As Stine admits, "This is the $64,000 question. Although we can model the atmospheric circulation most likely to produce and sustain a drought for centuries—a contraction of the polar cold fronts— we don't know what caused the circulation to change in the first place. We don't know where the crucial climate switch is located."[54] Somewhere in the globally coupled ocean-icecap-atmosphere system, however, there is a positive feedback mechanism that might allow a small increase in solar output or some other variable to produce a modern

Drowned forests revealed medieval megadroughts

drought in Southern California of medieval magnitude.* As California state climatologist Bill Mork has acknowledged, "If you were to project [the medieval] conditions into today, it's obvious that we couldn't survive in the present infrastructure with the agriculture and the cities that we've got. We just wouldn't have enough water."[56]

The likelihood of a return to what some researchers call the "Mayan scenario" may only be increased by global warming, which, ironically, could ensure greater frequency of both extreme drought and extreme flood conditions.[57] Some researchers, to be sure, believe that the mysterious persistence of El Niño warming in the Pacific between 1990 and 1995, followed so quickly by the super-Niño winter of 1997–98, signals that some kind of epochal climate shift is already under way.[58] Rising sea surface temperatures, at the very least, are having a cataclysmic impact on the marine food chain in the off-

---

* Recent studies of Greenland ice cores and North Atlantic seabed sediments provide unassailable evidence of an approximately 1,500-year cycle of "little ice ages" followed by warmer intervals like the Medieval Anomaly throughout the Holocene.[55]

shore California Current. In March 1995 Scripps Institute of Oceanography researchers stunned the environmental press with a report that over the past generation California coastal zooplankton populations had crashed by 80 percent, resulting in the decimation of some seabird species, as well as a 35 percent decline in fish catches.[59]

At the very least, there is a scientific consensus that Southern Californians must come to grips with not only the reality of catastrophic climate change during the past thousand years but also the "false norms" represented by the weather patterns documented since instrumental record keeping began in the late nineteenth century. To put it brutally, the "peaceful" Land of Sunshine is part fluke, part myth: every recent investigation, whether based on tree rings, lake sediments, seabed varves, or pollen cores, confirms that the Los Angeles region's climate over the past 150 years has been anomalously mild and, therefore, atypical.[60] Stine emphasizes that the modern period is "the fourth wettest of the past 4,000 years," while Graumlich confirms that it has been characterized by "one of the lowest rates for extreme events within the last 600 years."[61] The same thing is undoubtedly true of recent seismic history.

5. THE SEISMIC REGIONAL DEBT

Topography doesn't happen for nothing.
                              Geologist Jeff Unruh (1993)

Another scientific detective story, no less remarkable than Stine's uncovering of epic drought, began on 2 May 1983, when a magnitude (M) 6.3 earthquake rocked the small city of Coalinga in Fresno County, roughly midway between Los Angeles and San Francisco.*

---

* Although the daily press continues to confuse the two, the famous Richter scale, based on seismic wave amplitudes, has been superseded in scientific usage by the Moment Magnitude Scale (M), which takes account of all wave types generated by an earthquake. Technically, it measures "seismic moment": the area of fault rupture multiplied by average slip and shear energy.

Although no fault rupture appeared on the surface, the business district, composed of elderly brick and stone buildings, was almost entirely destroyed. The damage, however, was not confined to Coalinga. In seismology labs and geology departments from Berkeley to Caltech, a paradigm was collapsing.

Coalinga, it turns out, sits on subsurface folds of sedimentary rock that mark the structural boundary between the Coast Ranges and the San Joaquin Valley. Similar folds, known as "anticlines," also constitute much of the picturesque tectonic drapery of the Santa Monica Mountains as well as the underground topography of the Los Angeles Basin and its adjacent valleys. Until the Coalinga temblor—the first modern California earthquake "not associated with any previously known or suspected active fault"—the textbook view was that these folds were the products of gradual, nonviolent deformation. Anticlines were deemed "seismically benign." The real and present danger was believed to be the plate tectonic energy stored in classical "strike-slip" faults like the mighty San Andreas, whose scar is visible from space and which is inexorably conveying most of Los Angeles County in the direction of Alaska.[62]

The scientific postmortem on the Coalinga quake, however, confirmed the existence of a new species of fault zone, the blind thrust fault, "in which the surface expression of the earthquake is a fold."[63] The folded topography of much of coastal California was subsequently recognized as the work of violent spasms rather than gentle compression, further evidence for the neocatastrophic view of nature, California-style. Thrust faults, where crustal blocks override one another rather than grind past each other, were well known to geologists from their dramatic surface expressions in mountain ranges from the Himalayas to the San Gabriels.[64] In the Coalinga case, however, the thrust gave nothing away; it was buried under thousands of feet of sedimentary strata. Anxious seismologists could only wonder how many more of these deadly faults, with the potential energy of so many deeply buried hydrogen bombs, were hidden under the southern half of California.

The next piece of the puzzle fell violently into place on the morning of 1 October 1987 when an M 5.9 earthquake killed eight people and wrecked scores of older buildings in Richard Nixon's hometown of Whittier, just southeast of Los Angeles. (Twenty-five miles away in Echo Park, I was flung out of my bed as the foundations of my apartment house collapsed.) Although seismologists rushed to pin the blame on the Whittier fault zone, a well-studied strike-slip system, their data ultimately convinced them that the real culprit, as in Coalinga, was a previously unknown thrust fault underlying the nearby Puente Hills. Later studies of the "Whittier Narrows" earthquake revealed that the same fault extended northward under the Elysian Hills into downtown Los Angeles.[65] Other geophysical evidence suggested a dense thicket of buried thrust faults under the very heart of the metropolis.[66]

It was a stunning revelation. Whittier Narrows, wrote seismologists Jian Lin and Ross Stein, "raises the possibility that the principal source of future earthquakes in the Los Angeles metropolitan area comes not from strike-slip and reverse faults prominent at the surface, but from blind (or buried) thrusts that are intimately coupled to the development of the subsurface folds."[67] While disaster planners were still focused exclusively on the danger of the "Big One" on the San Andreas, geologists were studying more than 50 active faults directly underneath the heavily urbanized portions of Los Angeles, Orange, and Ventura Counties. The entire metropolis had suddenly become, at least in theory, "epicentral" to a massively destructive quake. As Lucy Jones, the U.S. Geological Survey (USGS) seismologist usually delegated to explain bad news to the public, summarized the new paradigm for a television audience after Northridge: "We probably have a close-to-comparable hazard over the whole region. That view is probably more suitable than finding individual fault strands and saying, 'worry about this one and worry about that one' . . . especially when all the strands are going to add up to most of the basin!"[68]

A devastating M 6.9 earthquake in Armenia in early December 1988, also caused by an unexpected rupture on a blind thrust fault,

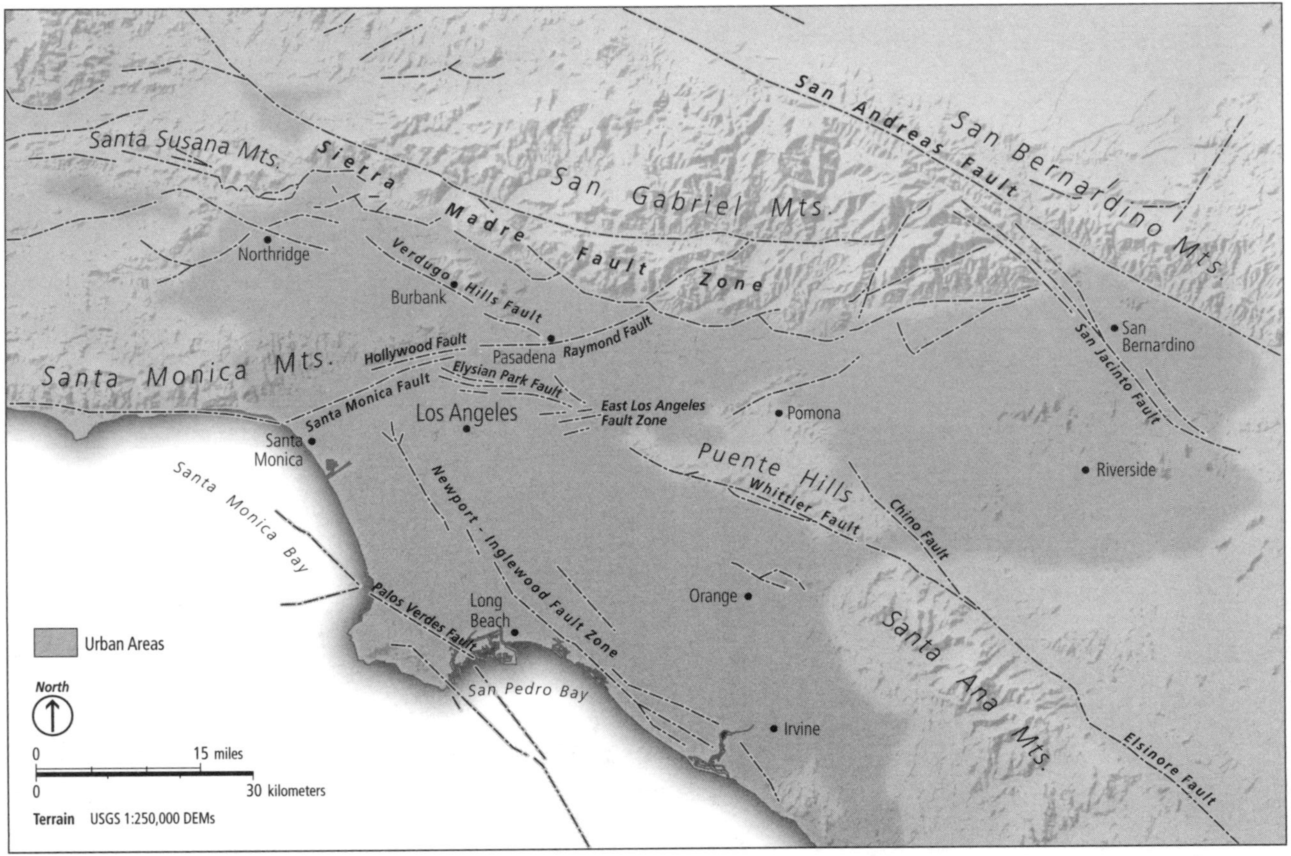

Seismic gridlock

North

Urban Areas

0   15 miles

0   30 kilometers

Terrain   USGS 1:250,000 DEMs

San Bernardino Mts.

San Andreas Fault

San Gabriel Mts.

Sierra Madre Fault Zone

Santa Susana Mts.

Santa Monica Mts.

San Jacinto Fault

• San Bernardino

• Riverside

Elsinore Fault

Santa Ana Mts.

Chino Fault

Puente Hills

Whittier Fault

• Pomona

• Irvine

• Orange

Raymond Fault

East Los Angeles Fault Zone

Pasadena

Verdugo Hills Fault

Burbank

Hollywood Fault

Elysian Park Fault

Santa Monica Fault

Los Angeles

Newport - Inglewood Fault Zone

Long Beach

San Pedro Bay

Palos Verdes Fault

Santa Monica Bay

Santa Monica

Northridge

injected new urgency into the hunt for hidden faults under Los Angeles. Ironically, some of the most important data on such faults had existed for years but was locked away in the vaults of oil corporations. Los Angeles is built on top of sandstones and shales that fill ancient ocean basins (in some places to a depth of 30,000 feet) and conserve the incredibly rich reservoirs of petroleum that made Los Angeles the land of the blue-eyed sheiks in the 1920s. No city in the world has had so many holes drilled into its deep subsurface, and the oil well logs kept by the corporations include invaluable descriptions of sedimentary unconformities diagnostic of blind thrust faults. Significantly, it was two oil industry geologists with an extracurricular interest in earthquakes, Thom Davis and Jay Namson, who pioneered the use of well data to locate buried thrust faults. They were also the first to tie the Whittier Narrows earthquake to the fault system responsible for the familiar corrugations of the Elysian Hills.[69]

Meanwhile, James Dolan and Kerry Sieh from the Seismology Lab at Caltech began to track a different set of clues. With the persistence of archaeologists hunting a fabled tomb or lost city, they spent countless hours combing nineteenth-century maps of Los Angeles for subtle topographical details, especially streambeds and hillocks, that, while now covered by urban development, might indicate prehistoric fault slippage or folding. They discovered two new strike-slip faults beneath MacArthur and Echo Parks "riding piggy back" on top of a major blind thrust structure, the Wilshire Arch.[70] They also excavated exploratory trenches across the faults at the feet of the San Gabriel and Santa Monica Mountains. Conventional wisdom held these faults to be inactive, but Dolan and Sieh found evidence that they were still active.[71]

On 28 June 1992, while the research community was absorbing the implications of these discoveries, a massive M 7.3 earthquake ripped through the Mojave Desert near the small town of Landers. It defied all existing seismic models by hopscotching along angled fault segments and setting off enigmatic tremors as far away as Yellowstone Park. "I think bizarre is a good word to describe it," said one senior geologist at the USGS regional headquarters in Menlo Park. "This is one of those rare moments in science when your observational systems bring you something that you've never seen before."[72]

Landers adventitiously coincided with a fundamental reconsideration of whether major earthquakes were predictable or not. Many seismologists had long believed that the assumed regularity of fault behavior would someday make earthquake prediction within reasonably narrow time bands possible. As a first step, the federal government in the early 1980s financed $20 million worth of instrumentation around the tiny town of Parkfield, California, where a moderate temblor on a local segment of the San Andreas fault ("the best understood in the world") was considered imminent "with a confidence of 95%." The public was given optimistic expectations of a dramatic breakthrough in earthquake forecasting.[73]

In 1990, however, geophysicist Wayne Thatcher—a true paradigm rebel in Thomas Kuhn's sense—had published an iconoclastic article arguing that great earthquakes are unique historical events, with variable, not constant parameters that cannot be predicted by simple extrapolation from recent fault history. The Landers temblor, which defied all standard theories, accorded well with Thatcher's "chaos" theory of earthquake frequency. So did the complete failure of the Parkfield prediction experiment: the model quake, predicted for 1988, had not occurred when the statistical window of probability closed in 1992. (Indeed, in early 1998 forlorn USGS seismologists were still waiting for their seismic version of Godot.)[74]

Thus a quiet revolution in earthquake science was already under way when the first P-waves, traveling at more than 12,000 miles an hour, struck the Northridge Meadows apartment building in the northern San Fernando Valley at 4:30 A.M., 17 January 1994. A few seconds later the more violent S-waves arrived and the shoddily built 164-unit building began to collapse on top of its screaming residents.* Sixteen people were crushed to death.

---

* The stored tectonic energy released in an earthquake produces two kinds of elastic waves in the surrounding crust. The primary (P) waves, which arrive first, compress the crust, while the subsequent secondary (S) waves twist or shear it.

A "lucky near miss"?

Although the total death toll (72) was mercifully small when compared with Armenia (25,000 plus) three years earlier, or Kobe (6,000) one year later, 12,000 people were injured and at least 437,000 housing units were damaged.[75] Shell-shocked residents (25,000 of them homeless) not surprisingly found it almost impossible to assimilate reassurances from geologists that the M 6.7 quake was a "lucky near miss" since 80 percent of its energy had been directed northward toward the sparsely populated Santa Susana Mountains (which promptly grew by 18 inches) and the Santa Clara River valley. "What kind of hell," asked a newspaper columnist, "would a 'direct hit' entail?"[76]

The scientific response to the Northridge disaster was perhaps the most intensive public research effort, outside of wartime and apart from medical research, in recent American history. While scores of structural engineers combed through the rubble, seismologists debated the exact provenance of the unknown thrust fault that nucleated almost 11 miles below Northridge. (Pressured by the press to give the enigmatic fault a name, USGS spokesperson Lucy Jones simply christened it "Fred.")[77] Dolan and Sieh, meanwhile, joined with other veteran geologists to reassess the earthquake hazard in the greater Los Angeles area. Their report, published on the first anniversary of Northridge, focused on the problem that haunted most researchers: the "moment deficit paradox."[78]

Quite simply, geodetic surveys as well as paleoseismic studies of active faults suggest an earthquake frequency in the Los Angeles region over the past several millennia that is dramatically higher than the record of the past two centuries. There have, in other words, been too few quakes to relieve the accumulation of stress generated by plate tectonic motion as Los Angeles hitchhikes northward on the Pacific Plate.[79] As Dolan told Science News, "Los Angeles appears to have been settled in a quiet period in terms of earthquakes, and that can't last forever. At some point, we're going to have to relieve all the strain that's built up over that period."[80] As he added later, "Seventeen [Northridge-size] events should have occurred during the past 195 years, but we have experienced only two."[81]

This deficit, Dolan and his colleagues emphasized, is a real debt, owed to the restless Pacific Plate, that must eventually be paid in full—either as a deadly swarm of Northridge-size quakes (M 6.7) or as a single monster event (M 7.2 to M 7.6) right under the basin. Arguing the case for a single large quake, they pointed out that "it has been at least 210 years since such an event has occurred in the region, indicating that we are within the expected average recurrence time for an earthquake of this size." Either scenario, however, would produce a scale of destruction that "would certainly strain the ability of the region (and the nation) to absorb the resultant losses."[82]

These estimates of Los Angeles's quake debt and possible modes of payment were seconded by Susan Hough, a USGS researcher who used satellite measurements of tectonic compression in the Los Angeles Basin to confirm that modern earthquakes have been too infrequent to relieve the accumulated strain. A group report for the Southern California Earthquake Center, meanwhile, warned that, in addition to the thrust fault hazard under Los Angeles, there was a higher risk than previously estimated of a major earthquake on the San Andreas and San Jacinto faults where both—a few miles apart—sliced through schools, freeways, and residential neighborhoods in the suburban San Bernardino Valley. Overall, the report indicated, there was an "80% to 90% probability of an M 7 or greater earthquake somewhere in Southern California before 2024." Finally, the center tacitly acknowledged the epistemological revolution taking place in seismology by noting that a "cascade" of quakes across disjoint faults was now considered a real possibility.[83]

At a meeting at Caltech, a few months after Northridge, Kerry Sieh speculated apocalyptically that an entire thrust fault system might rupture in synchronization with a San Andreas quake. "Perhaps the really big quakes tend to come all at once," he remarked. Two years later, David Jackson, scientific director of the Southern California Earthquake Center, revived Sieh's multiple-fault scenario in a controversial article that argued the case for rare but huge earthquakes of M 8 or greater in Southern California. The infrequency of such large quakes might postpone the day of reckoning by a building boom or two, but (as Jackson dryly noted) the eventual interest charges would spell a permanent end to fun in the sun: "Dollar losses could be in the *trillions*."[84]

Although some authorities discount Jackson's theory as mechanically implausible, there is new evidence that the great 1857 Fort Tejon quake—the last rupture on the southern San Andreas fault—did detonate some hidden thrust faults in the San Joaquin Valley.[85] Since Landers, moreover, there has been growing interest in how faults interact with one another across what were previously conceived of as insuperable barriers. Indeed, some researchers have made the epistemic leap to the radical view that all of Southern California's hundred or so active faults are a single, "wired" system with long-distance communication to other families of faults in central California and the Great Basin. "Faults are talking to one another," asserted one prominent seismologist.[86]

Exploiting this emergent paradigm, USGS geologists Ruth Harris and Robert Simpson have proposed a solution to the puzzle of Los Angeles's 150-year-long seismic drought. Great earthquakes, they argue, reorganize seismic stress throughout regional fault systems—increasing the strain on a few faults, but reducing it on most. They describe these areas of temporarily reduced seismicity as "stress-relaxation shadows," and they marshal impressive evidence that the twin shadows cast by the (M 8) 1857 Fort Tejon and the (M 7.5) 1952 Kern County earthquakes have been primarily responsible for the modern moment deficit.[87]

But what of the near future? The recent series of quakes suggests that Los Angeles has now emerged from the protective shadow of past seismicity. In a survey of earlier seismic cycles, a team of UCLA geophysicists has found compelling evidence that great quakes on the San Andreas and related faults are ordinarily preceded by swarms of intermediate-magnitude events. Thrust fault quakes, in other words, can be the precursors of great San Andreas–type quakes.[88]

Alternatively, former Carter science advisor Frank Press and Caltech emeritus professor Clarence Allen have proposed that the San Andreas system and the Los Angeles thrust belt take turns as the dominant locus of seismic release in the region. According to their model, Los Angeles may still be in the early stages of a thrust fault earthquake cluster: Dolan and company's multiple-quake mode of paying back Pacific Plate Savings and Loan. Like other researchers, they also find evidence that faults can "communicate" at great distances through transfers of stress. They see a particularly strong correlation between temblors in the Gulf of California and the Great Basin of eastern California and Nevada and later ruptures on the San Andreas system.[89]

Prognosis became even more complicated in March 1998 when teams from the USGS and the Southern California Earthquake Center ignited new controversy with revisionist claims that the seismic deficit had been overestimated. The *Los Angeles Times*'s account of their unpublished research created the impression that the deficit had been little more than a mirage based on the undercounting of nineteenth-century earthquakes. In fact, the USGS team assumed that a great earthquake comparable to the 1857 Fort Tejon event would occur within the next 50 years: hardly a cause for celebration. Another report to the same scientific meeting, moreover, announced the discovery of a dangerous blind thrust fault in the San Joaquin Hills surrounding Newport Beach and Laguna Beach.[90]

Regardless of the differences in calculation and scenario, there is a growing scientific consensus that Southern California is awakening from its long seismic siesta, and that the Northridge disaster—God help us—was little more than a yawn.

6. THE GREAT ANOMALY

How can we claim to build for events that might happen in the next 1,000 years, when our ideas don't hold up for 20 years? ("I am sorry, but the warranty on that research expired last year.")

                                     Seismologist Thomas Heaton (1995)

If there has been a single, fatal flaw in the design of Southern California as a civilization, it has been the decision to base the safety of present and future generations almost entirely upon shortsighted extrapolations from the disaster record of the past half-century. If the average human lifetime is defined biblically as 62 years, then native Californian cultures spent at least 142 lifetimes nourishing an intimate knowledge of the environment as a dynamic system. In contrast, Anglo-Americans have occupied the region for little more than two and a half lifetimes. Most of the major water, flood control, sewage, energy, communications, and transportation infrastructures are less than one lifetime old. These spans are too short to serve as reliable proxies for ecological time or to sample the possibilities of future environmental stress. Bureaucratic faith in the immortality of public works derives exclusively from attenuated, almost meaningless official time frames. In effect, we think ourselves gods upon the land but are still really just tourists.

For example, the current water allocation to Southern California and the rest of the booming Southwest under the Colorado River Compact is based on a 21-year record (1899–1921) of river flow at Laguna Dam, near Yuma, Arizona, that water planners took as a historical norm. In fact, subsequent tree ring analysis of precipitation trends in Western forests shows that this was a period of high, persistent runoff, "the greatest and longest such anomaly in the last 450 years." As a result, the long-term average Colorado River water supply was overestimated by at least 1.5 million acre-feet per year—a fact of great concern to the Los Angeles area, which depends on augmented supplies of Colorado River water to survive droughts as in 1987–92.[91]

Likewise, Southern California's multibillion-dollar flood control system was built to control a statistical abstraction called the "hundred-year flood," which, in fact, has already occurred twice in this century.* But how would storm channels, debris basins, and dams stand up to an event like the two-hundred-year "Noachian Deluge" of 1861–62, which transformed most of coastal Los Angeles and Orange Counties into an inland sea? (You could have rowed from the Los Angeles Civic Center to Newport Beach along the present route of Interstate 5.) As urbanization, moreover, has relentlessly eroded flood control capacity by paving over watershed and reducing surface absorption, more than 110,000 homes adjacent to the Los Angeles River and Rio Hondo have

---

* Climatic recurrence intervals—for example, a "50-year storm" or a "200-year flood"— are simply well-informed guesses, based on brief instrumental records, of the average frequency of such events. They do not imply that storms or floods occur in fixed cycles or with regular periodicity. For flood control purposes, the hundred-year event is usually taken as the design standard in engineering dams and runoff channels.

become vulnerable to the next hundred-year event. In October 1997, FEMA designated a 75-square-mile area of low-lying subdivisions and industrial land as a "special flood hazard area" where inundation up to eight feet deep is possible.[92]

Similarly, state and local seismic safety regulations consist entirely of grudging responses to moderate earthquakes such as Long Beach in 1933 (M 6.3) and San Fernando in 1971 (M 6.7). But Northridge cost a thousand times more than the Long Beach quake, and it has been recently estimated that the Big One on the southern San Andreas fault or a "direct hit" on a downtown blind thrust fault will produce physical destruction in excess of $200 billion. Economic damage has increased by almost an order of magnitude between each of Los Angeles's major twentieth-century earthquakes. The same inflationary pattern holds elsewhere: since the Kobe disaster, which cost $200 billion, the projected cost of the next great Tokyo earthquake has been ratcheted upward to an incredible $1.2 trillion.[93]

EARTHQUAKE DAMAGE INFLATION

Location	Magnitude	Damage Cost (unadjusted millions)
Long Beach (1933)	M 6.3	$ 40
San Fernando (1971)	M 6.7	$ 500
Northridge (1994)	M 6.7	$ 42,000
"Direct hit" (?)	M 7+	$ 200,000+
Tokyo (?)	M 8+	$1,200,000

In Southern California, the classical uniformitarian assumption that the present is the key to the past, and therefore to the future, is likely to prove a dangerous fallacy. As science over the past decade has laid the foundations for a true environmental history of the Los Angeles region, the modern era has come to look increasingly anomalous. Recent research on past climate change and seismic activity has transformed the question "Why so many recent disasters?" into the truly unnerving question "Why so few?" The urbanization of the Los Angeles area has, it seems, taken place during one of the most

The 1933 earthquake (Jefferson High School, Long Beach)

unusual episodes of climatic and seismic benignity since the inception of the Holocene; or put another way, twentieth-century Los Angeles has been capitalized on sheer gambler's luck.

The tempo of actual disaster, moreover, has been oddly attuned to the business cycle. All the major twentieth-century floods and earthquakes have coincided with recession or slow-growth years. (The apparent exception, the 1987 Whittier Narrows earthquake, occurred two weeks before Black Monday's stock market crash.) Incredibly, there were no "ordinary" disasters during the great booms that extended from 1919 to 1929 and 1945 to 1968. Cataclysm, therefore, has never interrupted a major business expansion, while it has providentially offered excuses for Keynesian, countercyclical spending during recessions—most notably in 1934, 1938, and 1994, when Democratic presidents used disaster aid to leverage votes in Southern California. It is easy to imagine, by contrast, how different the modern image of Southern California might be if thousands of tourists had perished in the Long Beach Deluge of 1921 or the Great Disneyland Quake of 1963.

I don't mean this facetiously. Natural disasters on several famous occasions have decisively influenced the Darwinian competition among American cities and regions. Houston, for example, might today be a suburb of Galveston if not for the epic hurricane and flood that destroyed the latter in 1900. Los Angeles and Oakland, likewise, gained population and capital at the expense of San Francisco following the great earthquake in 1906. The Miami hurricane of 1926 and the Lake Okeechobee hurricane of 1928, which together killed 2,079 tourists and residents, put South Florida out of competition with Southern California for an entire generation. (Crying crocodile tears, the Los Angeles Chamber of Commerce raised pennies— "Help Florida, Only $1000 More Needed"—for miserable Miamians.) And the dustbowl drought of the 1930s, which ravaged parts of Texas and Oklahoma, furnished Southern California with a cheap supply of labor for its wartime shipyards and aircraft factories.

Now the tables appear to have turned, as Los Angeles faces the likelihood of future disasters that will impose real economic and competitive costs on the region. The crucial questions are what can it do, and how can it afford, to mitigate the impacts of these expected "ordinary" disasters? Although El Niño–induced storms and protracted drought raise great concern, seismic safety is the problem in the foreground of all disaster planning. In an era of more frequent and very likely larger earthquakes, nothing would bolster the confidence of residents and investors as much as dramatic improvement in the stability and safety of the built environment.

7. KILLER PULSES AND BURNING SKYLINES

Until this last year I was never truly scared. Now, I am.
                                    Seismologist Kerry Sieh (1995)

What, then, are the lessons of Northridge? Although this medium-size quake vented most of its wrath on the Santa Susana Mountains, ground shaking at some locations in the San Fernando Valley exceeded building code standards by as much as 400 percent. Researchers were startled by the uneven pattern of damage, with unusual clusters of destruction in Tarzana, Hollywood, the Crenshaw district, and Santa Monica, all far from the epicenter. This seemingly erratic pattern was partly a function of soil geology, with several dramatic instances of site "liquefaction," where moist sands and silts in ancient channels of the Los Angeles River turned into quivering Jell-O.[94]

The more important cause of damage distribution, however, was the amplification of the earthquake's energy through resonance with the subsurface topography of the Los Angeles Basin. Concavities in basement rock—the harder metamorphic rock underlying sedimentary strata—acted as lenses to focus wave energy on surface targets. Thus the promiscuous pattern of surface damage reflected invisible contours of the sedimentary-bedrock interface thousands of feet below the surface.[95] Similar resonance effects within an ancient sedimentary basin were partly responsible for the collapse of nearly two hundred high-rise buildings during the Mexico City earthquake in 1985, and seismologists are now greatly concerned about their destructive potential in Los Angeles's urban core.[96] One research team recently calculated that wave amplitudes within the Los Angeles Basin might be "ten times larger than those at sites outside the basin" at comparable distances from a San Andreas rupture. Another study reached the unnerving conclusion that quake energies could be amplified 200 to 400 percent directly underneath the Los Angeles Civic Center.[97]

Los Angeles skyscrapers, whatever the amplification factor, are poised to become rubble or towering infernos in future quakes. For decades the public has been reassured that steel-frame high-rises are virtually earthquake proof. The Northridge temblor, however, fractured critical joints in at least 150 steel-frame buildings: some of them brand new, some nearly 20 miles from the epicenter. Later laboratory tests showed that the metal alloy used for welded joints failed at stress levels far below design specifications.[98] It was easier, however, to make the diagnosis than to prescribe the multibillion-dollar cure. Despite dire warnings of future deaths, the astronomical cost of retrofitting the nine-hundred-odd high-rise buildings in the Los Angeles area has discouraged any serious debate about the problem. In the face of landlord protests, city hall even retreated from a modest proposal for the mandatory inspection of vulnerable buildings.[99]

But even with failsafe welds, some skyscrapers would most likely be doomed in Los Angeles's next major seismic blowout. The 1992 Landers quake provided the first conclusive evidence of a species of seismic wave, called a "killer pulse," that could prove especially lethal to high-rise structures. USGS seismologist Thomas Heaton—long fascinated with "why so many tall redwoods [during the 1906 San Francisco earthquake] were snapped off two-thirds of the way to their tops"—had predicted the existence of such pulses based on an analysis of seismograms from the Mexico City earthquake.[100] Killer pulses differ from ordinary seismic shaking in that they literally yank the ground out from underneath structures (researchers call it "seismic fling"): up to 15 feet in a few seconds. As Heaton explained, "If you move the base of a building a large distance, basically you're knocking the legs out from underneath it. It's very important in a tall building that the columns stay vertical. If they tilt very much, they're in trouble."[101]

Following Northridge, Heaton teamed up with Caltech engineer John Hall to test exactly how far a typical 20-story skyscraper would be "flung" under the impact of pulses from an M 7 thrust fault quake. In their laboratory simulation, the answer was far enough for the unlucky building to immediately topple over. Even a state-of-the-art, "base-isolated" building, designed to withstand massive earthquakes, could be wrecked by such pulses. The seismic engineering theory of the 1970s from which so much in Southern California's building codes derives now looks "pretty poorly founded," according to Heaton and Hall. Nevertheless, Heaton's proposals for an immediate moratorium on high-rise construction and a 1 percent tax on all new development to go to seismic research received a glacial reception from local officials desperately hoping for a revival in office construction.[102]

The killer pulse problem needs to be appreciated in the context of recent research on tall-building fire hazards. In the wake of the 1987 Whittier Narrows quake, fire expert Mark Kluver warned building officials that contemporary skyscrapers with automatic sprinkler systems are actually more fire-prone than their ancestors. To encourage the adoption of sprinkler systems, modern building codes in Los Angeles and elsewhere have traded away the traditional structural fire protection of office compartmentation. At the same time, developers have been allowed to use combustible plastic as a construction material and to pack interior ducts with thousands of miles of plastic-coated wiring. Yet research indicates that sprinkler systems will quickly fail during any major earthquake, while "due to decreased compartmentation and other relaxations of fire-safety provisions, modern high-rises have the potential for very large [postquake] fires," especially in light of "the increased combustibility of today's building contents."[103]

Los Angeles also lacks the firefighting resources to deal with several simultaneous high-rise blazes as might occur during any large earthquake. In 1987 it took half of the ladder companies in the city to combat a single fire in the First Interstate tower downtown.[104] Yet a burning skyline is not even the worst-case possibility in official disaster planning literature. That distinction is reserved for the multiple fires that could engulf the huge petrochemical complex that surrounds the adjacent ports of Los Angeles and Long Beach. In a 1989 simulation of a rush-hour M 7 event along the axis of the 1933 Long Beach quake, California Division of Mines planners raised the specter of a "major conflagration" in the harbor area, where "an earthquake cocktail of aging refineries and soft soil is a firestorm waiting to happen."[105]

Nor was the Northridge experience exactly reassuring about the ability of the understaffed and underfunded Los Angeles Fire Department—Cinderella to its greedy big sister, the LAPD—to deal with the five-hundred-plus major fires predicted to erupt simultaneously during a Newport-Inglewood, San Andreas, or thrust fault "direct hit."[106] Although crews responded with traditional heroism to more than a hundred house and trailer fires ignited by broken gas mains, they faced a near breakdown in lifeline services: 35 firehouses were damaged, the entire power grid was blacked out, older gas pipelines ruptured, six freeways went down, and so many water mains were broken that crews had to pump water from swimming pools (providentially abundant in the Valley).[107] In its postquake report, the state's Seismic Safety Commission emphasized that "good fortune played a critical role in keeping fires from spreading: there was no wind, and the area was not experiencing a dry spell."[108]

This 1951 refinery inferno dramatized the fire hazard at L.A. Harbor

Moreover, a large portion of the emergency communications network failed, and fire department paramedics were unable to communicate with local hospitals, 14 of which were in any case put out of
commission by the main shock.[109] State officials later estimated that
barely 20 percent of Los Angeles area hospitals met the standards of
the 1973 Hospital Facilities Seismic Safety Act, enacted after 47 people were killed in the collapse of the Veterans Administration Hospi-

tal in San Fernando during the 1971 earthquake. (The Hospital Council of Southern California had successfully lobbied the Legislature to exempt older hospitals from obligatory compliance.)[110] Although Los Angeles County's two largest medical centers, UCLA and County-USC, functioned throughout the emergency, subsequent inspection led their administrators to claim an astonishing $2.3 billion in combined structural damage.[111]

Many older school campuses may be even more dangerous than antiquated hospitals. By sheer chance, none of the last 10 major earthquakes in California has occurred during school hours. But if the Northridge quake had struck in the middle of a regular school day, according to the Los Angeles Board of Education, "thousands of children would have been injured or killed by falling debris, furniture and lighting."[112] The Los Angeles Unified School District did, however, have to temporarily suspend operations after a staggering 5,600 school buildings suffered quake damage.[113]

Similarly, in a daytime quake, hundreds would have perished in the Valley's caved-in shopping malls and parking structures. The destruction of Bullock's department store in Northridge Fashion Center was officially described as "the type of collapse where no one survives," while its sister store in Sherman Oaks Fashion Square looked like it had been hit by a cruise missile. Structural engineers who examined the damage concluded that the huge, precast concrete department stores, together with concrete parking structures of similar construction, are particularly prone to catastrophic failure. Essentially houses-of-cards made of 100-ton slabs, these structures demonstrate, according to one expert, the "dangerous combination of inadequacies in building codes and an increasing drive to cut costs by designing for the minimum."[114]

But killer department stores and garages are only a small subset of Los Angeles County's nearly three thousand precast concrete buildings. This homicidal building type, which includes warehouses, factories, offices, discount stores, and schools, failed spectacularly during the 1971 San Fernando quake and was directly responsible for most of the slaughter in Armenia in 1988. The precast concrete hazard has been dramatically amplified in the Los Angeles region by the popularity of

Bullock's department store, Northridge

siting warehouses and superstores in floodplains and former coastal wetlands, where liquefaction is inevitable during any major quake.[115]

Most disturbingly, Northridge revealed a massive, hidden crisis in the quality of residential construction. After inspecting thousands of homes, structural engineers concluded that at least one-third or more of quake damage was directly attributable to shoddy construction. (The situation has gotten worse with every building boom: "Ironically, houses in neighborhoods developed prior to 1950 often sustained less damage than houses in areas developed after 1960.") In smaller, single-family homes, these building defects meant astronomically higher costs of repair than disaster planners had ever foreseen but seldom caused serious injury or loss of life. In larger apartment buildings, however, construction quality became a life or death issue. As the Northridge Meadows tragedy made clear, Los Angeles's myriad stucco apartment complexes, especially those precariously perched over carports and garages, are quite simply death traps.[116]

If Northridge was a small-scale trial run for a prospective "direct hit," Los Angeles failed miserably. From the defective welds in the new Metropolitan Transportation Authority skyscraper looming over Union Station, to a missing shear wall in a middle-income dream-house on a quiet cul-de-sac—postquake engineering surveys illuminated scores of potentially fatal flaws in the precarious architecture of the Southern California dream. However, when the cost estimates for lifesaving repair soared into the billions, the light was abruptly turned off. Despite the grim reminder from Kobe, public discussion of seismic safety reform withered away in 1995, as lobbyists dug in their heels and politicians moved on to happier agendas.

In Sacramento, where Republican governors in recent years have vetoed dozens of earthquake safety measures, the long-awaited report on Northridge from the state's Seismic Safety Commission proved a compendium of cowardice. After bitter internal debate that postponed its publication for six months, a majority of the commissioners opted for inaction on the hazard of steel-frame construction (more study recommended) and a virtually meaningless 25-year deadline for compliance with local seismic retrofit ordinances. If anything, the report actually defused what sense of crisis remained. In Los Angeles, Mayor Richard Riordan was too busy being a beacon of the post-riot, post-Northridge optimism ("L.A. Is Back!") to fret about the dangers of precast concrete or blind thrust faults. Massive rebuilding, moreover, was removing the tangible evidence of disaster. What earthquake? In Southern California we bury our dead, then forget.

8. POLITICAL AFTERSHOCKS

First the earthquake, then the disaster.
Graffiti on side of damaged house in
San Fernando Valley (1994)

Disaster amnesia is a federally subsidized luxury. Los Angeles's boosters would not have found it so easy to put the Northridge earthquake behind them if the Valley were still littered with quake-rubble ghost towns, vacant lots, abandoned businesses, and thousands of displaced residents. This would almost certainly be the grim landscape today had the coordination and financing of recovery efforts been left strictly in the governor's hands in Sacramento. After stealing kudos from voters for reopening the Santa Monica Freeway in record time (with federal money), Governor Pete Wilson turned his back on Los Angeles. Reminding Northridge victims that "aid is not an entitlement," he canceled a crucial housing assistance program and blocked passage of a quarter-cent sales surtax for quake relief. After a statewide earthquake bond measure failed, Wilson astonished federal authorities by forcing the city of Los Angeles to lend the state money to pay its small counterpart share of relief.[117]

Governor Wilson's decision to play Scrooge, however, allowed President Clinton to play Father Christmas to stricken homeowners in the vote-rich precincts of the Valley and northern Los Angeles County. The Clinton administration, then chock-a-block with Southland power brokers like Warren Christopher and Mickey Kanter, broke all records in speeding $13 billion in earthquake relief to Los Angeles. Setting aside an amendment to the 1974 Disaster Relief Act that required state and local governments to pay 25 percent of all recovery costs, the White House gallantly assumed 90 percent of the burden.[118] It was a dramatic contrast, not only to the Bush administration's benign neglect of South Central Los Angeles after the 1992 riots, but also to its relatively tight-fisted efforts in Florida after Hurricane Andrew in August 1992.

Although insured losses were higher in South Florida, Los Angeles received nearly eight times more federal aid. Part of the discrepancy can be attributed to the greater magnitude of damage to freeways, hospitals, and public buildings in Los Angeles, but the decisive factor, as every political analyst in the country recognized, was political.[119] Washington worried that earthquake damage might prolong the recession in Southern California, which was already slowing national economic recovery. Even more important, the so-called New Democrats, whose eyes never stray far from the stars in Hollywood, were determined to put California in the bag for the president in 1996. George Bush, on the other hand, had treated South Floridians as so much "trailer trash"—more a law-and-order problem than a possible electoral windfall.[120]

"For the Clinton Administration," one veteran reporter explained, "the Los Angeles earthquake has provided a politically salable reason for doing what it has sought to do for most of its first year in power: pump billions of dollars into Southern California's ailing economy."[121] FEMA ended up providing assistance to a larger population than the city of Denver, while the Small Business Administration, in its quake relief role, became the largest mortgage lender in Los Angeles County. In some cases, including the big university hospitals, the city sewer system, the Los Angeles Coliseum, and various county office buildings, "disaster aid," loosely construed, was a de facto public works program that financed expensive upgrades as well as simple repairs. With extraordinary charity, moreover, federal relief was showered on rich and poor alike. Nearly 1,400 households in Beverly Hills 90210, for example, received FEMA grants.[122]

Although it took more than a year before the patient fully responded to the treatment, seismic Keynesianism played a major role in Los Angeles's robust recovery from the worst recession in a half-century.[123] In the balmy view of the media and the chamber of commerce, Los Angeles had been put back together again. Clinton, in return, not only transformed his 1992 margin in California into a landslide in 1996 but also won grateful new allies, including Los Angeles Mayor Riordan, a moderate Republican.

Unlike the postman, however, such serendipity only rings once. "Should another disaster of the same magnitude as Northridge occur in the reasonable future," predict researchers for the prestigious California Policy Seminar, "neither private insurers nor federal or state agencies will be willing or able to respond with a comparable level of rebuilding assistance."[124] Since Hurricane Andrew and the Northridge earthquake, the political economy of disaster has been profoundly reshaped. The insurance industry has shown a steely will to use economic terrorism against homeowners if necessary to defend its bottom line against future earthquakes. Congress, meanwhile, has retooled the game rules for disaster relief: in order to disarm competition between "heartlanders" and "coastlanders," the interests of the urban poor and middle-class homeowners in disaster-prone environments are now directly counterposed.

In the next earthquake, to begin with, homeowners and landlords are certain to face huge unrecoverable losses. At the time of the Northridge earthquake, the owner of a relatively new, wood-frame house worth $200,000, and suffering $100,000 in structural and contents damage, would have received 78 percent of the loss under her old insurance policy. Today, under the controversial new California Earthquake Authority (CEA), established by the legislature after private insurers threatened to cut off the supply of homeowners' coverage, the same quake victim would recover only 43 percent of her loss.[125] In the event of a new disaster, of course, the shortfall in homeowners' coverage under the CEA combined with a larger number of uninsured victims will translate into poignant demands for increased federal relief. Will Washington be willing to assume that burden?

Before the Los Angeles riots and Hurricane Andrew in 1992, federal disaster aid had simply been added to the national debt with little or no impact on other federal programs. However, the soaring cost of federal relief ($33 billion between 1989 and 1994) galvanized deficit hawks in Congress to join forces to stall passage of the 1993 Midwest flood relief bill until disaster expenditures were offset with tax increases. Although they were easily swept aside by a bipartisan majority, a new anti-relief bloc composed primarily of midwestern representatives emerged six months later when, faced with the huge demands of the Northridge disaster, Congressman David Obey (D-Wisconsin) proposed replacing FEMA with voluntary, state-level insurance schemes. "Millions of people choose to live in coastal areas and in earthquake zones because of other compensating attributes of those areas. I don't see why taxpayers in the rest of the country have to subsidize that decision."[126]

With Machiavellian cunning, the new Republican Speaker, Newt Gingrich, defused this potential disaster-aid war between the states by proposing to finance the final installment of Northridge aid with counterpart cuts in social spending. The White House endorsed the deal after the Republicans, in the ill-famed and confusing episode of the 1995 "recision bill," kidnapped the $6.6 billion disaster relief bill and held it hostage until the Democrats agreed to $16.3 billion in cuts to already budgeted domestic spending.*

As a result of this compromise, earthquake victims in Los Angeles, including the unfortunates in Beverly Hills 90210, continued to receive relief payments and low-interest loans. Freeways were rebuilt and hospitals reopened. But all this was financed by counterpart cutbacks in low-income housing and environmental protection programs, as well as the termination of "unnecessary spending" on rural health grants, the urban parks and recreation program, and summer youth employment funds for 1996. For his part, Speaker Gingrich was able to boast of a new ally in his crusade against entitlements for the urban poor—an angry and evidently Republican-oriented lobby of one, Mother Nature. Congress, with the barest

---

* The president, who had not mounted a heroic resistance, ended up embracing the Democratic defeat as a bipartisan victory. "The budget cutting in this bill is exactly the kind of thing we should be doing ... cutting unnecessary spending but maintaining our commitment to education, to health care, to the environment." It was difficult not to wonder whether Clinton was suffering from the notorious "Stockholm syndrome."[127]

dissent, had replaced traditional deficit financing of disaster aid with a new, bipartisan policy of "pay as you go" offsets in domestic spending. It was an ingenious strategy for recycling natural disaster as class struggle.[128]

The implications of this new(t) dispensation have failed to percolate very far beyond the Beltway. Yet disaster relief could potentially cannibalize a significant portion of what remains of discretionary social spending. In addition to Southern (and Northern) California's own exceptional vulnerability to seismic debt collection, there are potent reasons, ranging from global warming to the fad for second homes on hurricane-prone barrier islands, to suspect that the current clustering of climatic and geological disaster will continue.[129] As if the poor do not already have enough to worry about, they now face the bizarre prospect that if Malibu burns or Hilton Head is blown away in a hurricane, they will have to foot the bill.

The fate of inner-city areas of Los Angeles in the aftermath of the Northridge earthquake vividly illustrates how people of color are doubly punished by natural and political disasters. The first casualty of the temblor was any residual official interest in economic recovery efforts and job creation in the neighborhoods traumatized by the 1992 riots. Rebuilding the Valley supplanted "Rebuild L.A." At the same time there was a virtual media blackout about the extensive quake damage in the northern part of the Crenshaw district, the retail and cultural heart of African-American Los Angeles, where housing sprawls over former *cienegas* and stream channels.

The Crenshaw district earthquake assistance center, which received 6,726 applications for relief, was the busiest in Los Angeles County. But two-thirds of the applicants for Small Business Administration loans (widely used to cover deductibles on private insurance claims) were rejected because of insufficient savings. These quake victims, often elderly African-Americans on fixed incomes, had to wait two years or longer before they qualified for a last-resort city program for low-income homeowners. Community leaders bitterly contrasted the bureaucratic haste to repair the La Cienega section of the Santa Monica Freeway, whose collapse had forced white commuters to drive through black neighborhoods, with the prolonged neglect of damaged homes and apartments in the same area.[130] In the meantime, landlords simply walked away from damaged properties in poorer areas, worsening the rental housing shortage and adding a new crop of derelict buildings and empty lots to the large inventory still remaining from the 1965 and 1992 riots.

9. STRANGE ATTRACTIONS

Most natural disasters are characteristic rather than accidental features of the places and societies where they occur.
Geographer Kenneth Hewitt (1983)

In the fall of 1996 Chinese authorities announced plans for the world's first earthquake theme park in Tangshan, a hundred miles southeast of Beijing. In 1976, an M 7.8 quake killed as many residents of this large industrial city as a direct hit by a nuclear warhead might have. The official death toll was 250,000, but U.S. intelligence agencies suspected that it was closer to 800,000. The proposed "Earthquake City," to be partially financed by foreign investors, would incorporate ruins from the 1976 catastrophe, "most notably the preserved college whose intact four upper storeys remain perched on the rubble of the collapsed ground floor." Simulated earthquakes would give visitors the adrenaline rush of surviving the Big One. "The chief aim of the park is said to be education rather than tourism, but there's little doubt that the park scheme is intended to attract visitors and their money to a region that currently sees only 1,000–2,000 foreigners a year."[131]

Perhaps there is a lesson here for Los Angeles. In the event that half of the metropolis is wrecked in the next earthquake (or riot, for that matter), Disney and Dreamworks can collaborate to reshape the ruins into a really stunning version of what Saint John of Revelation claimed to see at the end of time. Then the tourists' shekels will flow in like the Los Angeles River at floodtide. In the meantime, and while there is time, the 17 million people in the Los Angeles region need to take careful heed of what environmental historians, earth scientists, structural engineers, consumer advocates, and a handful of elected officials have been trying to tell us about the dialectic of ordinary disaster.

Los Angeles fatally lacks the emergency capacity—engineers would call it "redundancy"—to deal with larger or more frequent earthquakes, as well as great floods, chaparral firestorms, and protracted droughts. The cheapest and most sensible form of redundancy, of course, would have been "hazard zoning" to exclude intensive development from the most disaster-prone terrains, combined with a conservative water ethic. Historically, there has been no shortage of prophetic voices urging the region's leaders to mitigate inevitable disaster and enhance quality of life through the regulation of urbanization in the foothills and wetlands; but they were almost uniformly ignored, and as a result, there is scarcely any open space left to act as a buffer against temperamental Mediterranean nature.

In addition, vulnerability to disaster has an inflationary dimension. Uncontrolled horizontal growth of the megalopolis relentlessly undermines existing infrastructures and raises the cost of protecting suburbia from nature. To deal with the impact, for example, of the recent residential boom in the Puente Hills and the west end of Riverside and San Bernardino Counties, the Army Corps of Engineers is being forced to spend another $1.5 billion on massive improvements in flood control systems, while Southern California's already existing pharaonic public works are rapidly aging. In some cases, their careers may last less than an average human lifetime. In his superb cautionary essay, "Los Angeles against the Mountains," John McPhee tells the sobering story of Pasadena's Devil's Gate Dam, built to last centuries, which filled up with debris in less than 50 years. It is now a sand and gravel quarry.[132]

Metropolitan Los Angeles's political systems are as single purpose and inflexible as its physical infrastructures, and they also fill up with debris almost as quickly. In a region where rapid economic growth has been the one sustaining ideal and common goal, the 1990–95 recession has left a much deeper political imprint than riot, earthquake, or flood. There is less tolerance than ever for environmental regulation that interferes with the short-term investment climate, nor are there any significant local tax resources left in tax-slashing Southern California to pay for new programs. In Sacramento, underfunded campuses battle overcrowded prisons for the last scraps from the governor's table.

Yet the Northridge earthquake has redefined the meaning of seismic safety and raised its cost by a full order of magnitude. We now know that all high-occupancy structures, including steel-frame office towers, are at risk from even a moderate earthquake directly under the Los Angeles Basin. We also know that hundreds of thousands of family homes and apartment buildings urgently need expensive seismic reinforcement, and that precast concrete buildings are probably too dangerous to be tolerated in areas of unstable soil. We need, in a nutshell, to spend billions in mitigation in order to prevent hundreds of billions in damages. But nothing is less politically realistic in the present climate, and the ostrichlike consensus is to ignore problems that are too big to fix.

This all boils down to an unhappy but obvious proposition: the continuing clustering of disaster on "ordinary" or extraordinary scales will inevitably erode many of the comparative advantages of the Southern California economy. Certainly, other metropolitan regions, especially the Bay Area, Wasatch Front, Puget Sound, and South Florida, face comparable risks of natural disaster over the next generation, but none bear Los Angeles's heavy burdens of mass poverty and racial violence. What is most distinctive about Los Angeles is not simply its conjugation of earthquakes, wildfires, and floods, but its uniquely explosive mixture of natural hazards and social contradictions. Not even Miami, that other fallen paradise, can approach the conflagrationist potential of Los Angeles.

But I am not summoning Armageddon. Despite the wishful thinking of evangelicals impatient for the Rapture or deep ecologists who believe that Gaia would be happiest with a thin sprinkling of hunter-gatherers, megacities like Los Angeles will never simply collapse and

Will the poor now be forced to rebuild the rich?

disappear. Rather, they will stagger on, with higher body counts and greater distress, through a chain of more frequent and destructive encounters with disasters of all sorts; while vital parts of the region's high-tech and tourist economies eventually emigrate to safer ground, together with hundreds of thousands of its more affluent residents. Aficionados of complexity theory will marvel at the "nonlinear resonances" of unnatural disaster and social breakdown as Southern California's golden age is superseded forever by a chaotic new world of strange attractors.

2

HOW EDEN LOST ITS GARDEN

The ambitious time traveler, *pace* popular science fiction, doesn't need to know anything about Lorentz transformations or black holes—a good road map of Los Angeles County will suffice. Thirty miles north of Downtown, just past the 41-story-high "Superman" ride at Six Flags Magic Mountain but before the exit for the county sheriff's enormous jail complex at Castaic, the traveler should turn west on California Highway 126. Following the channel of the Santa Clara River as it cuts through spectacularly colored sandstone and shale formations to the ocean at Ventura, this eucalyptus-arbored, two-lane blacktop turns back time to a Southern Californian golden age when garden cities nestled in millions of acres of orange, lemon, and avocado groves.

More than a generation after the last fruit trees were bulldozed to make way for tract houses in the San Fernando and San Gabriel Valleys, the Santa Clara River Valley still looks much as it did before 1940. Here, the formal order of the orchards offsets the wild angularity of the sedimentary hills. The citrus towns of Piru, Fillmore, and Santa Paula initially strike the hyperreality-hardened visitor as movie sets or nostalgia theme parks with all the hackneyed charm of Norman Rockwell paintings. There are no minimalls or fast-food strips, just quiet main streets with old-fashioned stores, soda fountains, and the town movie theater. It is shocking to realize that these are, in fact, real towns, homes to orchard owners and their Mexican workers, and not just clever simulations designed for the pleasure of tourists.

Time machine: Santa Clara River Valley (1995)

Perhaps most disconcerting is Camulos, once the estate of the Del Valle family, where Helen Hunt Jackson during the winter of 1882 conceived the setting and plot of her famous novel *Ramona.* Although the Del Valles passed on long ago, this working rancho, with its regiments of orange trees sloping down to the Santa Clara River, is almost indistinguishable from its portrait on turn-of-the-century postcards. Apart from a television aerial on the ranch building, the most striking emblem of modernity in sight is a 1949 flathead Ford pickup.

This picturesque landscape, of course, masks the citrus industry's long history of paternalistic exploitation, social segregation, and labor violence. ("Oppressive society and rich beautiful countryside," as geographer Yi-Fu Tuan points out, "are fully compatible.")[1] Still, what shocks some visitors even more than the surprising endurance of the unsimulated past in the valley is that most of the mailboxes in front of the tidy Victorian cottages and 1920s bungalows are stenciled with last names like Gonzales and Hernandez. That such a luscious setting so close to Los Angeles has not yet been devoured by million-dollar homes, gated subdivisions, antique malls, and white-flight commuters is surely remarkable.

The very beauty of the valley can't help but prompt thoughts about the near extinction of such landscapes elsewhere in urbanized Southern California. Millions of newcomers were once drawn to the Los Angeles area by the promise of homes and orchards soaking in sunshine at the foot of snow-peaked mountains. Postcards and orange-crate labels advertised this idyllic image to the world for decades, and unlike so much else about the region, it was not entirely fake. Even at the end of the Second World War, metropolitan Los Angeles still possessed inestimable scenic capital as well as compelling if utopian visions of how the city might yet use its open spaces to make itself more beautiful and more egalitarian. What happened? Why is the Santa Clara River Valley the last refuge of Southern California's most famous dream?

1. THE UNDERPRODUCTION OF PUBLIC SPACE

Continued prosperity will depend on providing needed parks. . . . In so far . . . as the people fail to show the understanding, courage, and organizing ability necessary at this crisis, the growth of the Region will tend to strangle itself.
> Frederick Law Olmsted, Jr., Parks, Playgrounds
> and Beaches for the Los Angeles Region *(1930)*

In March 1930 the most distinguished citizens' committee in Los Angeles history submitted its final report to city and county authorities. A letter of transmittal signed by movie stars like Mary Pickford, bankers like Irving Hellman, and corporate lawyers like John O'Melveny warned of a situation "so disquieting as to make it highly expedient to impress upon the public the present crisis in the welfare of Los Angeles."[2]

With nearly one-quarter of the city out of work in that grim depression year, it might be presumed that the report, so urgent in tone, was about unemployment relief or soup kitchens for the hungry. In fact, the attention of the 162 prominent members of the Citizens' Committee on Parks, Playgrounds and Beaches was concentrated on the "parks and recreation crisis." This was less strange than it might seem.

As the report's authors, the celebrated urban design firm of Olmsted Brothers (with planner Harlan Bartholomew as an associate), pointed out, accessible open space was the foundation of an economy capitalized on climate, sports, and outdoor leisure, but the region's scenic beauty was being eroded on all sides by rampant, unregulated private development. They warned that Los Angeles's future prosperity was directly threatened by the increasing discrepancy between tourists' buoyant expectations and their disillusioning experiences in the Land of Sunshine.

> The widely-advertised attractions of climate and scenery bring thousands to the Los Angeles Region every year. They find the climate fully equal to expectations but the facilities by which the out-of-doors may be enjoyed prove a surprise and disappointment. . . . The beaches, which are pictured in the magazines to attract eastern visitors, are suffering from the rapid encroachment of private use; the wild canyons are fast being subjected to subdivision and cheek-by-jowl cabin construction; the forests suffer annually from devastating fires; the roadsides are more and more disfigured by sign boards, shacks, garages, filling stations, destruction of trees.[3]

Frederick Law Olmsted, Jr., and Harlan Bartholomew further observed that "the things that make [Los Angeles] most attractive are the very ones that are the first to suffer from changes and deteriorate through neglect." Although Los Angeles spent more than other cities to advertise its charms, it invested less to preserve or enhance them. The deficiency of parks was "positively reprehensible," and the region fell "far short . . . of the minimum recreation facilities of the average American city." Moreover, as the authors acknowledged, "all this has been realized for years."[4]

Indeed, at the turn of the century, Charles Fletcher Lummis, editor of *Out West* and impresario of the local franchise of the Arts and Crafts movement (the "Arroyo set"), had thundered against Los Angeles's Victorian elites for "impoverishing the future" through their reckless alienation of the original pueblo lands.

> As late as 1856 the city owned eighty per cent of its area of some 17,000 acres. It gave this priceless heritage away—generally for nothing, and altogether for next to nothing—without even once getting an equivalent or a good bargain. . . . We would have the finest parks in the world, and the finest public buildings—and all endowed beyond the dreams of avarice. As it is, nothing was left the city but the Plaza and some riverbed when we began to take notice.[5]

By the early 1900s, even this remnant was under threat, as the once arcadian landscape of the Los Angeles River was pressed into service as a sewer for the city's expanding industrial district. The Reverend Dana Bartlett, planning advocate and settlement house pioneer, battled the corporate "octopus" of the Southern Pacific Railroad (the largest floodplain landowner) in an unsuccessful crusade to reclaim the riverbed as a nature preserve and playground for the children of the "congested areas" east of Downtown.[6]* Middle-class Progressives, meanwhile, indicted Los Angeles's meager and poorly maintained parks as the "shame of the city": "Some of our parks are filthy to the grade of a public nuisance and should have been condemned long ago."[8]

In his 1907 report to the Los Angeles Municipal Art Commission, Charles Mulford Robinson, the renowned apostle of the City Beautiful, advocated a comprehensive plan for parks, boulevards, beautifi-

---

* Labor leaders, who supported Bartlett's struggle against the railroads, also blamed traction magnate Henry Huntington for refusing to lay track to newly donated Griffith Park while keeping fares so high on his Ocean Park line that working people could not afford to go to the beach.[7]

Hollywood in 1905

cation of the Los Angeles River, and a civic acropolis on Downtown's Bunker Hill.[9] In order to finance his heroic proposals, he urged the city to "grasp the big idea" and become a land developer in its own right.

> There will be great gain if the city can obtain that authority which the cities of Pennsylvania and Ohio have already secured, and by which the great municipal improvements of Europe and South America have been financed—the right to acquire property on the edge of a public improvement, in order to protect that improvement, and to recoup the cost of making it by the resale of the property at the enhanced value which the improvement bestows.[10]

He cautioned that "the tourist metropolis of the country . . . simply cannot afford to stand still, or, rather, with your increasing population to go from bad to worse in congestion, in city discomfort and ugliness." Robinson hinted that if Los Angeles wavered in its commitment to public space, other "more beautiful" cities would usurp its destiny (was he already thinking of Seattle?).[11]

By the time Olmsted and Bartholomew surveyed the same problem 20 years later, nearly two million more people, the equivalent of the population of Philadelphia, had moved to the Los Angeles region. Their 1930 report was, first of all, a stinging critique of the giddy twenties building boom, which after its collapse in the oil scandals of 1926–28, left 175 square miles of vacant, unsold lots on the city's fringes, but only a few hundred acres of new parkland.[12] Developers had stubbornly ignored official pleas to dedicate parks for their subdivisions, and powerful homeowners' groups had opposed every attempt to pass specific assessments for parks or recreation; thus, as the population soared, per capita recreation space shrank drastically. By 1928 parks comprised a miserable 0.6 percent of the surface of the metropolis, and barely half an inch of publicly owned beach frontage was left for each citizen of Los Angeles County.[13] No large city in the United States was so stingy with public space.

A selfish, profit-driven presentism ruled Southern California. As Olmsted and Bartholomew paraphrased the dominant attitude, "The benefit of parks bought now will accrue largely in future years and even to future generations. We can get along without them a while longer, anyhow. And if land at those prices is a good purchase, we would rather use our money to get lots on speculation for personal profit than give it up in taxes for our share of a park system."[14]

Indeed, speculation—"excessive and fictitious prices for raw land"—was the crux of the landscape crisis. The "high capitalization of future rental values" in even the most marginal or hazardous of terrains made a comprehensive program of park building prohibitively expensive.[15] Ironically, the entire inflationary process was subsidized by local government. Olmsted and Bartholomew were especially critical of the costly public outlays for roads, sewers, fire protection, and flood control meant to encourage promoters to subdivide scenic canyons, streambeds, and foothills.

> It costs so much in the long run to adapt rough mountain lands satisfactorily to ordinary intensive private uses that their real net value as raw material for such use is generally far less than their value for watershed protection and for public recreation. Unfortunately in the local speculative land market this fact is

often ignored and subdivision sales are made which commit the community to extravagant wasteful private and public expenditures for converting a good thing of one kind into a poor thing of another kind.[16]

The Gordian knot of land speculation, however, could be cut with a single, decisive blade: *hazard zoning.* Since the "burden of wrong development does not fall on the purchaser alone, and scarcely ever on the vendor, but most heavily on the community at large," the municipality could justifiably invoke its powers to limit or even bar development of floodplains and hillsides (and, by implication, of known earthquake fault zones and chronic wildfire corridors).[17]

Together with radically enlarged public ownership of ocean frontage, the redemption of Los Angeles's riparian landscapes was the key to Olmsted and Bartholomew's elegant design for a unified regional system of beaches, parks, playgrounds, and mountain reserves. At their 1924 conference, Los Angeles County pioneer regional planners had already recognized the crucial role of river courses as the "easiest and often the shortest connection between the mountain and the beach playground areas." In addition to advocating public ownership

Hollywood in 1925

of the oceanfront, the conference recommended "that all principal natural drainage channels be acquired and controlled by the community for the highest public use."[18] Olmsted and Bartholomew argued that greenbelts (or "pleasureway parks," in their slightly awkward terminology) flanking these channels could simultaneously provide flood control, recreation, and transportation. Using hazard zoning to force land values downward and "stop the ill-directed spread of the population," they proposed to transform the major flood channels and associated wetlands into a 440-mile network of multipurpose parkways reminiscent of Frederick Law Olmsted, Sr.'s famous 1887 "emerald necklace" design for Boston's Back Bay fens.[19]

"Parkways should be greatly elongated real parks . . . several thousand feet in width," parallel to broad natural flood channels and offering a variety of recreational experiences. Regional highways would be embedded in these attractive, tree-lined corridors, screened from adjacent industrial and residential developments.[20] Parkways thus designed would reinforce the role of natural hydrology in dividing up the otherwise monotonous coastal plain into attractive, well-defined community landscapes. Finally, Olmsted and Bartholomew's plan explicitly redistributed park and open space resources to the advantage of the neglected working-class districts south and east of Downtown. "Those of lower incomes generally live in small-lot, single-family home districts, and have more children and less leisure time in which to go to distant parks and recreational areas. These families comprise 65 percent of the population, and they should be given first consideration."[21]

2. KILLING THE LOS ANGELES RIVER

The main purpose of flood control is to waste water.
Richard Lillard, Eden in Jeopardy *(1966)*

The 1930 report is a window into a lost future. A heroic culmination of the City Beautiful era in American urban design, it was also the final fruit of the Olmsted Brothers' intense, decade-long involvement in California landscape planning. (The firm also prepared master plans for Los Angeles County highways, the state park system, Balboa Park in San Diego, and the preservation of watershed in the East Bay hills, as well as designing the acclaimed suburb of Palos Verdes Estates.)[22]

Frederick Law Olmsted, Jr., and Harlan Bartholomew were quiet, conservative reformers whose personal utopia was park-rich Minneapolis, not Soviet Russia. Yet if their proposals had been implemented, the results would have been virtually revolutionary. The existing hierarchy of public and private space in Los Angeles might have been overturned. A dramatically enlarged commons, not the private subdivision, might have become the commanding element in the Southern California landscape. Preserved natural ecosystems (Olmsted was a passionate champion of native flora) might have imposed clear boundaries on urbanization. The speculative real estate market might have been counterbalanced by a vigorous social democracy of beaches and playgrounds.

Needless to say, such extravagant conceptions of public space alarmed guardians of Los Angeles's reputation as the capital of anti-radicalism and the open shop. (One of the major local events of 1930 was a brutal attack by the police on a peaceful crowd celebrating May Day in Pershing Square.) The *Los Angeles Times*, in particular, disdained proposals to municipalize almost 100,000 acres of private land and to triple the area of public beach frontage. It crusaded against legislation to establish a metropolitan park district to carry out the Olmsted plan, denouncing it as "the greatest combination of power, taxation and bonding burden in history." Under pressure from the *Times*, 27 prominent members of the Citizens' Committee withdrew their support from the park legislation, thus killing the Olmsted plan before the final report had reached the printer.[23]

But even if an encompassing civic consensus had existed, neither the city nor the county had the wherewithal, in the bleak early days of the depression, to undertake a massive park-building program. Only Washington had the resources. Ironically, when New Deal agencies finally came to the fiscal rescue of Los Angeles, local government used federal capital to pave over the wetlands and streams that were so central to Olmsted and Bartholomew's vision. The death of the Los Angeles River, in particular, was a dismal portent of the continuing role of government in reshaping and degrading the regional environment.

For most modern visitors, the very concept of a "Los Angeles River" has always seemed like an old Jack Benny joke. This is because none of them have ever seen it in full flood. As the Army Corps of Engineers has often reminded its critics, Los Angeles, sited in an alluvial plain at the foot of a rugged, rapidly eroding mountain range, has the worst flood and debris problems of any major city in the Northern Hemisphere. Before 1940, at least half of the city's flatland area was subject to periodic overflow from the Los Angeles River.[24]

Olmsted and Bartholomew emphasized in their report that flood control could be accomplished by different combinations of landuse planning and public works. Their preference was to strictly limit private encroachment within the 50-year floodplain. They wanted to conserve broad natural channels in which storm waters could spread, irrigating and fertilizing the riverside landscapes that out of flood season would serve the public as nature preserves, recreational parks, and scenic parkways.[25]

The opposing solution was to deepen and "armor"—that is, pave—a narrow width of the river's channel in order to flush storm runoff out of the city as efficiently as possible, and thus allow extensive industrial development within the floodplain. Beneficial to large landowners, this strategy would force the natural river into a concrete straitjacket—destroying the riparian ecology and precluding use of the riverway as a greenbelt. Not surprisingly, support for this approach was first organized and financed early in the century by Paul Shoup of the Southern Pacific Railroad.[26] Shoup's so-called Flood Control Committee portrayed the river as an apocalyptic threat to the city's "humble homebuilders." "It should be remembered," read one of its campaign ads, "that prior to 1824, the Los Angeles River, when in flood, flowed southwest through the present location of the city into Santa Monica Bay. If we had another flood like that of 1889, and a steel bridge fell

1938 flood (Echo Park)

into the river and dammed it, this might happen again, causing a calamity equal to that of Johnstown or Galveston."[27]

The unprecedented loss of 87 lives in the great deluge of 1938, which turned 300,000 acres of the San Fernando Valley and Orange County into inland seas, seemed to justify the flood control lobby's morbid predictions. There was broad agreement that the urban-riparian interface had to be reconstructed to take account of the huge population explosion of the 1920s. Urbanization, of course, had itself inexorably increased the menace of such floods by reducing the porous surface area available to absorb runoff. But Olmsted and Bartholomew's greenbelt alternative, with its explicit assertion of communal sovereignty over private interest, was never seriously debated. Nor did anyone seem to pay much attention to the Olmstedian proposition that it was cheaper to keep property away from floodplains through hazard zoning than to keep floods away from property through vast public works.

A decisive political factor was the promise that flood control construction would generate thousands of temporary jobs for the unemployed. Fletcher Bowron, Los Angeles's new reform mayor, was under tremendous pressure from his trade union allies to expand public works employment in coordination with Washington. As a result, both local New Dealers and the city's traditional Republican elite campaigned for the comprehensive plan that Congress eventually approved as the Flood Control Act of 1941. The Army Corps of Engineers was authorized to reshape the county's natural hydrology into a monolithic system of concrete storm sewers. The Los Angeles River—the defining landscape of the nineteenth-century city—was sacrificed for the sake of emergency work relief, the preservation of industrial land values, and a temporary abatement of the flood problem.

In the same period, the city also came perilously close to killing Santa Monica Bay. Since the citrus revolution of the 1880s, most Southern California towns had recycled their sewage to farmers as valuable irrigation water and fertilizer. In 1894, however, Los Angeles, whose population was growing faster than nearby farmers' demand for fertilizer, began discharging its raw sewage into the ocean

Paving the Los Angeles River (1940)

through an outfall at Hyperion Beach. A primitive screening process was finally introduced in the early 1920s after a storm of protest against the unspeakable beach pollution. But waste treatment was unable to keep up with the population explosion, and with the huge migration of war workers and GIs in the early 1940s, the system broke down entirely. As a result, thousands of swimmers and picnickers contracted bacillary dysentery. In 1943, in order to forestall the more lethal threats of full-fledged typhoid and poliomyelitis epidemics, the state Board of Health declared a "gross public health hazard" and closed 10 miles of fetid beaches.[28]

Indeed, a decade after Olmsted and Bartholomew's report, the "parks and recreation crisis" had become a comprehensive environmental crisis. With biblical implacability, floods and sewage spills in the bay were accompanied by massive beach erosion from improper groining and breakwater construction, land subsidence from oil drilling, and saltwater intrusion into the underground water supply. The first smog attack in 1943—an eerie "darkness at noon" over the Los Angeles Basin—caused almost as much consternation as had Pearl Harbor.[29]

3. BATTLE OF THE VALLEY

It's a dream! This charming, gleaming white home tucked way among the flowers. Patio, view, snooty den. Located on Florida Avenue, the most secluded street in the San Fernando Valley. You'll love it. Bargain at four thousand, nine hundred and fifty dollars.

> Theodore Pratt, The Valley Boy (1946)

At a symposium of the region's leading architects and planners on the eve of the Second World War, Richard Neutra, the architectural representative on the new State Planning Board, denounced the reckless disfigurement of Los Angeles's hillsides, the dispiriting uniformity of most of its subdivisions, and, above all, the corrosive impact of extreme privatism. "Beautiful and broad views from individual dwellings," he argued, "can hardly atone for the lack of a comprehensive and convincingly landscaped neighborhood design and for lost communal opportunities." Large-scale government housing projects rather than private developments, Neutra argued, offered the best opportunity for integrated community design.[30]

Neutra's derision of private homes in the hills rings odd today since it is for precisely such projects that he and other first-generation Los Angeles design modernists are most remembered. Yet, in the war years, domestic architecture scarcely made an appearance in the Los Angeles–based *Arts and Architecture* magazine. The war mobilized an unprecedented coalition of architects, planners, and New Deal reformers committed to a common vision of regional planning, slum clearance, social housing, and environmental conservation.

In a score of federal housing projects, as well as in several exemplary private subdivisions, Southern California's leading modernists attempted to define an alternative urbanism based on medium-density groupings of bungalows and garden apartments around dramatic common spaces. If Neutra's Channel Heights project, built to house shipyard workers in the Los Angeles Harbor area, is justifiably recalled by architectural historians as the finest single design of the period, then Baldwin Hills Village has been the most successful enduring community. Completed in 1942 after a long struggle to obtain federal financing, the village consists of 630 row houses and apartments, in five styles, arranged in a continuous **S** plan around garden courts opening onto three large greens connected by tree-shaded malls. Uniquely for Los Angeles, automobile traffic is confined to the project's periphery, while the center is an oasis of pedestrian calm. At every level of organization, the village's design sustains a superb dialectic between private and communal space. After more than a half-century—integrated and ungated—it remains one of Los Angeles's most vibrant neighborhoods.

In its original context, moreover, the village was envisaged as a prototype "democratic community," an alternative urban building block to the automobile-dominated private subdivision. One of the most influential contemporary advocates of this new urbanism was Robert Alexander, a member of the architectural team that created the village and a future partner of Richard Neutra. Appointed to the Los Angeles City Planning Commission at the end of the war, Alexander boldly attempted to use agricultural greenbelts—much in the spirit of Olmsted and Bartholomew—to force postwar suburbanization along a new design path, based on the commons-centered, pedestrian-scaled examples of Baldwin Hills Village and Channel Heights.

Alexander foresaw that the voracious postwar demand for housing, if left to the speculative marketplace, would simply repeat the 1920s boom on a larger and more destructive scale. The remaining agricultural areas of coastal Southern California, especially the San Fernando and San Gabriel Valleys, would immediately become enormous real estate casinos where speculators and builders would lay their bets on farmland and wait for population growth to pay off. In the San Fernando Valley, in particular, rural and urban landuses were already precariously balanced. As one writer described it in 1946:

> Modest cottages and estates of the master-bedroom-swimming-pool class were often side by side. There were walnut groves, and peach and apricot and persimmon. There were fancy chicken and rabbit ranches and fancier establishments of cowboy movie stars. A few genuine old farmhouses peered apologetically, with unpainted faces, out from beneath great white oaks. Vacant fields were covered with a chiffon of yellow-green polka-dot wild mustard. Gaily colored pennants waved briskly in a fresh breeze in front of real estate offices. On the outdoor signboard of one office was the assurance, "Horses Okay Here."[31]

Such areas, Alexander feared, would be transformed overnight into a monotonous mosaic of tract houses and vacant lots. The orchards and truck farms that formed the historical matrix for

Baldwin Hills Village Green (1941)

already existing suburban garden cities would be uprooted and new development would coalesce into a shapeless amoebic mass.

Alexander and city planning director Charles Bennett recognized that the San Fernando Valley, under tremendous pressure from real estate speculators, would be the first and most decisive battlefield. Accordingly, they proposed a zoning strategy that opened the Valley to hundreds of thousands of house-hungry ex-GIs and aircraft workers but concentrated new development at medium-density levels around 16 existing suburban nodes permanently separated by 83 square miles of citrus and farm greenbelts.[32]

Alexander's implicit vision was of a *virtuous circle* in which the protection of open space through strict zoning simultaneously preserved landscape integrity, promoted clustered housing, reduced the costs of school and utility provision, and ensured sufficient population densities to sustain rapid transit systems, including the famous interurban "red cars." This new urban fabric would, he believed, be especially conducive to strong neighborhood identity and to increased democratic participation—key values in the New Deal paradigm of planning.[33]

At the end of the war, greenbelt zoning for the Valley was actually passed into law by the city council, but it lacked the broad political support to survive the relentless counterattack of developers and landowners. As Alexander explained in an unpublished memoir, something more sacred than quality of life was at stake:

> With a vast pent-up demand and a sure market, it would have been quite profitable for developers to buy undeveloped lots in any of the existing town centers. They could even acquire adjacent unsubdivided land, . . . but nothing would satisfy their greed. Instead, they obtained options for practically nothing to buy the cheapest land zoned for agricultural use and applied for changes in [zoning]. Sometimes accompanied by a veteran wearing an American Legion hat, they found willing cooperators in the planning director and four of the commissioners who needed no urging to respond to the hysteria of the housing shortage. They gained untold riches as they converted "greenbelts" to densely packed urban town lots.[34]

As politically naive planners were shocked to discover, other units of government became active accomplices in the destruction of Los Angeles's agricultural periphery. The county tax assessor, for example, increased the pressure on farmers to sell out by reappraising their land as prime residential real estate—"a self-fulfilling prophecy which spread like wildfire."[35] The Federal Housing Administration, already notorious among African-Americans for its endorsement of racially restrictive covenants and white-only suburbs, refused to lift a finger to preserve natural landscapes or to discourage leapfrog development.

Alexander's virtuous circle was inexorably transformed into a *vicious circle:* the total loss of horticultural landscape, excessive accumulation of vacant lots, expensive utilities and schools, a dramatic imbalance of homes and jobs, minimal community cohesion, and low-density populations transportable only by private cars. By the early 1960s, instead of a "balanced self-sufficient constellation of communities" bordered by greenbelts, the valley had become a paved-over "undifferentiated slurb" of nearly one million people.[36]

4. GREENING THE URBAN DESERT?

The traditional view toward private ownership of property that permits the temporary owner a proprietary interest has been outmoded by new knowledge of man's relationship to nature and to the community. This knowledge demands a new attitude toward ownership of land, substituting the concept of trusteeship for exploitation.

EDAW, The Urban Metropolitan
Open Space Study (1969)

In 1958 sociologist William Whyte—author of *The Organization Man*—had a disturbing vision as he was leaving Southern California. "Flying from Los Angeles to San Bernardino—an unnerving lesson in man's infinite capacity to mess up his environment—the traveler can see a legion of bulldozers gnawing into the last remaining tract of green between the two cities, and from San Bernardino another legion of bulldozers gnawing westward." When he reached New York he wrote an article for *Fortune* magazine, describing the insidious new growth form that he called "urban sprawl."[37]

After the debacle in the San Fernando Valley, there was negligible political or bureaucratic opposition to the obliteration of the rest of Southern California's picture postcard landscapes. Although Los Angeles County paid homage in its 1941 master plan to the "major importance" of protecting choice agricultural land from subdivision, its actual landuse policies continued to encourage sprawl. In a 1956 report, for example, the Regional Planning Commission confirmed that all the remaining citrus orchards in the eastern San Gabriel Valley would soon be bulldozed and subdivided. The commission's only concern was that "this transition to urban uses should be encouraged to take place in an orderly manner" to minimize the "dead period"

Los Angeles Times Annual Midwinter

JANUARY 2, 1948

Real Estate
and
Development

★

Part 4

Sprawl devours the garden

between land clearance and home construction.[38] But the speculative homebuilding frontier of the 1950s produced the same glut of subdivision relative to demand—"ghost towns in reverse"—that so shocked Olmsted and Bartholomew during the 1920s.

EAST SAN GABRIEL VALLEY: CHANGES IN LANDUSE INVENTORY, 1940–60

Landuse Type	1940	1960	1940–60 Change
Residential	1.3%	15.5%	+14.2%
Agricultural	72.4	19.5	−52.9
Vacant	19.4	42.4	+23
Other	6.9	22.9	+16

Source: Los Angeles County, Regional Planning Commission, *East San Gabriel Valley* (Los Angeles, 1966), p. 12.

For a decade, meanwhile, at least one thousand citrus trees were bulldozed and burned every week. Between 1939 and 1970, agricultural acreage in Los Angeles County south of the San Gabriel Mountains (the richest farmland in the nation according to some agronomists) fell from 300,000 to less than 10,000 acres. One of the nation's most emblematic landscapes—the visual magnet that had attracted hundreds of thousands of immigrants to Southern California—was systematically eradicated.[39]

Hillside and canyon environments fared little better. Both Olmsted and Neutra had denounced the privatization of hillside vistas, and Olmsted had urged public ownership of key tracts in the Santa Monica Mountains. A 1945 county citizens' committee, after reminding political leaders that the quality of recreational landscape was "the goose that lays our golden eggs," proposed extensive open space conservation in the Palos Verdes, Baldwin, Montebello, Puente, San Raphael, and Verdugo Hills. But the postwar demand for "view lots" was virtually unquenchable. Within Los Angeles County as a whole, more than 60,000 house sites were carved out of the mountains and foothills during the 1950s and early 1960s.[40]

URBANIZATION OF THE SANTA MONICA MOUNTAINS
(WEST OF CAHUENGA PASS ONLY)

Year	Dwellings
1930	3,000
1940	5,000
1950	12,000
1960	21,000

Source: Adapted from David Weide, "The Geography of Fire in the
Santa Monica Mountains" (M.A. thesis, Department of Geography,
California State University, Los Angeles, 1968), p. 145.

The automobile also devoured exorbitant quantities of prime land.
By 1970 more than one-third of the surface area of the Los Angeles
region was dedicated to the car: freeways, streets, parking lots, and
driveways.[41] What generations of tourists and migrants had once
admired as a real-life Garden of Eden was now buried under an estimated three billion tons of concrete (or 250 tons per inhabitant).[42]

Southern California sprawl eventually became a national scandal.
Thanks to the crusading efforts of Whyte, federal responsibility for
the "exploding metropolis" was subjected to unprecedented scrutiny
and debate. Despite fierce opposition from the National Association
of Home Builders, the Kennedy administration officially acknowledged the social costs of sprawl and introduced legislation in 1961 to
support the conservation of urban open space.

In California, the state legislature was prodded by the Sierra Club
and California Tomorrow (a regional-planning advocacy group) into
authorizing a major study of the state's "open space crisis." The eminent San Francisco firm of Eckbo, Dean, Austin, and Williams (known
acronymically as EDAW), which dominated environmental planning in
California during the 1960s and 1970s, was hired to consult. Although
Edward A. Williams wrote the final report for the State Office of Planning in 1965, the overarching influence of the firm's most prominent
partner, Garrett Eckbo, in this and subsequent studies was evident.

Eckbo is justly regarded as a pioneer of modernism in American landscape architecture. "A green Californian from the frontier," he arrived at Harvard in the late 1930s just as Bauhaus leader-in-exile Walter Gropius was launching a mini-revolution in its architecture department. But European modernism was only one of many influences in the evolution of Eckbo's unique personal philosophy. In equal measures he was to become a regionalist, ecologist, and radical social democrat who conspired to turn the aristocratic inheritance of landscape design on its head. Since his early days with the Farm Security Administration, designing yards and gardens for farmworker housing, Eckbo had been preoccupied with "the contradiction between social relations and individual land use . . . between the interests of ordinary citizens and those of free enterprise elements who see no values beyond their own private profit."[43]

In *Landscape for Living,* his postwar manifesto for a new philosophy of environmental design, Eckbo decried the "sordid chaos" of "general commercial speculation" and argued that it was "no more than democratic Americanism to say that such forces can be analyzed, exposed and placed under proper public control." Rejecting the reservation of the lushest areas for the rich, he advocated a "truly democratic organization" of the landscape that would replace "the sterile formality of authority" with the "tremendous tree symphony of the future." Indeed as authentic democracy began to achieve "cultural expression in the landscape . . . the present scale of landscape values will tend to reverse itself."

> Instead of moving from the ugly city toward the peak of wilderness beauty, it will be possible to move from the wilderness through constantly more magnificent and orderly rural refinements of the face of the earth, to urban communities composed of structures, paving, grass, shrubs, and trees, which are rich, sparkling, crystalline nuclei in the web of spatial relations that surrounds the earth—peak expressions of the reintegration of man and nature.[44]

The Urban Metropolitan Open Space Study that Eckbo and his partners submitted to Governor Pat Brown in 1965 as the keystone of a proposed state development plan resonated with the bold values and motifs of *Landscape for Living.* Indeed some Sacramento bureaucrats must have found little to choose between EDAW's theses and those of contemporary radicals in Berkeley's Sproul Plaza. The study warned that all of California's remaining Mediterranean valleys and foothills, including the exquisite Santa Barbara–Ventura coast, as well as the famed vineyards of Sonoma and Napa Counties, were threatened with the same fate as Los Angeles's citrus belt. It condemned county governments for their "weak, timid and unimaginative" use of zoning powers and denounced a tax system that rewarded land speculators and punished farmers. It also stressed how landscape-destroying sprawl at the urban edge devoured the bulk of regional tax resources and accelerated neighborhood decay in the center.[45]

"A clearcut crisis situation," the authors found, "exists in the Southern California urban-metropolitan area." Once again, suburbanization had entirely outpaced the production of new public space. By the most minimal standards of per capita provision of recreation space, Los Angeles County was facing a 100,000-acre shortfall of regional parks, while at the municipal level the discrepancy was frequently much worse. Indeed, the open space situation throughout the Los Angeles Basin—"1,500 square miles of low grade, monotonous suburban construction"—was so hopeless that the study focused instead on stopping sprawl at its periphery.[46]

In 1965 significant farm and foothill belts still defended Ventura-Oxnard, San Bernardino, Riverside, and San Diego from engulfment by greater Los Angeles. Although local environmentalists had targeted the Santa Monica Mountains as the most important conservation area, the study focused instead on the Puente Hills and Chino Plain, which separated the San Gabriel Valley from suburbanizing San Bernardino and Orange Counties. As "the center of the greatest population pressure within the region . . . they should become the most highly prized and zealously protected open-space resource."[47]

The second regional priority was "from Conejo to Hidden Hills, between Los Angeles and Ventura, an area of beautiful rolling hills and valleys, peculiarly vulnerable to destruction by careless and indifferent development, yet peculiarly pregnant with possibilities for rich and imaginative design." Other environmental battlegrounds were the undeveloped parts of the Oxnard Plain, the Elsinore-Temecula corridor in southwest Riverside County, and the coastal mesas and valleys between San Diego and Vista.[48] (EDAW's prescience was subsequently borne out by the frenzy of subdivision in each of these areas during the late 1970s and 1980s.)

The study also briefly surveyed the dismal trajectory of urban overspill into the Mojave and Colorado River deserts. "The entire desert seems to be subdivided and covered with a gridiron of graded streets; such development destroys the desert as landscape and as open space, replacing [it] with nothing but the empty wasteland of exurbanism." Moreover, the elaboration of community designs suitable to the desert environment appeared to be simply "beyond the capability of [existing] planning processes."[49]

In 1966, Eckbo was asked by *Cry California* magazine (the publication of California Tomorrow) to comment on the issue that the study had deliberately sidestepped: how to expand open space resources within the congested and overdeveloped Los Angeles Basin. After observing that "no comparable urban region in the nation even remotely approaches the basin's inadequacy [in parkland]," Eckbo made a characteristically audacious proposal for "greening the urban desert." He suggested that the county redevelop suburbs into parks by relocating 10 percent of the population ("from various income groups") into new higher density housing. Estimated cost: seven to nine billion dollars.[50]

Six years later, in 1972, EDAW produced another major open space survey: this time an exhaustive study of the Santa Monica Mountain coastline for the California legislature. Given the Santa Monicas' incalculable recreational and landscape value, EDAW expressed incredulity at the county's projected population of 405,000 for the environmentally sensitive Malibu area.[51] They pointed out that Malibu, apart from major problems with earthquakes, flooding, and landslides, also had a fire history "unique in intensity, devastating in effect, and heightened during Santa Ana wind conditions"; and echoing Olmsted and Bartholomew, they decried the ease with which developers in high-risk areas shifted the costs of fire and flood protection onto the taxpayers at large. They proposed a stringent permit system to keep new construction at a minimum while the legislature evaluated options for expanding public ownership in the Santa Monicas.[52]

The EDAW reports were seminal documents in the renaissance of regional planning and landscape conservation. Californians were suddenly forced to confront the cultural and ecological costs of their postwar wonderland, and from Eureka to San Diego, they were shocked by what they saw.

In the San Francisco Bay Area, a unique heritage of Brahmin conservationism provided Nob Hill support for successful efforts to protect wetlands and create a regional conservancy in the foothills. People for Open Space united the followers of John Muir and Lewis Mumford—environmentalists, planners, and philanthropists—in a common defense of San Francisco's great natural beauty and fashioned the first comprehensive "antisprawl" plan for any American metropolitan area.[53]

Southern California's counterpart movements crusaded to stop flagrant tract development in the Santa Monica Mountains and other foothill and coastal areas. Unlike Bay Area activists, however, they found little institutional support. The Los Angeles County Regional Planning Commission was theoretically the chief custodian of the regional landscape. Yet commission members, according to critics, had historically functioned as "expediters for fringe growth," producing planning documents that were seldom more than "blueprints for sprawl." As the League of Women Voters complained, the commission's efforts to preserve the Santa Monicas amounted to "color[ing] the vacant land green on its master plan."[54] After soliciting environmental development guidelines from a distinguished panel of natural scientists in 1970, the commission brazenly discarded them in order to double the area of land targeted for urbanization.[55]

At stake were the remaining fragments of the greenbelts identified by Eckbo and Williams in their 1965 study. The commission proposed to feed hungry developers another million acres of priceless agricultural and foothill landscape, while a coalition of environmental groups argued in a landmark lawsuit that population growth should be accommodated by investment within the existing urban fabric to revive declining neighborhoods and pockets of blight.[56] In 1979 the controversy over open space management suddenly erupted into full-fledged public scandal. A grand jury investigation exposed the inner workings of a regional planning system dominated and corrupted by development interests. As critics had long charged, key planning officials had advised developers in the Santa Monica Mountains and Antelope Valley on how to circumvent public hearings and environmental regulations by illegally partitioning their property among relatives and dummy corporations. An astounding *13,000* individual cases of fraudulent lot division were alleged. Further, when planning staff recommended against environmentally destructive projects in Diamond Bar and Santa Clarita, they had been summarily overruled by the commission majority.[57]

Although public outrage eventually forced the resignation of the commission's chairman, it was a modest, even a Pyrrhic victory for the environmental movement. The brief light focused on corruption within the Regional Planning Commission was never allowed to illuminate more fundamental conflicts of public and private interests within the Board of Supervisors. Once the commission reformed its most egregious practices, the steam went out of the largely legalistic battle to stop the fringe development juggernaut. To appease the court, the county was finally forced to officially designate some 62 "significant ecological areas" (SEAs), but no legislation was ever enacted to guarantee their preservation. To rub salt in environmentalists' wounds, the majority of appointees to the commission monitoring the SEAs have been and continue to be full- or part-time consultants to developers.[58]

As a result, suburbanization has completely devoured each of the open space buffer zones thought crucial by Eckbo and Williams.

While the population of the Los Angeles region grew by 45 percent from 1970 to 1990, its developed surface area increased by 300 percent.[59] Small environmental gains—notably by the Santa Monica Mountains Conservancy—have been parried and checked by relentless subdivision. Unlike in the San Francisco Bay Area, there have been no unqualified victories for open space preservation, just an accumulation of worthless environmental impact reports and toothless development guidelines. In part, this striking difference in outcomes must be attributed to the dissimilar political cultures and power structures in California's two major metropolitan regions. County government in Southern California is so hopelessly captive to the land development industry that sweeping electoral reforms, comparable to California's Progressive revolution of 1911, are probably the prerequisite for overthrowing the "new octopus" and transforming landuse priorities.

Yet 1970s environmentalism in Los Angeles County was also compromised by its own parochialism and historical amnesia. There was little discussion, in the spirit of New Deal modernists like Neutra and Eckbo, of the role of parks and other open areas as the "functional skeleton of the community." More often than not, environmental battles were fought piecemeal by local organizations with scant consideration of overall regional strategy and seldom in coalition with other constituencies. The class and racial dimensions of the recreational crisis were pointedly ignored. Ecology, in other words, stopped short of the more subversive but necessary politics of urban design.

5. THE LAST LANDSCAPE

At Newhall Ranch, nature has been given primary consideration.

Advertising brochure (1997)

January 1998. Time travel is becoming increasingly difficult. Traffic on California 126 is halted while a convoy of huge bottom-dump semis, each filled to the brim with the dark rich soil of the Santa Clara River Valley, lumber onto the asphalt. Farther west, even larger Caterpillar graders are leveling roadbed for the four-lane widening of Highway 126. A wrathful dust devil whirls in front of the lead grader.[60]

Eventually to be widened to eight lanes, Highway 126, once a bottleneck blocking the urbanization of the Santa Clara River Valley, will become the conduit for rapid and overwhelming growth. Transport planners already foresee its fate in the early twenty-first century when, gridlocked from Ventura to Santa Clarita, it will accommodate a staggering 360,000 trips per day. The major cause of this congestion will be Newhall Ranch, a master-planned city of 70,000 which will occupy a 10-mile corridor along the Santa Clara River. The Newhall Land and Farming Company, one of the West's largest developers, will begin building it in the year 2000.[61]

This project should be a legal impossibility. More than 25,000 housing units are designated for an agriculturally zoned floodplain of a wild river that is one of the most important SEAs in Los Angeles County and contains several endangered species protected by the state of California. Newhall Land and Farming, however, has the kind of political "juice" that makes the eyes of politicians pop. A lavish contributor to the campaigns of three of the five Los Angeles County supervisors, the company is also one of Governor Wilson's most faithful corporate supporters. By promising to preserve an 800-acre beauty strip along the Santa Clara River, and counting a large area of nearby undevelopable mountainside as integral "open space," the company purchased enough environmental legitimacy to satisfy its undemanding political allies. By the beginning of 1998, Newhall Ranch had easily cleared most of the principal zoning and regulatory hurdles.[62]

The stakes for the company are immense. Over its 30-year development schedule, each completed phase of the Ranch will further raise the value of remaining raw land within the 19-square-mile parcel. Similarly, the growth of Newhall Ranch and the addition of more workers and consumers will consolidate the role of adjacent Valencia—an earlier Newhall Land and Farming Company community—

The "New Urbanism"?

as the industrial, retail, and cultural hub of northern Los Angeles County. The Ranch will also become an Archimedean lever inflating land values and ensuring urban development in the nearly 16,000 acres of orange and lemon groves owned by the company west of the Ventura County line.

Opposing the Ranch is a small band of ranchers, artists, and environmentalists known as the Friends of the Santa Clara River. They are acutely aware that northern Los Angeles County is evolving into a second Orange County, fueled by white flight from the aging suburbs of the San Fernando Valley. The population of the region, which has tripled since 1980, is expected to reach one million sometime around 2010. As the Friends have argued cogently but futilely to the Regional Planning Commission, unrestrained development on this scale will soon destroy the landscape "amenities"—including clean air, beautiful vistas, abundant open spaces, and relatively uncongested highways—that have attracted so many thousands to northern Los Angeles County in the first place.

Likewise, the continuing exodus from Los Angeles of so many middle-class taxpayers (led by several thousand police officers and sheriffs), inevitably followed by businesses and jobs, will only accel-

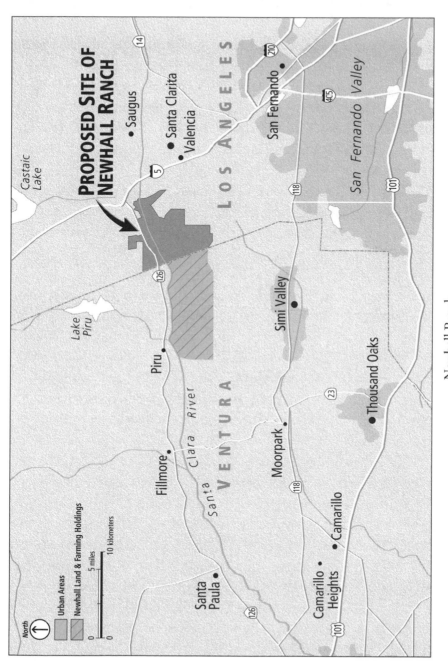

Newhall Ranch

erate the decay of older suburban neighborhoods. Taxpayers in these areas subsidize their own decline through gas taxes for new peripheral freeways and higher water rates to amortize the costly California Aqueduct that irrigates the new edge cities. Public action mitigates the environmental crisis primarily for the top 10 percent of the population who benefit from the conversion of wetlands into marinas, and from hidden subsidies for hillside living. For the other 90 percent, Southern California remains radically unplanned, undesigned, and out of control.

The Newhall Land and Farming Company, of course, would vehemently disagree. Newhall Ranch, like the dozens of other master-planned communities that offer "prestige lifestyles" in the white-flight belts of northern Los Angeles, eastern Ventura, western Riverside, southern Orange, and northern San Diego Counties, is meticulously planned down to the last cul-de-sac and red-tiled roof. The company claims, moreover, to have designed Newhall Ranch in conformity with the deepest longings of Southern Californians for an idealized "hometown America." Using "psychographic" surveys and focus groups, the company found that 98 percent of potential homebuyers want to live near nature and that "vast majorities said they wanted entertainment opportunities, to feel safe, and to avoid the homogeneity of many of today's suburban tracts."[63]

Newhall Ranch, the company promises, will be this utopia. Like Disney Corporation's model community of Celebration in Florida, it has been planned to the fairytale standards of the "New Urbanism," with all homes located in traditional villages ("Riverwood," "Oak Valley," "The Mesas," and so on), a short walking distance away from shops, open areas, and sports facilities. Billed as "A Community by Nature," it will supposedly "re-create elements of the lifestyle prevalent in Southern California before World War Two."[64]

The Friends of the Santa Clara River are quick to point out the dark irony in the nostalgic trappings of Newhall Ranch. The last authentic landscape of that prewar way of life—Eden's last garden—will be destroyed in order to build its suburban simulation. The classic tenets of good planning advocated by Olmsted, Alexander, and

Eckbo—repackaged as "New Urbanism"—will become sales points for the next generation of supersprawl.

The widening of Highway 126 is then a primal scene—the familiar tremor heralding an eruption of growth that will wipe away human and natural history. Suburbanization is like another one of Southern California's natural disasters—recurrent, inexorable. The big machines shifting dirt along the Santa Clara River today are the direct descendants of the bulldozers that ripped freeway corridors through the San Gabriel Valley and Orange County in the 1950s. The cast is the same, but the play is now in its final act. After the Santa Clara River Valley dies, there is only desert to feed the developers' insatiable hunger.

3

THE CASE
FOR LETTING
MALIBU BURN

Late August to early October is the infernal season in Los Angeles. Downtown is usually shrouded in acrid yellow smog while heat waves billow down Wilshire Boulevard. Outside air-conditioned skyscrapers, homeless people huddle miserably in every available shadow. A few blocks away, in poorly ventilated garment sweatshops, thousands of *operadoras* pant for breath in front of their sewing machines. Irritable bosses, their dress shirts stained with sweat, bark endless orders in Spanish, Armenian, Korean, or Cantonese.

Across the Harbor Freeway, the overcrowded tenements of the Westlake district—Los Angeles's Spanish Harlem—are intolerable ovens. Suffocating in their tiny rooms, immigrant families flee to the fire escapes, stoops, and sidewalks. Anxious mothers swab their babies' foreheads with water while older children, eyes stinging from the smog, cry for *paletas:* the flavored cones of shaved ice sold by pushcart vendors. Shirtless young men—some with formidable jail-made biceps and mural-size tattoos of the Virgin of Guadalupe across their backs—monopolize the shade of *tienda* awnings. Amid hundreds of acres of molten asphalt and concrete there is scarcely a weed, much less a lawn or tree.

Thirty miles away, the Malibu coast—where hyperbole meets the surf—basks in altogether different weather. The temperature is 85 (20 degrees cooler than Downtown), and the cobalt blue sky is clear enough to discern the wispish form of Santa Barbara Island, nearly 50 miles offshore. At Zuma surfers ride the curl under the insouciant gazes of their personal sun goddesses, while at Topanga Beach, horse

Malibu erupts—the view from Santa Monica (1993)

trainers canter Appaloosas across the wet sand. Elsewhere along the coast, naked screenwriters poach in Point Dume jacuzzis, au pairs trade gossip in French (*quelles familles bizarres!*) over cappuccinos at Malibu Colony Plaza, and tourists get lost in the hills searching for a view of Streisand's elusive palace. Indifferent to the misery on the "mainland," the residents of Malibu suffer through another boringly perfect day.

Needless to say, the existential differences between the tenement district and the gilded coast are enormous at any time. But late summer is the beginning of the wildfire season in Southern California, and that's when Westlake and Malibu suffer a common lot: catastrophic fire.

According to recent estimates, Westlake (including adjacent parts of Downtown) has the highest urban fire incidence in the nation: one of its two fire stations was inundated by an incredible 20,000 emergency calls in 1993.[1] Some tenements and apartment-hotels have continuous fire histories dating back to their construction in the early twentieth century. The notorious Hotel St. George, for instance, experienced fatal blazes in 1912, 1952, and 1983. Moreover, almost all of the deadly tenement fires in Los Angeles since 1945 have occurred within a one-mile radius of the corner of Wilshire and Figueroa, Downtown.

FATAL TENEMENT FIRES, 1947–93: DOWNTOWN/WESTLAKE

Date	Location	Deaths
1947	656 Maple	1
1952	St. George	7
1960	906 E. Sixth	1
1969	320 S. Rampart	8
1970	Ponet Square	19
1972	Barclay	3
1973	Stratford Arms	25
1976	335 S. Witmer	10
1979	Oxford	2
1982	Dorothy Mae	24
1983	St. George	1
1986	116 S. Flower	5
1993	330 S. Burlington	10
1993	1100 S. Grand	3
	Total	119

Sources: *Los Angeles Examiner* and *Los Angeles Times.*

Malibu, meanwhile, is the wildfire capital of North America and, possibly, the world. Fire here has a relentless staccato rhythm, syncopated by landslides and floods. The rugged 22-mile-long coastline is scourged, on the average, by a large fire (one thousand acres plus) every two and a half years, and the entire surface area of the western Santa Monica Mountains has been burnt three times over this century. At least once a decade a blaze in the chaparral grows into a terrifying firestorm consuming hundreds of homes in an inexorable advance across the mountains to the sea. Since 1970 five such holocausts have destroyed more than one thousand luxury residences and inflicted more than $1 billion in property damage. Some unhappy homeowners have been burnt out twice in a generation, and there are individual patches of coastline or mountain, especially between Point Dume and Tuna Canyon, that have been incinerated as many as eight times since 1930.[2]

MALIBU FIRESTORMS, 1930–96
(10,000+ ACRES)

Date	Locality	Acres	Homes	Deaths
1930 October	Potrero	15,000		
1935 October	Latigo/Sherwood	28,599		
1938 November	Topanga	16,500	350	
1943 November	Woodland Hills	15,300		
1949 October	Susana	19,080		
1955 November	Ventu	12,638		
1956 December	Sherwood/Newton	37,537	120	1
1958 December	Liberty	17,860	107	
1970 September	Wright	31,000	403	10
1978 October	Kanan/Dume	25,000	230	2
1982 October	Dayton Canyon	54,000	74	
1993 November	Calabasas/Malibu	18,500	350	3
1996 October	Monte Nido	15,000	2	
	Total		1,636	16
	Plus smaller fires		app. 2,000	

Source: Los Angeles County Fire Department records.

In other words, stand at the mouth of Malibu Canyon or sleep in the Hotel St. George for any length of time and you eventually will face the flames. It is a statistical certainty. Ironically, the richest and poorest landscapes in Southern California are comparable in the frequency with which they experience incendiary disaster. This was emphasized tragically in 1993 when a May conflagration at a Westlake tenement that killed three mothers and seven children was followed in late October by 21 wildfires culminating on 2 November in the great firestorm that forced the evacuation of most of Malibu.

But the two species of conflagration are inverse images of each other. Defended in 1993 by the largest army of firefighters in American history, wealthy Malibu homeowners benefited as well from an extraordinary range of insurance, landuse, and disaster relief subsidies. Yet, as most experts will readily concede, periodic firestorms of this magnitude are inevitable as long as residential development is tolerated in the fire ecology of the Santa Monicas.

On the other hand, most of the 119 fatalities from tenement fires in the Westlake and Downtown areas might have been prevented had slumlords been held to even minimal standards of building safety. If enormous resources have been allocated, quixotically, to fight irresistible forces of nature on the Malibu coast, then scandalously little attention has been paid to the man-made and remediable fire crisis of the inner city.

1. THE FIRE COAST

Homes, of course, will arise here in the thousands. Many a peak will have its castle.
    John Russell McCarthy, These Waiting Hills (1925)

From the beginning fire has defined Malibu in the American imagination. In *Two Years Before the Mast,* Richard Henry Dana described sailing northward from San Pedro to Santa Barbara in 1826 and seeing a vast blaze along the coast of José Tapia's Rancho Topanga Malibu Sequit. Despite—or, as we shall see, more likely because of—the Spanish prohibition of the Chumash and Tong-va Indian practice of annually burning the brush, mountain infernos repeatedly menaced Malibu through the nineteenth century.[3] During the great land boom of the late 1880s, the entire latifundio was sold at $10 per acre to the Boston Brahmin millionaire Frederick Rindge. In his memoirs, Rindge described his unceasing battles against squatters, rustlers, and, above all, recurrent wildfire. The great fire of 1903, which raced from Calabasas to the sea in a few hours, incinerated Rindge's dream ranch in Malibu Canyon and forced him to move to Los Angeles, where he died in 1905.[4]

From the time of the Tapias, the owners of Rancho Malibu had recognized that the region's extraordinary fire hazard was shaped, in large part, by the uncanny alignment of its coastal canyons with the annual "fire winds" from the north: the notorious Santa Anas, which blow primarily between Labor Day and Thanksgiving, just before the first rains.[5] Born from high-pressure areas over the Great Basin and Colorado Plateau, the Santa Anas become hot and dry as they descend avalanche-like into Southern California. The San Fernando Valley acts as a giant bellows, sometimes fanning the Santa Anas to hurricane velocity as they roar seaward through the narrow canyons and rugged defiles of the Santa Monica Mountains.* Add a spark to the dense, dry vegetation on such an occasion and the hillsides will explode in uncontrollable wildfire: "The speed and heat of the fire is so intense that firefighters can only attempt to prevent lateral spread of the fire while waiting for the winds to abate or the fuel to diminish."[6]

Less well understood in the old days was the essential dependence of the dominant vegetation of the Santa Monicas—chamise chaparral, coastal sage scrub, and live oak woodland—upon this cycle of wildfire. Decades of research (especially at the San Dimas Experimental Forest in the San Gabriel Mountains) have given late-twentieth-century science vivid insights into the complex and ultimately beneficial role of fire in recycling nutrients and ensuring seed germination in Southern California's various pyrophytic flora.[7] Research has also established the overwhelming importance of biomass accumulation rather than ignition frequency in regulating fire destructiveness. As Richard Minnich, the world authority on chapar-

---

* The same canyons, however, also allow cool ocean air to refresh the polluted San Fernando Valley. The Santa Monica Mountains, according to air-quality researchers, are the most vital "airshed" for metropolitan Los Angeles.

The Rindges' Shangri-la in the 1920s

ral brushfire, emphasizes: "Fuel, not ignitions, causes fire. You can send an arsonist to Death Valley and he'll never be arrested."[8]

A key revelation was the nonlinear relationship between the age structure of vegetation and the intensity of fire. Botanists and fire geographers discovered that "the probability for an intense fast running fire increases dramatically as the fuels exceed twenty years of age." Indeed, half-century-old chaparral—heavily laden with dead mass—is calculated to burn with 50 times more intensity than 20-year-old chaparral. Put another way, an acre of old chaparral is the fuel equivalent of about 75 barrels of crude oil. Expanding these calculations even further, a great Malibu firestorm could generate the heat of three million barrels of burning oil at a temperature of 2,000 degrees.[9]

"Total fire suppression," the official policy in the Southern California mountains since 1919, has been a tragic error because it creates enormous stockpiles of fuel.[10] The extreme fires that eventually occur can transform the chemical structure of the soil itself. The volatilization of certain plant chemicals creates a water-repellent layer in the upper soil, and this layer, by preventing percolation, dramatically

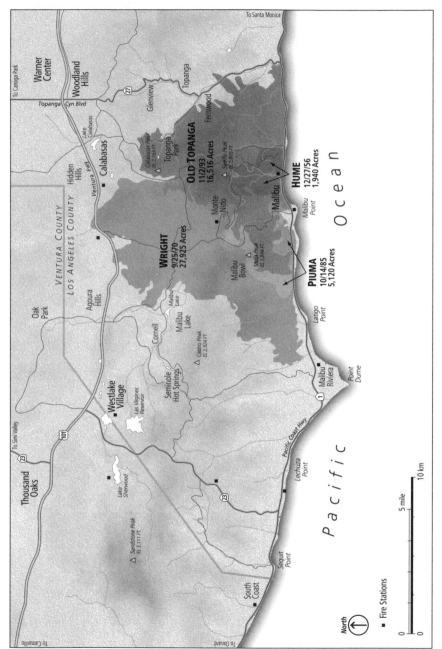

The Fire Coast

accelerates subsequent sheet flooding and erosion. A monomaniacal obsession with managing ignition rather than chaparral accumulation simply makes doomsday-like firestorms and the great floods that follow them virtually inevitable.*

For a generation after Rindge's death, his widow, May, struggled to keep the family Shangri-la isolated and intact in the face of state attempts to push a highway through the rancho. Like one of the iron-fisted heroines played by Barbara Stanwyck, the so-called Queen of the Malibu closed the ranch roads in 1917, strung barbed wire along the perimeter, and posted armed fence-riders with orders to "shoot to kill." In one episode during the 1920s, Rindge cowboys provoked a tense confrontation with deputy sheriffs after driving away a road survey crew at gunpoint. Hysterical newspaper headlines warned of "Civil War in Peaceful Southern California!"[12]

But the pressure during the 1920s boom to open the coastal range to speculative subdivision was unrelenting. In the hyperbole of the era, occupation of the mountains became Los Angeles's manifest destiny. "The day for the white invasion of the Santa Monicas has come," declared real estate clairvoyant John Russell McCarthy in a booklet published by the *Los Angeles Times* in 1925.[13] In anticipation of this land rush, the county sheriff had been arresting every vagrant in sight and putting them to work on chain gangs building roads through the rugged canyons just south of Rancho Malibu. (Radical critics at the time denounced this system as "deliberate real-estate graft" meant only to enhance land values in mountain districts "which the population of this city does not even know exists.")[14]

Widow Rindge, in any event, would not be allowed to stand in the way of "the march of adventuring Caucasians," as McCarthy put it. After one of the most protracted legal battles in California history, the

---

* Minnich has compared in great detail the contrasting fire histories of Southern California and neighboring Baja California. Hundreds of millions of dollars have been spent on fire suppression in Southern California's increasingly urbanized mountains, while fire control is virtually nonexistent in Baja's wild northern uplands. As a result, only Southern California is plagued by recurrent firestorms. Baja wildfires are more frequent, but smaller, "patchier," and never catastrophic.[11]

Conquering the Santa Monicas

court granted the state right-of-way through Rancho Malibu. Opened to traffic in 1928, the Pacific Coast Highway gave delighted Angelenos their first view of the magnificent Malibu coast and introduced a potent new source of ignition—the automobile—into the inflammable landscape.

The indefatigable May Rindge continued to fight the road builders and developers in the courts, but in the end the costs of litigation forced her to lease choice parts of Malibu beachfront to a movie colony that included Jack Warner, Clara Bow, Dolores Del Rio, and Barbara Stanwyck herself. The colony's unexpected housewarming was a lightning-swift wildfire that destroyed 13 new homes in late October 1929.[15] Exactly a year later, walnut pickers in the Thousand Oaks area accidently ignited another blaze, which quickly grew into one of the greatest conflagrations in Malibu history.

The 1930 Decker Canyon fire was a worst-case scenario involving 50-year-old chaparral and a fierce Santa Ana. Faced with a five-mile front of towering flames, 1,100 firefighters could do little except save their own lives. As the firestorm unexpectedly wheeled toward the Pacific Palisades, there was official panic. County Supervisor Wright, his nerves shaken by a visit to the collapsing fire lines, posted a hundred patrolmen at the Los Angeles city limits to alert residents for evacuation. Should the "fire raging in the Malibu District get closer," he gasped, "our whole city might go."[16] Ultimately, this apocalypse (which may have given Nathanael West the idea for the burning of Los Angeles in his novel *Day of the Locust*) was avoided—no thanks to human initiative—when the fickle Santa Ana abruptly subsided.

In hindsight, the 1930 fire should have provoked a historic debate on the wisdom of opening Malibu to further development. Only a few months before the disaster, Frederick Law Olmsted, Jr.—the nation's foremost landscape architect and designer of the California state park system—had come out in favor of public ownership of at least 10,000 acres of the most scenic beach and mountain areas between Topanga and Point Dume.[17] Despite a further series of fires in 1935, 1936, and 1938 which destroyed almost four hundred homes in Malibu and Topanga Canyon, public officials stubbornly disregarded the wisdom of Olmsted's proposal for a great public domain in the Santa Monicas.[18] The county of Los Angeles, for example, squandered an extraordinary opportunity in 1938 to acquire 17,000 acres of the bankrupt Rindge estate in exchange for $1.1 million in delinquent taxes. At a mere $64 per acre, it would have been the deal of the century.[19]

Instead, in December 1940, an impecunious and heartbroken May Rindge was forced to put her entire empire on the auction block. Potential buyers were advised to make "an early selection" of "ocean-front lots, sites for villas, hotels, golf clubs, estates, beach and yacht clubs, income and business lots, small summer home places, ranchitos, 100–640-acre ranchos, and acreage for further subdivision."[20] The disconsolate Queen of the Malibu died two months later.

During the Second World War—severe drought years on the West Coast—hundreds of firewatchers were sent into the Southern California mountains to guard against rumored Axis saboteurs. A few months after the watchers were withdrawn, 150 Malibu homes were

The 1938 Topanga fire

incinerated in another November fire. Yet this new disaster failed to discourage a postwar migration of artists, printers, bookdealers, poets, screenwriters, and architects (including Olmsted himself)—many of very modest means, some seeking to escape the scrutiny of McCarthyism—who envisaged Malibu as Carmel south. In an engaging memoir of this period, UCLA librarian Lawrence Clark Powell described a genial way of life devoted to Mozart and beachcombing.

He also provided a classic account of the onslaught of the terrible firestorm of Christmas week 1956, which, burning its way to the sea, retraced the path of the 1930 blaze.[21]

> The wind was still savage when we went to bed at ten, the sky swept clear, aglitter with stars, Anacapa flashed its warning light. The cypresses, pines and eucalyptuses were noisier than the surf. Cats' fur threw sparks when stroked. We slept in spite of the sinister atmosphere.

> I woke abruptly at four to see a fierce glow in the sky. . . .
> God, the whole face of the mountain was burning, in a long line
> just below the summit, and moving toward us on the wind.
> Fear dried my mouth. I knew doom when I saw it.[22]

A Forest Service analysis of this disaster, which killed one person and destroyed one hundred homes, stressed the impossible challenge of combating such erratic and untamable natural forces.

> Malibu fires combine most known elements of violent, erratic
> and extreme fire behavior: fire whirls, extreme rates of spread,
> sudden changes in speed and direction of fire spread, flash-
> overs of unburned gases complicated by intense heat and
> impenetrable smoke held close to the ground.[23]

Indeed the conflagration, which coincided with a waxing of Cold War anxieties, had unexpected political repercussions. "If the government could not defeat wildfires in the Santa Monicas," critics asked, "how would it deal with possible nuclear holocausts?" Accordingly the Eisenhower administration acknowledged the Malibu blaze as "the first major fire disaster of national scope," and Congress—more concerned with the credibility of a vast civil defense establishment than with the tragedy of local homeowners—debated how to provide "complete fire prevention and protection in Southern California."[24] (Large Malibu fires, moreover, would later be used by researchers to model the behavior of nuclear firestorms.)[25]

According to fire historian Stephen Pyne, the Malibu blaze also marked the transition from the traditional forest fire problem to a "new fire regime" characterized by the "lethal mixture of homeowners and brush." This artificial borderland of chaparral and suburb magnified the natural fire danger while creating new perils for firefighters who now had to defend thousands of individual structures as well as battle the fire front itself. "Whereas it was often remarked that chaparral, particularly that composed largely of chamise, is a fire-

1956: a national turning point

climax community, it is now joked that the same is true of the Southern California mountain suburb."[26]

Ultimately the 1956 fire—followed by two blazes, one month apart, in 1958–59 that severely burned eight firefighters and destroyed another hundred homes[27]—proved the beginning of the end for bohemian Malibu. A perverse law of the new fire regime was that fire now stimulated both development and upward social succession. By declaring Malibu a federal disaster area and offering blaze victims tax relief as well as preferential low-interest loans, the Eisenhower administration established a precedent for the public subsidization of firebelt suburbs. Each new conflagration would be punctually followed by reconstruction on a larger and even more exclusive scale as landuse regulations and sometimes even the fire code were relaxed to accommodate fire "victims."* As a result, renters and modest home-

---

* After the 1978 fire, for example, many rebuilding Malibu homeowners were exempted from the new standards governing water pressure and width of access roads adopted by the county during the 1960s.[28]

owners were displaced from areas like Broad Beach, Paradise Cove, and Point Dume by wealthy pyrophiles encouraged by artificially cheap fire insurance, socialized disaster relief, and an expansive public commitment to "defend Malibu."

In the absence of fire-risk zoning of the sort that Olmsted had earlier advocated, the only constraint on development was the limited supply of water for firefighting and domestic consumption. The completion of a trunk water line, connecting Malibu to Metropolitan Water District reservoirs, was the signal for a new land rush. The county's Regional Planning Commission promptly endorsed developers' wildest fantasies by authorizing a staggering 1,400 percent expansion of the Malibu population over the next generation: from 7,983 residents in 1960 to a projected 117,000 in 1980.[29] Although the California coastal acts of 1972 and 1976, under the populist slogan "Don't Lock Up the Beach!" eventually slowed this real estate juggernaut (as well as squelching such nightmarish proposals as a Corral Canyon nuclear power plant and an eight-lane freeway through Malibu Canyon), the urbanization of the Malibu coast—Los Angeles's "backyard Big Sur"—was a fait accompli.[30]

Yet, even as they were opening the floodgates to destructive overdevelopment, county and state officials were also turning down every opportunity to expand public beach frontage (a miserable 22 percent of the total in 1969). Nor did they show any interest in creating a public land trust in the mountains, which were now entirely under private ownership, right down to the streambeds.[31] Consequently, most of Malibu remained as inaccessible to the general public as it had been in the Rindge era. (For people of color, moreover, it was absolutely off-limits.)* As historians of the coastal access battle put it: "The seven million people within an hour's drive of Malibu got Beach Boys music and surfer movies, but the twenty thousand residents kept the beach."[33]

---

* Once in the 1950s there was a rumor that Nat King Cole might attempt to move to Malibu. Art Jones, the Colony Association's "dictator," vowed that "he would personally head a vigilante group to burn him out."[32]

Returning for a final look, UCLA librarian Powell bitterly decried the aristocratization of his beloved coast:

> In a feverish buying and selling of land, the coast has become utterly transformed and unrecognizable. Each succeeding house, bigger and grander, takes the view of its neighbors in a kind of unbridled competition. . . . Once lost, paradise can never be regained. . . . Developers have bulldozed the Santa Monicas beyond recovery.[34]

The Malibu nouveaux riches built higher and higher in the mountain chamise with scant regard for the inevitable fiery consequences. The next firestorm, in late September 1970, coupled perfect fire weather (drought conditions, 100-degree heat, 3 percent humidity, and an 85-mile-per-hour Santa Ana wind) with a bumper crop of combustible wood-frame houses. According to firefighters, the popular cedar shake roofs "popped like popcorn" as a 20-mile wall of flames roared across the ridgeline of the Santa Monicas toward the sea. With the asphalt on the Pacific Coast Highway ablaze and all escape routes cut off, terrified residents of the famed Malibu Colony took refuge in the nearby lagoon. Firebrands fell like hellish rain on the beach, and day became night under the gigantic smoke pall. Coalescing with another blaze in the San Fernando Valley, this greatest of twentieth-century Malibu firestorms ultimately took 10 lives and charred 403 homes, including a ranch owned by then-governor Ronald Reagan.[35]

Furious property owners—ignorant of the true balance of power between fire suppression and chaparral ecology—denounced local government for failing to save their homes and demanded new, expensive technological "fixes" for Malibu's wildfire problems.* Elected officials, acutely sensitive to Malibu's national prominence in political

---

* Thus Malibu homeowners' leader and state Democratic chieftain Paul Ziffren, after the 1970 fire: "What I don't understand is how we can do all those things like playing space basketball and yet we're still fighting fires the same way we did 25 years ago."[36]

fund-raising, were quick to oblige. A celebrated example occurred in the late 1970s when the Malibu Colony was being pounded by the heaviest surf in a quarter-century. Larry Hagman, *Dallas*'s J. R. Ewing, is reported to have told Jerry Brown, the governor of California: "Jerry, do something. Goddammit, we're in real trouble. Get your ass down here!" In short order, Malibu was declared a disaster area and National Guardsmen were helping sandbag Hagman's—and sometimes Brown date Linda Ronstadt's—homes.[37]

Meanwhile, developers—racing to stay ahead of proposed "slow growth" coastal legislation—redoubled their subdivision efforts. The subsequent boom only provided more fuel for the three successive "Halloween" fires that consumed homes in October 1978, 1982, and 1985. The first two blazes both began in Agoura and roughly followed the route of the 1956 fire through Trancas Canyon, while the third repeated the itinerary of the 1930 Decker Canyon conflagration.

The 1978 fire, which consumed million-dollar homes in the Broad Beach area (where Powell had lived in the more humble 1950s), also

"Balls of flaming fur"

set a new speed record: the fire crossed 13 miles of very rugged terrain in less than two hours (the 1970 fire had taken twice the time). One eyewitness described how the rampaging fire front "turned thousands of wild rabbits into balls of flaming fur that darted insanely about, only to start new fires at the spots where they fell." The surviving beasts— domestic pets and wild animals alike—"mingled in chaos with human evacuees along the beach at Point Dume while oblivious surfers rode the waves."[38] Traumatized Malibu residents, also battered by disastrous floods and landslides in 1978 and 1980, could be forgiven for imagining that nature was getting angrier at them.

2. THE BURNED-OVER DISTRICT

Furnaces with chimneys. You couldn't build better boxes to fry people in if you tried.

A Los Angeles firefighter (1973)

On 25 March 1952, spectators outside 115 East Third Street were mesmerized by the desperate figure hanging from the third-story windowsill of the burning skid row tenement. They shouted to him to hang on. "He clung there for several minutes before his grip loosened, and he fell, screaming, to his death in the paved alleyway below."[39] Meanwhile every available ambulance in the city was rushing toward the building. Scores of injured tenants—some with third-degree burns and multiple fractures—sprawled piteously on the sidewalks while skid row missionaries prayed over them and grim-faced firefighters scaled ladders onto the blazing roof. They would eventually recover six more bodies from the Hotel St. George. And, for a few days, debate over such avoidable but chronic fire tragedies would chase Korean War news out of the headlines of Los Angeles's four daily papers.[40]

Like wildfires in Malibu, Los Angeles's tenement holocausts have been astonishingly faithful to a fundamental fire ecology (or perhaps we should say "disaster algorithm" since none of the variables

Threatening to jump (1952 Hotel St. George fire)

involved are natural). Consider, for example, the infamous and amazingly still extant Hotel St. George. It hardly ever seemed to stop burning: scores of fire alarms over the decades were climaxed by fatal blazes in 1912 (six dead), 1952 (seven dead), and 1983 (one dead). Moreover, 10 of the 11 fatal tenement fires that followed the 1952 disaster broke out in structures of strikingly similar configuration, and all 11 occurred within the same three-square-mile fire zone overlapping Downtown and Westlake.

The brief if brutal debate over responsibility for the 1952 fire, which pitted Councilman Davenport, chairman of the Police and Fire Committee, against Fire Chief Alderson, exposed widespread official culpability. On the one hand, Chief Alderson pointed to the city council's repeated failure to enact new fire safety regulations recommended by his department three years earlier. On the other hand, Councilman Davenport excoriated the chief for failing to enforce existing regulations. At the time of the fire, the Hotel St. George was in blatant violation of almost every section of the fire code: "bolted nailed door at bottom of rear stairs; unusable drop ladder; rotten standpipe fire hoses; landings of stairways blocked with furniture storage"—the list was endless. Raising the specter of corruption in the fire department, Davenport acidly told the press:

> It looks to me that there is evidence here of dereliction on the part of the fire inspectors. It might even develop that the whole building should have been closed. . . . For some reason—which I won't even guess at—[Chief Alderson] lets these old buildings get away with murder.[41]

This vicious circle of inadequate regulation and negligent enforcement was compounded by the lethal design of the most common tenements. Built of cheap brick and soft mortar, without steel reinforcement, these structures had been promoted as a safety innovation in the wake of the great San Francisco earthquake and conflagration of 1906: "the modern, fireproof answer" to the old-fashioned combustible wooden building. Brick construction in Los Angeles received additional impetus in 1924 after 24 children were burned to death in "an ancient wooden home for mentally deficient girls" in Del Rey, and another 35 died in a blaze at a claptrap Venice hotel.[42]

Originally designed mainly as two- to six-story "economy" hotels for often elderly tourists, who arrived at a rate of a thousand per day each winter season, these brick structures were built by speculators who sold them to middle-class investors, especially doctors and dentists, as "rent mines."* The typical plan featured large, open stairwells, steam heat, shared hallways, common lavatories, high ceilings, and fold-down murphy beds. In 1980 there were still 1,079 of these hotel and apartment tenements—comprising 46,000 units and housing 137,000 residents—in Los Angeles, primarily in Downtown and the Westlake and Wilshire districts.[44]

The deadly propensities of these unreinforced masonry buildings were revealed during the March 1933 Long Beach earthquake, when hundreds of them collapsed, crushing more than 120 people to death and injuring thousands more. New brick construction without steel reinforcement was quickly outlawed, although almost a half-century passed before seismic retrofitting was required for the thousands of pre-1933 unreinforced structures that remained. In the meantime, as auto courts and motels began to coopt the tourist trade, the economy hotels quickly metamorphosed into squalid tenements for the depression's lost souls. (Robert Aldrich's 1955 film version of Mickey Spillane's *Kiss Me Deadly* offers an extraordinary noir tour of the decaying residential hotels that before demolition in 1961 crowded the flanks of Los Angeles's Bunker Hill neighborhood.)

Fire officials soon recognized that these structures were as much damned by fire as by earthquake. Their most diabolical feature was the ubiquitous open stairwell that in a blaze invariably acted as a huge flue spreading fire through the upper stories. A similar stairwell-as-chimney design—also advertised as "fireproof"—had been responsible for the terrible Winecoff Hotel holocaust in Atlanta which killed 120 in December 1946, still the worst hotel fire in American history.[45]

Although open stairwells were barred from all new construction by a 1947 ordinance, the city council—yielding to the same "slumlord lobby" that delayed reparations for seismic safety—refused to make

---

* A chamber of commerce study in 1919 found that 20 percent of winter tourists leased bungalows or homes, 33 percent rented apartments, while the rest made do with sleeping rooms in boardinghouses or tourist hotels. There was a chronic shortage of accommodation for poorer tourists as well as for the large number of Eastern workers seduced to the coast by the false advertising of plentiful jobs.[43]

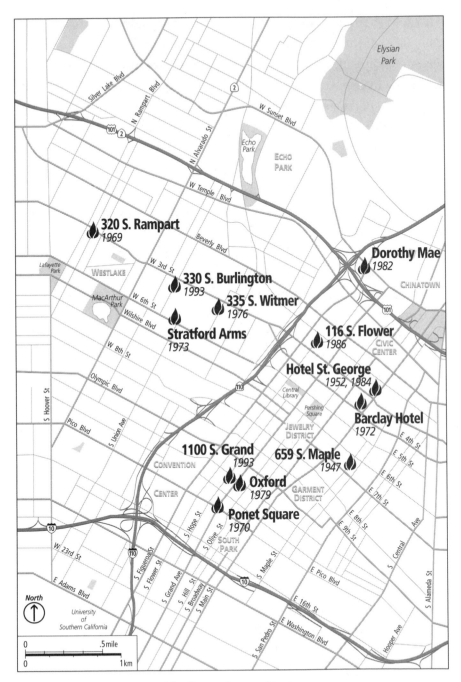

320 S. Rampart
1969

330 S. Burlington
1993

335 S. Witmer
1976

Stratford Arms
1973

Dorothy Mae
1982

116 S. Flower
1986

Hotel St. George
1952, 1984

Barclay Hotel
1972

1100 S. Grand
1993

659 S. Maple
1947

Oxford
1979

Ponet Square
1970

Elysian
Park

Echo
Park

ECHO
PARK

CHINATOWN

Lafayette
Park

WESTLAKE

MacArthur
Park

CIVIC
CENTER

Central
Library

Pershing
Square

JEWELRY
DISTRICT

CONVENTION

CENTER

GARMENT
DISTRICT

SOUTH
PARK

University
of
Southern California

Silver Lake Blvd

N Rampart Blvd

N Alvarado St

W Sunset Blvd

W Temple Blvd

Beverly Blvd

W 3rd St

W 6th St

Wilshire Blvd

W 8th St

Olympic Blvd

Pico Blvd

S Hoover St

S Union Ave

W 23rd St

E Adams Blvd

S Figueroa St

S Flower St

S Grand Ave

S Hope St

S Olive St

S Hill St

S Broadway

S Main St

S Maple St

S San Pedro St

E Washington Blvd

E 16th St

E Pico Blvd

E 4th St

E 5th St

E 6th St

E 7th St

E 8th St

E 9th St

S Central Ave

S Alameda St

Hooper Ave

North

0 .5 mile

0 1 km

The burned-over district

the standard retroactive.[46] The controversy surrounding the St. George tragedy, while dramatizing the stairwell-as-flue danger, failed to shift the council majority on this matter. In the same period, Los Angeles's public housing coalition of trade unions, civil rights groups, and liberal churches, which had been crusading since the late 1930s to demolish Downtown firetraps and rehouse the poor, suffered a crushing electoral defeat. California voters, inflamed by the *Los Angeles Times*'s and *Oakland Tribune*'s statewide campaign against "socialist housing," passed a constitutional amendment in November 1952 requiring two-thirds-majority local approval for public housing construction. As a result, not a single unit of new public housing has been built anywhere in Los Angeles County since 1953.[47]

For nearly a generation politicians were able to forget about the tenement fire problem. Although serious blazes, often with casualties, were reported virtually every month in skid row or the Westlake district, there were no headline-grabbing tragedies. Then, on 12 October 1969, a ground-floor fire broke out in a 1920s wood and masonry structure on Rampart Boulevard, just west of MacArthur (formerly Westlake) Park. Following the deadly pattern of the Hotel St. George fire, superheated gases literally exploded up an open stairwell. With the front fire escape cut off by flames, dozens of tenants had no choice but to jump from the upper stories. The eight dead included a pregnant woman killed in a leap from a third-floor window.

Eleven months later, a virtually identical fire broke out in the lobby of the Ponet Square, a four-story Downtown apartment-hotel built in 1910. According to an incident analysis later released by investigators, flames from a deliberately set fire raced up the fluelike stairwell at a velocity of five feet per second. At each landing, fire "back-drafted" down the hallways. Fire escapes at the ends of those hallways were engulfed in flames before residents could reach them. Within a few minutes, the temperature in the stairwell and hallways reached the same extreme heat as a mountain firestorm: about 2,000 degrees. Dozens of residents, meanwhile, were trapped inside their rooms with the temperature rapidly climbing to 400 degrees. Again the only choice was to jump or be baked to death. "I could hear bod-

"I could hear bodies hitting the ground" (1970 Ponet Square Fire)

ies hitting the ground all around me," said Fire Captain James Williams. Demolition crews worked for a week to recover the bodies of the last of 19 victims.[48]

The back-to-back Rampart and Ponet Square disasters finally forced the council to require the retrofitting of pre-1947 tenements. Owners were given the options of installing sprinkler systems, enclosing stairwells with fireproof doors, or simply demolishing their buildings. With sharp teeth, the "Ponet Square" ordinance might have made a serious difference. But the council, ever solicitous of property owners, gave them a four-year grace period to make improvements and exempted all two-story structures—loopholes which condemned scores more to death by fire.

Three years later, only 6 percent of owners cited had bothered to bring their buildings into compliance with the law. On the evening of 15 November 1973, a fire started in a lobby sofa near an open stairwell in the ancient, unretrofitted Stratford Hotel near MacArthur

Park. It proved an uncanny repeat of the previous conflagrations. Although firefighters reached the building within five minutes of the alarm, 25 tenants were already dead. It had taken no time at all for the blast-furnace heat to burn through their thin apartment doors. In one room, five dead children were found huddled around the body of their mother.[49]

Over the next decade, one fire tragedy after another exposed the defects of the Ponet Square ordinance. A few days before Christmas in 1976, for example, 10 Central American and Mexican immigrants were killed when another open-stairwell fire destroyed a two-story tenement in the Westlake district. A firefighter who had been at the scene wrote a letter to the *Los Angeles Times* complaining that "vested interests" had blocked the extension of the stairwell ordinance to hundreds of dangerous two-story structures. "It's the old story: Cost versus Safety."[50] His point was grimly reinforced by more fatal tenement fires in 1979 and 1981.[51]

Meanwhile, in the 1970s, the elderly white population in the Downtown and Westlake firetraps was largely replaced by poor immigrant families--*recien illegados*—from Mexico, El Salvador, and Guatemala. Poverty and overcrowding ensured that fires would claim even higher body counts. Responding to the 1976 Witmer blaze, for example, firefighters were amazed to discover 75 adults and children crammed into nine single-room units on one floor, with a single shared kitchen and toilet.[52] The new immigration also transformed the economics of slumlordism. As no affordable new residences were being constructed, the owners of older tenements found themselves with a monopoly on bottom-end housing. As a result, the percentage of total income that the poorest families paid for rent soared from 37 percent in 1977 to 60 percent by 1987. Rents, profits, and overcrowding increased in lockstep, while standards of maintenance and building safety deteriorated rapidly from their already scandalous levels.

Savage budget cuts, meanwhile, in the wake of California's 1978 tax reduction revolution (Proposition 13), shrunk the fire department by 15 percent at a time when demand for its services had increased by more

"Little Salitre"

than 50 percent. Local fire stations, undermanned and overwhelmed by emergency calls, began to neglect regular fire inspection. Slumlords, in turn, routinely disregarded citations for fire code violations. When investigators did have time to pursue noncompliance cases, they typically found ownership not only unresponsive but often undiscoverable, having been disguised behind various fronts and straw men.[53]

The Dorothy Mae Apartments—a four-story brick tenement built in 1927—was a microcosm of new immigrant life on one of these rent plantations. Most of its residents had migrated together—an entire transplanted village—from El Salitre in the state of Zacatecas, Mexico. Fathers and mothers worked together in Downtown garment sweatshops, while grandparents and older children took care of toddlers and infants. On the weekends "Little Salitre" celebrated christenings in the Dorothy Mae parking lot or held communal picnics and soccer matches in nearby Elysian Park. They paid rent to an abstraction called HLL Management Company, a facade as it turned out for attorney Hiram Kwan and his 10 anonymous partners. Although the Dorothy Mae was equipped with fireproof "Ponet doors," these were illegally propped open. The absentee owners had pointedly ignored repeated citations from fire inspectors.

The ensuing tragedy on 8 September 1982 was a virtual repeat of the fire at the Hotel St. George 30 years before. A blaze in a first-floor utility room burned through to the stairwell and within seconds became a miniature firestorm sucking every molecule of oxygen out of the building. The 200 residents had almost no warning: 24 died (including 7 members each of the Diaz and De La Torre families), 150 were injured. Little Salitre was devastated.[54]

Eight months later, while the city council was supposedly debating a "Dorothy Mae" ordinance mandating automatic sprinklers and smoke-activated fire doors, the postwar history of tenement fire came back, full circle, to the Hotel St. George. The skid row crematorium's latest owner was a Palos Verdes millionaire who had changed nothing

They never had a chance (1982 Dorothy Mae fire)

but the name (to the "LA Six Motel"). He was under criminal investigation for 121 separate health, building safety, and fire code violations. The six-story structure's misdemeanors included fire escape doors that opened the wrong way, missing fire hoses, inoperative smoke detectors, and substandard wiring. There were gaping holes in the walls, cracks in the ceilings, no heating, sagging floors, and one of the largest vermin populations on the West Coast. Superior Court judge Dickran Tevrizian, who toured the former St. George in 1982, called it "a time bomb."[55]

It went off on 13 May 1983. Although an elderly man was burnt to death, alert firefighters, primed to the perils of the hotel, stopped the blaze before it became "a major catastrophe." Fire Chief Donald Manning then urged the city council to pass the Dorothy Mae ordinance. The response of Robert Farrell, chairperson of the Building and Safety Committee, spoke volumes about communications between the fire department and the council. "What ordinance?" he demanded.[56]

3. NOUVELLE INFERNO

This is hell, dude!

Malibu resident fleeing fire (1993)

As in 1970, when Ponet Square and Malibu went up in flames in the same few weeks, tenement fire and wildfire were again in stark counterpoint to each other in 1993. If Southern Californians seemed unprepared for this trial by fire, they had no one to blame but themselves. The conflagrations of 1993 came down grimly familiar pathways—and there was no shortage of omens.

Harried fire inspectors, for example, knew the tenement at 330 South Burlington Avenue only too well. Since 1988 they had repeatedly cited its owners for failure to repair defective smoke detectors and fire doors. Building and safety officials had also slapped the sprawling 69-unit structure with a notice of substandard maintenance, while health inspectors had responded to innumerable tenant com-

plaints about broken plumbing, leaking ceilings, and obscene infestations of rats, cockroaches, and fleas. True, there were other tenements
in the Westlake district with comparable dereliction, but they were 60
to 85 years old. The Burlington Apartments had been built in 1985.[57]

The belief that Los Angeles's tenement problem would gradually be
reduced by the sheer attrition of blighted buildings was confounded in
the 1980s by the appearance of huge four-story stucco boxes precariously supported by their parking garages. These poorly constructed
"super-cubes," containing from 36 to 112 cramped units, were scarcely
more than instant slums designed to exploit a desperate demand for
cheap shelter in the central city. Speculators—typically headquartered,
like the Burlington's owners, in the affluent western end of the San Fernando Valley—took advantage of federal tax exemptions and Los
Angeles's unreformed zoning code to impose exorbitant new population densities (amplified by tenant overcrowding) on poor neighborhoods in the Westlake, Mid-City, and Hollywood districts.

When fire inspectors visited the Burlington on three separate occasions during April 1993, they found people living in closets and
infants sleeping in dresser drawers. They also discovered that the
Ponet fire doors were nailed open and that few of the smoke alarms
actually worked. After the first inspection they ordered the owners to
post an emergency 24-hour firewatch until the violations were cor-
rected. The owners—Sidney and Frances Kaufman of Woodland
Hills—did not comply. A week later, after two further visits, the
inspectors reissued the order. Once again the Kaufmans disregarded
it. At this point departmental regulations required the inspectors to
take the citations to the fire marshal for an emergency hearing and
possible prosecution. They failed to do so.

Two weeks later the predictable tragedy occurred. Breaking out on
the second floor, fire erupted through the open fire doors to the third
floor, then blasted out the windows facing the interior courtyard. Residents—many of them Kanjobal (Mayan) Indians from Guatemala—
were trapped between the inferno in the hallways and the toxic
smoke which quickly filled the tiny courtyard. Desperate parents
dropped screaming babies and toddlers from upper-story windows

Ten died (1993 Burlington fire)

into the arms of people on the street. A local Eighteenth Street gang member, Carlos Ingles, became an instant neighborhood hero when he caught six children, then, hearing cries, entered the building to rescue a young couple from their blazing bedroom. Still, it was too late for 10 victims, including two pregnant women.[58]

The wildfires came six months later. The rains of the previous winter had produced exorbitant new brush growth, now dried and highly combustible. As in other recent fire years, the Santa Anas began howling just before Halloween. On the morning of Tuesday 26 October, Southern California woke up to perfect fire weather. Los Angeles Fire Chief Donald Manning accurately assessed "a potential day for disaster" and dispatched 10 city engine companies to the rim of the San Fernando Valley where chaparral meets suburb. And shortly after lunch, a blaze flared up in that crucible of so many Malibu fires: just across the Ventura County line in the grassland corridor between Agoura and Thousand Oaks. A regional fire war room was quickly established in the Los Angeles County Fire Department's new headquarters in the Montebello Hills.

Early Wednesday morning, as a 50-mile-per-hour Santa Ana whip-sawed power lines and ripped the fronds off palm trees, fires erupted one after another in Chatsworth (northwest San Fernando Valley) and Santa Paula (eastern Ventura County). Meanwhile, a transient, camping in Eaton Canyon along the flank of Mount Wilson, tried to keep warm by kindling a small fire which immediately spread to century-old, unburnt chaparral. Within 24 hours it would destroy 118 homes in Altadena and Sierra Madre. As dawn broke on the 27th, the Thousand Oaks/Malibu, Chatsworth, and Altadena fires were out of control, five firefighters had already been critically injured, and new blazes were being reported throughout five Southern California counties. As local forces were overwhelmed, statewide mutual aid agreements kicked in, and 100 engine companies were sent southward on Interstate 5, sirens screaming, from Bay Area and San Joaquin Valley fire departments.

They arrived too late to save the two dozen homes destroyed by the first Malibu fire, which ultimately incinerated 39,000 acres. But events in Malibu were overshadowed by the fire that began on Thursday just after lunch and with incredible speed consumed Laguna Beach "as if it had been soaked in gasoline." Twenty-seven thousand residents were evacuated from the path of a conflagration whose coming had been long predicted and long disregarded.

> The narrow streets of wood homes with shake roofs finally suc-cumbed to the devastation that for decades officials had warned was the region's destiny. After the Oakland fire two years ago, Orange County Fire Captain Dan Young said com-munities such as Laguna Beach were "designed for disaster."[59]

The Laguna Beach blaze—the biggest Orange County fire since 1948—injured 65 firefighters, destroyed 366 homes (most of them valued at over $1 million), and caused $435 million in damage. It seemed to be the dramatic denouement to a catastrophic fire week. In fact, it was only the first act.

The second began on the morning of 2 November near a pair of water tanks on Mount Calabasas. Within a few minutes the Santa Anas transformed a careless—or deliberate—spark into the seed of a great firestorm. Two off-duty volunteer firefighters, driving up Old Topanga Canyon Road, spotted the initial plume of smoke and managed to hook up a hose to a hydrant, but they were quickly overwhelmed by the fire's explosive growth. "I immediately thought it was arson," one commented. "I don't exactly know why."[60]

While county crews were still racing to the scene, the implacably advancing fire ambushed its first victims at a ranch a few hundred yards downhill from the water tanks. Miscalculating the fire's velocity, residents Ron Mass and Duncan Gibbins attempted to defend their home with a garden hose. They recognized their mistake almost immediately, but it was already too late. Mass jumped into his jeep, but the fire caught him before he could get out of the driveway. Hideously burned, he managed to stagger to the edge of Old Topanga Canyon Road where firefighters found him: his blistered arms "outstretched like a scarecrow." Gibbins, who had dashed back to rescue his cat, ran right into the fire's deadly thermal pulse. It charred 95 percent of his body. Paramedics later discovered him, barely conscious, in the ranch's swimming pool. "I don't want to die," he said over and over. Smoke poured from his mouth, and he talked in the painful high-pitched squeal of a man with lungs scorched beyond repair.[61] Gibbins died later in the hospital, but Mass surprised doctors by surviving his terrible third-degree burns.

By the early afternoon the summit of the Santa Monicas was a funeral pyre. The ridgeline network of fuel breaks failed to slow the Santa Ana–fanned conflagration. Veteran county fire crews, aided by air tankers and helicopters, gamely defended their fire line on Old Topanga Canyon Road, but it was impossible to stop a 30-foot wall of flames, driven by 70-mile-per-hour winds, from cascading down the steep ravines and gorges that led to the Malibu coast. Multimillion-dollar estates in Carbon and Las Flores Canyons—some built on the ashes of humbler houses destroyed in 1956 and 1970—became so much fire fuel.[62] The situation was now out of control. From Los

Angeles International Airport (LAX) or West L.A., the dark nimbus billowing above the Santa Monicas looked like a volcanic eruption. At 1:30 P.M. a sheriff's helicopter ordered Malibu Colony residents to evacuate their beach houses.

Meanwhile, in the hills above the ocean, overwhelmed firefighters and terrified residents fought for their lives. Some had to drive through barricades of fire, while others saved themselves in empty swimming pools. Sean Penn and Ali McGraw, among scores of others, saw their homes burn to the foundations. Time and again, firefighters were betrayed by the feeble water pressure in hydrants or trapped in the labyrinth of narrow mountain streets. In upper Los Flores Canyon, an Alhambra fire crew miraculously survived a fireball that incinerated their truck.

Don and Amy Yarrow were not so lucky. An elderly couple who lived in a modest trailer at the top of Carbon Canyon, they had been Malibu residents since the 1940s. They tried to outrun the firestorm in their Toyota pickup, but the flames were faster. They were engulfed a mere hundred yards down the road. It took several days to identify their charred remains.[63]

At dusk that day, Malibu was a surreal borderland between carnival and catastrophe. On the pier nonchalant crowds played video games while television news helicopters hovered overhead and the Coast Guard cutter Conifer stood offshore, ready to evacuate residents. Beneath the flaming hills, the Pacific Coast Highway was paralyzed by a hopeless tangle of arriving fire trucks and fleeing Bentleys, Porsches, and Jeep Cherokees. Hundreds more trekked out on horseback, by bike, or on foot. A few escaped on roller blades. Three hundred sheriff's deputies were brought in to guard against looting. The chaotic exodus was oddly equalizing: panicky movie stars, clutching their Oscars, mingled with frantic commoners. Confronted once again with its destiny as a fire coast, Malibu replied in the vernacular. "This is hell, dude," one resident told the Los Angeles Times. "I'm expecting to see Satan come out any time now."[64]

The crisis also tested Malibu's strange, bespoke morality. When the firestorm temporarily cut off the highway as an escape route, trapped

Not everyone was evacuated

residents had to make some tough choices. The *Malibu Times* celebrated the case of two intrepid housewives from the Big Rock area who loaded their jewels and dogs into kayaks and took to the sea, where they were eventually rescued by blond hunks from Baywatch Redondo. Only the fine print revealed that, in saving their pets, they had left their Latina maids behind. (The abandoned maids managed a narrow escape down the beach to Topanga.)[65]

Firefighters, meanwhile, began to have the eerie sense that they were struggling against supernatural cunning. After feigning a thrust

at Malibu Colony and Pepperdine University, the fire suddenly piv-
oted eastward toward Tuna Canyon. As frantic fire crews battled
walls of flame in the lower canyon, the swirling red center of the
firestorm easily outflanked them on the north, heading straight for
Topanga, the Getty Museum, and, ultimately, the fat neighborhoods
of the Palisades (where 70 city fire engines were already waiting).

By the early morning of 3 November, deputy county fire chief
Donald Anthony had deployed 7,500 firefighters—some from as far
away as Oregon and Oklahoma—for a last-ditch stand in Topanga
Canyon. No one had ever seen such a gigantic mobilization of personnel and equipment. The urban ladder rigs, forestry pumper
trucks, and bulldozers stretched almost bumper to bumper for 11
miles. Courageous helicopter pilots ignored their safety manuals to
fly dangerous night water drops. At dawn they were relieved by C-
130s capable of bombing the chaparral with 3,000 gallons of fire
retardant at one time. Still the fire shrewdly parried each human tactic, repeatedly leaping over fire lines to ignite brush on the east side
of the road. The battle raged savagely until late Wednesday afternoon
when the firestorm literally ran out of fuel and wind at the edge of the
ocean. It had lasted 36 hours.

As in previous years, the prime-time drama of a Malibu fire produced an extravagant outpouring of sympathy from government agencies and common citizens. FEMA director James Lee Witt assured fire
victims that the Clinton administration, having declared Malibu a federal disaster area, would provide "all the aid they need to rebuild
homes and lives." Meanwhile, scores of trendy restaurants, bistros,
and boutiques acted as an upscale equivalent of the Red Cross (which
was also on the scene). Insurance adjusters set up camp in Winneba-
gos next to the Malibu pier. The county promised tax relief. A group
of German architects offered to work for free. Fire victims formed a
support network. Anthony Hopkins offered an apartment to Dick Van
Dyke. Zsa Zsa Gabor gave shelter to some homeless horses.[66]

Eleven days later, while the tabloids were still shedding crocodile
tears for burned-out movie stars, another fire—invisible to most of

the media—killed three residents and critically burned twelve others in a dingy Downtown residential hotel. The death toll was the same as in the Malibu blaze, but property damage differed by several orders of magnitude. Once again, the double standard of fire disaster was rubbed in the faces of the poor—in this case, Mexican and Guatemalan garment workers. The owners of the Grand Avenue tenement—mere spitting distance from Ponet Square—had a notorious record of fire, health, and safety code violations. They had ignored long-standing tenant complaints about locked fire escapes, inoperable smoke detectors, vermin infestations, and crack addicts who monopolized the common bathrooms. When an evicted tenant threatened to burn the building down, however, the landlords did call the police. "They never came down. They said that if anything happens, call 911." A police spokesperson later explained, unconvincingly, that it had been "an awful busy day."[67]

4. THE INCENDIARY "OTHER"

I was extraordinarily liberal until I came to Malibu, now I'm a fascist.

Prominent screenwriter (1984)

The LAPD's phlegmatic attitude toward tenement arson stood in sharp contrast to official hysteria about suburban wildfire. The 1993 firestorms, following so close on the heels of the Rodney King riots, opened a Pandora's box of white fear. One disaster was, not necessarily logically, superimposed on the other. From Laguna to Ventura, rumors spread that "some new breed of terrorist, or worse, several, were on the loose." Public officials openly speculated that black gangs were at last making good on supposedly long-standing threats "to burn rich white neighborhoods." In private, some even hinted darkly about a possible "Muslim connection" to New York's World Trade Center bombing.[68] Ironically, the burning hills had been full of hundreds of present and former gang members: all risking their lives on state and county fire crews. (In addition, several thousand state prison inmates served bravely on Malibu fire lines.)[69]

The homeless also cast demonic shadows in Southern California's social imaginary. The Eaton Canyon fire, accidentally triggered by a transient, seemed to confirm the worst fears of mountain and canyon homeowners: that an invisible army of careless, embittered strangers was lurking in the brush. Clandestine hobo encampments, like those in Tuna Canyon along the Malibu coast, were singled out as intolerable fire hazards. Blazes of indeterminate origin were routinely ascribed to the homeless.[70]

As media-hungry politicians commuted from one fire scene to another, their rhetoric became inflammatory. Republican Governor Pete Wilson, desperately trying to toughen his image, compared arson with child molestation and proposed life sentences for the guilty. This failed to satisfy two even more bloodthirsty Orange County Republicans—Congressman David Drier and Assemblyman Ross Johnson—who insisted on the death penalty for instigators of fatal blazes. Drier even demanded one-year prison terms for those who caused fires accidentally.[71]

Fire investigators, for their part, zealously emulated the federal-local task force model first deployed during the 1992 riots. In an unprecedented effort, Bureau of Alcohol, Tobacco and Firearms (ATF) agents joined city and county fire officials, sheriff's deputies, and local homicide detectives to search for the arsonists believed to be responsible for setting 19 of the 26 recent wildfires. Thanks to private contributions, the reward for apprehension of the Malibu arsonist—initially described as a mysterious figure in a "blue pickup"—rose to $350,000.[72]

The normally temperate *Los Angeles Times* blew an editorial fuse over the arson issue. Livid that a few thoughtless environmentalists had characterized homeowners in the fire zones as the real firebugs, the paper reassured readers that it was "hardly a crime against nature . . . to choose to live in the mountains, at the urban/rural interface." Instead, it called for "a true paradigm shift in the way that [Californians] think about fire."

> Fire prevention and crime prevention in California are becoming one and the same. . . . Californians need to stop viewing brush fires solely as acts of God and start thinking of them as sometimes acts of criminal—even pathological—man. What the arsonists did to us in the last two weeks they can do to us next week, or the one after that, if weather conditions are right for their evil crime. . . . We are no longer fighting "it"; we are fighting "them."[73]

Ironically, the *Times*'s "paradigm shift" from "it" to "them" has been conventional wisdom in Southern California for generations. Although probably not more than one in eight blazes is caused by arson,[74] Anglo-Californians have always criminalized the problem of mountain wildfire. The majority have never accepted the natural role or inevitability of the chaparral fire cycle. (Conversely, there has been a persistent tendency to naturalize the strictly human causality of tenement fire.) Political as distinct from scientific discourse has long been obsessed with identifying an "incendiary Other" responsible for fire destruction.

In the early twentieth century, this "cruel-hearted and selfish man" (in Frederick Rindge's words) was portrayed as an Indian, a sheepherder, or, most frequently, a tramp. During the First World War, the Wobblies (Industrial Workers of the World) were believed to be lurking behind every burning bush in California. A decade later, major wildfires—like the 1930 Decker Canyon blaze—were usually blamed on itinerant farmworkers, especially the Okies. A year after Pearl Harbor, though, FBI agents and National Guardsmen were combing Las Flores Canyon for clues to the identity of "Axis saboteurs" responsible for the 1942 Malibu fire. Reflecting popular preoccupations during the Eisenhower era, the *Los Angeles Times* added new profundity to its reportage of the 1956 Malibu fire by linking arson to sexual perversion. According to a psychologist consulted by the

A new breed of terrorist?

paper, arsonists "set fires at night in order to see women run out of their homes in a state of undress."[75]

The political backlash to the 1993 firestorms, however, was unprecedented in its virulence and the scope of the blame that was leveled. Seedlings of neo-McCarthyism sprouted in the charred ruins of affluent subdivisions. Following the demagogic lead of Governor Wilson, conservatives claimed to trace the web of a vast conspiracy against the sacred rights of property. In addition to spectral "terrorists" directly responsible for the fires, vengeful homeowner and pro-development groups indicted such fellow travelers of arson as gays, liberals, the Sierra Club, and an endangered rodent.

In Laguna Beach, for instance, pro-growth forces attacked openly gay council member Robert Gentry, who had lost his home in the fire, for devoting "too much attention to AIDS victims and not enough on fire protection." Scorning the charge that homes with wooden roofs and siding virtually invited incineration, the so-called Laguna Coalition instead vilified environmentalists for opposing construction of a three-million-gallon reservoir.[76] On Orange County talk radio stations, the Sierra Club was denounced as "arson's fifth column."

In Riverside County, burned-out homeowners charged that federal regulations designed to protect the rare Stephens kangaroo rat had prevented them from clearing tall brush around their homes. "My home was destroyed by a bunch of bureaucrats in suits and so-called environmentalists who say animals are more important than people," claimed one distraught resident. "I'm now homeless, and it all began with a little rat." But the allegation that wildlife regulations prevented fuel clearance was a canard. In fact, the U.S. Fish and Wildlife Service had encouraged the *mowing* of grasses around homes as a reasonable fire safety measure. The problem has been that many homeowners find mowing too troublesome, preferring simply to rototill their ecosystem under.[77]

These attacks were, in effect, the opening salvos in a major new political offensive to unleash further pyromanic suburbanization. Thus, Congressman Ken Calvert (R-Riverside), supported by the powerful Riverside Building Industry Association and the Farm Bureau, proposed a radical revision of the Endangered Species Act in order to protect property rights. At stake were 77,000 acres of federally protected habitat that developers had long coveted. Likewise along the Laguna coast, pro-growth forces were orchestrating a similar hue and cry against the California gnatcatcher. This small, almost extinct bird was depicted as an arsonist through a bizarre syllogism that equated any undeveloped landscape or protected habitat with an ipso facto fire hazard.

In Malibu, local wrath fell on advocates of greater public access to beaches and critics of hillside development. It was a replay of an old battle. After the 1978 fire, the California Coastal Commission, which is mandated to protect public access to coastal areas, asked celebrity homeowners to provide rights-of-way to exclusive Trancas Beach. Governor Jerry Brown's Malibu friends, however, generated such an uproar against "government by extortion" that he denounced his own stunned commissioners as "bureaucratic thugs."[78] Four years later, while state officials were preoccupied with fighting the 1982 Trancas Canyon firestorm, local defenders of the status quo sabotaged a public access project at El Pescador Beach. "Tires were slashed, sand put in gas tanks, machinery pushed over the bluff, and site improvements trashed."[79]

In late 1993, Malibuites were again frothing at "radicals" who advocated more beachfront rights-of-way as well as stricter fire safety regulation of new and rebuilt housing. "They have forsaken our constitutional rights, and have shown a shocking insensitivity to [our] traumatic situation." Public access was equated with freedom of movement for arsonists. Residents demanded restricted access to mountain roads during periods of acute fire danger and raged against critics of the California Fair Plan, a state-mandated insurance pool that subsidizes fire-zone dwellers by spreading the costs among the mass of homeowners. Those who wanted the rich to pay a fairer share of the cost of protecting their homes were accused of instigating a "new class struggle between flatlanders and hillsiders." As in the wake of past fires, declarations of "victimhood" preempted any serious debate about the social costs of sustaining luxury lifestyles along the fire coast.[80]

By the end of summer 1994, however, the great arson manhunt had dissipated into a maze of false leads, misidentifications, minor arrests, and interagency squabbles. The evil "Fedbuster," whose menacing letters the previous fall had suggested a vast conspiracy ("They burned me now I'm going to burn back. I fight fire with fire. You like puns, chumps? Sizzle, sizzle"), turned out to be a delusionary former sex offender with no role in setting any of the fires. Similarly, the dramatic confession of a homeless Satanist that he started the Laguna Beach fire "in order to commune with a demon" left egg all over the face of Orange County District Attorney Michael Capizzi when it was discovered that the suspect had been in a Mexican prison at the time of the fire.[81]

Finally, the investigation of the Malibu fire came full circle to focus on the original heroes: the two off-duty firefighters on Mount Calabasas. The result was an unseemly tug-of-war between Sheriff Sherman Block, who publicly accused the two of setting the fire so that they could put it out and become heroes, and District Attorney Gil Garcetti, who refused to indict them for lack of evidence. As the firefighters were left to writhe in the agony of unproven accusation, the ATF assumed control of the bungled investigation but quietly abandoned it after several years of desultory effort.

There was no breakthrough in any of the fire origin investigations until the fall of 1997. Then suddenly in October, the chief legal counsel for the California Department of Forestry identified the serial arsonist believed responsible for six recent fires in the Los Angeles area, including an October 1996 Malibu blaze that injured 11 residents and firefighters. The suspect was none other than Southern California Edison, whose main office near Los Angeles was raided after its executives refused to cooperate with state investigators. The sweep by state officials—who confiscated records, equipment, even tree limbs—followed up earlier charges by Ventura County fire officials and the U.S. Forest Service that Edison had deliberately withheld, tampered with, and destroyed critical evidence that linked negligent power-line maintenance to the fires. California forestry officials told the press that the giant utility was being investigated under a criminal statute "that makes it a felony to 'recklessly' cause a fire that results in serious bodily harm."[82]

5. REDLINING FIRE SAFETY

Separate and unequal fire protection is only the tip of the iceberg.

Councilmember Michael Hernandez

Councilmember Mike Hernandez's field office is a suite of tiny rooms above a pool hall and El Pollo Loco restaurant. The principal decoration is a wall map of his First Council District, a sprawling archipelago of Spanish-speaking neighborhoods consolidated by 1980s voting rights litigation to increase Latino representation on the Los Angeles City Council. Half of Hernandez's quarter-million constituents are crowded, 50 per acre, into the fire tenements of the Westlake area; the other half live, 15 per acre, in the bungalow belt that extends from Echo Park across the Elysian Hills to Garvanza.[83] Westlake is an electoral desert, with the smallest percentage of registered voters in the entire city. As a result, Hernandez's predecessor devoted most of her attention to politically active homeowners and small businesses in the other half of her district.

Hernandez, a large, quick-witted man with the cherubic face of Diego Rivera, has tried to redress this inattention to Westlake's predominantly immigrant population. He and his staff daily confront slum conditions of Dickensian dimensions. Although Hernandez has no tolerance for private exploiters, his wrath is especially directed against public agencies that negligently dismiss Westlake as Los Angeles's Third World. Whether the issue is garbage collection, recreation, school crossing guards, street cleaning, library facilities, or housing inspection, Westlake is the city's orphan. "We are still light years away," Hernandez emphasizes, "from per capita equality in city facilities or services."[84]

Fire inspection is a major case in point. In 1993, shortly after the Burlington fire, the *Los Angeles Times* surveyed tenements in the Westlake district and discovered that, despite epidemic safety violations, fully two-thirds had not undergone the annual fire inspection required by law. Hernandez was outraged and ordered the city's chief administrative officer (CAO) to prepare an independent audit of the entire city. The CAO, sampling 10 inspection records in each of 30 fire stations, found that only half of the mandatory inspections had been made. He also confirmed that 62 percent of the inspected structures were in blatant violation of the fire code.[85]

Hernandez's indignation about the Burlington disaster also jolted the fire department into conducting its own internal audit, employing the *Times*'s methodology of randomly selected buildings. Despite frequent boasts by Fire Chief Donald Manning that his department had "the best fire inspection program in the nation," his own auditors uncovered a stark double standard. "Under the current system," they pointed out, "inspectors spend the least time in many of the areas with the greatest fire hazards." Annual fire inspection rates, for example, were almost three times higher in upper-income areas, like Bel

Air and Encino, than in poor and fire-prone Westlake or South Central. The auditors argued that such disparities were the inevitable result of the much higher levels of emergency response common in inner city areas. Overworked and understaffed fire companies, in other words, were too busy battling blazes to have time to complete their entire schedule of safety inspection.[86]

The auditors found it more difficult to explain other anomalies. There was, for example, the "startling pattern of neglect of fire prevention records," 85 percent of which did not even indicate when buildings needed to be reinspected; inspectors, moreover, were negligent in referring persistent code violators to the city attorney for prosecution.[87]

Hernandez scoffs at the idea of an unavoidable trade-off between fire suppression and fire prevention in the tenement belt. "A two-tier system of fire safety—one for the Westside, another for the inner city—is morally indefensible." What the audits really demonstrate, he argues, is an urgent need to redeploy resources to beef up fire inspection in areas like Westlake and South Central. Although acknowledging that the department is severely understaffed, having lost four hundred firefighters to budget cuts since the late 1970s, he is fiercely critical of what he characterizes as a "discriminatory policy of allocating personnel by the number of structures in an area rather than its population." Although they have roughly equivalent numbers of structures, for example, Westlake has almost 25 times the per acre population density of Brentwood, Bel Air, or the Palisades. Hernandez also complains that desperately needed fire units have been shifted from his district to tony new subdivisions in the northwest San Fernando Valley.[88]

When I first interviewed him in June 1994, Hernandez—together with council allies Jackie Goldberg (Hollywood) and Mark Ridley Thomas (South Central)—had spent a long, frustrating year trying to move city housing agencies and the fire department into action on proposed fire reforms. Their proposals ranged in graduated intensity from withholding rent from noncompliant owners to placing their buildings under city receivership. By the first anniversary of the Burlington tragedy, however, nothing had been accomplished.

Although the city council had ordered the housing department to submit regular fire safety progress reports, none had been issued. Nor had the fire department taken even the first steps to implement Fire Chief Manning's promised reforms, including the computerization of fire inspection records and the creation of a special task force for the Westlake area.[89]

Hernandez and Goldberg have also had to fight the formidable influence of the landlord lobby on the city council. Incorporating the "bottom-line recommendations" of both the CAO and the fire department, their proposed "Burlington ordinance" ordered the installation of sprinkler systems in some 5,600 hotels and apartment houses with more than 15 dwelling units, built between 1943 and 1990. At an estimated cost ranging from $450 to $900 per unit and stretched out over a compliance period of seven to nine years, the ordinance, according to Goldberg and Hernandez, would not be "cost prohibitive." Landlords, however, immediately denounced it as a "death-knell for affordable housing" and applied fierce pressure on the council to eviscerate the measure. Yet the Burlington ordinance (still under debate at time of writing) is the essential third leg of a tripod of comprehensive fire reform that includes a high-density-area fire inspection task force and new fire code sanctions incorporated into the city's slum abatement program.

In historical perspective, these initiatives are little more than a determined effort to complete the reforms begun after the Ponet Square fire a quarter-century earlier. Yet the struggle for basic fire safety remains desperately uphill. In spring 1997, Hernandez was still battling the mayor's office over the decision to open the city's only new firehouse, after a decade of cutbacks, in the San Fernando Valley. "I'm surprised that we continue to focus the projects where the children are not," Hernandez told reporters. "The mayor continues to cater to that population he believes votes."[90] A few months later, the Blue Ribbon Committee on Slum Housing blasted the city's building and safety department for its conjugal relationship with landlords as well as its continuing failure to enforce codes in the city's 108,000 rat-infested slum apartments.[91]

6. THE FIRE BOOM

I have this sense of impending doom. . . .

Fire historian Stephen Pyne (1993)

In 1981, in one of his last articles, Los Angeles's best-known environmental writer, Richard Lillard, challenged Frederick Jackson Turner's famous thesis that the American frontier—and with it, the frontiersman—disappeared in 1890. As a matter of fact, Lillard asserted, the frontier was alive and well in the Edenic canyons above Malibu and Hollywood. The unique challenge of the wild mountains so near the big city brought out the true grit in the self-selected population of hill dwellers. "The whole hillside and canyon ambiance, almost always fresh and wildsmelling, both attracts and holds the kind of individual that Frederick Turner and many a traveller, Tocqueville included, knew in the backwoods districts." The neighborly and self-reliant hill folk, moreover, were tempered to heroic mettle by the implacable constancy of the fire danger, "keeping an outlook for arsonists or children playing with matches, as their forefathers once kept alert for hostile aborigines."[92]

At the same time, however, Lillard warned harshly against the creeping threat of mountain society's nemesis: sloping suburbia.

> It is not habitation amid wilderness. Mankind has conquered
> nature instead of adjusting to it. Often the new instant enclaves
> have a supermarket, a cleaning and dyeing establishment, and a
> laundromat. The immigrating mini-city populace consists of
> country club types rather than hillsiders.[93]

Although Lillard was writing only a decade and a half ago, his mountain frontier is now extinct. "Country club types" have everywhere conquered and now monopolize the picturesque seacoasts and foothills. Despite brave but belated attempts at open space conservation, like those of the Santa Monica Mountains Conservancy,

Southern California's remnant natural landscape continues to be destroyed or privatized. As we saw earlier, fire itself accelerates gentrification and the replacement of bohemian lifestyles by snobbery and exclusiveness. The real impetus of this movement to the hills is no longer love of the great outdoors or frontier rusticity, but, as critic Reyner Banham recognized in the 1960s, the search for absolute "thickets of privacy" outside the dense fabric of common citizenship and urban life.

Hillside homebuilding, moreover, has despoiled the natural heritage of the majority for the sake of an affluent few. Instead of protecting "significant ecological areas" as required by law, county planning commissions have historically been the malleable tools of hillside developers. Much of the beautiful coastal sage and canyon riparian ecosystems of the Santa Monica Mountains have been supplanted by castles and "guard-gate prestige." Elsewhere in Southern California—in the Verdugo, Puente, San Jose, San Joaquin, and San Raphael Hills, as well as the Santa Susana, Santa Ana, and San Gabriel Mountains—tens of thousands of acres of oak and walnut woodland have been destroyed by bulldozers to make room for similar posh developments.

And the "flatland" majority—including the poor taxpayers of the Westlake district, most of whom have never seen a Malibu sunset—will continue to subsidize the ever increasing expense of maintaining and, when necessary, rebuilding sloping suburbia. As Richard Minnich points out, hillside homeowners, unlike tenement dwellers, have access to almost unlimited fire protection.

> The money flows to the Santa Monica Mountains instead of poor areas of Los Angeles because fighting firestorms is an emergency action. In fact, all wildland fires, even one acre spots, are treated as emergencies. The Forest Service and other land management agencies have no *a priori* budget. After the fire is suppressed, they just send a bill to the government. Budgeting is *a posteriori,* which means there are no strings. They can spend as recklessly as possible. Urban fires aren't treated this way.[94]

A Malibu castle

Meanwhile, the suburbanization of Southern California's remaining wild landscapes has only accelerated in the face of a perceived deterioration of the metropolitan core. As middle- and upper-class families flee Los Angeles (especially its older, "urbanized suburbs" like the San Fernando Valley), they seek sanctuaries ever deeper in the rugged contours of the chaparral firebelt. The population, for example, of the Thousand Oaks–Agoura Hills corridor—the crucible of almost all Malibu firestorms—has tripled since 1970 (to nearly 60,000), with hundreds of new homes scattered like so much kindling across isolated hilltops and ridges.[95]

Ignoring every lesson of the recent fires and earthquakes, two new megadevelopments, Newhall Ranch and Ritter Ranch, totaling 42,000 homes, are under construction in the environmentally sensitive, fire-prone Santa Clarita and Leona Valley areas of northern Los Angeles County. Statewide, some seven million inhabitants—the whitest and wealthiest segment of the population—now live in the suburban-chaparral border zone where wildfire is king. Excluding national parks and military bases, California suffered an incredible 10,000 wildfires per year during the 1980s.[96]

At the same time, suburban firestorms are becoming ever more apocalyptic. The social cost of fire has increased in almost geometric relation to the linear growth of firebelt suburb populations. Two-thirds of all the homes and dwellings destroyed by wildfire since statewide record keeping began in 1923 have been burnt since 1980. If, as Stephen Pyne has suggested, the 1956 Malibu fire inaugurated a new fire regime, then the 1991 Oakland fire ($1.7 billion insured damage) and the 1993 Southern California fire complex ($1 billion) marked the emergence of a new, "postsuburban" fire regime.

CALIFORNIA URBAN WILDFIRES, 1923–93

Period	Homes Destroyed	Percentage of Total Destroyed
1923–64	1,626	17
1965–79	1,539	16
1980–93	6,303	67
Total	9,468	

Source: Data (except 1993) from California, Department of Forestry and Fire Protection, *Fire Safety Guides for Residential Development in California* (Sacramento, 1993).

The increased dangers of this "fire boom" are most obvious to those who risk their lives every year fighting mountain firestorms. As Interior Secretary Bruce Babbitt complained while visiting the Malibu fire scene in 1993: "Fire-fighting is getting more expensive, more hazardous." To use a military analogy, the new density of hillside housing has transformed the battle against wildfire from a wide-ranging war of maneuver into the equivalent of street fighting. Firefighters' energies are now dispersed into house-by-house defenses, while traditional wildfire techniques, like the use of backfires, are vitiated by the threat to nearby homes. As a result, there is a dramatically increased risk of firefighters' being trapped by erratic and rapidly moving fire fronts.

This is exactly what happened to four engines from the Glendale and Los Angeles city fire departments on the second day of the 1996 Malibu fire. Although the fire did little property damage, it came close to wiping out an entire fire line of defenders. The firefighters had been dispatched to save some ridge-top homes perched above Malibu Bowl in Corral Canyon, when shifting winds suddenly fanned flames up a steep south-facing hillside. The captain in charge of the Glendale fire crew, who would normally have watched for such flare-ups, was preoccupied with laying line to protect the homes. As the fire unexpectedly erupted across the eucalyptus-planted ridge, "Engine 24's captain felt a blast of heat followed by a rain of embers. He ordered his personnel to abandon their hose line and run." One firefighter, 53-year-old William Jensen, held his position with almost suicidal courage in order to cover his fleeing comrades with spray from his hose. He was hideously burned over 70 percent of his body and, although he lived, required 16 separate skin-graft operations before he left the hospital four months later.

Meanwhile, nearby units from Los Angeles were desperately trying to escape from the closing circle of flames. The heavy smoke, however, stalled Engine 10, and "the four men on board were only able to open one of the aluminized blankets each carried as protection. Three crawled under it; the fourth—the captain—was only able to get his upper body under the shield." He was seriously burned. Two other Los Angeles crews suffered smoke inhalation after they were forced to drive through the red wall of flame. A subsequent internal review by the two fire departments narrowly, and probably unfairly, focused on the role of "inexperienced leadership" in the near catastrophe, while ignoring the larger issue of house-by-house deployment under dangerous firestorm conditions.[97]

Indeed, a growing risk of entrapment and death is inevitable as long as property values are allowed to dictate firefighting tactics. The exponential growth of housing in foothill firebelts, moreover, increases the likelihood of several simultaneous conflagrations and stretches regional manpower reserves to their limit, or beyond. As one national

Endangered firefighters

forest official observed: "These fires in Malibu prove that you could throw in every firefighter in the world and still can't stop it."[98]

Most experts agree that the most effective way to curb the rising fire danger is regular "prescriptive burning" every five to seven years to reduce fuel accumulation. This return to Tong-va practice, however, has proved almost impossible to implement in Southern California, outside of unpopulated national forest jurisdictions. All controlled burns entail some small risk of runaway fire, and local fire departments are understandably intimidated by their potential liability. Hillside homeowners' associations, moreover, vehemently oppose prescriptive burning because of the belief that "blackened hillsides and ash in the swimming pools reduce property values." In a typical case, the Los Angeles County Fire Department was recently sued by a Topanga Canyon resident who claimed that controlled burns would make it impossible to sell his home.[99]

Mountain homeowners also continue to reject any special fiscal responsibility for the defense of their precarious habitats. Penny-pinching Malibuites, for example, have resisted every effort to force them to update their notoriously inefficient water system or widen their narrow, winding streets. Yet thanks to their disproportionate political clout, they continue to expect that the general public will bear the exploding costs of a scientifically discredited strategy of total fire suppression. As Alan Kishbaugh, the president of the powerful Federation of Hillside and Canyon Associations of Los Angeles (which includes Malibu affiliates), recently put it: "We're sitting here in our homes, doing our part, and expecting the best protection available. . . . When it comes to fire protection, Californians are entitled to the best that exists."[100]

As in the aftermath of each previous fire tragedy, homeowners have invariably been seduced by the idea of a technological fix to the problem of wildfire ecology. The latest fetish is the CL-415 "Super Scooper": a gigantic amphibious aircraft capable of skimming the surface of the ocean and loading up to 14,000 gallons of water per fire drop. For years the Federation of Hillside and Canyon Associations has been fiercely lobbying state and local officials to purchase a fleet of these Canadian-built planes at $17 million each. Since the 1993 evacuation of Malibu, moreover, the federation has enjoyed the support of the powerful West L.A. Democratic machine as well as most of the regional media, including the *Los Angeles Times.* In 1996 the state introduced the big planes on an experimental basis.[101]

Once again, politicians and the media have allowed the essential landuse issue—the rampant, uncontrolled proliferation of firebelt suburbs—to be camouflaged in a neutral discourse about natural hazards and public safety. But "safety" for the Malibu and Laguna coasts as well as hundreds of other luxury enclaves and gated hilltop suburbs is becoming one of the state's major social expenditures, although—unlike welfare or immigration—it is almost never debated in terms of trade-offs or alternatives. The $100 million cost of mobilizing 15,000 firefighters during Halloween week 1993 may be an increasingly common entry in the public ledger. Needless to say, there is no comparable investment in the fire, toxic, or earthquake safety of inner-city communities. Instead, as in so many things, we tolerate two systems of hazard prevention, separate and unequal.

4

OUR

SECRET

KANSAS

This story begins, like a Sinclair Lewis novel, along the shaded main street of a drowsy but prosperous American town. It is a wet Saturday afternoon in late January 1918.[1] The accents in the street place most of the population between the Wabash and the Scioto, although there are also the occasional brass notes of Chicago and the clipped vowels of New England. Nothing much is in the news, apart from local complaints about a bicycle thief and reports of military training accidents in the East. A large banner between the Corinthian columns of the central library advertises a new Liberty Loan; the crack drill team of Company 40 of the Home Guards is practicing in the armory.

At the First Friends' Church a quarterly meeting is in progress when a strange vibration suddenly ripples through the pews, accompanied by a locomotive-like drone which quickly grows in pitch to a banshee scream. As the church walls tremble, the wind pops out a high window which falls dangerously close to the choir. There is "short-lived panic" until the Reverend Harry Rimmer begins "a lively hymn" that rallies the congregation. The violent shaking and deafening clamor soon subside.

Rushing outside, the Friends discover amazing destruction: overturned cars, toppled trees, exploded garages, and roofless homes. In the middle distance, a sinister funnel cloud leisurely vacuums its way through a residential neighborhood. A large star-spangled banner "with standard attached" is clearly visible in the upward swirling column of debris.

The first herald of the disturbance, on an otherwise clear day, had been the sudden development of a single, towering cumulonimbus

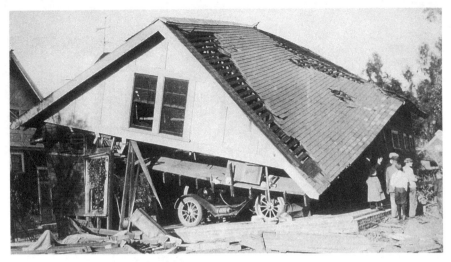

Miraculously, no one was killed (Pasadena, 1918)

cloud. According to eyewitnesses, the twister first touched ground near the high school. Roaring into the center of town, it began to feed hungrily on shingles, plate glass windows, fences, and other light material. As it steadily grew in intensity, its diet changed to sheds and small trees, then to house roofs, garages, and even hundred-foot-tall sycamores. Most of the time it was a "black, funnel-shaped column," but "once or twice it seemed to almost disappear, but then in not over five seconds would resume its old form."*

With pagan fury the tornado singled out symbols of local piety: unroofing the home of the Reverend H. T. Staats, pastor of Northside Congregational, and heavily damaging the Central Christian Church as well as the Lincoln Avenue Methodist Church. Central Christian was a gothic fortress built from huge concrete blocks, yet the twister "demolished the entire side, throwing down several solid blocks together which probably weighed several tons." At Lincoln Avenue Methodist,

---

* A *tornado* is "a violently rotating column of air in contact with the ground and extending from the base of a thunderstorm." They are most commonly spawned by large, rotating thunderstorms with powerful updrafts known as *supercells*. Tornadoes are popularly mistaken for their convection clouds or "funnels." As Charles Doswell of the National Severe Storms Laboratory points out, "since it is the wind associated with the rotating air column that does the damage, it is the moving air (wind) and not the cloud that constitutes the tornado."[2]

a few minutes later, the pastor and his family had a harrowing escape from death or serious injury. "The roof was lifted off [the pastorage] and the tornado played all kinds of havoc with the interior. When the roof went, the family took themselves to the basement, and to that alone probably owe their lives. The house was fairly torn inside out and the contents strewn around in pitiable fashion. The barn at the rear was lifted clear over the parsonage and set down in the front yard."

Whirling across the northeast corner of town, the tornado unroofed and damaged at least a dozen homes, destroying as well scores of barns and outbuildings. Indeed, all that was found of one garage was "the door knob, and it was blown through the radiator of an automobile close by." Shaken by the twister's ferocity, witnesses were equally amazed by its leisurely pace. "At times it seemed almost to stand still. It was as if a giant were amusing himself, and taking his time in doing so, by tearing trees up by the roots, unroofing houses and frightening people on every hand. To those in its path it seemed hours were consumed by the column in going two or three blocks. As a matter of fact, it probably took half an hour for it to cross the city."

With a damage corridor 50 to 200 feet wide, the twister most likely would rank as an F2 ("considerable damage") on the modern Fujita scale of tornado intensity.* Miraculously, no one was killed or seriously injured by its rotating scythe of deadly debris, though one woman was struck in the back by a falling rafter. In gratitude, the choir at the heavily damaged Lincoln Avenue Church opened the next day's Sunday service with "Safely through Another Week God Has Kept Us."

In the annals of the American heartland's perennial struggle with tornado devastation, the 26 January 1918 twister is probably close to the historical median in both intensity and damage. What distin-

---

* Devised by Dr. Theodore Fujita at the University of Chicago, this is a six-step (0–5) scale of wind damage intensity in which rotational wind speeds are inferred from an analysis of damage effects. Thus an event powerful enough to "rip roofs off frame houses, demolish mobile homes, and uproot large trees"—exactly as occurred in Pasadena—is classified as an F2 with an estimated wind speed of 110 to 150 miles per hour. It is important to keep in mind, however, that a tornado's intensity, and thus its F-scale rating, can change in the course of its brief life cycle.[3]

guishes the event, however, from thousands of similar small disasters in Texas, Oklahoma, Kansas, and Illinois is that it occurred in Pasadena, California, just 30 miles from the Pacific Ocean. One of the twister's major casualties was an orange grove, completely uprooted by its fierce winds. Yet just half an hour after its passage, "the sun was shining brightly, the wind had died down, the temperature was like a summer day."[4]

Ironically, Pasadena (formerly known as the "Indiana Colony") was traditionally sold to the midwestern émigrés who made up a majority of its population with the official assurance that "Southern California has no cyclones, hurricanes or blizzards."[5] It is not surprising, then, that residents reportedly "gazed at the swirling funnel in amazed disbelief," or that "immense crowds of sightseers thronged the afflicted quarters" to view the tornado damage firsthand. Thinking themselves in Oz (and in 1918, L. Frank Baum—Oz's creator—lived just over the hill from Pasadena in Hollywood), Dorothy and Toto were actually back in Kansas.

1. FREAK WINDS AND HOT SPOTS

Neither tornadoes nor tropical hurricanes are significant in the recent weather history of southern California.
  Harry Bailey, The Weather of Southern California *(1966)*

Pasadena's city fathers immediately characterized the tornado as a "freak windstorm" and invoked the authority of the Reverend Mr. Staats, an old-timer from the 1880s, to assure residents that the last wind disaster to savage Pasadena in 1891 had been "nothing like a tornado, but a steady blow" (in other words, an unusually strong Santa Ana).* The Los Angeles press meanwhile clamped a tight lid on

---

* Southern California's famous "devil wind," the Santa Ana, is produced by strong high-pressure systems over the Great Basin during the late autumn and early winter. Santa Anas sometimes gust to 80 to 90 miles per hour and can cause extensive property damage, injury, and occasionally death.[6]

reports of the Pasadena twister. The next day—Sunday, 27 January—was Southern California's annual "brag day" (timed to coincide with blizzards in the East), when both the *Times* and its Hearst rival, the *Examiner,* published nationally circulated "Come to California" editions. Obviously, they were not eager to advertise tornadoes or other blemishes on the face of Los Angeles's reputation for perfect weather. As a result, even many Southern Californians remained unaware of the spectacular damage in Pasadena.[7]

The incredulous reaction of Pasadenans in 1918—consternation followed by denial or, inversely, denial followed by consternation—has been the common response to episodically destructive tornadoes. Although tornadoes are ordinary citizens of Southern California's "normal" climate regime, they have been persistently construed as aberrations, like mountain lions in a suburban yard. "Freak winds" is the euphemism that has most often appeared in breathless newspaper accounts. Despite more than 75 destructive tornadoes in the southern coastal counties during this century, new twisters are still termed "bizarre" or "extremely rare."[8]

Indeed, Southern Californians seem to have ingested too much of their own propaganda about the "weather-beaten, cyclone-lashed" Midwest. Our cultural immune system, adapted to dealing with earthquakes, floods, and wildfires, autonomically rejects the equally inevitable probability of tornadoes and occasional hurricanes. They are categorized as exotic events whose existence requires radically different environmental contexts. "It just doesn't happen here" could be the Golden State's motto. Tornadoes, therefore, are a fascinating index of a larger problem in our cultural psyche: the occlusion of natural history by landscape ideology. They are, so to speak, a periodic litmus test of Southern California's environmental memory.

Science, for its part, has done little to increase public awareness of this homegrown tornado hazard. For many decades, the existence of local tornadoes was essentially a trade secret of meteorologists and a handful of weather buffs. Written accounts were confined to brief, if pioneering, descriptions of the 1918 Pasadena and the 1930 Vernon twisters in the columns of *Monthly Weather Review*.[9] Despite repeated flurries of tornado damage, little was known about their intensity or frequency until 1972, when the Lawrence Livermore National Laboratory, worried about natural threats to the nuclear power industry, published a brief synopsis of California tornadoes. Livermore consultants identified 48 events between 1950 and 1971. In 1979, this number was enlarged to 116 between 1951 and 1979 in a short report, *Windstorms in California,* issued by the California Department of Water Resources.[10]

These studies confirmed that California had a much higher statewide tornado incidence than anyone had guessed, but they did not profile tornado behavior in specific subregions. Only in 1983, in the aftermath of a particularly destructive tornado near downtown Los Angeles, did the National Severe Storms Forecast Center in Kansas City undertake a review of all evidence of California tornadoes between 1962 and 1983. One of the center's researchers, John Hales, with funding from the Nuclear Regulatory Commission, carefully reconstructed the associated meteorological features of 14 tornadic thunderstorms (28 individual tornadoes) responsible for damage in the Los Angeles area during the same period.[11]

Hales's groundbreaking 1983 study—the first to consider the weather system (or "synoptic") context of Southern California tornadoes—was followed nine years later by an even more comprehensive survey of California tornadoes that extended the record back to 1950. The study's authors, Warren Blier and Karen Batten of UCLA, compared the climatological features of the four subregions of intense tornadic activity: South Coast, Southeast Deserts, Central Valley, and North-Central Coast.[12] Finally, mining local newspaper archives, I have pushed the chronicle of Southern California twisters back to 1918, and even found evidence of a nineteenth-century twister.[13]

Hales's and Blier and Batten's research, as augmented by my additional data, points to some extraordinary conclusions:

Although repressed in public memory, tornadoes have left impressive trails of injury and property damage in modern Southern California. Twisters have wrecked at least 60 major structures, including a convention center, two airports, a movie studio, and a municipal wharf, as well as schools, factories, and packing plants. They have also destroyed or seriously damaged about 1,440 homes and small businesses and injured as many as 188 people. The absence of fatalities has been, by all accounts, miraculous.

Moreover, statewide reportage of tornado data has tended to conceal the existence of a tornado hot spot in the South Coast region, which includes Los Angeles and Orange Counties, coastal San Diego County, and the western portions of San Bernardino and Riverside Counties. Tornadoes occur nearly 10 times more frequently there than in the state as a whole. Indeed, coastal Southern California, with more than one hundred reported events since 1950 (or 2.5 tornadoes per year), has the highest tornado incidence west of the Great Plains.[14]

But that is only the beginning of the story. Within the South Coast region there is a distinctive "tornado alley" along the Los Angeles plain from Santa Monica to Newport Bay. Hales suggests that a "unique juxtapositioning of the coastline and mountains" steers unstable cold air into this convergence zone.[15] According to Blier and Batten, the post-1950 tornado incidence here (3.10 tornadoes per 10,000 square kilometers per year) is slightly higher than that for the state of Oklahoma (2.86 per year), universally conceded to be earth's tornado capital.[16] To sharpen the point, the Oklahoma City metropolitan area, considered to have the world's worst urban tornado problem, is hit by twisters, on average, every 4.0 years. Yet metropolitan Los Angeles, at an average of once every 2.2 years, is hit nearly twice as often![17]

Perhaps higher frequency is compensated by reduced intensity? Indeed, it's true that Southern California's nouvelle cuisine twisters tend to be less intense and shorter lived and have shorter path lengths than their corn-fed Oklahoma or Kansas cousins. Only a few long-lived South Coast tornadoes may have briefly reached the F3 threshold, and meteorologists do not believe that giant F4 and F5 events as portrayed in the 1996 film *Twister,* with winds well in excess of 200 miles per hour, are possible in coastal California.

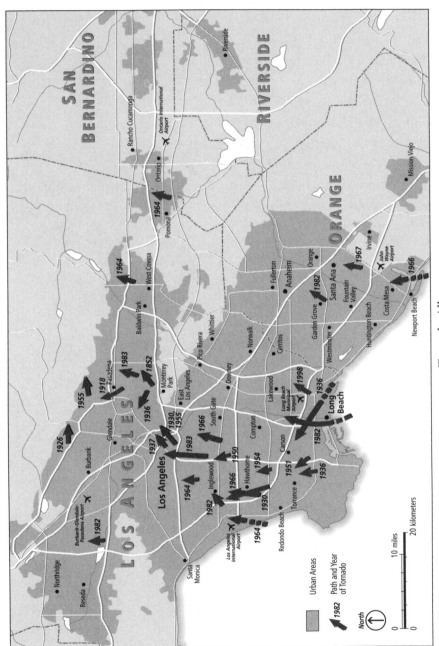

Tornado Alley

COMPARATIVE TORNADO INTENSITIES

Intensity	United States (1997)	Los Angeles Region (1950–92)	Fujita Magnitude
Weak (100 mph winds)	62%	93%	F0-F1
Strong (200 mph winds)	36%	7%	F2-F3
Violent (300 mph winds)	2%	0%	F4-F5

Source: U.S. figures from National Weather Service (Newport, N.C., 1997); Los Angeles figures from Warren Blier and Karen Batten, "On the Incidence of Tornadoes in California," *Weather and Forecasting* 9 (September 1994): 301–15.

This is small solace, however, since unlike in the Midwest the "greatest incidence of tornadoes [in California] occurs almost precisely in the area of highest population density."[18] Even "weak" F1 tornadoes in heavily urbanized areas can be deadly, especially when pedestrians, motorists, or mobile home dwellers are involved.[19] "Strong" F2 events are capable of inflicting stunning damage on Southern California's typical stick-built residential neighborhoods.

The two major concentrations of employment and traffic in Los Angeles County have frequently been caught in the crosshairs of tornadic storms. Downtown has been struck five times in this century, and the area around LAX, eight times. The tiny, square-mile community of Lennox, immediately east of LAX's main runway, has suffered significant tornado damage three times (1930, 1966, and 1982) in the twentieth century: a remarkable figure that should prompt concern about airline safety during thunderstorm episodes.[20]

By any standard, Los Angeles–area tornadoes constitute a significant natural hazard whose costs will only increase as urbanization puts more lives and structures in harm's way. But popular recognition of the tornado problem has not followed on the heels of increased tornado damage. On the contrary, one of Southern California's most dramatic natural phenomena remains culturally invisible, an alien presence locked away in the "X-Files" of regional memory. This fact in itself, however, reveals the popular mind at work: even the weather (or, rather, its normative representation) is subject to ideological construction. As our look at the public reactions to the 10 most destructive tornadic storms since 1918 will make clearer, Los Angeles's tornadoes are fascinating case studies in the politics of environmental perception and, in this instance, amnesia.

TEN MOST DESTRUCTIVE TORNADIC STORMS

| Date | Damage and Injuries | | |
	Major Structures	Homes/Businesses	Injured
1926 April 5–7	7	135	100
1930 March 15	13	161	3
1936 February 12	3	71	6
1966 November 7	2	208	10
1977 March 16	2	119	4
1978 February 10		47	6
1982 November 9	5	35	2
1983 March 1	3	197	33
1983 September 30		75	2
1993 January 14–18		148	

DESTRUCTIVE TORNADO INCIDENCE BY DECADE

Decade	Number
1900–09	0
1910–19	1
1920–29	5
1930–39	7
1940–49	1
1950–59	8
1960–69	11
1970–79	9
1980–89	17
1990–95	18
Total	77

Mere statistics, of course, cannot convey the human impact of tornado disaster in a region where such events are considered nothing short of extraterrestrial. Tornadoes are celebrated as not only the most violent but also the quirkiest windstorms in nature. Their capricious behavior—taking the cradle but leaving the baby safely asleep—constitutes an entire genre of American folklore. Likewise, Los Angeles is the greatest eccentricity in American urban culture. When such inherently weird atmospheric physics interacts with such an admittedly bizarre city, remarkable tales are sure to ensue.

2. WHEN THE BLACK RAIN FELL

The two men were killed when a miniature cyclone, generated by the overflowing of a huge oil reservoir, tore the roof from their farmhouse, crushing them in the timbers.

Los Angeles Examiner *(1926)*

In his 1941 novel about a fierce Pacific storm named "Maria," George Stewart wondered if "perhaps there was something about the human mind itself that made it feel comfortable to think of a storm as a person, not an equation."[21] Certainly, some invite the comparison. In the rogues' gallery of Southern California storms, the great Easter storm of 1926, which spawned five destructive tornadoes as well as the twentieth century's most violent display of sea-level lightning, had a most sinister personality—more like fiendish Professor Moriarty than the elemental but straightforward Maria.

Although the first rains arrived in Southern California around dinner time on Easter Sunday (4 April), the blustery mass of the storm did not cross the Tehachapi Mountains until the next day. The terrific downpour, the most intense in a decade, was accompanied by trillion-watt lightning strikes all over the Los Angeles Basin. The first fatality was a Nisei farmer named Hega who was working in his truck garden in the Bandini area. Struck directly in the face by a bolt of lightning, he burst into flames in full view of his horrified neighbors. Further east, near the citrus hamlet of San Dimas, where several inches of rain had fallen in a few hours, the dam under construction at Pudding-stone Reservoir collapsed, and local ranch families were barely evacuated before a 50-foot wall of water came roaring through their homes and orange groves.[22]

Meanwhile, in the small foothill community of La Crescenta, just above Glendale, the first of the storm's reported tornadoes sucked the roof off the Spooner pharmacy and damaged the grocery store next door.[23] But the real tornado drama was just beginning along the San Diego waterfront, 120 miles to the south. What harbor authorities later confirmed as a "twister" attacked the new Fifth Street Landing Wharf and tore off most of its roof. It also snapped the heavy anchor chains on a 900-foot-long log raft in front of the Benson Lumber Company, sending hundreds of violently bobbing logs toward the warships in the harbor. The skipper of the destroyer *Kennedy* had to take quick action to avoid being rammed by the logs. The tornado/waterspout simultaneously wrenched the fishing barge *Ike Walton* from its anchorage off Point Loma and hurled it toward the shore, where, as two crewmen managed to swim to safety, it broke up in the raging surf.[24]

As the hardest April rains in history continued to pound the city, a second waterspout materialized over San Diego Bay shortly before midnight on Monday.* Striking into the mudflats just south of the municipal wharf wrecked by the earlier twister, it devastated the waterfront section of National City—a blue-collar community of pre-fabricated bungalows, railroad shacks, and adjoining truck gardens. It then crossed over to Chula Vista and destroyed a large citrus packing plant before moving on to demolish another dozen homes.

> There was a sheet of hail, a blast of rain, a terrific roar, a terrible crash of lightning, and then the sound of falling timbers. Wires were down and lights were out. Men, women and children, thrown from their beds, began to creep from under the

---

* A *waterspout* is "an intense columnar vortex (not necessarily containing a funnel-shaped cloud) over water." Most tornado researchers now accept that "the distinction between a tornado and a waterspout is basically of little or no scientific value."[25]

ruins of their houses and scantily attired, floundered about the mud in the chilly night. Those who escaped injury were directed through the dark by the cries of others who were pinned under the wreckage.[26]

Photographs of the damage in National City reveal utter devastation within the 200-foot-wide tornado track. Twenty-one homes and businesses were demolished, while scores more were severely damaged. There were a dozen serious injuries, ranging from skull fractures to broken hips, as well as hundreds of minor cuts and bruises. The local hero of the disaster was George Gary, a staunch Seventh Day Adventist, whose house survived intact while the homes on either side were reduced to rubble. "Insurance agents have come to me time and again and wanted me to insure my home. I told them all to go away. I told them that the Lord would take care of my house and the Lord did."[27]

The next day, while the Red Cross was still organizing relief for the victims, a third storm-spawned tornado came onshore just north of downtown San Diego. "Striking the Kelley Laundry company garage, the 'twister' ripped off huge strips of corrugated iron from the roof of the building and wrapped them around telephone poles, arc lights and the corners of houses." After peeling off the roofs of a number of homes in nearby residential streets (one shingle "was driven into the side of a building as if it had been shot from a gun"), the twister lifted up and then touched down a quarter-mile away in Balboa Park, where it ripped out most of the trees in the beloved Pepper Grove picnic area. Continuing in a northeast arc, it set down again in East San Diego where it unroofed the Harmonial Institute on University Avenue. At least 50 homes were damaged along a path length of nearly five miles.[28]

After these three dramatic F2 events in San Diego, the twister that skipped across Santa Monica Beach on Wednesday (7 April) and unroofed five houses near Eighth and Pico rated barely a footnote.[29] The attention of the local and, indeed, national press was diverted instead to the San Luis Obispo area, 200 miles up the coast, where storm lightning had started a fire in the great Union Oil tank farm. Desperate local authorities immediately conscripted every able-bodied man in the county to battle the blaze. But a burning sea of crude oil overwhelmed defensive dikes and ignited most of the vast facility. Late Wednesday night the nearby town of Edna was evacuated and firefighters retreated to an outer defense line.[30] The next morning, while the San Luis Obispo inferno was raging out of control, the storm unleashed yet more lightning on another Union Oil tank farm, this one near Brea, in Orange County.

> Two huge reservoirs at the Brea tank farm exploded with a deafening roar when the lightning crashed into them, scattering wreckage for miles around. Buildings within an area of several miles were rocked to their foundations and windows were shattered when the two reservoirs, each containing 750,000 barrels of crude oil, exploded with a roar and burst of flames which shot heavy timbers a thousand feet into the air.[31]

As temperatures soared above several thousand degrees, both conflagrations—up to that time the largest oil fires in American history—grew into full-fledged firestorms, pumping so much energy into the surrounding atmosphere that they began to act as the superheated cyclonic cores of their own freakish weather systems. In both cases, as updrafts of air along the fire perimeter were sucked toward the center, violent tornadoes were the result. In Brea, while a crowd of 50,000 spectators was being drenched by black rain "like falling ink," a "miniature tornado" descended from the sky and wrecked a home more than a mile from the tank farm.[32]

Outside of San Luis Obispo, the result was more tragic. According to the local weather bureau observer, the five-day-long firestorm "produced hundreds of violent whirlwinds, many of tornadic character and force, probably the strangest meteorological phenomenon ever noted in connection with a fire. . . . Practically every explosion or 'boil-over' of a reservoir or tank produced whirlwinds or tornadoes. Melted cast iron fittings found at the scene of the fire indicate a temperature of between 2000 and 2500 degrees F." One of the larger of these fire-generated twisters was powerful enough to kidnap a cottage near the refinery and drop it in a field 150 feet away. Fifty-year-old A. Secber and his 25-year-old son perished in the wreckage. After a half-dozen attempts and through a bizarre chain of events, the angry storm of April 1926 had finally given birth to a killer.[33]

3. THE TERRIBLE TWINS

Los Angeles was struck yesterday by the first tornado in its history—at least, the first in the memory of the oldest inhabitants.

Los Angeles Examiner *(1930)*

The 15 March 1930 twister that roared through Los Angeles's southwestern suburbs also provoked a nomenclatural battle on the front pages of the city's daily press. As usual the *Times* could not say the forbidden "T word," so its restrained headline merely noted that "Roofs Go Flying in the Hawthorne Area." The *Record,* on the other hand, bannered "Hailstorm and 'Twister' Strike L.A.," while the *Examiner* shouted in 72-point type: "Tornado Unroofs L.A. Houses! Workmen Hoisted in Air." Indeed, the Hearst press, always striking the opposite note from its archrival, the *Times,* seemed to exult in the trail of cyclone damage that stretched from South Bay suburbs to the edge of downtown Los Angeles. Over dramatic photographs of the wreckage at the Santa Fe railroad yards and the Crown Carriage Works in the Vernon district, the *Examiner* crowed, "Was City Surprised as First Tornado Brought This!"[34]

In fact, the "first tornado" was two distinct events. Twister number one materialized out of a thunderstorm moving across the northern section of Los Angeles's "tornado alley." Just after eleven in the morning, the "tip of the tail hit the ground" in the Lawndale area and "bounced along like a rubber ball." As it barreled north through the city of Hawthorne's truck gardens and tiny chicken ranches, it

San Luis Obispo firestorm tornado

scooped up hundreds of chickens which it promptly discarded at the intersection of Chicago and Lawndale Avenues in a strange downpour of poultry.[35]

Continuing to cut a swath "sixty or seventy feet wide," the funnel cloud made a beeline for the Hawthorne municipal complex, where Saturday traffic court was in session. "Fireman William Dicks saw the twister coming and ran into court, notifying the judge that a dangerous storm was bearing down. Judge Thompson adjourned court immediately, and all present hurried to shelter. A moment later the whirling storm tore the tar roof off the fire department section of the building." In the surrounding residential streets, "many homes suffered heavily, with walls and porches torn off, and shot like arrows across space." In at least two instances, the F2 tornado lifted a two-car garage intact and hurled it a full city block.[36]

The angry vortex then spun into Mrs. Cecil Drew's driveway, picked up her car while blowing the roof off her next-door neighbor's garage, "then smashed the two cars together." Mrs. Drew, meanwhile, had grabbed her newborn baby and, with other terrified residents, taken refuge under a "ten-ton ditch-digging machine" parked on Wallace Street near Hawthorne Boulevard. A mechanic from the corner service station was sprinting to join them when the twister caught him: "It lifted me about six feet off the ground . . . then carried me about 30 feet and I fell beside the garage just as the side was ripped out." Somehow, he suffered only minor cuts and bruises.[37]

A flagpole sitter named Russell Fay had an even more unnerving encounter with the tornado. In the peculiar advertising custom of the day, he was perched on a tall pole in front of a Hawthorne dance hall, when the tornado suddenly bore down on him. He had only a few seconds to contemplate the absurdity of his predicament before he disappeared into the dark vortex of the funnel cloud. Horrified witnesses feared that he would be sucked into the sky, but Fay soon reemerged, triumphantly hugging the madly vibrating pole, though stripped of all of his clothing.[38]

Having unroofed approximately 150 homes and structures in Lawndale and Hawthorne, twister number one finished its morning's work in the tiny business center of Lennox: an unincorporated, "urban farm" district just east of Mines Field (now LAX). The editor of the *Lennox Tribune* and his wife saw the funnel approaching and ran out to rescue two kids playing in the street. "An instant after they snatched the children to safety the street was filled with flying debris and showering glass." The whimsical tornado, however, passed a nearby tent carnival "without even ruffling the canvas" and then disappeared in the direction of Venice.[39]

While incredulous South Bay residents were watching roofs and garages fly by, the rest of the Los Angeles Basin was being bruised by the heaviest hailstorm in living memory. As golfball-sized hailstones pelted streetcars and unhappy pedestrians, a second twister suddenly appeared near 28th Street and the Santa Fe tracks in the "exclusively industrial city"—as the official motto put it—of Vernon, just a few miles southeast of downtown Los Angeles. Working its way through the refineries and warehouses, the tornado occupied itself with unroofing buildings and hurling workmen about.[40]

The first tornado finished its work in Lennox (1930)

The twister then "leaped ten blocks" to McPherson Street where, in succession, it wrecked an auto-top factory, ripped the roofs off two other large plants, and blew down a long line of eucalyptus trees. As it crossed 23rd Street, it flung a heavy freight car off the tracks and against a nearby barn: evidence of possible windspeeds near the F3 threshold (156 mph). With full fury it then attacked the Santa Fe machine shops at 14th and Santa Fe, just inside Los Angeles. Some of the older buildings were totally destroyed, and two workmen were hospitalized with injuries from flying glass and debris.[41]

Twister number two was clearly visible from Downtown office buildings. "The funnel dipped down in a graceful sweep, the lower tip seemingly about fifteen degrees above the horizon, dipping and rising. The lower end was of a yellow-brown color." To more distant observers the funnel seemed to suddenly withdraw into a cloud bank, but an *Examiner* reporter claimed that the tornado "took a westerly twist after splitting its force by striking a monster gas tank of the Southern California Gas Company." "It then disintegrated and disappeared, leaving heaps of wreckage at the street intersection."[42]

Marion Dice, a General Petroleum geologist who recorded a short account of the episode, found the reactions of the onlookers almost as fascinating as the aerobatics of the tornado. "By watching spectators as they caught their first glimpse of the storm, one could immediately sort out the middle westerners from the native sons. Californians, most of whom had never seen a tornado, watched it with no thought of danger, while more experienced Kansans and Iowans were casting about for convenient shelters into which to dive if the whirl came closer."[43]

The twin tornadoes of 15 March 1930 may have been members of a larger outbreak, following the pattern of the January 1926 storm. A "freak wind" on the same day in 1930—most likely a waterspout— damaged five aircraft and moved a large hangar across a field at the Carpinteria airport on the Santa Barbara Channel. There were reports as well of a small twister in the Pasadena area and a water- spout which came onshore in Orange County, doing minor damage to farms in the Santa Ana area.[44] Indeed, the interaction of parental storm systems with the complicated topography of the Los Angeles coast appears to produce twisters in swarms.

During such outbreaks there is no fundamental distinction between onshore and offshore events, which has led some observers, vexed by the idea of twisters in the land of sunshine, to classify all local tornadoes as "waterspouts," with the implication that they are a qualitatively distinct phenomenon, smaller in intensity and scale than the "true" tornadoes of the Midwest. Thus, in characterizing the F2/F3 Vernon twister as a waterspout, the *Times* was only following in the footsteps of its ancestor, the *Los Angeles Star,* which reported a "very large waterspout" moving through the San Gabriel Valley on 20 February 1852 and making "that peculiar rumbling noise which is inherent to the phenomena."[45] Scientists now agree that the distinc- tion between tornadoes and "onshore waterspouts" is spurious. Whatever the label, the 1930s provided two further opportunities for residents of Los Angeles to study the formidable destructive powers of their own subspecies of tornado at uncomfortably close hand.

Funnel cloud over Vernon (1930)

4. THE TEMPESTUOUS DECADE

Screams of women and children could be heard above the din
of the gale. The crashing of timbers was like artillery fire.
Housetops were ripped loose.

Los Angeles Examiner *(1936)*

On Ash Wednesday (12 February) 1936, the entire Pacific Slope was
in the maw of a huge low-pressure system that had moved down from
the Aleutians. Gales lashed the fishing towns of Washington and Oregon; all construction on the great Bonneville Dam was suspended;
and Mary Astor and Melvyn Douglas, along with their film crew of
150, were marooned in the Sierra by a severe blizzard. In the western
San Gabriel Valley, just east of downtown Los Angeles, the chief concern was the relentless, heavy rain. Some nervous residents of the
foothills and canyons had already packed their automobiles for imminent flight. Their anxiety was understandable since two years before,
on New Year's Day 1934, more than 40 residents of nearby La
Canada Valley had died when similar storm conditions had precipi-
tated a catastrophic debris flow—a flash flood of the "consistency of
wet concrete . . . with boulders riding on top of the waves"—that
crushed scores of homes and cars under 20 feet of mud and rock.[46]

This time nature struck from an unexpected direction. A funnel
cloud, "roaring suddenly out of clouds surcharged with thunder and
lightning," touched down in the pretty bungalow town of Alhambra.
For five minutes the "baby cyclone" swirled through the residential
streets, but it was only the first half of a tornadic doubleheader.[47] A few
minutes later, just after four in the afternoon, a much meaner F2 began
its snakelike undulation across Long Beach, unroofing homes and toppling oil derricks. According to the *Examiner,* the "swath cut by the
heavy blow began at Twelfth street and American avenue and extended
for three miles in a northeast diagonal line toward the oil field section,
spending itself on the empty fields beyond. It was two blocks in width."
Harvey Connett, rescued by oil workers after his home was crushed by

a large derrick, suffered massive internal injuries and broken bones, while four other Long Beach residents were severely cut by flying glass. Several others narrowly escaped with their lives after a hundred-foot-tall derrick fell across busy State Street near Redondo Avenue.[48]

Heavy rains in the wake of the Long Beach twister only made the scene more forlorn. "Signs, awnings, and timbers floated in streets that were hissing rivers. Hundreds of cars were stalled. Pedestrians, drenched and frightened, sought shelter. Power was ordered shut off in the 'wind-whipped area' and several streets were blockaded, including State street, into the middle of which a large shed was catapulted by the wind." As the deluge overwhelmed local sewer capacity, "life guards stood by with rowboats to carry residents from homes flooded by the overflow."[49]

Contemporary newspaper accounts fail to clarify whether additional tornado damage in the Harbor City area of Los Angeles, where a house was blown off its foundations, and in the nearby city of Torrance, where toppled oil wells started a fire, was inflicted by the Long Beach twister—giving it a path length in excess of 10 miles—or resulted from a third tornado.[50] There was also debate about whether the Long Beach twister originated as a waterspout, since witnesses claimed that its rain had "a distinct salty taste."[51]

There was no disagreement, however, about the magnificent waterspout in Santa Monica Bay, nearly a year later (12 January 1937), that introduced one of "the most freakish afternoons" in Los Angeles history. At about 1 P.M., beachcombers were stunned by the spectacle of a funnel cloud "swirling half a mile offshore, amid crackling lightning and rumbling thunder. . . . It was of huge dimensions and revolved for several minutes before it swept from view into the fog." After several hours of short downpours punctuated by sunshine, a meteorologist was plotting storm paths at the weather observatory in downtown Los Angeles when the building came under a terrific hail bombardment. Looking outside, he was amazed to see lightning surging between the radio towers on Spring Street bank buildings and dancing across the tops of Broadway movie marquees.[52]

Then "at precisely 3:10 P.M., residents along North Broadway were startled by a mysterious rumble which quickly increased to a roar. Looking skyward, terrified spectators saw the air filled with flying timber which had been picked up by a twister from the Southern Pacific freight yards. Some of the pieces were twenty-five feet long and as much as eight inches thick." At least 12 pedestrians and railroad employees were hurt by wood shrapnel and flying glass, and "ambulances summoned by frantic residents, screamed through the lower business section as city hospitals dispatched first aid crews."[53]

The 1936–37 tornado outbreaks added spice to the depression-era conjugation of natural and social disasters. Nationally, economic collapse on Wall Street was mirrored by environmental collapse across the drought-stricken Great Plains. In Southern California, the 1930s represented a sharp spike in the short historical record of extreme events: the catastrophic Long Beach earthquake of 1933 (113 dead) was followed by major floods in 1934 (40 dead) and 1938 (83 dead). And just as the decade had opened with an unexpected tornado, it ended, on 24–25 September 1939, with a surprise tropical hurricane, or *cordonazo,* whose 65-mile-per-hour winds and 40-foot waves killed 45 people in the Los Angeles area.[54]

This tempestuous decade was then followed by 20 years of relative environmental quietus. Apart from the 1956 Malibu fire, suburbanizing Southern California was spared catastrophic natural disasters between 1940 and 1961. There were no earthquakes, floods, or storms comparable in magnitude to the lethal events of the depression years. The downturn in tornado and flood damage was largely due to the relative infrequency of major flood-making storms and the decline in the annual number of what meteorologists call "thunderstorm days." "In the 20 years between 1944 and 1963 precipitation . . . only one [year] exceeded 20 inches at Los Angeles (1952 with 24.95 inches), whereas in the first half of the precipitation record (1878–1920) totals at Los Angeles exceeded 20 inches in 11 out of 43 years." Moreover, "between 1944 and 1963 fully three-fourths of the years have brought less than 15 inches of rain annually."[55]

During this generation-long storm holiday, Los Angeles's tornado problem receded from sight. Twisters, of course, did not really disappear, but they did pass out of common memory, particularly with the influx of millions of new immigrants indoctrinated with stereotypes of Southern California's climatic exceptionalism. Consequently, the occasional public appearance of a tornado seemed especially uncanny, as on 22 December 1948, when a "great 'spout,' " estimated by lifeguards as at least 1,500 feet high, suddenly appeared in Santa Monica Bay. It was almost as if a Martian spaceship were hovering offshore. "Thousands rushed to the beaches and other vantage spots to view the phenomenon. Others, frightened, telephoned police for an explanation of the 'tornado at sea.' " At the base of the funnel, "the water was greatly agitated, flinging out huge clouds of spray. The heaving disturbance attracted thousands of sea gulls."[56]

5. ELECTION DAY DEMONS

It whirled entire roofs and garages 100 feet in the air, and at its worst impact points it left whole blocks looking like they had been bombed.

Los Angeles Herald-Examiner *(1966)*

The raw incidence of tornadoes in Southern California is closely synchronized to the fluctuation of wet (storm rich) and dry (storm poor) periods. So it is not surprising that the flood-generating storms which returned in greater numbers during the 1960s brought with them the synoptic conditions for increased tornado production. The magnitude of tornado damage, however, is also related to the post-1945 urbanization of the coastal plain. As farms, orchards, and open spaces have yielded to subdivisions and industrial parks, exponentially more property and lives have been placed in the path of tornadoes. (Development simultaneously enhances the destructiveness of twisters of all magnitudes by providing larger diets of deadly debris.) This is the same problem of "disaster inflation" that, in the case of wildfires, has resulted from the rampant development of the Malibu coast.

On 8 October 1961, a dying Mexican hurricane lurched to the coast of San Diego County. Newspapers all over the world published a remarkable photograph taken by a housewife early that morning: a dark funnel, taller than the Empire State Building, hovering ominously over Solana Beach. Astonished airline pilots had earlier reported a dozen massive waterspouts—a true tornado regatta—approaching the San Diego County coastline between Del Mar and Oceanside. "An undetermined number became tornadoes after reaching shore at Carlsbad and Oceanside, and ripped roofs, uprooted fences, and knocked down trees."[57]

In Carlsbad's Terremar district, three people, including a toddler, suffered facial cuts when winds hurled a large piece of plywood through their picture window as they were watching a waterspout make landfall. The same twister, as if competing in a pentathlon, levitated a massive cement bus bench five feet off the ground for several seconds, then hurled a catamaran the length of a football field. In Oceanside, meanwhile, several homes, a car dealership, and a Catholic high school were heavily damaged, while utilities reported that power lines had been knocked out by "water, wind and 'flying seaweed.' " A highway patrol officer complained that his battered car had been pelted first by "shreds of tomato crates" then by "machine-gun-like hail." When homeowners later called their insurance companies to report the damage, one incredulous adjuster exclaimed: "You can't mean a tornado!"[58]

The F1 tornado that plowed through the beach town of El Segundo, just south of LAX, on the morning of 9 November 1964 also probably originated as a sea spout. Sixty students were gathered in front of Center Street Elementary waiting to leave on a field trip when the "giant funnel bore down on them." As in a scene out of the film *Twister,* the principal and vice-principal quickly herded the terrified students into the school office, then braced themselves against the office door, which the tornado simply "blew off its hinges." Although the screaming students were severely shaken, there were no serious injuries.[59]

Moving on, the tornado plundered a parked semitrailer full of artificial Christmas trees. Forty thousand "Twinkle Twees" were sucked up into the vortex, then showered down on stupefied El Segundo residents. As the twister began to rip roofs off houses in the Bungalow Avenue area, "a strange and dangerous hazard was added to the tornado by jagged rocks torn from rock-and-tar roofs and hurled like projectiles by the roaring wind." This fusillade shattered car windshields as well as picture windows in nearby homes. As one couple recalled: "We could see the debris flying through the air. We were watching it through the living room window and when the rocks started hitting the house we ran for the hall. We were scared half to death." Two policemen who had been tracking the twister saw it vanish near the boundary of LAX, where air-traffic controllers merely recorded a sudden 40-mile-per-hour gust.[60]

In the Midwest, it is frequently asserted that tornadoes, like lightning, seldom strike twice in the same place. The opposite, in fact, may be closer to the rule. Thus the next family of twisters to visit Los Angeles—the "Election Day" outbreak of 7 November 1966—was led by a vicious F2 that meticulously retraced the route of the 1930 Hawthorne tornado. Postwar subdivision of the area's truck farms and chicken ranches—as well as a slightly longer tornado path length—ensured that property loss was much more extensive the second time around. Indeed, the *Times* reported that "hundreds of homes were damaged in the 150-foot to 200-foot-wide swath" as compared to the mere "dozens" damaged by the comparable F2 event 36 years earlier.[61]

The tornado dropped out of the sky shortly before 1 P.M. in the city of Lawndale. Like its predecessor in 1930, it made a beeline northward through Hawthorne and Lennox, coming within a thousand yards of LAX's main runway. But turning inland, rather than seaward, it continued through Inglewood, veering off into the clouds somewhere near Centinela Park. The eight-mile path length was an almost continuous corridor of damage and debris.[62] At Ramona Elementary School in Hawthorne, where 20 classrooms were severely damaged, teachers ordered 650 terrified children under their desks as windows shattered and ceiling tiles collapsed. "A giant eucalyptus tree in the school yard was shorn of its huge limbs and twisted apart as if struck by a bolt of lightning." In Lennox, "two whole blocks were torn apart like a battlefield," according to sheriff's deputies, while at a muffler shop in Inglewood, one employee was flung across the store, as the tornado absconded with the roof. Elsewhere, houses "virtually exploded," trailers were blown over, and scores of fires were ignited when flying debris collided with power lines.[63]

The *Herald-Examiner,* after interviewing local meteorologists, officially labeled the Election Day storms "California twisters": "strong and fearsome, but lacking the awesome destructive power of similar phenomena frequent in other parts of the country."[64] This reassurance was misleading. Although no public comparison was made at the time, the F2 twister that ravaged Vancouver, Washington, on 5 April 1972 provided an "awesome" demonstration of what one of the largest of the modern Southern California tornadoes might do if, without warning, it were to strike a crowded public space at lunch hour. Touching down first on the outskirts of Portland, the twister crossed the Columbia River to Vancouver and plowed through a busy shopping center and then a school. Six people were killed and nearly three hundred injured. Unlike Los Angeles, the metropolitan Portland-Vancouver area had no historical record of tornado occurrence, and local National Weather Service (NWS) staff were so shell-shocked that it took them two days to officially confirm that a twister was responsible for the carnage.[65]

In 1972, however, tornadoes were the last thing on the minds of Southern Californians. Despite the recurrence of severe weather, the 1966 twister outbreak was followed by a decade-long tornado "drought" interrupted by only two incidents of significant tornado damage. On 18 December 1967 a short-lived F1 twister caused havoc along South Main Street in Santa Ana, shattering storefront windows and scattering roofing materials. No one was injured.[66]

A far more powerful vortex was spawned from a violent "Sonoran" thunderstorm over the San Jacinto Mountains in Riverside County on 23 July 1974. At Ryan Field, just outside of Hemet, hundred-mile-per-hour winds accompanied by hail stripped the roofs off hangars and tossed aircraft and mobile homes around like straw. One woman was injured by flying glass, and eight aircraft were completely destroyed. Forest Service officials, who witnessed the cycloidal fury of the event and measured the winds, were perplexed: "no tornado cloud was observed, but the storm had virtually all the other characteristics of a full-fledged twister."[67] In fact, as research has subsequently confirmed, the absence of a visible funnel (or its incomplete extension to the ground) is "a typical feature of tornadoes in mountainous or elevated terrain."[68]

6. MONSTER STORMS AND EPISTEMOLOGICAL PUZZLES

Like beauty, a tornado is in the eye of a beholder.
Meteorologists Charles Doswell and Donald Burgess (1993)

Of the familiar occurrences of the natural world, extreme weather events are the most resistant to precise delineation. Victorian meteorology, for example, spent several generations debating the definition of a "storm" only to end up divided between two competing models that the twentieth century adjudged equally wrong. Tornadoes, as their frustrated pursuers never fail to point out, pose comparable problems of classification. Like those ultimate apocalyptic vortices, black holes, they exist in a baffling ontological niche between pure energy and matter. Consider, for example, their phenomenology in time and space. The lifespan of the typical F0–F3 tornado is equal to that of the most short-lived virus or bacteria: 2 to 20 minutes. A rare few F4s or F5s have roared on for as long as an hour. But no tornado has ever lived, or will ever live, as long as a fly or an amoeba. Tornadoes are fleeting things indeed.

But are they really "things"? Charles Doswell and Donald Burgess, senior researchers at "tornado central," the National Severe Storms Laboratory in Norman, Oklahoma, remind us that while storm events may have personalities, they are no more objects, in any stable sense, than Heraclitus's moving stream. "A tornado, no matter how one chooses to define it," they write,

> is a kinematic structure that renews itself from instant to instant via one or more dynamic processes. It is not a "thing" in the sense that a table or a book (neglecting atomic or molecular fluctuations) is the same from one moment to the next. Much confusion about tornadoes comes from thinking of tornadoes as objects rather than as the kinematic manifestation of dynamic processes.[69]

Over the past 20 years, a combination of high-resolution Doppler radar, sophisticated 3-D numerical cloud models, and detailed observations by teams of university-based "storm chasers" has provided vast amounts of new data about tornado dynamics. Yet, as Doswell and Burgess emphasize, increasing knowledge of tornadoes' complex behavior has not led to any elegant, conceptually streamlined model of their genesis. On the contrary, "the definition and classification of convective vortices and the storms which produce them have become more complex and, in many ways, more troublesome than ever before."[70]

Tornadoes, in other words, are epistemological puzzles in the same sense as other phenomena discussed in this book, like "nonlinear" mountain lions and "wired" earthquake faults. They belong to the messy, fractal, chaotic part of nature. Their complexity overpowers simple typologies and linear causalities, especially when these tornadic events are not associated with the classic supercell thunderstorms that dominate tornado production in the Plains states. With such short-lived events, moreover, much of the scientific record depends on the accuracy of reports provided by a volunteer cadre of "storm spotters." In Southern California this reliance on amateur judgment poses a double problem, since observers usually lack the expertise to accurately distinguish tornadoes from impersonators like microbursts and "gustanadoes," or from the local "straight line" winds like Santa Anas and coastal gales that commonly imitate the damage caused by tornadoes.

Understandably, then, as Southern California tornadoes finally became a legitimate subject of research in the 1970s, the NWS remained reluctant to accept "anecdotal" evidence without a confirming radar signature or an expert sighting. Inevitably, conflicts broke out between eyewitness accounts and radar observations. For example, when reports of widespread tornado damage in Orange County began to arrive at the NWS regional office on the evening of 16 March 1977, staff meteorologists attributed the devastation to unusually strong gales. Their radar had failed—as sometimes happens—to detect any rotation in the storm, and therefore, there was no official tornado.[71]

This NWS's denial roused the ire of witnesses and victims who had seen the F2 twister with their own eyes. One Buena Park woman, for example, told the *Los Angeles Times* that "she had just walked out of a restaurant when she saw a funnel pick up her automobile and smash it down, breaking the windows and springs." Likewise, firemen in Fullerton, where 99 homes and businesses (including two large canning plants) were damaged, confirmed that they had witnessed cars being levitated 20 feet in the air. Residents of the heavily damaged 1900 and 2000 blocks of Jacaranda Place, moreover, gave an unequivocal account of the twister's sinister approach that could have been lifted from a small-town newspaper in Oklahoma or Kansas.

"It was about 6:30," Edward Pena told reporters. "The TV started flickering. I looked out the back door and saw this greenish, weird, funnel-shaped cloud. We heard a rumbling sound, getting louder and louder. I thought it was a freight train that had jumped the tracks that aren't far away. Our windows began breaking. The house actually shook. And we heard our neighbors screaming."[72]

In addition to the devastation in Fullerton, other tornadoes (the number is unknown) damaged homes and automobiles in surrounding neighborhoods as well as injuring several workers at a nearby factory. Although the NWS eventually conceded that "part" of the Fullerton damage had been caused by a genuine tornado, they continued to insist that straight-line winds were responsible for shearing off block after block of telephone poles.[73]

"A sound like a freight train" (Fullerton, 1977)

The NWS was similarly cautious seven weeks later when another twister damaged 45 homes and businesses, including a hospital, in Long Beach. This time the NWS interviewed eyewitnesses and inspected wreckage before confirming that a new F2 tornado had revisited some of the same sites damaged by its ancestor in 1936. The Crestwood Convalescent Hospital was evacuated after losing most of its roof and windows. "When the windows started breaking we moved everyone into a central hallway," said an administrator. "We all held hands until it was over and no one got a scratch. God was really good to us."[74]

Nine months later (10 February 1978), tornadoes made yet another return to scenes of earlier crimes: this time to El Segundo, Oceanside, and Huntington Beach. These whirling triplets were progeny of what the *Los Angeles Times* characterized as a "monstrous storm—one of the worst in Southern California's history." In fact, this storm was a maritime version of the typical "squall line" so vividly familiar to any inhabitant of the Great Plains.* In addition to burying the tiny mountain community of Hidden Springs under a mudslide (13 dead), the storm also washed corpses out of a Verdugo Hills cemetery into nearby backyards, and freed three African lions from a flood-damaged zoo into a trailer park where they terrorized residents until shot by sheriff's deputies.[76]

Almost exactly a year later (31 January 1979), another winter megastorm unleashed a fourth brood of tornadoes across Los Angeles and Orange Counties. Accompanied by "hailstones the size of golf balls," two small twisters damaged several homes, a gas station, and a convenience store in Anaheim, while another again tore up a long block on south Main Street in Santa Ana. In Anaheim, a woman and her son were moving six heavy metal barbecue units from a sidewalk display when "there was this tremendous roar." She was knocked from her feet by the force of the wind at the same instant the twister snatched the barbecue units and threw them 150 feet away. The more powerful Santa Ana tornado flipped over parked cars, ripped off store awnings, unroofed apartment buildings, and

---

* A *squall line* is a band of intense thunderstorms which frequently precedes a rapidly moving cold front. Squall-line tornadoes are typically smaller than those generated by supercell thunderstorms.[75]

decapitated palm trees. Meanwhile, a fourth tornado demolished Manhattan, or rather its replica at Universal Studios, just north of downtown Los Angeles.[77]

7. THE EL NIÑO OUTBREAK OF 1982–83

Authorities termed it a "mini-tornado" although it left maximum destruction in its path.
Los Angeles Herald-Examiner *(1982)*

If tornadoes are the unruly children of thunderstorms, then their grandparents are the great weather fronts where hot and cold air masses collide in atmospheric combat. Such martial nomenclature is not accidental. Frontal theory, the conceptual cornerstone of modern synoptic meteorology, was developed by two Norwegian scientists, Vilhelm Bjerknes and his son Jacob (who later moved to UCLA), during the First World War. The Bjerkneses saw a clear analogy between the gridlock of monster armies in the trenches of France and the formation of huge cyclonic depressions through the violent opposition of polar and tropical air masses. Nowhere is the military metaphor more appropriate than in North America at the beginning of tornado season.

"Every spring, a battle ensues in the sky over the Midwestern United States. Each day the sun rises a little higher, and as it does it heats the waters of the Gulf of Mexico. Those waters evaporate and creep north into the United States. Somewhere over the Plains states, this tongue of warm humid air encounters cold, dry air left over from winter. Placing warm, moist air beneath cold, dry air is akin to dropping a match into a gas tank." As science writer Keay Davidson goes on to explain, the resulting thunderstorms ("as energetic as many atomic bombs") bring the heartland its annual surprise package of lightning, hail, and tornadoes.[78]

Does a comparably "explosive" mixture of air masses ever come together over Southern California? Before 1982 most meteorologists would probably have said no. It is now clear, however, that major El Niño episodes, by feeding warmer water ("storm fuel") into West Coast winter weather systems, dramatically amplify their violence.* The 1982–83 El Niño, the most intense ocean-atmosphere event of the twentieth century, demonstrated how major Southern California tornado outbreaks are frequently linked to the planetary heat engine of the tropical western Pacific.

This "super Niño" produced record warming in Southern California coastal waters while simultaneously inducing "an unprecedented development of the Aleutian low" as well as an intensified subtropical jet stream. The Aleutian low manufactures Southern California's typical winter weather, but during 1982–83 it pushed farther south than usual and the water under it was anomalously cold. As storms were generated in the heart of the low, they were transported eastward by the jet stream over the El Niño–warmed California Current. The sharp temperature gradient thus produced—cold, dry air moving over warmer water—was exactly Davidson's "match in the gas tank." The result was extreme storminess and extraordinary tornadogenesis.[79]

The correlation between the great El Niño of 1982–83 (as well as another powerful event in 1992–93) and the resulting spike in the number of "thunderstorm days" and reported tornadoes is striking. Over a 53-year record, the mean number of annual thunderstorm episodes reported at the LAX weather station is 4.1. Major El Niño winters can triple this figure and, as a corollary, the potential for tornado production. (Large El Niño events seem to have the opposite

---

* More than 40 years after he and his father first elaborated their theory of weather fronts, UCLA professor Jacob Bjerknes conceptually unified two previously distinct phenomena—a quasi-periodic see-saw in air pressure in the western tropical Pacific (Southern Oscillation) and warm water anomalies in the eastern Pacific (El Niño)—into a single model of Pacific Basin–wide fluctuations, the "El Niño—Southern Oscillation" (ENSO), with profound global climate impacts.

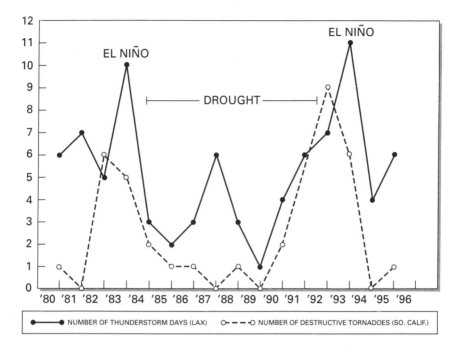

EL NIÑO EVENTS AND SOUTHERN CALIFORNIA TORNADOES

EL NIÑO

EL NIÑO

DROUGHT

'80 '81 '82 '83 '84 '85 '86 '87 '88 '89 '90 '91 '92 '93 '94 '95 '96

●——● NUMBER OF THUNDERSTORM DAYS (LAX)   ○─ ─ ─○ NUMBER OF DESTRUCTIVE TORNADOES (SO. CALIF.)

effect in the Great Plains, where they produce drought and reduced tornadic activity.)[80] That is why it is not surprising that the wild winter of 1982–83 was punctuated by two record-setting twister outbreaks.

November is usually Santa Ana season, but in 1982 it was a month of thundershowers and torrential rain generated by the anomalously low-latitude Aleutian depression. Embedded within the flow of unstable maritime air was an unusual "comma cloud" or small cyclone that went convectively berserk as it passed over the Los Angeles region.[81] The largest outbreak of tornadoes in modern Southern California history began at 9:30 A.M. on Tuesday, 9 November, when an F1 waterspout hit land at Malibu. Picking up an 18-foot catamaran (whose aerodynamic properties, as we saw in the 1961 Carlsbad outbreak, must be outstanding!), it hurled the boat 125 feet, through the third-floor window of architect Henry Gesner's studio. His wife Nan was on the floor below: "I was reading in bed when I saw a boat fly by."[82]

Two hours later, a more robust F2 descended on the San Fernando Valley, which acts as a huge bellows for Santa Ana winds but is usually sheltered from coastal tornadoes. This was the first modern twister to inflict significant damage there. It began by blowing down two hundred trees in the area between Van Nuys and Sepulveda Boulevards. Some of the falling timber crushed parked cars, while one towering eucalyptus sliced through two homes. Two nurses were seriously cut by flying glass as they tried to shield patients at a nearby hospital. At the corner of Raymer and Kester Avenues, the twister peeled the roof off a giant Fedco discount center, then flipped over two delivery trucks that were unloading behind the store. (As one truck driver, relishing his brief moment in front of the flashbulbs, told the press: "This doesn't happen every day, you know!")[83]

A half-hour later, at noon, a minor tornado revisited Lennox, while an ugly-tempered F2 plowed an eight-mile-long pathway through residential neighborhoods just west of the Los Angeles River in Long Beach. The most serious injury of the day occurred just after 1 P.M. when a fifth twister, after blowing the roofs off a half-dozen homes in Garden Grove, flipped over an eighteen-wheeler on the Santa Ana Freeway in the city of Orange, seriously injuring the driver and causing an immense traffic jam. The same tornado was probably responsible for knocking out the phones and stealing part of the roof from Orange County's Emergency Storm Center in Anaheim. As a result, emergency officials were unable to respond when an administrator at Saddleback College in Mission Viejo tried to report yet another F1 tearing up his campus. An instructor at Saddleback later told the *Los Angeles Times:* "It was extremely strange. What you were seeing didn't go with the sound. You were seeing huge trees split apart, flying past the window. It was the most silent thing and it happened very fast."[84]

While tornadoes were creating helter-skelter from Point Mugu to Mission Viejo, dozens of waterspouts were prowling the coastline. Few spectators, especially on Orange County beaches, will ever forget the haunting vision of funnel clouds dancing across the dark waters of the Pacific.[85]

8. "LIKE AN ATOMIC BOMB"

It wasn't just bad weather. A little heavy rain—even with the consequent flooding, mudslides, road closings and the like— we can accept. But a series of pyrotechnic thunderstorms? A pair of earthquakes, hours apart? Not one, but two torna- does? In L.A.? In a single day?

Los Angeles Herald-Examiner *editorial (1993)*

How much damage can a single tornado cause? The ultimate night- mare in tornado research circles, of course, is the image of a prime- time twister rampaging through the financial district of a major city, sucking stockbrokers and mortgage bankers into its hungry vortex. Yet the downtown areas of the largest midwestern cities have been curiously immune to tornado damage. Chicago, for example, has suf- fered heavy tornado losses in its outer suburbs (most recently with the 29 killed by the 1990 Plainfield twister), but the Loop has never been touched. Experts are unclear whether this is sheer luck, or the result of the destabilizing influences of "surface roughness" (that is, high-rise buildings) and urban "heat islands" upon tornado structure.[86]

Paradoxically, Los Angeles is the one great North American metrop- olis that has suffered from repeated tornado penetrations of its business core. As we have seen, F2 twisters inflicted substantial damage on the eastern, industrial side of Downtown in 1930 and 1937. Although these winds were pint-sized compared to true monsters, like the horrific F5 that pulverized downtown Waco, Texas, in 1953 (114 dead), they nonetheless had lethal potential. Indeed, there was probably much contemporary thanksgiving that they spent their fury on mere ware- houses and freight depots. But what if a tornado someday decided to track the morning commute right into the heart of Downtown, toward, say, the Convention Center when a big show was in progress?

Call this a worst-case scenario, but it is exactly what happened on the stormy morning of 1 March 1983. An F2, with winds in excess of 110 miles per hour, abruptly set down in a working-class black and Latino neighborhood just west of the Harbor Freeway. In full view of hundreds of awed freeway commuters a half-block away, the twister plowed through homes and small businesses, peeling the roofs and sides off bungalows, blowing down the walls of masonry storefronts, splintering garages and porches, and stacking cars on top of one another.

Those on the ground had no warning other than a sudden roar "like a thousand freight trains" before they were engulfed in a cloud of dangerous, swirling debris from exploding roofs and windows. Several thought an airplane had crashed into the neighborhood, while another said it was "just like an atomic bomb." Michelle Jones, who had arrived from Illinois three days earlier, had just risen "when a long, sharp spear-like stick—probably a fence post—came flying through the window. . . . The projectile hit her still-warm bed."[87]

As the twister passed over the streets north of Vernon Avenue and east of the Coliseum, it left bizarre calling cards. One resident, for example, looked out his broken window to discover a strange boat sitting in his backyard. ("I'll take an earthquake any day," he later told a reporter.) A few blocks away, a camper truck had been catapulted through a second-story apartment, while a trailer was perched precariously on the ledge of a roof. Elsewhere, the steel I-beams that supported three-story-high billboards were bent completely to the ground.[88]

The twister, meanwhile, veered slightly northeast and took direct aim at hapless commuters stalled in heavy rain on the Santa Monica Freeway overpass. Firefighter Ed Castle, homeward-bound after a 24-hour stint at the LAX fire station, had a perfect view of approaching catastrophe. Underneath the funnel cloud, he saw "a constant explosion of colors—flashes of green, blue and yellow from high voltage lines. I could see power lines going down and buildings disintegrating. I saw a couple of signboards explode off a roof; I saw a roof go up. . . . I thought we were going to eat it."[89]

Instead, the twister vaulted over the freeway and came down hard on top of an apartment building just south of the Convention Center. The dozen poor Latin families in the tenement escaped with their lives but lost everything else. "Everything," one garment worker later told the *Times,* "even my dinnerware that I was buying on the install-

"A bizarre calling card"

Residents inspect damage

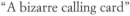

ment plan."[90] As a finale, the twister hovered over the Los Angeles Convention Center, tearing huge sections off the roof and littering the sidewalks with jagged pieces of sheet metal. Inside, terrified workers at a boat exposition feared the worst. "If it lasted any longer, the whole place would have been down. The roof started coming down in ashes, then the big blocks just caved in. It blew out like a bomb." The din inside the Convention Center became unbearable, then abruptly ceased. As unexpectedly as it had arrived, the Downtown twister simply evaporated.[91]

But its furious spirit was reincarnated a few minutes later in a second tornado that descended on Huntington Drive, just east of the tony suburb of San Marino, where it twirled a Cadillac in midair like a baton, then pitched it across several lanes of traffic. The driver suffered a broken back. As paramedics raced to his aid, the twister careened into the Sunnyslope Water Company near southeast Pasadena. Like a giant can opener, it peeled off the entire tin roof of a six-million-gallon reservoir, blew over some company trucks, then gutted the business office and pummeled a terrified secretary. Pieces of the reservoir roof fell like shrapnel over neighborhoods miles away.[92]

Across Southern California, torrential rains—at a rate of nearly an inch per hour—were inundating low-lying neighborhoods, piers in Santa Monica and Seal Beach were collapsing, and mudslides were carrying away million-dollar homes in Malibu. As the day went on, things only got worse. Just before noon, a third tornado slammed into a Santa Ana mobile home park, damaging 21 units. A few minutes later, shock waves arrived from a small, M 3.5 earthquake, centered in Inglewood. Meanwhile, flood control authorities were evacuating more than 1,400 Simi Valley residents whose homes were in the path of potential floodwaters from a cracked earthen dam.[93]

Local officials, inured to mudslides, collapsing piers, and floods, were flabbergasted by the ferocity of the Downtown twister. Veteran county supervisor Kenneth Hahn told reporters that it was the worst devastation he had seen "since the 1933 earthquake." In the face of national incredulity about a Los Angeles tornado, he challenged President Reagan to fly out to inspect the 193 wrecked homes and businesses. Mayor Bradley, for his part, was astonished that such extreme natural violence ("like a war zone") had resulted in only 32 minor injuries. "It's almost a miracle there were no deaths or serious injuries in this almost unique situation."[94]

9. UNACCEPTABLE REALITIES

When I came down Superior Lane, it looked like downtown Baghdad.

Orange County homeowner (1993)

If there is a sacrosanct interest in Los Angeles, it is downtown real estate. The earthquake-like damage from the March 1983 twister, which had come within a hairsbreadth of the financial district, briefly concentrated official attention on the local tornado hazard. The National Research Council's prestigious Committee on Natural Dis-

They could use a savior

aster, which conducts authoritative postmortems of major disasters, agreed to sponsor an inquiry led by Gary Hart, a professor from the UCLA Department of Civil Engineering. While his task force of engineers and meteorologists was being assembled, an anomalous storm on 30 September 1983 reminded researchers that the March event had not been a fluke.

It was highly unusual for a low-pressure system to break past the stationary Pacific High and move south so early in the fall. September 1983, moreover, was well on its way to becoming the hottest September on record when a cold air mass from the north overrode the wet, warm air along the coast. In addition to torrential rain, the resulting meteorological explosion generated a new outbreak of waterspouts and twisters, culminating in a possible F2 that demolished four homes and damaged seventy others in a middle-class Hawthorne neighborhood. A three-ton section of roof was ripped off a large apartment building, and three people were cut by flying glass.[95]

But neither this new outbreak nor any of the major antecedent tornadoes in Los Angeles were mentioned in the final version of the

National Research Council report. Indeed, the authors erroneously cited "the lack of historical tornadoes in the area" as a rationale for the police and fire departments' refusal to give credence to initial reports of a tornado moving up the Broadway corridor. Generally praising city officials (two of whom served on the committee), they acknowledged the absence of engineering standards for tornadoes in the building code but reassured the public (without further explanation) that proposed earthquake safety ordinances would deal with the tornado hazard as well. Surprisingly, there was no discussion of the March 1983 twister's near miss with rush-hour freeway traffic, nor any analysis of what would have happened had it veered into the crowded USC campus or the downtown financial district—both a few blocks from its actual path.

The report's most important conclusion was simply that "tornadoes are now an accepted reality in Los Angeles." Hart and his colleagues, moreover, were optimistic that researchers would soon be able to explain the distinctive meteorology responsible for local tornado outbreaks, while new storm-forecasting techniques might provide a feasible early warning system.[96]

There is a certain irony in revisiting these conclusions almost 15 years later. Thanks to the efforts of Hales and Blier and Batten there is now a historical baseline for assessing the incidence and pattern of Los Angeles tornadoes, but further research on the synoptic conditions of their generation has been stymied by a shortage of funding.* Although, as other researchers recently pointed out, "severe thunderstorms in California remain poorly documented,"[98] such research must compete against "sexier" topics, like global warming or El Niño disturbances, at a time when Congress is trimming the budget of the National Oceanic and Atmospheric Administration.

Similarly, public awareness of Southern California tornadoes once again vanished. As in previous periods, the clustering of tornado out-

---

* The biggest advance has been the conclusive demonstration, based on both radar and radiosonde data, that classic supercell storms *do* occur in California but have gone unrecognized because of "preconceived notions that such storms simply do not occur there."[97]

breaks was followed by more than a decade of relative meteorological quiescence. If the single El Niño winter of 1982–83 was responsible for 20 percent of all tornado damage in modern Southern California, the ensuing 14-year period (1984–97) has contributed only 4 percent of total residential damage with only one injury and no losses of major structures. The 1984–91 segment was a genuine "tornado gap" corresponding to a long regional drought and an abrupt decline in thunderstorm days—excepting the mild El Niño winter of 1986–87. (Nationally as well, the 1980s were the century's low point in violent tornado activity.) As we have seen, these low-intensity intervals are nurseries of illusion about the Los Angeles environment and the extreme events, including tornadoes, that constitute its ordinary metabolism.[99]

In this case, however, the subsequent storm failed to unthrone the illusory calm. The strong El Niño pulse which reached Southern California during the winter of 1992–93 more than doubled the number of thunderstorm episodes and produced more than a dozen damaging tornadoes and waterspouts. Across California, 19 twisters were recorded by the NWS during December 1992: an all-time record.[100] The severe January 1993 storms, which caused $1.3 billion damage statewide, brought a second outbreak. In Pomona (14 January), Debbie Lara "looked out the window [at about 1:30 A.M.] and there was so much stuff flying through the air that she couldn't see the house next door." A moment later, a 70-foot pine tree came crashing through the ceiling, narrowly missing her three sleeping children. In Buena Park, another twister, which some residents thought was the Big One, inflicted light damage on 110 homes and trailers.[101]

The most vicious tornado of the storm, however, struck three days later in the exclusive residential city of Lake Forest in southern Orange County. After vacuuming the roof tiles from dozens of homes and blowing over scores of trees, it briefly turned into a waterspout and flung boats out of a man-made lake. A young woman was catapulted 75 feet into a car and required attention from paramedics. A homeowners' association leader later compared the damage to "downtown Baghdad" after the U.S. cruise missile raids.[102] Yet few outsiders were aware of the destruction which went essentially unreported outside of Orange County.

Nor did media coverage and analysis measurably improve when an F1 twister ripped the roof off a Lucky supermarket and damaged several schools in the Los Altos section of Long Beach on 9 January 1998. Although the Long Beach area press bannered the event on their front pages with photographs of a sinister funnel cloud, the *Los Angeles Times* clung to its tradition of understatement with a short article that noted only reports of an "apparent tornado" and misleadingly reassured readers that they had little to fear from Southern California's "baby tornadoes." As usual there was no follow-up interview with disaster officials or Weather Service meteorologists after they had had a chance to assess the damage.[103]

As a result, the tornado hazard today is nearly as invisible as it was in 1918 when a strange thundercloud over Pasadena suddenly gave birth to a destructive black funnel. We can hope that when the next swarm of inevitable "freak winds" roar through tornado alley they will not collide with a 747 in its final descent over LAX or swoop down on the Coliseum during the annual USC–Notre Dame gridiron duel. If Los Angeles's luck holds out, they will simply demolish a few dozen homes and apartments, or wreck an elementary school or small factory. The dead and injured, in our secret Kansas, should not be much more than the average Friday night carnage on the freeways.

5

MANEATERS
OF THE
SIERRA MADRE

For Steve Berman, beachcombing is a favorite pastime in the wake of the big Pacific storms that start arriving after Christmas. Between the decaying barricades of giant kelp and the pounding surf, he loves to search for "mysterious messages from the sea." Choice finds among the tons of storm flotsam include gnarled redwood, derelict hatch covers, and, occasionally, the beautiful glass floats used by Japanese fishermen across the ocean.

In January 1995, however, the sea left a more disturbing message on Point Dume Beach—dozens of live snakes. "I almost stepped upon a large rattler sunning itself on the dry sand," recalled Berman. "I don't have a snake phobia, but it was an unnerving experience, like suddenly awakening—not out of, but into—a nightmare. It still sends shivers up my spine."[1]

For the rest of the winter, on beaches from Tijuana to Santa Barbara, each major storm was followed by further snake encounters. In early March, the *Los Angeles Times* headlined a story "Surfing Snakes Hit the Beach" after astonished lifeguards in San Diego County's Del Mar and Solana Beach were forced to close beaches while they collected scores of waterlogged, but still slithering "rattlers, rosy boas, king snakes, racers and gophers." A herpetologist at the San Diego Zoo explained that recent wet winters had "provided the high grass and bumper crop of insects and mice that can produce a snake population boom." Winter flooding, in turn, had washed the snakes into the ocean where they floated like driftwood until waves brought them back onshore. On an upbeat note, the *Times* opined that, "as far as

Beachcombing snakes

can be determined, the snakes are not some biblical curse visited on the region to punish the wicked and sybaritic."[2]

1. NATURE BITES BACK

A Malibu resident stumbled upon two mountain lions mating in his backyard. When he shined a flashlight at them, they just stared back. He let them get on with their business.
Naturalist David Wicinas (1995)

Native Californians might disagree. In the worldview of the Tong-va (or Gabrielinos), the original people of the Los Angeles region, snakes together with mountain lions are envisioned as special "messengers" (*tsatsnitsam*) of the messianic god Chengiichngech. Like the aboriginal Australians, the Tong-va believe several parallel worlds or realities are nested inside of one another, with the *tsatsnitsam* providing the connection between them. In times of ecological crisis and spiritual disorder, these creatures are omen bearers and, when necessary, the avengers of transgressions against nature.[3]

All the more prophetic, then, that the "surfing snakes" were followed within a few weeks by the first cougar attack on a human in the history of Los Angeles County.* On 20 March, 27-year-old freelance illustrator Scott Fike was pedaling his mountain bike up a fire road near the legendary White City, the ruins of Thaddeus Lowe's famous resort hotel and incline railroad, just above Pasadena, when a large mountain lion ("a house cat multiplied by ten") began loping along beside him.

> I yelled as loud as I could and jumped off my bike, trying to use it as a shield. But the lion clawed at the spokes and repeatedly

---

* "Cougar," "mountain lion," "puma," and "panther" are regionally interchangeable names for *Felis concolor,* an extraordinarily adept hunter capable of killing prey eight times its size. Leo Carrillo, the Los Angeles–born actor who as a teenager in the 1890s hunted mountain lions in Hollywood and Santa Monica Canyon, tells a story that may be apocryphal about a lion attacking an Indian woman in the early nineteenth century.[4]

bit the tire. In panic I ran about 25 yards down a steep embank-
ment, before I stumbled and fell. As the lion came after me, I
rolled into a ball to protect my face and throat. The lion clawed
at me and bit the back of my head. I managed to push her away
and pick up a rock. I hit the lion in the head and ran back up
the slope. I grabbed my bike and pedaled downhill as fast as I
could.[5]

Fike was examined at a nearby hospital but declined treatment.
The three superficial bites on his head were less serious than the
severe case of poison oak he contracted from rolling in the chaparral.
State and federal officials, meanwhile, issued a mountain lion alert
throughout the area. Three days later, expert trackers from the
Department of Agriculture discovered lion prints at the 4,500-foot
level of Mount Lowe. The next day they closed the hiking trails and
baited a dead deer near the spot where Fike was attacked. When they
returned a few hours later the deer was gone, and hunting dogs soon
picked up the scent of the lion, hiding 300 yards away in a canyon
bottom. After a short chase, the dogs treed the lion, which was then
killed by a tracker with a twelve-gauge shotgun.

In the well-studied archives of previous mountain lion attacks in
North America—by any standard, extremely uncommon events—the
individual animal was typically an immature male without an established range, a diseased and weakened adult, or a female defending
nearby cubs. The cougar killed on Mount Lowe, however, was an
unusually large, healthy female without nursing cubs. The aggressive-
ness of this magnificent animal in attacking the six-foot, four-inch
Fike, according to one veteran game warden, was "simply weird," an
abrupt departure from long-observed behavioral patterns. And it
raised a troubling question: were lions in Los Angeles County becoming habituated to humans?

"Definitely," said critics of Proposition 117, California's 1990 ban
on the sport hunting of cougars. In their view, the Fike incident was
further proof, following the deaths of two women hikers in other
parts of California in 1994, that the reclusive predators (whose popu-

lation was allegedly exploding in the absence of hunting) had become maneaters. "The mountain lions," one wealthy hunter explained, "need to fear man again, fear our scent as they used to." An anti-lion vigilante group sent Fike, who opposes cougar hunting, a T-shirt with the stark exhortation "Shoot, Shovel and Shut Up." At the same time, mountain lion encounters were being anthropomorphized in bizarre *Silence of the Lamb* terms. A man whose dog was attacked near Fillmore, 40 miles north of Los Angeles, complained that "it's like having Jeffrey Dahmer move next door," while a Monterey woman, startled by a lion while jogging, denounced the cats as "serial killers" whose numbers should be drastically culled for public safety. Worried fish and game officials warned the legislature that "public fear is reaching near hysteria."[6]

Yet the big cat—whom wildlife experts call "the Rolls Royce of North American predators"[7]—also had a noisy chorus of defenders. "The slaughtered cougar," wrote one angry reader about the *Times*'s coverage of the Fike attack, "had more sanctity, honesty and beauty than any of these blood-lusting humans." The previous spring, after 40-year-old Barbara Schoener was killed and partially devoured by a female mountain lion while hiking in a Sierra recreation area, 45 miles north of Sacramento, there was an extraordinary outpouring of empathy for the animal (subsequently killed by trackers). Sympathizers reportedly donated twice as much to a fund for the lion's orphan cubs than to the fund for Schoener's two small children.[8] People seemed to have only two images of cougars, both fantastic: as serial killers or as soft, cuddly toys.

In any event, the mountain lion hysteria, like similar panics in the face of beach snakes and other strange paranatural phenomena (including garbage-eating coyotes, black bears in hot tubs, plague-carrying squirrels, killer bees, and even goat-eating vampires) must be taken seriously as a symptom of a larger crisis in the relationship between the metropolis and its environment. As white flight and an anti-urban ethos drive the tract house frontier deeper into rugged foothills and interior valleys, suburbanites have acquired wild carnivores as unexpected and capricious neighbors. The result is a greater intimacy with nature than many had bargained for when purchasing their view lots or country estates. Although other urban areas in the American and Canadian West have wildlife problems, the six-county Los Angeles region is unique in the Northern Hemisphere for the intensity of interaction between humans, their pets, and wild fauna. This unusual distinction follows logically from two exceptional characteristics of Southern California's biogeography.

First of all, metropolitan Los Angeles, now bordered primarily by mountains and desert rather than by farmland as in the past, has the longest wild edge, abruptly juxtaposing tract houses and wildlife habitat, of any major nontropical city. Certainly, other North American cities, including Denver, Seattle, and Vancouver, have significant wildlife borders along their peripheries, but none *enfold* wild terrain in the complex fashion of Los Angeles. Only tropical Miami, on the edge of the Everglades, comes close. Los Angeles's wild edge, even by the crudest measure, is at least 675 miles long.[9] Moreover, it is steadily expanding as the widening megalopolis simultaneously consumes remnant agricultural areas while penetrating ever deeper into the wild desert and chaparral ecosystems that surround Southern California and make it, in the famous phrase of Carey McWilliams, "an island on the land."

Second, this is primarily a mountain edge, with development lapping at the slopes of the San Gabriel Mountains (usually called the Sierra Madre before 1940), one of the steepest ranges in North America.* Although 30 million "visitor trips" per year are made to the San Gabriels' most popular outlooks, streams, and picnic grounds, much of the 1,000-square-mile range consists of inaccessible canyons and ravines that act as wildlife redoubts. Thus they constitute the biogeographical core of an urban wilderness, sustaining the largest Southern California populations of coyotes (several thou-

---

* As naturalists Don Gill and Penelope Bonnett point out: "Few carnivores can tolerate high levels of disturbance; they are driven from their haunts as peripheral sprawl occurs. They are most likely to survive in those situations where housing encroaches upon areas of *sharp relief* thus creating an abrupt juxtaposition of the built and natural environments."[10]

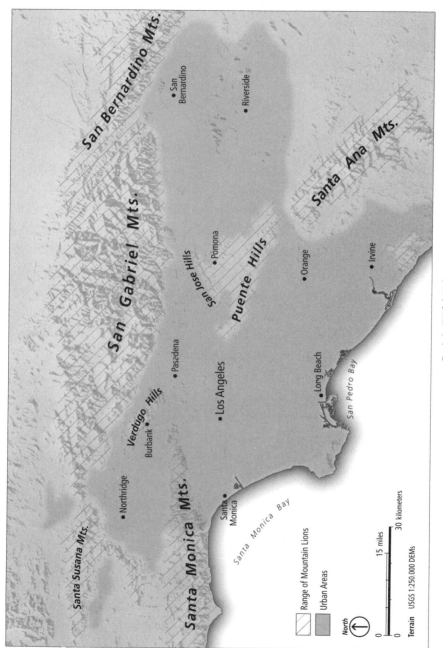

North

0

0   15 miles

0   30 kilometers

Terrain   USGS 1:250 000 DEMs

L.A.'s Wild Edge

Santa Susana Mts.

Santa Monica Mts.

San Gabriel Mts.

San Bernardino Mts.

Santa Ana Mts.

Verdugo Hills

San Jose Hills

Puente Hills

• Northridge

Burbank •

• Pasedena

• Los Angeles

Santa Monica •

• Pomona

• San Bernardino

• Riverside

• Orange

• Irvine

• Long Beach

San Pedro Bay

Santa Monica Bay

sand), black bears (perhaps 60 adults), and mountain lions (several dozen). Moreover, predators and larger fauna also survive in an archipelago of wild islands surrounded by densely urbanized areas. For example, Griffith Park, the Palos Verdes Peninsula, the Verdugo Hills, and the aptly named Coyote Hills preserve booming coyote populations, while perhaps a dozen urban cougars persist in the rugged defiles of the Santa Monicas, and probably in the recently suburbanized Puente Hills as well.[11]

On landuse and planning maps, of course, the division between "developed" and "undeveloped" areas is drawn as a straight-edged border. Spuriously precise boundaries likewise define parks, wildlife refuges, national forests, and official wilderness areas. In reality, there is an infinitely more intricate interpenetration of the wild and the urban. Fingers of chaparral and coastal sage provide informal wildlife (and wildfire) corridors into the very heart of the city. Throngs of deer, for example, descend nightly from the Hollywood Hills to browse on the lawns of Bel Air and Beverly Hills, while audiences at the Hollywood Bowl have grown accustomed to the coyote howls that sometimes accompany Bach and Gershwin. Conversely, urban pathologies, including illegal dumping, graffiti, gang violence, carjacking, paramilitary training, and plantation-scale marijuana cultivation, intrude so comprehensively into Los Angeles's wild hinterlands that *Newsweek* recently dubbed the Angeles National Forest, the "Prime Evil Forest." "More marijuana," *Newsweek* claimed, "is now grown in the Angeles and southern California's three other national forests than in all of the notorious 'emerald triangle' forests in northern California."[12]

The "wild" and the "urban," therefore, are best conceived as variable qualities or processes, rather than neatly bounded little boxes, a view which conforms to the growing preference in environmental studies for the "wild" as a richer, more dialectical concept than "wilderness." Leading environmental philosophers have devoted much ink to a critique of the "wilderness myth" and the fetish of the pristine. As David Rothenberg recently reminded readers, Thoreau invoked "Wildness," not "Wilderness," as the "preservation of the world." "The idea of wildness," Rothenberg explains, "has always been deeper than a place that exists because we place boundaries around it and call it a 'wilderness.' "[13] Although some revisionist writers like Irene Klaver have argued that the "wild" by definition should be intractable to definition, some approximation is surely possible.[14] My personal favorite is Gary Snyder's sly observation that "the wild is perhaps the very possibility of being eaten by a mountain lion. The risk, even if vanishingly remote, is an evolutionary trigger to heightened awareness and enjoyment of an environment shared with large animals."[15] As the Fike incident proves, Los Angeles is one of the few large cities that passes Snyder's gustatory wildness test.[16]

It seems almost a truism that the wild and the urban must be inversely related to one another: the growth of the latter must involve a net subtraction from the former. In fact, the relationship is far more paradoxical. Certainly, there is a distinct tendency for native biodiversity to decline as aboriginal landscapes are supplanted or fragmented by artificial landscapes. Indeed, entire Southern California ecosystems, including salt marshes, native grasslands, Engelmann oak savannas, and vernal pool communities, have become virtually extinct over the past century and a half. Speaking of endangered species, a U.S. Fish and Wildlife Service official called Southern California "this agency's Vietnam," while a major scientific study in early 1997 singled out the Los Angeles region as one of two major "hot spots" (the other is Hawaii) of endangered diversity in the United States.[17] Yet because of a massive naturalization of alien plant and animal species, total biodiversity has actually increased. Moreover, because of their adaptive flexibility or the removal of their key predators, populations of certain native birds and mammals have experienced dramatic surges after urbanization.*

---

* The broad range of microclimates and ecological niches in the Los Angeles region has also sustained incredible invertebrate diversity, including an estimated three to four thousand insect species, in the face of urbanization. In his celebrated study of local insect fauna, the entomologist Charles Hogue claimed that "we have several times more insect species here in the Los Angeles Basin than exist in any other large metropolitan area in the United States."[18]

This does not mean, however, that the impact of urban growth in Southern California has been biologically benign. Although some ecologists might contest such value judgments, the urban environment, with its alternative food chain based on garbage, tends to favor the selection of species undesirable from a human standpoint. As Anne Spirn pointed out in her pioneering study of urban nature: "The form of the city limits both the abundance and diversity of those wildlife [songbirds and migratory fowl] that would be an amenity. At the same time, most wildlife that do thrive in the city become pests."[19] As a rule of thumb, opportunist species, adapted to a variety of habitats, tend to survive and even prosper, while specialist species, fine-tuned to microenvironments, tend to perish.

The list of Southern California "pests" includes the lowly and the sublime. Crows, ravens, jays, skunks, raccoons, deer, and coyotes probably exist in far greater numbers than at the moment of initial European contact in the late eighteenth century. Pigeons, sparrows, and rats—species commensal with humans—were introduced by Spanish colonists, while starlings and red foxes are modern arrivals from the East. Although population estimates of mountain lions are controversial (and some populations in places like the Santa Ana Mountains, the Puente Hills, and the Santa Monica Mountains have recently become isolated, and are, perhaps, doomed), the various censuses in Southern California support the idea of a considerable increase in their numbers. As Maurice Hornecker, the recognized world authority on the species, reminds us, "There are more mountain lions in the Los Angeles area than in Yellowstone."[20] This directly contradicts the typical textbook assertion that "large predators such as wolves, mountain lions, and bears are conspicuously absent from the mammal community of urban habitats."[21]

Transactions between the wild and the urban take place within the spatial framework of what ecologists call an "ecotone": a zone of transition between biological communities whose boundaries may be relatively abrupt (as between chaparral and lawns) or gradual (as between domestic, feral, and wild animals). Science, moreover, has long recognized a special "edge effect" in ecotones—a greater species diversity that results from "an inter-mixture of species some of which are the most tolerant members of the adjacent communities and others which are edge species peculiar to the ecotone itself."[22] The opossum, which first arrived in California in 1910, is a good candidate for the paradigmatic "edge species." Although notoriously dumb (its cranial capacity is only 10 percent that of a fox), it is perfectly adapted to nocturnal foraging in such disturbed, interstitial habitats as vacant lots, woodpiles, freeway landscaping, and cemeteries. It is the only mammal common to both skid row and the foothills.[23]

The wild-urban ecotone, in other words, can be best envisioned as an ecosystem in its own right, albeit more dynamic, nonlinear, and unstable than its constituent communities. A major characteristic is the sometimes bizarre reshaping of food chain and predator-prey relationships. Deer, for example, become greedy lawn browsers, while coyotes end up addicted to junk foods scavenged from garbage cans. Bobcats add *Felis (catus) domesticus* to their diet, and booming raven populations follow roadkills. Wildlife, in other words, becomes more urban in its basic subsistence patterns, while, at the same time, domestic species go feral. In the industrial wastelands of south Los Angeles, wild dog packs now threaten the lives of small children, and in affluent west Los Angeles, escaped parrots, flourishing in several wild colonies, startle passersby with their insolent chatter. AWOL landscape plants, like the indestructible arundo, have become doomsday weeds supplanting indigenous flora on an ever widening scale.

This hugely complex system of shifting biological interactions along Los Angeles's wild edge is only episodically visible to most suburban residents, and then in a phantasmagorical mode. The unexpected appearance of large wildlife in the city's backyards is occasionally charming, but more often threatening. Coyotes and cougars, in particular, have become symbols of urban disorder. These *tsatsnitsam* are unwelcome heralds of a breakdown in the clear-cut, impermeable, but essentially imaginary boundary between the human and the wild. The ideal suburb is adjacent to nature but never directly implicated in it. Wild creatures are no more welcome across the crabgrass threshold of a subdivision than are urban ones. Indeed, in the minds of most suburbanites, the unruliness in the center of the metropolis is figuratively recapitulated at its periphery. It is not surprising that predators are criminalized as trespassers and discursively assimilated to "serial killers" or "gangbangers." Reciprocally, the urban underclass is incessantly bestialized as "predators," "wilding youth," and "wolf packs" in an urban "wilderness."

In ripe Hegelian fashion, then, the social construction of nature is typically mirrored by the naturalization of purely social contradictions. In what follows, I offer a symptomatic history of this strange choreography of the wild and the urban in Southern California. Needless to say, the politics of wildlife almost always presents a double aspect. On the one hand, it concerns the formation of human attitudes toward animals; on the other, it concerns class or ethnic conflict refracted through the symbolic role of wildlife in distinguishing the ethical universes of competing social groups. Los Angeles's wild edge, in other words, is the place where natural history and social history can sometimes be read as inverted images of each other.

Like all "dialectical fairy tales" (to adopt a phrase of Walter Benjamin's), this story has two parts, linked together by strange ironies. The first part takes up the history of human interaction with wildlife in Southern California, a relentless chain of slaughter and extinction stretching from the casual brutality of nineteenth-century ranching and market-hunting practices to the systematic predator extermination campaigns of the twentieth century, mounted in the name of "scientific" game management. In the second part, however, the surviving wild creatures, led by the astonishingly adaptive cougars of the Sierra Madre, begin to bite back, with often startling social consequences.

2. "SHOOTING EVERYTHING IN SIGHT"

*Like God, whose fabrication of man set off chain reactions
involving evil and good, of which the end is not yet, Southern
California man, in setting out to redo nature, to take over
godly prerogatives, has started more than he has finished.*
                                     Richard Lillard, Eden in Jeopardy *(1966)*

It is a founding conceit of American history that certain white men
were privileged to see the face of God in the beauty of untrammeled
Wilderness. Yet, apart from some high mountain summits, the
famous explorers, scouts, and colonizers moved strictly within cultural landscapes reconnoitered, named, and transformed by indigenous people over at least 10,000 years of continuous occupation.
Southern California was no exception. Humans and Mediterranean-
type biota have been coevolving since the end of the last ice age.
Anthropologists now recognize that native cultures like the Tong-va,
Chumash, and Cahuilla, once derided as lowly "diggers" for their
lack of agricultural technology, were potent "fire farmers" who used
their firesticks to extensively modify the local vegetation. The coastal
grasslands and black oak savannas, so admired by the mission fathers,
were the domesticated products of millennia of selective burning. As
environmental historians Thomas Blackburn and Kat Anderson have
emphasized, the diversity of native plants and habitat types was
"deliberately maintained by, and essentially dependent upon, ongoing human activities of various kinds."[24] Moreover, native Californians deftly manipulated the fire cycles of different plant communities
to increase the seasonal browse for deer and small game.

It is likely that these first people influenced the animal landscape of
the Southern California coast in less conservative ways as well. Periodically, the discovery of ancient bones or possible hunting artifacts
raises the possibility that humans were lurking in the bushes when the
Los Angeles Plain was a Pleistocene Serengeti. Some researchers have

even suggested that Paleo-Indians participated in the extinction of the fabulous Rancholabrean megafauna of mammoths, mastodons, saber-toothed cats, giant bison, and dire wolves. But as a recent publication of the Southern California Academy of Science notes, rather drily, "Cooperative seasonal hunting of late Pleistocene large herding animals is not confirmed in the archaeological record of the region."[25] The grooves on smilodon bones from the La Brea Tar Pits once attributed to hunters are now known to be formed by a natural process, while burnt mammoth remains from Santa Rosa Island could as easily be the result of wildfire as of campfire. More compelling is evidence for a later "prehistoric tragedy of the commons." According to this hypothesis, the Tong-va and the Chumash depleted marine mammal populations through the wholesale slaughter of young sea lions and fur seals in their coastal rookeries.[26]

Yet even with its diminished populations of marine mammals, Southern California was an extraordinary menagerie in 1769 when an impecunious Spanish Crown, worried about Russian and British intruders, began its belated effort at defensive colonization.[27] Although no comprehensive inventory of fauna was undertaken by any naturalist before 1900, it is possible to piece together earlier accounts into a rough mosaic. Thus the *pobladores* who founded Pueblo de Los Angeles would have seen whales of several species in Ballona Lagoon and San Pedro Bay, beaver in Ballona and Malibu Creeks, herds of white-tailed pronghorn in the Baldwin Hills and on the Tustin Plain, condors with 13-foot wingspans over Mount Hollywood, sea otters off Palos Verdes and Dead Man's Island, rainbow trout in the Rio Porciuncula (Los Angeles River), weasels in La Cienega, spotted and red lynx in the Arroyo Seco, gray wolves near Mission San Gabriel, and, everywhere, on what has been called "the best grizzly range on Earth," *Ursus horribilis,* the great brown bear. In the San Gabriels there were also badgers, bighorn sheep, and golden and southern bald eagles; and in Southern California's mountain fringe, in Riverside and eastern San Diego Counties, possibly jaguars (which in the early years of our century were still to be found in the delta of the Colorado River).[28]

The first impressions of nineteenth-century visitors were often defined by extraordinary visions of wildlife. For Richard Henry Dana in the 1830s, it was the spectacle of San Pedro Bay churning with whales who smashed dangerously against anchor chains and threatened to overturn longboats. "Turning our heads, we saw a great, rough, hump-backed whale, slowly crossing our fore foot, within three or four yards of the boat's stem. . . . He was a disgusting creature; with a skin rough, hairy, and of an iron-grey color."[29] Augustin Janssens, just arriving from Mexico in 1834, was impressed by the "great she-bear" that chased him down the road to Santa Inez.[30] Likewise, Horace Bell, who arrived in the early 1850s, was dumbfounded to discover that grizzlies were "more plentiful than pigs" and made "the rearing of cattle utterly impossible . . . in Topango Malibu, La Laguna de Chico, Lopez and other places."[31] Hugo Reid (in 1832) and Harris Newmark (in 1853) at the other end of the faunal scale were mesmerized by the vast rodent metropolis that covered the plains north of San Pedro. Reid complained that the squirrels, rabbits, and gophers "had so honeycombed the surface of the ground as to make it dangerous to ride anywhere off the roadway faster than at a walk." The horrified Newmark, who mistook the thousands of ground squirrels "for ordinary rats," felt as if he had "landed on another planet."[32]

The epiphanic experience shared by visitors as diverse as William Shaler (in 1805), General James Rusling (in 1866), and Prince Ludwig Salvator, archduke of Austria (in 1877) was the sight of the great wintering colonies of wildfowl along the road from San Pedro Bay. General Rusling, who recalled his drive from Wilmington to Los Angeles as "one of the fairest recollections of a life-time," left the most indelible description:

> The marshes about Wilmington, and the Plains beyond, were a halting place for vast flocks of wild geese, on their annual migration north, and they thronged the country in countless thousands. Off on the Plains, where they were feeding on the young and succulent grass, they whitened the ground sometimes for acres, and were so careless of danger, you might knock them over with a club. General Banning said they were

even more numerous in former years, but we had never seen anything to equal them. As we drove along, they rose by the roadside in flocks of thousands, and fairly deafened the air with their multitudinous konkings.[33]

Travelers skirting the edge of the great swamps that once extended southward from Bolsa Chica Mesa to Newport Mesa (today's coastal Orange County) encountered even larger populations of migratory wildfowl belonging to 83 separate species. "This section of the country," according to a local historian, "... was one of the greatest natural habitats for wildlife and game birds in the world."[34]

During the first century of Los Angeles's existence, its regional economy was largely based upon the comprehensive looting and destruction of this extraordinary biological endowment. The 22 million acres of coastal prairie, stirrup-high in tall grass, constituted the finest virgin grassland left in the world (largely ungrazed since the extinction of the megafauna eight thousand years earlier), while offshore kelp forests sustained staggering populations of sport fish and marine mammals.[35] Although foreign trade was officially proscribed during the Spanish period, the southern half of Alta California quickly became the economic colony of Nantucket sea captains and Boston merchants. The New Englanders needed otter pelts to trade in Canton and cowhides for the shoe factories of Connecticut and Rhode Island. The Californios, on the other hand, were desperate for manufactured products of every kind. Although the ranchos are often depicted as self-sufficient islands of a lazy and romantic feudalism, they were in fact franchises of dynamic Yankee capitalism. In this era of what Marx called "primitive accumulation," local wildlife was caught between the pincers of the fur trade and the hide-and-tallow market.

The first native fauna to pass into extinction was the sea otter. Although the major otter hunting grounds were in the Pacific Northwest and peninsular Alaska, American ships began to turn toward Alta California as early as 1796. Southern otter fur was not as valuable, but the rookeries were less depleted, and the missionized natives less dangerous than the bellicose tribes of the Northwest. From 1803 to 1813 the Americans "poached along the California coast on halves with the Russians, the latter providing Aleut and Kodiak hunters and kayaks and the former ships." The superb Aleutian hunters may have killed as many 50,000 otters, leaving only a tiny, remnant population for a new partnership of Americans and Mexicans to hunt during the 1820s. Sometime before the Mexican-American War, the animal disappeared entirely from its traditional habitats in the coastal waters of Baja and Southern California. In the same period, the Hudson's Bay Company and American mountain men trapped out most of the beaver, river otters, and minks in the state.[36]

The scrawny longhorns that the mission fathers turned loose on the Los Angeles Plain, direct descendants of the animals that Columbus had brought from the Canaries to Hispañola in 1493, caused ecological catastrophe on a far larger scale. New World cattle frontiers have been described as speculative and highly destructive exercises in "soil mining." Whether on the llanos of Colombia and Venezuela, the pampas of Uruguay and Argentina, the *sertão* of Brazil, the prairies of Texas, or the coastal plains of Southern California, nature raised cattle with little human intervention. Indeed, historians talk about the Spanish simply "seeding" the grasslands with livestock.[37] Supplementary fodder was virtually unknown, and rancho water resources consisted of natural streams and *cienegas,* on rare occasions augmented with small runoff dams and artificial ponds. The principal work of ranching still closely resembled hunting, and the long-horned cattle retained the instincts and behavior of wild game. Introduced into largely ungrazed ecosystems, the cattle acted as so many bulldozers in denuding the aboriginal landscape.

In her recent history of the environmental consequences of the conquest of Mexico, Elinor Melville has used modern research on the exponential population dynamics of "ungulate irruptions" among deer, sheep, and cattle to explain the devastating and often irreversible impact of Spanish pastoralism on New World ecosystems. Together with the destruction of native vegetation, intensified grazing produced soil compaction that led to increased runoff and acceler-

Californios at the Roundup

ated erosion. By the late sixteenth century once thriving croplands in central Mexico had deteriorated into depopulated wastelands.[38]

Thanks to a million mission cattle, a similar "conquest landscape," as Melville calls it, had emerged in the Los Angeles area by the 1830s; indeed, the introduction of cattle probably quintupled erosion rates and left the plains scarred with deep arroyos.[39] Even before the end of the eighteenth century, Spanish officials were already worrying about overstocking on local ranges. And they had reason: one recent study claims that the longhorn population had far surpassed the carrying capacity of the grasslands as early as 1821. The huge herds—120,000 hides were shipped out of San Pedro alone in 1834—did irreparable damage to fragile prairie and oak savanna ecosystems.[40]

In addition to "cattle on a thousand hills," Southern California also had myriads of *mestenos* (mustangs), so far in excess of possible demand that the best saddle horses sold for only 50 cents.[41] The draconian solution adopted after 1805 was the institution of periodic *matanzas* (slaughters) to reduce the grazing pressure from supernumerary cattle and *mestenos.* In 1812 alone, as many as 30,000 wild horses may have been killed throughout Alta California.[42] Horse killing was considered a basic civic responsibility, and slackers like Don Juan José Dominguez were bitterly denounced by their neighbors. (It took Dominguez's assiduous successor, Antonio Maria

Lugo, two years of hard work to exterminate Rancho San Pedro's prolifigate *mestenos*.)[43]

Yet the populations were quickly rebuilt, and *mestenos*—like those thundering across the San Fernando Valley in an early painting by James Walker—remained the most striking emblem of the rancho economy.[44] Even as late as the 1850s, Horace Bell was still marveling at "the vast herds of horses," while the German communist settlers at Anaheim fought desperate battles to keep the mustangs from trampling their precious vineyard.[45]

Feral horses and cattle, moreover, spilled beyond the ecological boundaries of the rancho economy and provided new cultural capital for native Californian societies struggling to adapt to the shock of conquest. On the peripheries of Southern California, in the southern San Joaquin Valley and in the high desert, a unique horseback culture, which adopted horsemeat as its staple food, arose among the heterogeneous bands of Yokuts, Paiute, Mojave, and runaway Chumash and Tong-va. Without the malaria and smallpox epidemics of the 1830s that killed at least three-quarters of the unmissionized native population, California's history might have turned out quite differently. As Woodrow Borah, the first historian to focus on the impact of the horse upon aboriginal California, has hypothesized:

> By the 1840s there was building up in the interior of California a reinvigorated and changed Indian society that was developing the tactics and the means for coping with Hispanic settlers. . . . A new Apache culture probably would have developed that would have given as good an account of itself as the Apaches and Commanches of the Southwest did in their defence against the Mexicans and Anglo-Americans.[46]

Meanwhile, the grazing pressure from hundreds of thousands of cattle and tens of thousands of horses abetted an unparalleled floral invasion. In the opinion of the leading authority on California grasslands, "few places on earth, if any, have had such a wholesale replacement of native plants by introduced species."[47] Hardy Mediterranean grasses and weeds, probably transported as seeds in the straw used to pack religious items, quickly displaced the native prairie. Unlike the indigenous perennial bunchgrasses, the invading annuals had evolved over thousands of years of stress from herbivores and thus were optimally adapted to conditions on the overstocked ranges. Simultaneously, a host of other invaders—plant and animal—including such now universal species as wild mustard, poison hemlock, the pepper tree, the house mouse, the Argentine ant, and the honeybee, were insinuating their way into the environment. Among larger mammals, the pronghorn antelope was pushed out of coastal grasslands by horses and cattle, as was its chief predator, the gray wolf (rarely seen after 1850).[48]

The opportunistic grizzly, however, adapted with gusto to a new cuisine of beef and horsemeat. Although grizzlies were increasingly hunted for sport, and sometimes even pitted against fighting bulls in the plaza, their population seems to have soared during the cattle era.

> They multiplied in mission and Mexican days because they were able to feast on livestock and on the carcasses the ranchers in the hide-and-tallow business threw away, giving the bears one of the largest free food supplies in ursine history. Grizzlies ate horses shot during droughts, consumed offal from deer killings and whaling operations, and raided sheepfolds and apiaries. They hid in the willows along the Los Angeles River and killed horses that wandered in for shade. They ate grapes in San Gabriel vineyards.[49]

The gold rush gave a second life to the rancho economy after the collapse of the hide-and-tallow trade in the early 1840s. One hundred thousand hungry prospectors in the foothills of the Sierra provided an instant market for all the beef that Southern California could produce. By the late 1850s, however, the southern ranches were competing with new cattle ranges stocked with higher-quality steers in the Central Valley, as well as longhorns driven all the way from Texas. As beef prices fell, local ranchers expanded their herds in a desperate attempt to preserve gross income. The overstocking that ensued was a reckless form of wagering on the weather. The Southern Californians lost.

The greatest storm in California history began on Christmas Eve 1861. Falling with little interruption for 45 days, the rains transformed most of the coastal plain from present-day Hollywood to Newport Beach into a giant inland sea. Entire communities, like the New Mexican settlement at Agua Mansa in San Bernardino County, were destroyed, and thousands of livestock drowned. This Noachian deluge was followed by a relentless drought that lasted from the summer of 1862 through the fall of 1864. While the attention of the rest of the world was riveted on Antietam and Gettysburg, Southern California's hybrid Yankee-Mexican squirearchy was watching hundreds of thousands of cattle die. The climax of the drought was an environmental disaster of Sahelian proportions. Dying, crazed cattle and horses stripped the desiccated landscape of every green stalk or leaf. What scant vegetation remained was consumed by a plague of *chapules* (locust) that suddenly appeared in 1864. The willow stockade built by the Anaheim colony to keep out *mestenos* now became a defense against famished cattle.[50] The rains, when they finally came again, carved hundreds of arroyos in the bare ground, carrying away nearly a quarter of the fertile topsoil. Once verdant valleys were transformed into deserts.[51]

Contemporary accounts emphasized the silent desolation: "Wide reaches of range utterly devoid of vegetation, great stretches of earth trampled to a powdery dust, caught up by wind devils as they raced across the parched plain." Another settler mourned the "empty land, empty of people and towns, of trees and cultivated fields."[52] Yet the ghostly cattle ranges were soon restocked with tens of thousands of sheep, as sheepmen from the Monterey area, fat with profits from the Civil War wool boom, bought up the southern ranchos at firesale prices. The sheep era—which largely justified John Muir's complaint that the animals were simply "hoofed locusts"—lasted barely a decade before a new drought, coinciding with worldwide El Niño–induced famines and plagues, once again decimated the herds. As a last resort, thousands of sheep were fed to hogs or driven across the desert toward the Colorado River. With biblical inevitability, the slaughter of the sheep was punctually followed by crop-devastating infinities of *chapules.*[53]

As one would expect, the environmental disasters of the mid-1860s and the mid-1870s were calamities for local wildlife communities as well. The great die-off of cattle sharply curtailed the grizzly populations that had grown with the herds. Yet grizzlies had roamed Southern California for centuries and would likely have survived the drought of even these two punishing decades. What they could not survive were the new Yankee overlords of the region, who, using repeating rifles, steel bear traps, and strychnine, were transforming bear hunting from an occasional sport into a campaign of extermination.

The victims fell quickly. One group of local cowboys killed half a dozen bears in a single two-week trip to Prairie Fork in the San Gabriels,* and grizzly meat was a regular item on local restaurant menus in the 1860s and early 1870s.[55] The paws from adult bears and the flesh from young cubs were deemed particular delicacies.[56] By the end of the 1880s, the slaughter of the great brown bears had been carried out so efficiently that some experts asserted they were already extinct everywhere in the state. The *San Francisco Examiner* disproved this claim in late 1889 when it unveiled the cage containing "Monarch," a huge male found on Mount Gleason in northern Los Angeles County. Although the *Examiner* published heroic accounts of the beast's capture by one of its reporters, "Monarch" had in fact been purchased from a syndicate of Los Angeles sportsmen. The only California grizzly in captivity, he died in 1911.[57] Five years later, the last wild grizzly in Southern California was shot by a rancher in lower Big Tujunga Canyon, at the edge of the San Fernando Valley. The final member of the distinctive California subspecies was killed in the southern Sierra in summer 1922.[58]

---

* The record Southern California grizzly hunt, however, was conducted by Benjamin Wilson in 1845. While on an expedition to punish Indian horse raiders, his posse killed 22 bears in the area subsequently known as "Bear Valley" in the San Bernardino Mountains.[54]

Roping a grizzly (1870)

The grizzly was not only the official state emblem, but also the state's peak predator. According to the scientific taxonomy of the time, the grizzly defined the dominant ecosystem in coastal Southern California: as late as the 1950s, textbooks still referred to the "Broad Sclerophyll–Grizzly Bear Community." In this sense, chaparral without the grizzly was the scientific equivalent of the short-grass prairie without the bison. The parallel extermination of these two most iconic American species took place during a national orgy of over-hunting. Indeed, the period from 1865 to 1890 probably saw the largest deliberate slaughter of wildlife in history. Fish and game officials later calculated that "from 50 to 95% of [California's] game has been killed off within one generation."[59] One infamous goal of this carnage was to destroy the ecological basis for independent native American life, but the ethos of "shooting everything in sight" was also driven by powerful market forces, including seemingly insatiable demands for fresh game from restauranteurs and for decorative feathers from manufacturers of women's hats.

California restaurants, north and south, were world-famous for the quality of their wildfowl, and the state was the nation's largest single market for fresh game—over one million ducks and 20,000 deer per year by 1890.[60] Game jobbers relied on professional hunters drawn from the ranks of a distinctive social stratum of poor whites: the "Pikes." Named after the famous county in Missouri that sent "Sweet Betsy" and thousands of other impoverished pioneers westward, the predominantly Scots-Irish Pikes were nomadic pig raisers and notorious squatters who were frequently embroiled in armed clashes with ranchers and sheriffs. According to the aristocratic English outdoorsman Horace Annesley Vachell, who lived in Southern California in the 1880s, they were also peerless small game hunters. Vachell describes one "capital fellow" of his acquaintance near Los Angeles:

> He was what is called a "market hunter"; and none was more familiar with the habits and habitat of game. He seemed to know by instinct where the big trout might be found, and could catch them with his hands; he was the finest stalker I have ever met; he used to come striding into town [Los Angeles] with dozens of quail, when other market hunters would tell you that there were no birds in the country; he could always predict the coming of the snipe and wild duck, of which he shot thousands annually.[61]

In the Los Angeles area, a small army of market hunters provisioned scores of restaurants, as well as a local quail cannery that had been established in 1881. As nineteenth-century civic leader Boyle Workman fondly recalled more than a half-century later, an "epicurean cuisine" of fresh game was "absurdly cheap" in this era: "Quail, dove and cottontail rabbits were 50 cents a dozen. . . . Venison steaks and roasts were 10 cents a pound."[62] Giant-bore fixed shotguns were used to annihilate migratory birds whole flocks at a time, while the use of hunting dogs ensured that hunters could reliably kill 50 to 60 deer each week in the San Gabriels above Pasadena. Antelope in the Lake Elsinore area and the western Mojave Desert were gunned down from railroad cars and later from automobiles. Commercial fishermen used dynamite to harvest trout by the ton in

San Gabriel Canyon as well as albacore off Santa Catalina, where rifle experts like to practice on the famed flying fish. For the souvenir trade, small boys were employed to trap horned lizards and tarantulas for sale to astonished tourists from the East. "The harmless, extremely useful and interesting California Condor," on the other hand, "was lassoed and dragged and strangled when full of food and clumsy, or shot just for the sport of it." With the arrival of several hundred thousand tourists and new residents during the boom of 1887–89, the exploding demand for wild game threatened to deplete what once had seemed a cornucopian supply.[63] Unregulated commercial hunting and fishing also endangered the new "English-style" hunting and fishing clubs that were all the rage among Los Angeles's nouveaux riches.

3. THE GOLDEN AGE OF THE HUNT

From down the valley, filtering through the windbreaks of the eucalyptus trees, comes softly on the wind the flute-like tremulo of the horn—the adios of the huntsman and his hounds.

Charles Holder, Life in the Open *(1906)*

"Outdoor sport" in early Los Angeles consisted of horse racing, "rooster pulling," informal rattlesnake and coyote hunts, grizzly-versus-bull combats in the old plaza (the bull generally won), and, most popular of all, public lynchings.[64] The ideal of hunting as a genteel Anglo-Saxon pastime, governed by an etiquette of "fair play," came to Southern California only with the arrival of wealthier eastern and British immigrants (like Horace Annesley Vachell) during the 1880s. The promotion of Los Angeles as "Nature's Garden" coincided with a national campaign, instigated by George Bird Grinnell in his *Forest and Stream Weekly,* to restrict commercial overhunting. In a famous dinner speech in December 1887, Grinnell's good friend

Theodore Roosevelt proposed the formation of an elite sportsmen's organization to protect other game animals from the tragic fate of the bison. Although named after homespun heroes, the Boone and Crockett Club only recruited from the bluest bloods on the Mainline and Beacon Hill, including du Pont, Pratt, Stimson, Whitney, and their peers. Teddy provided a heroic role model as an athletic hunter who pursued game in a sporting manner, killed "cleanly," and abhorred the cruelty of "market-hunters and savages." Later, when scientific management became the gospel of the Progressive bourgeoisie, the Boone and Crockett Club became a leading advocate of game preserves and the management of wildlife as a renewable resource.[65]

In Southern California, the Boone and Crockett point of view was eloquently represented by Charles Frederick Holder, a distinguished naturalist and biographer of Agassiz who taught zoology at Pasadena's Throop Institute (predecessor to Caltech). A friend of Roosevelt and Grinnell, as well as of illustrious Californians David Starr Jordan (president of Stanford) and Henry Huntington (traction baron), Holder moved to Pasadena for his health in 1885, on the eve of the great boom. Comparing contemporary Pasadena to Florence and Nice, he described it as "the wealthiest city of its size in the world."[66] With peerless enthusiasm for the Southern California outdoors, he preached the sporting life in the saddle to his patrician friends. Holder's hunting circle quickly evolved into the Valley Hunt Club, the inner sanctum of early-twentieth-century Pasadena society. A decade later, enraged at commercial overfishing in local waters, he founded the equally celebrated and exclusive Tuna Club in Avalon to encourage competitive amateur sportfishing as an alternative to the dynamite and gill nets of the "callous marketmen."[67]

By Theodore Roosevelt's second term, the Los Angeles area boasted nearly 40 gun and tackle clubs, including exclusive duck clubs which leased huge tracts of coastal wetlands in Playa del Rey, Bolsa Chica, Alamitos Bay, and Newport Bay. Many of the larger surviving ranchos like Lucky Baldwin's Rancho Santa Anita or the Irvine

Ranch sponsored regular mounted hunts.[68] Far more than the half-dozen fledgling golf clubs, these hunting clubs provided a distinctive social matrix for the new elites that emerged in the aftermath of the late 1880s boom. They defined a faux seignorial lifestyle that combined the Boone and Crockett postfrontier ethos of honorable adventure with the "romance" of the "Spanish ranchos." Holder's fascinating 1906 book *Life in the Open: Sport with Rod, Gun, Horse and Hound in Southern California* portrays wealthy transplants from Boston and Chicago, now dressed in serapes and sombreros, charging through orange groves on their favorite Indian ponies in pursuit of fox, lynx, and coyote.

Holder, with his fine naturalist's eye, captured Southern California at that extraordinary historical moment when wildness and urbanity held each other in precarious balance. "There is hardly a village, town, or city," Holder bragged, "where wild country is not available in some form in a short distance."[69] The newly popular bungalow was still just a glorified hunting cabin next to an orchard or arroyo, and good hunting began at the Los Angeles city limits. (Indeed, Boyle Workman recalled being able to shoot wild duck from his front porch in Boyle Heights—across from Downtown—as late as the 1870s.)[70] Despite the near extinction of local grizzlies, pronghorn antelope, condors, and bighorn sheep, which he deplored, other wild species remained indelible parts of the landscape. There were still heron in back of Playa del Rey, incredible sandhill cranes in the Centinela Hills, bald eagles above Malibu, and a myriad of ducks in the "sea swamps" along the coast. The fishing camps in San Gabriel Canyon, like the popular Creel and Bait clubs, angled prodigious numbers of trout, and countless quail still swarmed over the Laguna and Puente Hills. Pasadena huntsmen regularly chased bobcats through Highland Park and tracked deer in the Arroyo Seco and La Cañada, while their counterparts in Orange County's Santiago Hunt Club boasted of the best fox hunting west of the Shenandoah.[71]

At every opportunity, Holder contrasted the noble ethic of the Southern Californian sportsman with the crass brutality of the typi-

Charles Frederick Holder

cal market hunter or plebian poacher (both of whom were often immigrants or nonwhites). Coursing rabbits into enclosures, for instance, is described as "a cowardly, brutal game," while 20 mounted gentlemen and their greyhounds, by contrast, are engaged in "a hard, furious, dangerous sport, the hare having an open country and by far the advantage." Similarly, "to go out with a rifle and shoot the coyote would be to descend to the level of the pot-hunter, but to hunt one of the swiftest of wild animals in the open, follow it on horseback, taking the country as it comes, is fair and honest sport to be commended."[72]

The "extraordinary complexity" of Los Angeles's arroyo and foothill topography ensured continuous challenge and unprecedented excitement to the newcomer accustomed to the more gentle terrain of eastern hunt country. Holder conferred almost mythic stature on huntsmen prepared to face the extreme conditions of the local mountains. "There is no more difficult sport," he bragged, "than to hunt deer in the Sierra Madre without dogs." Likewise, "it is assumed that the angler of Southern California is a lover of mountain climbing."[73] This romanticizing of the outdoor life, of course, was meant to ennoble its participants. Thus, a hard ride through the woody Arroyo Seco or a long trek up the rugged West Fork of the San Gabriel River held out the possibility of transforming overweight bankers and henpecked real estate men into bully facsimiles of T.R. himself.

Yet this vigorous "life in the open" with all of its furious dashing back and forth across the countryside, inevitably produced social friction as it rubbed against the sedentary culture of the majority. "Part of the fun," Holder conceded, was charging through the obstacle course of people's yards and gardens. Tense confrontations with angry sheepmen or citrus ranchers were routine parts of the hunt, and Holder comes close to admitting that his high-minded sport often amounted to hooliganism. "We inevitably ran down game. If it were not a coyote, fox, or wildcat, it would be a Chinaman, a burro, or a dog."[74] In the long run, a mounted Rooseveltian gentry was not compatible with garden cities or the automobile. Land development trumped lifestyle.

As sprawling suburbs devoured wild places, some of the more romantic old money left Pasadena for Santa Barbara where the equestrian charade of Spanish California—rich automobile dealers mounted as "dons" on silver-bridled stallions—persists to the present day. Other wealthy outdoorsmen simply moved their hunting lodges and duck blinds to the Sierra and Imperial Valley, which became recreational colonies for Los Angeles's elites.* Yet others sublimated the hunt into the new craze for polo, promoted by Will Rogers from his baronial estate in the Pacific Palisades. But the majority of the 1920s Social Register simply abandoned blood sport—its passions and dangers—for the golf course and the yacht club.

Even as his beloved hunt culture was beginning its slow decline, Holder joined with other upper-class sportsmen like Count Jaro Von Schmidt of the Bolsa Chica Gun Club and James Irvine of the great Irvine Ranch in a struggle to regulate the hunting franchise to exclude both marketmen and traditional subsistence hunters. As president of the Wild Life Protective League of America, he enjoyed the support not only of the gun and tackle clubs but also of the California Federation of Women's Clubs (to which most sportsmen's wives belonged) as well as nature groups like the Audubon Society and the Sierra Club.[76] Their campaign for the "non-sale of game," together with related demands for game preserves, game wardens, hunting licenses, and a cleanup of corruption within the Fish and Game Commission, was a classic example of a Progressive-era reform movement with an interlocking ethnic, class, and regional agenda.[77]

In the Progressive imagination, the moral universes of contending races and ethnic groups were clearly differentiated by their attitudes toward wild nature. Wildlife conservation "reflected the culture of 'Anglo-Saxon' America against that of the new immigrants and the values of the middle class against those of the 'lower orders.' "[78] The campaign against market hunting seamlessly coalesced with a nativist crusade against Chinese shrimpmen, black and Italian birdtrappers, white-trash Pikes, and native Californian subsistence hunters who did

---

* There has been a recurrent vision of turning some corner of Southern California into an artificial Serengeti. In 1925, for example, Southern California women's clubs mobilized thousands of members to defeat the Pacific Coast Sportsmen's Club's scheme to stock a 50,000-acre game preserve in the Tehachapi Mountains with imported "lions, tigers, leopards, wild boar and buffalo." However, 65 years later, fish and game agents found the "skulls, heads and hides of mountain lions, Bengal tigers, spotted leopards, black leopards and jaguars" on a ranch in the Lockwood Valley 60 miles north of Los Angeles. According to the agents, "big game hunters," many from overseas, paid up to $3,500 to shoot surplus zoo animals chained to poles.[75]

not honor the "animal loving ethos of the Anglo-Saxon." As the renowned hunter-zoologist William Hornaday put it, "No White Man calling himself a sportsman ever indulges in such low pastimes as the killing of [songbirds] for food."[79] Thus the reformers fought for a $25 hunting fee for noncitizens as well as stiff penalties for poaching that effectively criminalized poorer immigrant and native hunters while causing little inconvenience to wealthy British and Canadian tourists.

The class politics of game regulation, on the other hand, was seldom expressed as blatantly as its ethnic politics. At the beginning of the twentieth century, the free right to hunt was still widely conceived in eighteenth-century terms as a constitutive American freedom, one counterposed to Old England's notorious panoply of game warrants, forest officers, and the Black Act which sent yeomen poachers to the gallows. Unlike Europe's anciens régimes where game was the private property of the nobility, wildlife on the Jeffersonian frontier traditionally had been community property subject to household need (as well as brazen commercial exploitation). Any restriction of popular hunting custom at the end of the frontier period, therefore, had to be justified by appealing to other egalitarian values.[80]

This produced competing polemical claims. Progressive advocates of regulation (primarily based in Southern California), for their part, defined the issue as a struggle against de facto monopoly imposed by commercial hunters and the restaurant and hotel industry: "The wild game belongs to the people in their sovereign capacity and as such should be enjoyed by the people and cared for and preserved for their benefit." The market value of game, from this perspective, was "infinitesimal" compared to its recreational and aesthetic importance.[81] By contrast, hotel spokesmen and allied Union-Labor Party orators (primarily based in San Francisco) denounced the proposed game laws as "class legislation—that is, legislation against the masses and for the benefit of the wealthy," whose private hunting grounds and game preserves already monopolized wildlife resources near the big cities.[82]

Holder was exceptional in his blunt advocacy of noblesse oblige as the most effective system of game conservation. The Tuna Club's strategy, for example, was to discourage the overcatch by offering rewards to anglers who took the largest fish with the lightest tackle. Only relatively wealthy sportfishermen who could afford the requisite $75 tuna reels and $40 rods were likely to participate in the competition. Likewise, exclusive duck-shooting clubs, whose membership was only open to "gentile gentlemen of the highest standard," leased huge tracts of coastal wetlands. The result, according to Holder, was entirely beneficial to the preservation of migratory wildfowl. "Almost every foot of good duck shooting in Los Angeles County, and from Santa Monica to Laguna, is taken by private clubs; were this not so, every duck and goose on the coast would be killed off by the pot-hunter, the running mate of the man who dynamites trout streams."[83]

4. THE WAR AGAINST PREDATORS

The destruction of the mountain lion is not an easy task.
Naturalist Harold Bryant (1917)

The newly developing legal and cultural distinctions between "sportsmen" and "poachers" were soon projected into the faunal realm, where an analogous conflict between "protected wildlife" and "outlaw predators" quickly emerged. Exploiting traditional Anglo-American phobias about wolves and other forest carnivores, an unusual tripartite coalition persuaded Congress in 1914–15 to federalize the extermination of wolves, coyotes, mountain lions, bobcats, and raptors. The economic interest of Western ranchers, particularly wool growers, in predator control was self-evident, as was sportsmen's desire to increase deer and elk populations; but the moral self-righteousness that characterized the anti-predation crusade would come from the third party in the coalition—amateur naturalists, birdwatchers, and vegetarians. The burgeoning "humane" movement, which harvested a long accumulation of Victorian sentimentality about animals,* proposed to pull the teeth and claws from sanguinary nature by eliminating the big carnivores. "Gen-

---

* Kindness to animals, Dutch biologist Midas Dekkers observes, was "the most satisfying Victorian charity. Among animals there were no socialists, who would sooner or later bite the hand that stroked them."[84]

MANEATERS OF THE SIERRA MADRE | 229

teel nature appreciation," as historian Thomas Dunlap points out, "reinforced prejudice. Predators were 'cruel.' They 'murdered' the 'innocent' deer and songbirds."[85] Accordingly, the Audubon Society, the most prestigious nature organization in the country, lobbied hand-in-hand with stockmen and elite hunters for the establishment of the Division of Predator and Rodent Control within the U.S. Department of Agriculture's Bureau of Biological Survey.

Leading naturalists enthusiastically signed death warrants for predatory species. William Hornaday, the famed explorer and director of the New York Zoological Society, was "one of the most prominent cheerleaders for the search-and-destroy operations." His famous 1913 call to arms, *Our Vanishing Wildlife,* made little distinction between wanton overhunting, which he blamed particularly on immigrants, and the role of predators in the wilderness food chain. For example, he labeled a photograph of a Cooper's hawk "A Species to be Destroyed."[86] E. A. Goldman, a leading biologist in the Bureau of Biological Survey, was equally blunt: "Large predatory mammals destructive to livestock and game no longer have a place in our advancing civilization."[87]

The humane movement ideal of pacified nature had a special resonance in the garden cities of Southern California, where it converged with the regional goal of a scientifically managed landscape. The citrus industry, whose links to university research, hydroelectric technology, and mass production made it the high-tech sector of the 1900s, was particularly smitten by the fantasy of total engineered control over the wild environment represented by the Sierra Madre. As late as 1880 the range was still so dominated by large predators—grizzlies and cougars—that visitors were advised to "go equipped as walking arsenals" and shepherds slept on 12-foot-high *tepestras* (platforms) for protection.[88] The Orange Belt's leadership (the core of California's Progressive movement) fought for the incorporation of the mountains as a federal reserve (achieved in 1892), the construction of a vast system of defenses against floods and debris flow, a policy of total fire suppression to be implemented by full-time firefighting crews, and the planting of millions of trees in a scientifically misguided attempt to reforest lower mountain slopes. They also energetically supported the extermination of the remaining predator populations. Progressive opinion, which visualized deer herds as a harvestable "crop," analogously saw mountain lions and coyotes as faunal "weeds in the garden."[89]

With the extinction of the grizzly, however, it was difficult to find, no less define, a serious predator problem in Southern California. In his exhaustive inventory of local wildlife resources, Holder emphasized that cougars were famously reclusive and "rarely seen." (A dramatic exception was the lion killed on the grounds of Pasadena's Raymond Hotel in 1898.) Coyotes, although not uncommon, were principally confined to the Repetto Hills, east of Downtown, where they annoyed Basque shepherds and their herds without causing significant economic damage. Holder's main predator complaint had to do with the "Mexican custom" of keeping the "half-breed offspring of coyotes and town dogs as pets," thereby weakening the racial purity of the distinction between hound and wolf that was so important to the aristocratic ideology of the mounted hunt.[90]

In the absence of attacks on humans, the only compelling case for predator control in Southern California was the belief, shared by sport hunters and animal lovers, that mountain lions and coyotes were "wanton killers" who—out of human sight—decimated local deer and wildfowl populations. The cougar was a particular target of scorn. Writing for the California Fish and Game Commission in 1917, the prominent naturalist Harold Bryant asserted, on the basis of hunting lore alone, "It is a well-established fact that the mountain lion . . . is the most important enemy of deer. . . . A lion often kills more than it is able to eat."[91] Jay Bruce, a legendary hunter hired by the commission to rid the state's wildlife refuges of cougars, claimed to have calculated the annual dollar value of the depredations inflicted by an animal he considered to be uniquely evil and harmful. The mountain lion, he wrote,

> is the only predatory animal in California which is apparently of no economic benefit to the human race. Even the wildcat and the coyote generally do more good than harm by preying prin-

cipally upon rats, mice, gophers, ground squirrels and jackrab-
bits. . . . On the other hand, the mountain lion . . . is simply a
liability which probably costs the state a thousand dollars a year
in deer meat.[92]

The official war against predators in Southern California and the
rest of the state began in October 1907 when the state offered a $20
bounty (raised to $30 for females in 1917) for mountain lion skins. In
1913 and 1915 large parts of the Angeles and Cleveland National
Forests, including the hearts of the San Gabriel, Santa Ana, and Palomar Mountains, were dedicated as game preserves. In 1919, Bruce
was hired to exterminate the cougar populations in these ranges and
16 other game preserves throughout California, while federal hunters
eliminated predators from the state's national parks. Simultaneously,
the Fish and Game Commission mounted an educational campaign
to encourage cowboys, stockmen, and weekend hunters to kill every
lion in sight. One article cautioned against the temptation of keeping
cougars as pets, while another urged hunters to locate and kill all cubs
after slaying a female lion. (This was called "denning.") The commission also responded to a "question often asked by the zealous nature
advocate"—"Is mountain lion meat suitable for the table?"—by
answering that lion "resembles fine, tender veal." The article provided helpful tips for incorporating cougar steaks and roasts into the
family diet.[93]

In the early years of the war against predators, state and federal
hunters were able to sustain astonishing kill rates. The wolf was driven
into extinction throughout the Great Plains and the Southwest, while
mountain lions (already extinct everywhere east of the Rockies except
in Florida) were being slaughtered in numbers that optimistic game
officials believed were far in excess of natural reproduction. In 1923
Bruce, who alone could boast of 30 cougar kills each year, estimated
that there were fewer than 500 lions left in California, with about 100
remaining in the southern counties.[94] Eight years later, the chief
forester of Los Angeles County noted with grim satisfaction that only
one lion bounty had been paid in the county during the 1930–31 fiscal

Hunters near Pasadena display a cougar skin (1920s)

year as opposed to 26 in 1929–30. "The heavy decrease is no doubt largely responsible for the increase in the number of deer."[95]*

Mountain lion kills peaked in most parts of Southern California in 1927–32, with the remaining cats presumably driven into the most inaccessible parts of their ranges. Although there are no overall regional statistics for predator kills, a San Bernardino County animal control officer estimated that, in addition to personally shooting 109 cougars between 1920 and 1940, he had also exterminated more than 10,000 other predatory animals, chiefly coyotes, bobcats, and foxes. Like his counterpart in Los Angeles County, this official believed that the cougar "had been virtually eliminated" and applauded the increase in the deer population

---

* A lone voice of dissent in this period was D. H. Lawrence. One day in Taos in 1923 he encountered two hunters exulting over the magnificent cougar they had tracked and killed. In rage he wrote:

And I think in this empty world there was room for me and a mountain lion.
And I think in the world beyond, how easily we might spare a million or two of humans
And never miss them.
Yet what a gap in the world, the missing white frost-face of that slim yellow mountain lion.[96]

that was the supposed result.[97] Coyote control was a less consistent local priority than cougar extermination and less effective in its outcome. Yet in the first eight months after the Los Angeles Board of Supervisors adopted a coyote control program in 1938, 650 bounties were paid.[98] According to official reckoning, the taming of Southern California's wild edge was proceeding according to schedule.

BOUNTIED MOUNTAIN LION KILL IN SOUTHERN CALIFORNIA, 1907–50

County	Total Kill	Peak Year
Los Angeles	188	1929
Orange	16	1941
Ventura	168	1927
Santa Barbara	440	1927
San Bernardino	176	1931
Riverside	108	1935
San Diego	281	1929
State Total	10,558	1908

Source: Data from D. McClean, "Mountain Lions in California," *California Fish and Game* 40 (April 1954): 162–63.

By the end of the 1930s, however, there was disturbing evidence from across the West that predator persecution was not creating a peaceable kingdom. By removing natural constraints on deer and rodent population growth, it was instead producing biological catastrophes. The most famous of these, an outdoor version of Frankenstein's laboratory, took place on Arizona's Kaibab Plateau on the north rim of the Grand Canyon (which Theodore Roosevelt had set aside in 1906 as a model national game preserve). In little more than a decade, federal hunters had exterminated the plateau's entire predator community: 674 cougars, 3,000 coyotes, and 120 bobcats. As a result, the deer population exploded from an estimated 3,000 in 1906 to more than 100,000 by 1924. Tourists and animal lovers marveled at what the Forest Service boasted was "the biggest deer herd in the world" tamely browsing in a parklike landscape of open forest (actually the result of defoliation by the deer). Then, in the winter of 1925, with range resources depleted, the great die-off of the huge deer herd began, and the once teeming Kaibab was reduced to a silent faunal desert: the paradigmatic example in modern wildlife management textbooks of the need to balance game population against available range.[99]

The Kaibab experience was recapitulated a decade later in California's Mount Hamilton area, where the elimination of mountain lions by intensive bounty hunting in 1934–36 led to a deer population explosion that peaked in 1940, when hundreds of starving deer suddenly invaded the vineyards and orchards of the neighboring Santa Clara Valley (today's "Silicon Valley"). However, the most nightmarish example of the inadvertent consequences of predator control occurred in Los Angeles's own backyard, the southwest corner of the San Joaquin Valley. On the night of 24 November 1926 an estimated 100 million house mice overran the gritty oil town of Taft (population 5,000). "The mice," according to a local history, "invaded beds and nibbled the hair of horrified sleepers, chewed through the sides of wooden storehouses to get at food supplies, and crawled boldly into children's desks at Conley School."[100]

The battle against the mice lasted months and increasingly resembled the script of a science fiction film. At first local authorities tried to destroy the advancing rodent hordes with mechanical harvesters, but the blades "became choked with fur, flesh and blood to the resemblance of a sausage mill." They then surrounded Taft with a network of trenches sown with strychnine-impregnated straw. Although hundreds of thousands of mice were killed, myriads more overwhelmed the defenses.

> Advancing to the southwest, mice killed a sheep and devoured the carcass in less than a day. A column slipped past poison-filled trenches to touch off an exodus of women from Ford City, an unincorporated community adjoining Taft. Another column captured the Petroleum Club golf course after token opposition from fleeing golfers. To the north, hordes swarmed over the Taft-Bakersfield Highway, where thousands were ground to death under car wheels, making the highway dangerously slippery.[101]

Federal men killing mice

Turning down advice from the army chief of chemical warfare to use poison chlorine gas against the mice, desperate Taftites advertised "Fabled Pied Piper Needed." The Bureau of Biological Survey promptly sent in Stanley E. Piper, their chief wildlife poisoner.[102] With 25 local recruits ("promptly dubbed the Mouse Marines") Piper set up camp outside of Taft and began a systematic chemical extermination campaign. Although he made steady headway, the mice were ultimately defeated not by poison but by a plague, the rodent septicemia bacillus. Three months after it had begun, and with Taft on the verge of a collective nervous breakdown, the great mouse invasion suddenly ended.[103]

This, however, was only the beginning of a memorable scientific debate over the causes of the extraordinary rodent irruption. E. Raymond Hall, a Berkeley biologist fresh from fieldwork in the Kaibab, attributed the Taft event to the efficiency of the Biological Survey's predator control campaign in Kern County during 1924–25, which had eradicated natural mouse enemies like coyotes, skunks, and redtailed hawks.[104] Piper, on the contrary, ardently defended the survey, blaming the outbreak instead upon a bumper crop of maize in the irrigated bed of former Lake Buena Vista, which became available as agricultural land in 1925 after the diversion of flood runoff from the

Kern River. But other prominent members of the American Society of Mammalogists (ASM) like Johns Hopkins's A. Brazier Howell quickly came to Hall's defense. Although most conceived of "rodent plagues" as multicausal in origin, they were incensed by the Biological Survey's self-serving denial that carnivores had played any significant role in regulating rodent populations.[105]

Indeed, the ecological debacles on the Kaibab and Mount Hamilton, as well as at Taft and elsewhere, gradually forced a rethinking of the scientific premises of game management and a new recognition of the destructive potential of out-of-control deer populations. Wildlife managers gained a better appreciation of the ecological role of predatory mammals and raptors (and their surrogates: human hunters) in adjusting populations to carrying capacity. A watershed 1931 report, endorsed by the ASM, objected to the Biological Survey's indiscriminate poisoning of carnivores and deplored "the propaganda of the Survey which is designed to unduly blacken the character of certain species of predatory mammals, giving only part of the facts and withholding the rest, propaganda which is educating the public to advocate the destruction of wildlife."[106] Yet the protestors emphasized that "we make no mention of wolves and mountain lions which, whatever their values from an aesthetic viewpoint, are truly killers and are destructive."[107] This scientific exemption for the "wanton killer species" allowed wildlife managers to embrace the new ecosystem perspective in good faith while simultaneously escalating the war against mountain lions throughout the West.

In Southern California by the early 1930s, optimistic game officials thought a few more years of systematic hunting might succeed in vanquishing the cougar—like the California grizzly—once and for all. Accordingly, the number of full-time state lion hunters was increased to four (Bruce retired in 1946 with a lifetime record of 581 kills), while the Second World War provided a new arsenal of chemical predacides and booby traps, including the superpoison sodium fluoroacetate and a widely adopted device that fired cynanide bullets into predators' mouths. Yet in 1954, the California Fish and Game Commission complained that the campaign against the cougar was "just holding the number about even or possibly losing a little ground."[108] Even in urban centers like Los Angeles County, the surprisingly resilient lion refused to go the way of the wolf and grizzly, clinging with superb tenacity to the wild recesses of its mountain ranges.* The perennial trickster, the coyote, on the other hand, relied on its astonishing reproductive powers to survive the onslaught of poison traps and bounty hunters, compensating for higher mortality rates with increased fertility.†

The pacification of nature in Southern California, in other words, had experienced its first inexplicable failures. Although predator control programs did keep cougars, coyotes, bobcats, and foxes virtually invisible to the postwar urban millions, a wilderness, defined by the survival of these carnivores, continued to border the increasingly fractal edge of development. Then, suddenly, in the 1980s, baffling numbers of predators reemerged from the foothills and became routine visitors to suburban neighborhoods. This was most dramatically a "return of the repressed," and the initial charm of such encounters quickly gave way to hostility and panic as predators began devouring pets and attacking small children.

5. RETURN OF THE LION

We have a saying in Descanso: "When you enter the park, you enter the food chain."

Local rancher (1994)

The first person to die was three-year-old Keely Keene of Glendale on 26 August 1981. She was playing in the front yard of her home in the

---

* Having been hunted to extinction almost everywhere east of the Rockies (except in the Everglades), how did the cougar manage to survive the intense persecution of California's bounty era? Part of the answer undoubtedly lies in the extreme ruggedness of much California terrain, especially the San Gabriels with their steep middle-altitude slopes covered with manzanita chaparral, dense and impenetrable, at least to humans.

† As Hope Ryden points out, the coyote also has the extraordinary ability to mate with both wolves and domestic dogs to produce, respectively, coy-wolves and coy-dogs. "The coyote, unlike almost every other known species, is capable of interspecific breeding; it can mate with either the dog or the wolf and produce offspring that are not sterile."[109]

then newly developed San Rafael Hills section of the city when she was attacked by a coyote with such ferocity that she was nearly decapitated. It was the first fatality blamed on a coyote in modern American history. When Glendale Humane Society officials were unable to locate the culprit, the county attempted to stem local hysteria by sending in professional trappers to exterminate the entire coyote population in the surrounding foothills. They were amazed to recover 57 carcasses from a single square-mile area around the Keene home. This unexpected density—"a teeming coyote ghetto," in the words of one alarmed resident—was attributed to the bountiful supply of garbage, possibly augmented by deliberate feeding, that had transformed the San Rafael Hill coyotes into "bag animals." Experts were perplexed by the aggression, although one ventured (somewhat improbably) that "attacks may be made by female coyotes suffering false pregnancies who attempt to adopt young creatures."[110]

In the five years after Keely Keene's death there were several other, nonfatal coyote attacks on children along Los Angeles's wild edge, but none attracted media attention or caused a political uproar. There was an entirely different reaction, however, to the first cougar attack in Southern California history. On 23 March 1986, five-year-old Laura Small was hunting for tadpoles in the shallow creek that flows through the Ronald Caspers Wilderness Park northeast of the famed mission town of San Juan Capistrano. As her horrified mother watched, an animal "that looked like a big dog" suddenly wrenched Laura into the underbrush. Following her child's screams, the mother, joined by her husband and another hiker, plunged downstream until they confronted a large mountain lion with Laura's head in its jaws. After they drove off the cougar, Laura was evacuated by a paramedic helicopter to a nearby hospital where a team of specialists saved her life, though she was left disfigured, partially paralyzed, and blind in one eye. Later that fall, another youngster hiking in Caspers Park was attacked by a cougar, and authorities were forced to close the park to minors. The Small family eventually won a $2 million suit against Orange County for "negligence" in failing to post mountain lion warning signs.[111]

In the meantime, Laura was adopted as the poster child of a campaign by pro-hunt groups, including the National Rifle Association, to restore seasonal mountain lion hunting in California. In 1963 the state had abandoned its traditional cougar bounty as too costly to administer, and in 1972, following a surge of public sympathy for endangered predators, the legislature had imposed a moratorium on the sport hunting of the animal, now classified as a protected species. (Coyotes, however, were still treated as noxious varmints.) In 1986 legislators voted to renew the moratorium, but the bill was vetoed by Republican Governor George Deukmejian, whose appointees to the Fish and Game Commission, citing the Caspars Park attacks, drafted a plan for open lion hunting. The pro-hunt forces loudly publicized a claim by the Fish and Game Commission that the statewide mountain lion population, only 500 to 600 in 1920, had reached an all-time high of 6,000—greater than the estimated cougar population (5,800) of the entire continental United States in 1942! The commission also asserted that at least 1,000 lions were "stalking" the urban periphery of Southern California.[112]

Most wildlife biologists, understanding the extraordinary difficulty of accurately estimating even the smallest local population of such a famously reclusive creature, scoffed at these figures. But Deukmejian's anti–mountain lion offensive did galvanize a coalition of wildlife advocates and environmental groups to establish the Sacramento-based Mountain Lion Foundation, which quickly won a temporary injunction blocking the proposed cougar hunt. Emboldened by their success, pro-lion forces, including the powerful Conservation League and the Sierra Club, gathered more than half a million signatures to place Proposition 117, the California Wildlife Protection Act, on the the 1990 ballot. It won handily: a stunning vindiction of the cougar's new status, along with the wolf and the grizzly, as a romantic icon of a disappearing wilderness.

In addition to permanently banning the sport hunting of mountain lions, Proposition 117 enraged many conservatives by allocating nearly $1 billion over a 30-year period for the conservation of wildlife habitats for cougars, deer, and other large mammals. To stanch fears about "killer lions," the act continued the provisions in the old moratorium that authorized special permits for the destruction of individual animals whose behavior signaled that they were a threat to humans or livestock. Public safety was treated as an entirely separate issue from trophy hunting. Unfortunately, this fundamental distinction was obscured as the guns-and-ammo lobby exploited a new wave of predator panic in the early 1990s.

The six-year-long California drought of 1987–92, possibly the worst in four centuries,[113] drove unprecedented numbers of wildlife into irrigated urban oases. In the San Fernando Valley, for example, hillside homeowners were besieged by hungry mule deer who defoliated flower beds, while in the flatlands, animal control officers struggled to deal with myriad complaints about opossums, 1,600 of which were trapped there in 1990 alone.[114] Carnivores soon followed prey in their drought-induced exodus from the foothills. Throughout the Valley, coyotes became brazen daytime visitors. Their preference for poodles, cats, and other small coddled creatures led to a sudden rise in the number of forlorn notices, usually tacked to telephone poles, that begged for the return of "Fluffy," "Whispers," and other favorite pets. More disturbingly, residents in some neighborhoods began to find the remains of deer killed by cougars in their backyards. Then lions were observed watching children in Laurel Canyon and Granada Hills. Mountain lion warning signs began to appear in city as well as county parks.[115]

In the same period, pandemonium broke out episodically in the tier of affluent former citrus towns along the southern edge of the San Gabriels. In Bradbury, a walled private city of million-dollar homes bulldozed out of the foothills, residents were horrified by the sight of a large lion swaggering down a street in broad daylight with a helpless white poodle in its jaws. Paranoid suburbanites immediately began to equate wild predators with urban street gangs. "Do you want to move to a neighborhood where there are drive-by shootings?" asked a resident who had earlier bragged to reporters about trying to run over a mountain lion with his car. "No, that's just stupid. Would you want to move to a place where animals roam the streets and could kill your child? It's the same thing."[116]

Further consternation was caused by lions who killed guard dogs in
La Crescenta and Glendora. In Upland a full-grown cougar terrorized
shoppers in a popular mall before it was shot by police. In nearby
Monrovia, a couple surprised a black bear (a species introduced into
the San Gabriel Mountains by the National Forest Service during the
1930s) enjoying a dip in their hot tub. Other bears blundered through
neighborhoods in Arcadia and Azusa, and a teenager was badly
scalped by one at a summer camp in the San Bernardino Mountains.[117]

As the drought abated, however, a widely predicted decline in
human-predator contacts failed to occur. Naturalists began to specu-
late that mountain lions, bears, and coyotes were adapting to the new
subsistence and prey opportunities at the interface of the urban and
the wild. Children in particular remained at risk. In March 1992, a
man beat off a cougar who attempted to drag away his nine-year-old
son in Gaviota State Park, north of Santa Barbara. In September
1993, a lion invaded a popular campground in the Cuyamaca Mountains, 50 miles east of San Diego. Ignoring more than 60 adult
campers, some of whom cowered on picnic tables while others
barked like dogs, it lunged at a fifth-grader who was playing catch
with her father and brother. "Daddy yelled for me to stand still," said
10-year-old Lisa Kowalski. "Then I looked around and saw the
mountain lion and I screamed. The mountain lion sniffed me and
then bit me real hard." She would have been mauled but for her pet
Labrador which boldly charged the lion while Lisa escaped to the
family car. The angry cougar milled around the campsite for another
10 minutes or so before departing.[118]

The incident at Cuyamaca proved the beginning of a new and more
violent cycle of predator contacts. Over the course of the next year,
"serious mountain lion incidents," as defined by the Fish and Game
Commission, increased by 20 percent to a statewide record of 350,
with most encounters occurring on the periphery of metropolitan
regions or in heavily used weekend recreation areas. More than half
occurred in Southern California, including a dozen within the Los
Angeles city limits. One group of "mountain lion victims" organized
their own therapy and support group. Meanwhile, anxious animal

control officials warned that predators "were developing a taste for humans," and if politicians refused to provide protection, "people will take it into their own hands."[119] Wildlife activists accused pro-hunt fish and game bureaucrats of deliberately fomenting hysteria with unconfirmed incidents that "require only a telephone call to report,"[120] but an ugly strain of vigilantism was already emerging in the "cougar hot spot" of Descanso, a small town near the campground where Lisa Kowalski was attacked.

In the early twentieth century, this picturesque backcountry hamlet had been a retreat for persecuted Socialists and Wobblies from San Diego. Modern Descanso, however, is better known for its racial intolerance and pseudo-hillbilly lifestyle. Although locals had been complaining about aggressive cougars for several years, rangers at nearby Cuyamaca State Park were convinced that the real problem was a single rogue female which had been scaring campers for several months before it attacked Lisa Kowalski. After tracking and killing this cat, which turned out to be diseased and underweight, park officials reassured disbelieving residents that the mountains were once again safe.[121]

Fifteen months later, in December 1994, after five more Cuyamaca cougars (all healthy this time) had been tracked and killed for their "threatening behavior," Iris Kenna, a popular high school counselor from San Diego, was bird-watching along the trail to Cuyamaca Peak. She was probably running from the lion when it broke her neck from behind. After finding her half-eaten body in the brush, one tracker compared her wounds to the results of a chain saw. (Experts say that cougars always eat the heart, liver, and stomach of their prey first.) The park, a favorite weekend destination for San Diegans, was closed indefinitely.[122]

Furious Descanso residents, wearing "Beware! Cougar" T-shirts and brandishing magnum sidearms, openly boasted that they were ready to solve the lion problem frontier-style. (As one rancher told a reporter, "It's not hard to bury a dead cougar.") To quell local fears, as well as head off possible confrontations between rangers, wildlife advocates, and armed residents, elite state and federal "animal dam-

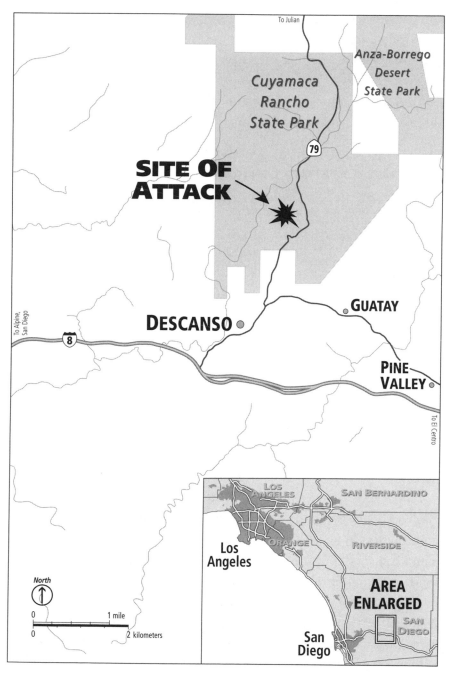

The panic zone

age control specialists" were sent into the Cuyamacas. Throughout 1995 they tracked and killed lions in response to reports from hikers and horseback riders that they had been stalked. Wildlife managers, meanwhile, began to take seriously what biologists had always assured them was impossible: maneating on an epidemic scale among at least one population of cougars.[123]

MOUNTAIN LION ATTACKS ON HUMANS IN CALIFORNIA, SINCE 1900

Year	County	Victim(s)	Injuries
1909	Santa Clara	Wilson and Kennedy	Died of rabies
1986	Orange	Small (age 5)	Severely mauled
1986	Orange	Mellon (age 6)	Minor injuries
1992	Santa Barbara	Arroyo (age 9)	Minor injuries
1994	Santa Barbara	Foote (age 6)	Minor injuries
1994	Sacramento	Schoener (age 40)	Killed
1994	San Diego	Kowalski (age 10)	Minor injuries
1994	San Diego	Kenna (age 56)	Killed
1994	Mendocino	Two couples charged by lion	Man loses thumb
1995	Los Angeles	Fike (age 27)	Minor injuries

Source: Compiled from newspaper reports cited above and from Paul Beier, "Cougar Attacks on Humans in the United States and Canada," *Wildlife Society Bulletin* 19 (1991): 403–12.

Not surprisingly, the Cuyamaca attacks, together with the death of Barbara Schoener in the Sierra foothills in spring 1994, provided new ammunition to old foes of mountain lion protection like state senator Tim Leslie, a Republican from the Lake Tahoe area, and Terry Mansfield, the chief of the Wildlife Division of the California Department of Fish and Game. In fall 1995, Leslie won legislative approval for a March 1996 referendum on returning control of cougars to the pro-hunt Fish and Game Commission. Proponents made little effort to disguise the fact that Proposition 197 was a trojan horse for the California Sportsman's Lobby, reinforced by agribusiness and corporate political action committees that opposed the $30 million annual set aside for cougar habitat preservation.[124]

In the increasingly bitter and expensive battle over Proposition 197, proponents, supported by Republican Governor Pete Wilson, consistently depicted "killer lions," like street gangs and welfare chislers, as the result of a breakdown in the traditional hierarchies of authority. The abolition of open hunting, they argued, had taken away the cougars' innate fear of humans—God's chosen peak predators—and encouraged them instead to become depraved maneaters. As a result, claimed a pro-197 argument in the state voters' pamphlet, "two small children woke up one morning without a mother because a lion ate her."[125]

Scornful wildlife advocates, for their part, pointed to British Columbia, where cougar hunting had been legal and relentless throughout the twentieth century (an average of two hundred lions killed annually) and where, correspondingly, the "fear of man" should be greatest. Yet 57 percent of all cougar attacks on humans since 1890 had occurred there, a percentage completely out of proportion to the number of cougars in the province. If hunting had any correlation with cougar behavior, they claimed, it seemed to be associated with increased rather than diminished lion ferocity, perhaps due to natural selection as hunters culled the less aggressive or less competent predators from the population.[126]

The opponents of Proposition 197 accused the pro-hunt forces and the Wilson administration of inflating a few aberrant events into mass hysteria. They compared the actual probability of being mauled by a lion to "pianos falling out of the sky."[127] Their bible was Paul Beier's painstaking 1991 study of all recorded mountain lion attacks in the United States and Canada since 1890. He had discovered only 9 fatal and 44 nonfatal incidents in the course of an entire century, thus confirming the opinion of old-time lion hunters like Jay Bruce that attacks on adult humans were extraordinarily rare.[128] Outdoor recreationists, anti-197 literature pointed out, face far greater danger from bees, snakes, lightning, hunters, and their own pets. More than 600,000 Americans, for example, require medical treatment for dog bites every year.[129]

Beier, the only lion researcher with extensive local field experience (he had conducted a four-year study of telemetered cougars in

Orange County's Santa Ana Mountains), wrote in 1992—before the Descanso incidents—that he had "seen no evidence that cougars are habituated to humans." On the contrary, to him the lions seemed as wary as ever; the problem lay largely with the humans who were intruding ever deeper and more frequently into the lions' habitat. He warned that an exaggerated concern with public safety was ultimately incompatible with the enjoyment of wild places.

> If cougars are dangerous enough to require a warning, then warnings for many other hazards—from rattlesnakes to cliffs to poison oak—will also be needed throughout thousands of square miles of wildlands. . . . This raises the specter of wilderness areas blighted with guardrails and warning signs, or, worse yet, "wildlands" that are sanitized for the visitor's protection.[130]

In March 1996, a majority of California voters endorsed the preservation of "unsanitized" wildness by rejecting Proposition 197. The mountain lion referendum, originally envisioned by the right as a wedge issue and an integral part of Governor Wilson's tough "law and order" agenda, became instead a major victory for a wilderness coalition led by the Sierra Club and the Mountain Lion Foundation. Leslie and his supporters were singularly unsuccessful in convincing the electorate that seasonal trophy hunting would be effective in removing dangerous animals. The lions, moreover, showed exemplary self-interest and political discipline by refraining from attacking or eating any voters during the final phase of the campaign. National media attention only made them into celebrities.

The defeat of Proposition 197 temporarily defused the "predator crisis" as a political issue, but the underlying ecological tensions between humans and large carnivores remain. Mountain lion sightings in populated areas continue to increase, while coyotes adapt in ever larger numbers to the pet-and-garbage ecology of the suburbs.[131] Attacks by black bears, meanwhile, have raised the specter of a "Yellowstone syndrome" in the San Gabriel and San Bernardino Mountains—"deviant" behavior by a majority of bears leading to their piecemeal elimination and eventual extinction.[132]

At the same time, residential subdivisions continue to push ever deeper into the chaparral belt from all sides, further fragmenting predator habitats. Coyote survival is not in question, but the much smaller local cougar populations depend on tenuous wildlife corridors, linking major mountain and foothill habitats, to maintain minimal thresholds of genetic diversity. If these corridors are severed, as happened in the San Joaquin Hills above Laguna Beach in the late 1970s, isolated mountain lion populations can quickly die off. (The San Joaquin cougars were extinct by the early 1990s.) This puts the recent mountain lion "population boom" (if Fish and Game Commission figures can be believed) in a different light: short-term population increase may belie an erosion of ecological conditions essential to long-term survival.[133]

Troubling questions also persist about predator, and especially mountain lion, reactions to the increasing stresses of urbanization. If the opponents of Proposition 197 had logic and science on their side, they nonetheless fudged certain crucial issues in their election literature. Cougar attacks, for example, may still be rare, but their increase has been nothing short of explosive, a trend not at all predictable from past records. Indeed, if an anomalous incident in 1909 involving a rabid cougar is set aside, *all* mountain lion attacks in twentieth-century California have occurred since 1985, two-thirds of them in the heavily urbanized southern counties. Moreover, these attacks seem independent of such traditional explanations for cougar aggression as disease, weakness, and immaturity. Neither statistics nor hunting lore explicate current behavior. As Mark Palmer, executive director of the Mountain Lion Foundation, conceded after the killing of Iris Kenna, "Something weird is happening at Cuyamaca."[134]

In fact, as leading cougar researchers like Maurice Hornocker and Paul Beier acknowledge, lions remain fundamentally mysterious animals. Serious scientific study of *Felis concolor,* based on long-term observation of telemetered populations, only began in the 1980s, and many basic aspects of its behavior remain unknown; it is not even clear, for example, how large a deer population must be to support a lion population of a particular size. Without such knowledge as a foundation, cougar responses to environmental changes cannot be anticipated—certainly not when "the cougar's 'qualitative environment,' " as Beier told me, "is undergoing radical and unpredictable changes that exceed anything in the historical record."[135]

Can environmental instability on this scale produce drastic and abiding changes in animal behavior? This is another vital question that the Proposition 197 debate failed to address. Most of the popular literature about large carnivores like bears, wolves, and big cats assumes an inflexibly normative pattern of adaptation, interrupted here and there by outbreaks of "deviant" or "problem" behavior. Yet this is essentially the same epistemology that for generations has produced such disastrous results in application to social problems like crime and deliquency. But current research in animal ethology, if not in criminology, now embraces "nonlinear" behavioral models that incorporate elements of chaos theory. There is a growing recognition that even small environmental fluctuations, if they occur at certain "thresholds," can sometimes produce "behavioral catastrophes" in animal populations. To borrow an example from Stephen Budiansky, the writer who has done most to publicize the anti-Newtonian turn in ecological research, predator response to changing prey abundance may sometimes take the form of an abrupt shift rather than an incremental adjustment.

> Suddenly, a critical point is reached; beyond that point the smallest additional change in prey abundance triggers a total flip-flop in the predator's behavior. A predator that has been a total specialist, feeding on a single prey species, will abruptly shift to opportunistic behavior.[136]

Coyotes are paradigmatic flip-floppers. They are the textbook example of a protean, "unfinished" species that is capable of rapidly altering its habits and diet to exploit new opportunities or to survive unexpected crises. A population of urban coyotes in Los Angeles's Griffith Park, for example, has been observed in continuous behavioral improvisation over the course of decades. In the 1960s the coyotes replaced their staple wild rodent and rabbit cuisine with exotic birds and mammals pilfered from the old Los Angeles Zoo. When the zoo animals were rehoused in more secure quarters, the coyotes quickly learned how to topple trash cans to retrieve picnic leftovers. As their population expanded, so did the radius and boldness of their foraging. Loping down Hollywood and Toluca Lake sidewalks in broad daylight, as they search for garbage, house pets, and occasional handouts, the brazen coyotes are now an integral part of the street scene.[137]

Mountain lions, however unlikely as street hipsters, may also be less hardwired and more polymorphous in their behavior than previously assumed. Certainly, their unexpected survival in the face of state and federal extermination campaigns suggests an inherent mutability. In that case, the Descanso and Pasadena attacks may be the alarm bells warning us that a "critical point" has been reached. What we are witnessing, then, may be nothing less than a behavioral quantum jump: the emergence of nonlinear lions with a lusty appetite for slow, soft animals in spandex.

6. PLAGUE SQUIRRELS

The microbe is nothing; the terrain is everything.
Pasteur on his deathbed

Mountain lions, like grizzlies, have the charisma of wild power to make them natural symbols of fear and sublimity. Yet the small, ordinary mammals of the chaparral belt—vectors rather than predators— pose far graver threats to human life. Those punctilious night visitors to so many suburban yards—skunks—are the principal hosts of rabies in Southern California, while the deer mouse population has recently been shown to harbor the deadly hantavirus pulmonary syndrome that caused 32 deaths and widespread panic in the Four Corners region of the Southwest in 1993.[138] Opossum fleas are responsible for periodic outbreaks of murine typhus among residents of the San Gabriel foothills, while many Malibu residents believe that deer ticks, which also burrow in rodents, are currently causing an epidemic of Lyme disease in their community, although public health officials are more skeptical about the scale of infection.[139] But the most dangerous animal of all is perhaps the most charming: the ubiquitous ground squirrel *Spermophilus beecheyi.* It has killed many times more Californians in the twentieth century than all large carnivores combined.

Although their normal diet is acorns and seeds, ground squirrels, along with pigeons, crows, and coyotes, have become voracious scavengers of Southern California campsites, playgrounds, and picnic areas. According to one naturalist, they have an inordinate fondness for "potato chips, corn chips, and cheese puffs."[140] They have prospered, accordingly, from the weekend and vacation overcrowding of local foothill recreational areas. Unlike their distant cousins, rats, ground squirrels are irresistibly attractive to humans, especially small children, and this constant intimacy generates myriad opportunities for the transmission of the deadly bacilli engorged in the bellies of their fleas. The California ground squirrel is one of the earth's most important biological reservoirs for the bubonic plague, the Black Death.[141]

Like a pilot light in a furnace, the plague bacterium, *Yersinia pestis,* burns quietly in the squirrel population, waiting for the right environmental conditions to suddenly burst again into conflagration. The particular strain of plague carried by the squirrels probably originated in China in the second half of the nineteenth century and raced around the world for 40 years, killing more than 13 million people in 52 countries. It then retreated into dormancy as a flea-rodent epizootic that in the Western Hemisphere is confined to the American West (especially Southern California and the Four Corners area), the Andes (where it may also be transmitted by human fleas), and northeast Brazil. If most Southern Californians are oblivious to the present-day plague hazard in their parks and playgrounds, that is in part because they are ignorant of the plague epidemics that caused so much political controversy and racial turmoil in early-twentieth-century San Francisco, Oakland, and Los Angeles.

The history of this "third plague pandemic," as it is called, can be briefly summarized. Officially, a "pandemic" is a deadly epidemic that is persistent in time (up to centuries in duration) and continental or global in scope. Justinian's plague, which halved the population of the Mediterranean world during the apocalyptic second half of the sixth century, was the first recorded pandemic. Procopius characterized it as the "pestilence by which the whole human race came near to being annihilated." The second pandemic was the Black Death of the fourteenth century, which one French historian has described as the "biological equivalent of nuclear war." In Western Europe it killed more than a quarter of the population and erupted episodically for more than three hundred years.[142]

The third pandemic broke out in the late 1860s in the war-torn southern Chinese province of Yunnan near the Burmese border. Infected rodent populations were dispersed by the turbulent movement of armies and refugees. By 1894, plague had killed 180,000 people in Canton alone and was entrenched in the port of Hong Kong. Plague rats stowed away in cargo holds disseminated the pandemic along all the major shipping routes.[143] The resulting port quarantines briefly threatened the structure of world trade, but protégés of Pasteur and Koch were able to crack the 1,500-year-old mystery of the disease: identifying the rod-shaped bacillus in 1894 and producing the first antiserum in 1896. The crucial role of rat fleas was proposed by another researcher two years later. The benefit of these breakthroughs, however, was largely denied to poor colonial subjects. In India alone, the plague slaughtered 12 million people between 1898 and 1928, with 1.3 million dying in the single year of 1907. The iron-fisted military response of the Raj was primarily designed to protect British residents from the plague-infested masses. Extensive search-and-detention operations in poorer villages and urban neighborhoods sparked widespread rioting and stimulated the emergence of modern Indian nationalism.[144]

In Hawaii and California, the arrival of the plague coincided with rising "Yellow Peril" agitation and provided a public health pretext for repressive measures against the Chinese community. Thus, on 20 January 1900, one month after the first plague case was identified in Honolulu, Chinatown was cordoned off by police and Anglo vigilantes and burnt to the ground. The five thousand people left homeless by the fire were then interned in military detention camps. Anti-Chinese demagogues on the mainland began to advocate the "Honolulu fire" as the solution to their own "Oriental problem,"* while Jack London penned a genocidal short story that celebrated the Western powers' deliberate employment of bubonic plague to depopulate China.[145]

Two months later, a young public health physician diagnosed plague from the grotesquely swollen lymph nodes, or buboes (hence, "bubonic"), of a body found in the basement of a cheap Chinatown hotel in San Francisco. The Board of Health, supported by the federal Marine Hospital Service, immediately ordered the police to seal off the 18 tenement blocks, congested with 25,000 people, that formed the heart of Chinatown. The quarantine polarized the city's medical community, press, and political leadership. In his flagship papers, the *San Francisco Examiner* and the *New York Journal,* William Randolph Hearst supported the Board of Health's draconian measures and greeted the Black Plague's arrival at the Golden Gate with apocalyptic headlines and quotations from Daniel Defoe's *Journal of the Plague Year.* Hearst's sensationalism infuriated the business elite on Montgomery Street, and the rival *San Francisco Bulletin* was soon roaring: "Our City Blacklisted All Over America as a Plague-Ridden Spot; Randolph Hearst of the *Examiner* Floods East-

---

* Citing the Honolulu precedent, the Orange County city of Santa Ana in 1906 used a leprosy scare to force the evacuation of their local Chinese community, then burned their homes and businesses to the ground.

ern Cities with Gross Libel on San Francisco." Governor Henry Gage bowed to anti-quarantine sentiment and established an investigating committee, exclusively composed of physicians for Chinatown's Six Companies, who denounced the plague diagnoses as incompetent, even fraudulent.[146]

As one member after another of the besieged Board of Health was forced to resign in the face of *Bulletin* accusations that they were "perpetrators of the greatest crime that has ever been committed against the city," the plague continued to make headway in the Chinatown tenements. It took fully two years and 119 deaths, along with the spread of the pestilence to Mexico and the subsequent closure of its Pacific ports to California shipping, before San Francisco's major business organizations finally endorsed a comprehensive anti-rat campaign in Chinatown.[147]

Before the project had much effect, however, the great 1906 earthquake and fire dispersed plague-infected rodents throughout the ruins of the city. Although white residents had previously been reassured that "the plague has a strong preference for yellow meat," a flare-up that began in May 1907 was concentrated in Caucasian neighborhoods, where 89 eventually died. With fashionable Nob Hill in peril, the official reaction to this new outbreak was a crash program, involving four hundred inspectors and poisoners, to "rat-proof" the entire peninsula. In the course of the campaign, which killed a million rats, 1,713 houses in poor areas were destroyed—the equivalent of a second earthquake.[148]

In 1908, while San Francisco was still exterminating rats, the plague suddenly appeared across the bay in Oakland and rural parts of Alameda and Contra Costa Counties, where it continued to claim victims in episodic outbursts until 1925. Struck by the fact that a number of the first victims had recently eaten squirrel meat, U.S. Public Health Service researchers were able to verify the lethal bacilli in squirrels collected from widely separated areas of the East Bay. The discovery of squirrel-borne plague also solved the mystery of three earlier plague deaths in Contra Costa County, as well as the

The plague reappears in San Francisco

death of a little Los Angeles boy who had been bitten by a ground squirrel in August 1908.[149] The news that plague had "jumped" from rats to squirrels (or, more precisely, from rat fleas to squirrel fleas) caused national alarm. Experts predicted that the Black Death might now threaten the entire nation through relays of infected wild rodents.

The American Medical Association's official journal, *American Medicine,* warning of a potential continental epidemic with "an appalling number of deaths," attacked San Francisco authorities for the "crime" of letting the plague escape. Disregarding the responsibility of the city's business elites for sabotaging the first quarantine, however, the magazine blamed the "ignorant working classes," and, by implication, universal suffrage, for the election of a malfeasant city hall incapable of halting the epidemic:

> All men are not equal, and low morality is generally a result of low mentality. English workingmen for generations refused to be represented by any one except a "gentleman." . . . They are now sending their own representatives, and it is hoped the experiment will turn out better than in San Francisco, a city which . . . must accept the contempt of the civilized world for permitting plague to enter the country and create a menacing situation which may require hundreds of millions of dollars, if the infected ground squirrels are not promptly destroyed.[150]

Fortunately, the lightning swift advance of the rodent plague so feared by *American Medicine* failed to occur, and the epizootic was confined to California until the mid-1930s.* On the other hand, a massive campaign launched by the Public Health Service in 1908 to create "squirrel-free zones" around major California cities was a failure. Premature declarations of victory in 1917 were followed by discoveries of diseased animals near major urban areas, and then in 1919 by an epidemic of the hypervirulent pneumonic form of the plague in Oakland which took 13 lives. Scientists again confirmed that a ground squirrel, not a rat, was the source of the initial infection.[152] Then, in the fall of 1924, *Yersinia pestis* finally arrived in Los Angeles—a city that had been braced for plague ever since the original San Francisco outbreak in 1900. Health officials and housing reformers had long feared that the pestilence would someday gain a foothold in a rat-infested Mexican shantytown down the street from Los Angeles's old plaza. This was indeed where Jesus Lajun, a laborer on the streetcar system, came home ill on the second day of October.[153]

---

* In 1935 plague was detected among ground squirrels in Oregon and Montana; the next year among wood rats in Nevada and Utah; and, finally, in 1938, among prairie dogs in New Mexico.[151]

From plague to pogrom: burning a Mexican village near downtown Los Angeles (1924)

His case was originally confused with the flu but was probably bubonic plague. However, by the time the pathogen killed his daughter two days later, it had already turned into the greatly feared pneumonic strain which can spread from one human to another. The focus of official concern soon shifted half a block away, to a tidy Victorian cottage which would soon be renamed the "death house." Here, between 19 October and 8 November, the plague killed 9 members of the Sarmarano family and 21 of their visitors, friends, and neighbors. City officials, meanwhile, had imposed "cubicle isolation," the equivalent of house arrest, on the 2,500 Spanish-speaking residents of the eight-block neighborhood.[154] The quarantine was later extended to four other Mexican areas, including the Belvedere district just outside the city line. Four hundred burly "quarantine guards," recruited from unemployed world war veterans, accompanied the poison squads as they ripped the sides off homes and jacked them above their foundations to get at rats. No less than 2,500 homes were badly damaged or destroyed, without compensation, in the course of this brutal "sanitation campaign."[155]

As in San Francisco, racial intolerance combined with unseemly rivalries between health officials and bitter denunciations of the quarantine by local boosters, who discerned a plot to "ruin Los Angeles." At the same time, an important scientific drama was taking place. In a staggering effort, more than eight million baited traps had been placed around Los Angeles County, and 130,000 dead squirrels and rats were then examined by forensic technicians. As the locations with heavy numbers of infected rodents were carefully plotted on a wall map of the county, a coherent ecological pattern began to emerge. Although no one could be completely certain, the plague appeared to have been transmitted from central California, possibly years before, through infected ground squirrel populations, then passed on to rats around Los Angeles's numerous hog farms where populations of both rodents intermingled. Corroborating earlier findings in the East Bay, Los Angeles medical officers noted that "rats and ground squirrels live in intimate contact, frequently occupying the same burrows; also that rat fleas infest the ground squirrel, as do the ground squirrel fleas infest the rat."[156]

THE BLACK DEATH IN CALIFORNIA, 1900–1925

Years	Location	Cases	Deaths	Vector
1900–1904	San Francisco	121	113	Rats
1903–1909	Contra Costa County	4	2	Squirrels
1907	San Francisco	160	78	Rats
1909	Oakland	16	8	Squirrels
1909	Los Angeles	1	0	Squirrels
1910–14	East Bay	13	4	Squirrels
1915–24	East Bay	3	3	Squirrels
*1919	Oakland	14	13	Squirrels
1920–24	Central California	4	2	Squirrels
*1924–25	Los Angeles	39	34	Squirrels/rats

*Pneumonic plague.
Source: Adapted from California, State Board of Health, *Pneumonic Plague: Report of an Outbreak at Los Angeles, California, October–November 1924,* Special Bulletin 46 (Sacramento, 1925), p. 28.

The 1924–25 Los Angeles epidemic, which Caltech historian William Deverell believes killed at least 40 people, was the last major outbreak of the pneumonic plague in the United States, and the investigation of its complex ecology and multivector mode of transmission was displaced by other public health priorities. The plague, of course, did not disappear; it merely went to sleep. From time to time, bubonic cases would arise and, if not promptly treated with tetracycline, would contribute a fatality or two to California's plague record. "The most deadly microorganisms," one expert emphasizes, "have infinite patience. It is almost as if the plague is waiting for our memory to fail. And every so often it ventures out to test the defenses."[157]

These shows of pestilential force, moreover, have a definite logic. Most researchers now accept that there are powerful linkages between the climate-regulated supply of rodent food (acorns, pine nuts, etc.), periodic spikes in rodent populations (like in Taft in 1926), and the potential transmission of rodent-borne diseases, like plague and hantavirus, to urban areas. Thus, in the spring of 1995, following several wet winters and the death of a Kern County man from pneumonic plague, public health authorities began nervously monitoring squirrel populations near major recreational centers in the San Gabriel and San Bernardino Mountains. In August they quarantined several mountain campgrounds and a popular picnic area. Half of the trapped squirrels from those areas had tested positive for plague, as had one camper's dog.[158] Later that fall, San Bernardino County health officials were alarmed when plague-infected squirrels were discovered in a Fontana park about 500 yards from a residential subdivision.[159]

Yersinia pestis reemerged during the spring and summer of 1996. By the eve of the long Fourth of July weekend, authorities were racing to close heavily used picnic sites in Tujunga Canyon, on the eastern flank of the San Fernando Valley. Two months later, the discovery of more infected squirrels forced the closure of campgrounds throughout the popular Big Bear area. "There is no reason to be paranoid," cautioned one entomologist, "but the public should be concerned."[160]

Exactly how "concerned," of course, is a big question. Certainly, the ecological prerequisites for an urban epidemic still exist. Despite sporadic extermination campaigns, ground squirrel populations— adapted to any open, grassy habitat—are thriving on junk food diets in parks and recreation areas. So, too, are big-city rats. In Los Angeles, rats even fall from the sky on occasion. (Actually, they knock each other out of the crown fronds of palm trees.) Hollywood is notorious for its acrobatic roof rats (*Rattus rattus*), as well as its back-alley sewer rats (*Rattus norvegicus*). Los Angeles's multitudes of free-ranging dogs, meanwhile, are the rats' accomplices: rummaging through garbage and leaving it strewn for rats to eat. (Rats also feed on the 50,000 tons of dog feces generated every year in Los Angeles.)* And rat-infested tenements are far more numerous and widespread today than they were in the much smaller Los Angeles of 1924.

If plague were to return for a second act early in the twenty-first century, it would be challenged by a powerful arsenal of antibiotic weapons. With prompt treatment, especially with streptomycin, it is estimated that no more than 15 percent of plague cases would prove fatal. Medical self-confidence, however, is built on the assumption that the plague bacillus has stopped evolving. As Charles Gregg emphasized in a 1978 study, this may be a fatal underestimation of the genus *Yersinia*'s cunning. "The more that modern antimicrobial drugs are used to combat serious plague infection and protect the contacts of plague victims," he warned, "the more likely it becomes that a multiple drug-resistant strain will arise." Plague baccilli, as laboratory experiments have repeatedly demonstrated, can also "borrow" drug-resistant genes from common bacteria like the *E. coli* that populate the human gut.[162]

The most recent plague outbreaks suggest that some kind of mutation—with or without human assistance—may already be under way. The 1994 Surat epidemic, for example, had so many puzzling features that Indian authorities hypothesized that it was caused by an engineered strain that had escaped from a former Soviet biowarfare laboratory. In California, meanwhile, epidemiologists are seeing an increased frequency of isolated outbreaks of pneumonic plague, as in

---

* In his study of the ecology of stray dogs, Alan Beck suggests that strays "might be used as indicators of environmental deterioration, since their presence is generally correlated with excessive garbage, which in turn is presumably correlated with rat density."[161]

a 1984 case in eastern Los Angeles County and the 1995 fatality in Kern County, that indicate the possible emergence of a "neo-plague." In any event, residents of Los Angeles's wild edge would be best advised to give ground squirrels, those adorable little carriers of humanity's most deadly scourge, a wide berth.[163]

7. LAND OF HONEY

Gimme your honey, or your wife.

"Killer Beez" (John Belushi)

Now we come to the place where natural history intersects with Holly-wood nightmares. Los Angeles will soon become the first great Northern Hemisphere city to be colonized by the Africanized honeybee. Those "killer bees," like their predecessor from South America, the opossum, are irresistible immigrants, moving implacably northward as far as the climate will suit their hot-blooded temperament. Agricultural officials predict that they will quickly take over all the wild hives in the state.[164] Although the bees do not deserve the apocalyptic reputation they have won in the popular imagination, they are considerably more dangerous than the soothing image ("just leave them alone, and they will leave you alone") presented by county agricultural agents and vector control officials trying to reassure an anxious public. Moreover, they are ineradicable and radically unpredictable. Far more than mountain lions or coyotes, they are certain to test Los Angeles's tolerance of wild nature at its doorstep.

The first African bees—a tropical race or subspecies of the honey-bee *Apis mellifera*—were imported to Brazil from the Transvaal in 1956 by Brazilian geneticist Warwick Kerr in the hope of boosting local honey production. He believed that their hyperaggressiveness would be moderated by breeding with European bees. Instead, Africanized escapees formed the nucleus of a feral population that exploded into its new ecological niche.* In 30 years, 26 renegade queens produced more than 100 million individual colonies.[165]

Moving north 100 to 300 miles each year, the bees reached Colombia in 1980 and Panama in 1982. As panicky American officials debated how to keep them south of the border, they considered a range of loony schemes. These included proposals to establish a deadly radiation kill zone across Panama with tactical nuclear weapons, to create a 50-mile-wide no-man's-land sown with the toxic chemical malathion, or to establish a 100-foot-high wall of gas-fueled flames along the north bank of the Panama Canal. Finally, the United States and Mexico joined together in 1989 to build a pesticidal Maginot Line across southern Mexico. It was an expensive debacle. In October 1990 a swarm crossed the Rio Grande near Hidalgo, Texas. The first attack on a human took place seven months later, and south Texas was placed under a quarantine restricting the movement of commercial hives.[166]

Over the next four years, the bees finished colonizing Texas and began to fan out over the other Southwest states. On 24 October 1994, incredulous guards discovered an Africanized nest at Chuckwalla Valley State Prison near Blythe, on the California side of the Colorado River. ("Poor things," sympathized a waitress at a nearby truck stop. "It's 150 miles from anywhere, 100 miles from nowhere and two feet from hell.")[167] Five months later, another swarm was found atop a "no trespassing" sign at an elementary school in Heber, a farm hamlet in Imperial County.[168] In October 1995, after killing many animals in the Mesa area, 35 miles east of Phoenix, the bees stung an elderly woman more than a thousand times. "At the hospital, a nurse used a plastic card to flick the stingers out of [the woman's] skin. A relative said the stingers littered the floor like cigarette ashes." Doctors were horrified to find scores of attackers still

---

* Kerr, a distinguished scientist and resolute opponent of Brazil's military dictatorship in the 1960s, was scapegoated by the government as the "Doctor Frankenstein" responsible for the bee plague and ensuing deaths.

writhing inside her mouth and nasal passage. A month after the woman's death, bees attacked two tree trimmers clearing limbs from a power pylon outside of Blythe. One terrified worker described how the swarm continued to pursue them down a frontage road hundreds of yards from their truck.[169]

In the deserts southeast of Los Angeles, the diurnal bees quickly established an unusual condominium with nocturnal cougars. According to Suzanne Goode, an ecologist for the state park system, one species slakes its thirst while the other satisfies its craving for mutton. "The African bees are hopscotching across the Anza Borrego Desert by using wildlife guzzlers [water feeders] as oases. These guzzlers were originally installed to save endangered bighorn sheep, whose water sources have been dried up by invading tamarisk plants. After innumerable attacks by the African bees, the sheep have adapted to their presence by going to the guzzlers at night, only to be devoured by waiting mountain lions."[170]

With the bees established as far west as the Palm Springs area, their arrival in the suburbs of Los Angeles is not only inevitable but overdue. Indeed, anxiety is already high, and the misidentification of European bees as killer bees has already incited several instances of mass hysteria.* "It's like we're dressed up for the party, but the guest of honor is late," says Dr. Jack Hazelrigg, chief entomologist and manager for the Greater Los Angeles County Vector Control District. Hazelrigg emphasizes that Southern California's newest immigrants are a threat that must be tolerated. "We have no choice. Forty years of containment efforts have failed. Africanized honeybees cannot be eradicated or quarantined. Their range will expand to natural climate limits." Most authorities expect that the bees' West Coast invasion will stop around the year 2000 somewhere in southern Oregon. (Sweeping up from Texas through the Southeast, they may eventually reach the Carolinas on the Atlantic seaboard.)[172]

---

* When a queen bee landed on their picnic table, for example, all the employees of a firm in Anaheim near Disneyland locked themselves inside their factory until fire officials managed to convince them that it was safe to come out.[171]

Welcome to
California:
a prison guard holds
dead African bees

By any standard, the bees have proved a stunning ecological success. Despite the popular misconception that they are larger and more menacing in appearance, Africanized bees are virtually indistinguishable from the friendly European bees in everyone's backyard. Originating in Asia several million years ago, *Apis mellifera* evolved into distinct subspecies as it adapted to the contrasting challenges of tropical and temperate latitudes. To cope with cold winters, for instance, European bees invest most of their energy in nest building and honey production. Sun-kissed African bees, on the other hand, collect less honey and build only rudimentary nests. Their energy instead is channeled into frenetic reproduction and migration. ("Work harder and die younger," says one expert.) Whereas a European hive may divide only once or twice in a season, an Africanized colony and its offspring can generate 64 separate swarms.[173]

African ferocity, by the same token, is a Darwinian response to higher rates of predation by insects and mammals. Indeed, it is probably in part a "man-made" trait arising out of hundreds of thousands of years of honey gathering by humans and their hominid ancestors. It is, in any case, a singularly effective tactic. "With five times as many guards in their nest as Europeans, half the [African-ized] population pours out of the hive at a rate three times greater than Europeans, [inflicting] eight- to ten-times more stings."[174] The provocation need only be trivial: killer bees are enraged by a broad spectrum of stimuli including vibrations, loud noises (espe-cially lawnmowers and chain saws), and even dark colors. Their response is an explosion of sheer fury unrivaled in nature. In 1986 a young botantist in Costa Rica who accidentally stumbled over a nest was stung eight thousand times. Indeed, few people can sur-vive more than a dozen stings without some kind of systemic re-action: fainting, abdominal pain, nausea, or respiratory collapse (anaphylaxis).[175]

In an urban setting the danger is magnified by the Africanized bees' penchant for building nests in almost any structure. Typical apiaries include old tires, junk cars, woodpiles, empty oil drums, patio awnings, and air-conditioning ducts. Swarms also systemati-cally invade European hives, killing the old queens and installing their own usurpers. After a few rounds of hyperactive mating, the local honeybee population becomes genetically Africanized and far more belligerent. This succession has been made even easier by the tracheal and varroa mite epidemics, combined with unusually cold winters, that have devastated the European bee population of the United States. In vast sections of the country, including much of Cal-ifornia (the leading honey-producing state), free-ranging Europeans are now extinct, and commercial hives have suffered drastic declines. Africanized colonies, on the other hand, have greater (pos-sibly genetic) resistance to mites and a correspondingly higher sur-vival rate. Infection has only accelerated their conquest of the southern tier of American states.[176]

In the 1977 B-movie classic *The Swarm,* the entire Pentagon, nukes and all, is mobilized against a deadly cyclone of killer bees threatening to pollinate Houston. But Los Angeles–area residents should not expect President Clinton to bring troops home from Bosnia or the Gulf to battle bees in Sherman Oaks or Hawaiian Gardens. In the era of shrinking government, all that stands between the nuclear family and the winged hordes is Jack Hazelrigg's tiny, cash-strapped agency. Since its formation during an encephalitis epidemic in 1952 that killed 50 people, the Southeast Mosquito Abatement District (as it was then called) has diligently toiled to protect the city of Los Angeles and 26 adjacent communities from mosquito-borne diseases.[177] Recently rechristened the Vector Control District, the 28-person agency now occupies the front line against both the Africanized bee and deadly exotic diseases, like dengue and hemorrhagic fevers, that may be introduced by infected alien mosquitos. It is the entomological version of the Border Control, without the latter's huge budget.[178]

Indeed, Los Angeles's anti-bee armada may be viewed any weekday, parked in front of the district's headquarters on a grimy industrial street in the blue-collar suburb of South Gate: four pickup trucks, each mounted with spray guns, each with "Africanized Honey Bee Suppression Unit" stenciled on its side. In addition there are blue buckets for capturing swarms ("Bees love blue," according to Hazelrigg) and dozens of white containers—"bee traps"—otherwise used for takeout Chinese food. That's it: no sci-fi superlasers or malathion-spewing helicopters. The district's entire thousand-square-mile Africanized bee program has been financed with a $200,000 annual grant and the hiring of two additional employees.

Since the fiasco in Mexico, the federal government has pulled out of the front lines of the bee war, and localities are left to their own devices. In the Los Angeles area, a countywide Africanized Bee Task-force has devised a bare-bones defensive plan against the invading insects. If humans or their pets are attacked, local firefighters will use fire-retardant foam to rescue victims. Then, according to the script, vector control will move in with soapy water and their chow mein traps to mop up the angry survivors. Hazelrigg's crews will also respond to migrating swarms and nests on public property. Should the bees decide to build a cozy home in a residential garage or fireplace, residents will be solely responsible for their eviction. The county claims that it does not have the present resources to undertake systematic bee abatement, if such a thing is even feasible. Instead, homeowners, according to their finances, will have to rely on private pest control firms or else devise their own ad hoc solutions. The county coroner will, however, promptly remove the bodies of foolish, do-it-yourself exterminators.*

In an interview, Hazelrigg said that his greatest worry is not the bees but the media-induced hysteria that inevitably will follow the first serious attacks. "Past experience suggests that it takes the public about two years to overcome its panic and accept the bees as an ordinary hazard, like lightning or snakebites."[180] But are the bees only an ordinary hazard? The experience of urban Latin America is chastening. In 1988–89, for example, Managua had six hundred serious attacks, and Venezuelan cities report dozens of deaths each year. In Mexico, 175 people have been killed by the bees in the past decade. It is uncertain how the famous Southern California lifestyle would adapt to this level of apiarian aggression, or how tourists would respond to bee attacks at Disneyland or Universal Studios.

The magnitude of hazard, of course, will depend on how well the Africanized bees prosper in their new home. In preferred terrains, feral populations build up rapidly, and it is not uncommon to find densities of 20 or more wild colonies per square mile.[181] Here it is possible to quote the incomparable authority of John Muir, who loved to watch the spring swarms harvesting honey in the foothills above Pasadena. "California," he enthused, "is still, as far as I know, the best of all the beelands of the world."[182]

---

* In California, state and local agencies offer uniform advice in the event of an encounter with Africanized bees: "Get away quickly. While running away, try to protect face and eyes as much as possible." It helps to be a track star since, as the official literature fails to point out, enraged Africanized bees will pursue victims for as far as a kilometer. In southern Africa people don't run, they roll on the ground, throwing up clouds of dust or sand to protect themselves against the bees.[179]

8. MONSTERS AND MESSIAHS

Perhaps the goatsucker is Nature's revenge for what we have done to the environment.

Scientist in Mexico (1996)

The wild is predator. It is the unexpected and the unpredictable. It is also dream. The Tong-va of Los Angeles, like other first peoples, made no ontological distinction between everyday animals and those that appeared only in dreams or at the end of vision quests. Their bestiary, for example, encompassed the *nunas-i-s,* dreaded creatures who survived from the time of the Ancestors, like the monster scorpion dwelling in a cave at the eponymous Rancho El Escorpion in the west San Fernando Valley, or the great inland whale that lived in Big Bear Lake (in Tong-van, "the lake that cries") high in the San Bernardino Mountains. There were also different species of were-animals—were-cougars, were-bears, were-sealions, and so on—in whom masqueraded the spirits of the most powerful shamans.[183]

Of course, the cougar that found its way onto the cover of the *Los Angeles Times* is not necessarily less imaginary than a giant cave scorpion or a mountain whale. Our bestiaries, deprived of the Tong-vas' continuous, intimate, and deep knowledge of their fauna, come closer to two-dimensional cartoons based on random encounters and behavioralist clichés. Too often, wildness is equated with urban disorder, and wild animals end up as the symbolic equivalents of street criminals; or conversely, they acquire all the psychopathic connotations of sentimentalized pets or surrogate people. The Otherness of wild animals is the gestalt which we are constantly refashioning in the image of our own urban confusion and alienation. Where nature is most opaquely unknowable, as in the "character" of animals, we intensely crave the comfort of anthropomorphic definition and categorization. And where it is the human world that threatens, this impulse is mirrored in our desire to give our fears shape: as beasts.

Bestiaries, by definition, are hierarchies of allegorical fauna (including familiar species in their double role as social symbols) crowned by monsters.[184] And monsters, by embodying inchoate fears in concrete forms, are sometimes messiahs of consolation.

If Los Angeles's bad dreams in recent years have conjured monsters out of its own wild periphery, they have also laid out a welcome mat for monstrous tourists. In early July 1996, for example, the famous goat-sucking vampire from Puerto Rico, El Chupacabra, took up residence in the Latino barrio of Pacoima, in the northwest San Fernando Valley. A hybrid fad, midway between the hula hoop and the Devil in Salem, mass culture and mass hysteria, the Chupacabra was simultaneously an avatar of poor people's deepest fears and an exuberant, tongue-in-cheek emblem of Latino cultural populism. I am not sure that the notoriously ill-tempered creature, with its bottomless appetite for *cabra, gallina,* and *pato* (not to mention the odd Doberman pinscher or two), would enjoy being called a "messiah," but it certainly has been a lightning rod for immigrant anxiety. In a vast, strange metropolis—sometimes more desolate than a desert and more dangerous than a jungle—the Chupacabra has brought the reassurance of familiar monstrosity. For rural immigrants, it is also a telluric symbol of the power of the countryside over the city.

Like Southern California's parched coyotes during the early 1990s, the Chupacabra was brought out of the hills and into the city by drought. Both in Puerto Rico, where the "goatsucker" first appeared in the town of Canovanas, 20 miles east of San Juan, in December 1994, and in northern Mexico, where scores of incidents were reported throughout 1996, there is good reason to credit local claims of a dramatic increase in mysterious attacks on livestock and pets. Puerto Rico was recovering from two years of drought and massive hurricane damage, while northern Mexico, together with the U.S. Southwest, had been suffering through the driest period since the dust bowl era of the 1930s. In both cases, as Puerto Rican veterinarians and Mexican agricultural officials demonstrated in detailed investigations, there was an unusual, drought-related hike in the number and ferocity of wild dog and coyote attacks. (In Sinaloa, a zoological task force blamed pollution rather than drought: "There's no goatsucker, but pollution is now so bad that it's driving ordinary animals mad, giving them the behavioral trappings of crazed alien creatures.")[185]

From the beginning, however, folk culture was suspicious of "expert" explanations—"Who, after all, has ever seen a dog kill a goat, like that?"—and preferred the agency of monsters and vampires. Indeed, the Chupacabra may be an echo of the mythic bestiary of the Tainos, Puerto Rico's extinct aboriginal culture. At any event, its image underwent a fascinating evolution as sightings passed from the oral grapevine into the Spanish-speaking tabloid press, then into primetime tabloid television, before a final apotheosis as an episode of *The X-Files*. Thus the original witness at Canovanas described an apparition "just like the Devil . . . 4 or 5 feet tall with red eyes and a hideous forked tongue." A month later the Chupacabra grew a horn, which a mechanic, attacked by the creature just before Christmas 1995, amended to long, spiked hair or fur. Its body was portrayed as a hideous combination of rat and kangaroo.[186] After the Chupacabra's immigration to Mexico in early 1996, however, its image was remolded yet again, as the bugged-eye rat face and punk rocker hairstyle were replaced by bat wings and a space alien's head. In Puerto Rico, there had been intense speculation that the Chupacabra was a mascot or pet left behind by extraterrestrial visitors; now, according to Mexican UFO experts, there was "proof" that the Chupacabra was ET himself.[187]

The Mexican left, on the other hand, declared that the Chupacabra was actually Carlos Salinas de Gortari, the runaway ex-president who "had sucked the blood of his country," and T-shirts with Salinas's visage, bald and big-eared, on the body of the Chupacabra soon became a popular rage. So did El Chupacabras, a masked wrestler and social activist, who began to appear regularly at some of the nearly one thousand antigovernment protests held in turbulent Mexico City during 1996. Elsewhere in Mexico, the beloved devil-rat-alien, Latino if not literally *raza,* was supplanting Mickey Mouse and the Power Rangers as popular icon: bars offered *chupacervezas,* foodstands sold *chupatacos,* and mariachis sung *chupacarridos.* The delirious embrace of *chupacabrismo* by Mexico was, first and above all, a celebration of

Chupacabra taco stand in Hollywood

the national sense of humor. Despite all the setbacks and infamies of the Salinas era, Mexico still owned its laughter. Yet, as in Puerto Rico and Florida (where a Chupacabra panic broke out in the Sweetwater district of Miami in March 1996), there was also genuine terror. Scientists, government ministers, even President Zedillo went on television to calm hysteria, while local investigators gathered irrefutable evidence of feral dog and coyote attacks on farm corrals.[188]

In Los Angeles, the Chupacabra craze was something of an antidote to the monomania of the Simpson trial. While O.J. was saturating English-language television in the late spring and summer of 1996, the Spanish-language media, dominated by the huge Univision chain, was covering Chupacabra sightings in Sinaloa and Baja California and debating whether the terror would strike in Southern California. Chicano political cartoonist Lalo Alcaraz, to be sure, had already suggested that "El Chupa"—bloated on the blood of immigrants—was currently residing in the governor's mansion in Sacramento.[189] Others, however, awaited a more prosaic monster.

In early July, two rabbits and a goat were found dead in a barnyard near Pacoima. (Pacoima may possess some kind of occult locational significance since the Virgin Mary was widely believed to have appeared in nearby Lopez Canyon in 1990.)[190] Although no one actually saw the Chupacabra, there were telltale puncture wounds on the animals' necks, and their bodies, quite vampirishly, were totally drained of blood. Some people locked themselves in their houses and refused to send their children to school. Others had trouble sleeping and were afraid to take the trash out at night.[191] The majority, however, simply chuckled: just as Los Angeles had recently acquired a first-rate *futbol* team, now it also had a genuine Chupacabra to prove its Latin-Americanity. Meanwhile, in the chaparral-covered hills above Pacoima, a pair of very well fed coyotes were howling their own delight.

THE LITERARY
DESTRUCTION OF
LOS ANGELES

A sweltering day in Los Angeles, 1962. A pretty girl ("she reminded him of well water and farm breakfasts") is absentmindedly taking off her clothes at a bus stop. The corner newsboy gawks in delight, but most passersby simply glance and continue on their way. A nerdish mathematician named Potiphar Breen comes to the rescue. As he wraps his coat around her, he explains that she is the victim of a strange epidemic of involuntary nudism known as the "Gypsy Rose virus."

It is a small omen of approaching chaos. Breen has discovered that Los Angeles is the global epicenter of a sinister convergence of pathological trends and weird anomalies. All the warning lights are beginning to flash in unison: the mercury soars, skies darken, dams creak, faults strain, and politicians wave rockets. And at this worst possible moment, suburbanites are gripped by a death wish to water their lawns.

> Billions in war bonds were now falling due; wartime marriages were reflected in the swollen peak of the Los Angeles school population. The Colorado River was at a record low and the towers in Lake Mead stood high out of the water. But Angelenos committed communal suicide by watering lawns as usual. The Metropolitan Water District commissioners tried to stop it. It fell between the stools of the police powers of fifty "sovereign" cities. The taps remained open, trickling away the life blood of the desert paradise.[1]

Epic drought is quickly followed by flood, earthquake, nuclear war, plague, a Russian invasion, and the reemergence of Atlantis. It is the ultimate cascade of catastrophe. Breen hides out in the San Gabriel Mountains with his new girlfriend, amusing himself by shooting the odd Soviet paratrooper. Then, when the worst seems over, he notices an unusually large sunspot. The sun has begun to die. . . .

So ends Robert Heinlein's tongue-in-cheek 1952 novella, "The Year of the Jackpot." In crowning Los Angeles the disaster capital of the universe, Heinlein anticipated the cornucopia of imaginary disaster to come. According to my own bibliographic research, the destruction of Los Angeles has been a central theme or image in at least 138 novels and films since 1909. More precisely, since Heinlein's heroine first took off her skirt, the city and its suburbs have been destroyed on average three times per year:

Pre-1920	2
1921–30	5
1931–40	7
1941–50	8
1951–60	16
1961–70	21
1971–80	29
1981–90	31
1990–96	19
Total	138

As the millennium approaches, the carnage may be accelerating. On multiplex screens alone, during the summer of 1996, Los Angeles was parboiled by aliens in *Independence Day* and reduced to barbarism by mega-earthquakes in both *The Crow: City of Angels* and *Escape from L.A.* One year later, reckless subway construction provoked a volcanic eruption near Farmer's Market and sent a river of molten lava down Wilshire Boulevard (*Volcano*)—all to the delight of millions of moviegoers. The City of Angels is unique, not simply in the frequency of its fictional destruction, but in the pleasure that such apocalypses provide to readers and movie audiences. The entire world seems to be rooting for Los Angeles to slide into the Pacific or be swallowed by the San Andreas fault.

1. DOOM CITY

This is so cool!
> *A typical Angeleno, in* Independence Day *(1996)*

No other city seems to excite such dark rapture. The tidal waves, killer bees, H-bombs, and viruses that occasionally annihilate Seattle, Houston, Chicago, or San Francisco produce a different kind of frisson, an enjoyment edged with horror and awe. Indeed, as one goes back further in the history of the urban disaster genre, the ghost of the romantic Sublime—beauty in the arms of terror—reappears. The destruction of London—the metropolis most persecuted in fiction between 1885 and 1940—was imagined as a horrifying spectacle, equivalent to the death of Western civilization itself. The obliteration of Los Angeles, by contrast, is often depicted as, or at least secretly experienced as, a victory *for* civilization.

Thus, in *Independence Day,* a film that Bob Dole endorsed as a model of Hollywood patriotism, devastation wreaked by aliens is represented first as tragedy (New York) and then as farce (Los Angeles). Although it could be argued, in an age of greedy suburbs and edge cities, that all traditional urban centers are equally expendable, the boiling tsunami of fire and brimstone that pours down Fifth Avenue is genuinely horrifying, consuming as it does genuine human beings. When the aliens turn to Los Angeles, however, who could identify with the caricatured mob of hippies, new agers, and gay men dancing in idiot ecstasy on a skyscraper roof to greet the extraterrestrials? There is a comic undertone of "good riddance" when kooks like these are vaporized by the earth's latest ill-mannered guests. As one of Dole's senior advisors quipped: "Millions die, but they're all liberals."[2]

Good riddance? (*Independence Day*)

The gleeful expendability of Los Angeles in the popular imagination is in no small part due to Hollywood, which, when not immolating itself, promotes its environs as the heart of darkness. No city, in fiction or film, has been more likely to figure as the icon of a really bad future (or present, for that matter). Post-apocalyptic Los Angeles, overrun by terminators, androids, and gangs, has become as much a cliché as Marlowe's mean streets or Gidget's beach party. The decay of the city's old glamor has been inverted by the entertainment industry into a new glamor of decay.

Although it risks spoiling the fun—who doesn't enjoy a slapstick apocalypse now and then?—Los Angeles's reigning status as Doom City is a phenomenon that demands clarification. The city's propensity for spectacular disaster—its "chief product" according to some postmodernists—obviously provides a quasi-realist context for its literary destruction, but environmental exceptionalism only takes us part of the way toward an explanation of why Los Angeles is the city we love to destroy. There is a deeper, Strangelovian logic to such happy holocausts.

In the pages that follow, I explore the underlying tides and currents in Los Angeles disaster fiction, emulating the heroic methods of jazz historian Gunther Schuller. In his magisterial survey of the swing era, he decided "to hear every recording of any artist, orchestra, or group that would come under discussion—and to listen systematically/chronologically in order to trace accurately their development and achievements." This feat entailed careful attention to some 30,000 recordings and took Schuller more than 20 years to accomplish.[3]

In my case, "systematic" reading has been a much more modest enterprise, involving only a hundred or so novels and a few dozen films. In addition to pulp fiction and "serious literature," I purposefully sought out ephemera—religious rants, privately printed tracts, occult speculations, soft-core pornography, and B-movies. These eccentric works, I hoped, might offer uncensored access to some of the secret sexual and racial fantasies that rule the genre's unconscious. Before I opened the first book, moreover, I searched for a vantage point that offered some view of how imagined disaster fits into the larger landscape of Los Angeles writing. The bibliographic equivalent of the view from Mulholland Drive is Baird and Greenwood's superb inventory of California fiction to 1970.[4] Out of 2,711 separate entries, I found 785 novels that obviously qualified as "Los Angeles based." Nearly two-thirds of this vast output was, unsurprisingly, devoted to either murder (255 crime and detective novels) or Hollywood (224 novels), with considerable overlap between the two categories. There were also 50 novels with specific disaster themes, 6 percent of the total, which put disaster fiction just ahead of cult fiction (39 titles) and citrus fiction (30 titles), and just behind historical novels (66 titles).

Statistics like these, however, are extremely crude indexes of relative popularity, let alone influence. Chandlerian noir (including Ross MacDonald and James Ellroy), for example, continues to define Los Angeles in the eyes of most critics, yet it makes up only a small subset, fewer than 40 titles, within the larger universe of regional fiction. Literary census methods, even when augmented by careful surveys of Los Angeles–based films and post-1970 novels, must quickly yield to other kinds of analysis. As with the interpretation of swing jazz, the goal is the "isolation and emphasis of certain themes or threads" that either pervade the entire genre or provide compelling criteria for the distinction of subtypes. In the case of Los Angeles disaster fiction, three fundamental propositions, based on my "Schullerian" reading, provide a critical framework for discussing individual books and films.

First, there is a dramatic trend over time toward the merging of all Los Angeles fiction with the disaster or survivalist narrative. Like some monstrous blob from a 1950s sci-fi movie, the form has slowly absorbed every competitor. Despite the critical obsession with Los Angeles as the home of hardboiled detective fiction, the disaster novel has long been an equally characteristic and symptomatic local export. Since 1980, in fact, a quorum of the region's best writers—including Octavia Butler, Carolyn See, Steve Erickson, Kim Stanley Robinson, and Cynthia Kadohata—have routinely sited their fiction in the golden ruins of Los Angeles's future. It is also true in the broader sense that disaster, as allusion, metaphor, or ambience, saturates almost everything now written about Southern California.

Second, almost all Los Angeles disaster fiction can be categorized into coherent subgenres like "romantic disaster" or "magical dystopia" fiction which have succeeded one another in a fairly orderly fashion over time. Although sorting out such subgenres is a notoriously subjective business, certain basic thematic patterns—the redemptive power of women, inadvertent biocatastrophe, the identification of cult with catastrophe, white survivalism in an alien city—made the process relatively straightforward in a form that is generally not known for its subtle literary qualities. The nine major story types of Los Angeles disaster fiction and their principal periods of popularity are:

Hordes	1900–1940
Romantic disaster	1920–30s
Cult-catastrophe	1930–50s
The bomb	1940–80s
Ecocatastrophe	1960–80s
Cinematic disaster	1970s
Armageddon	1980–90s
Alien invasions	1980–90s
Magical dystopia	1980–90s

In contrast to their relatively limited syntax of story types, such novels and films have managed to destroy Los Angeles in a remarkable, even riotous, miscellany of ways. If nuclear weapons have been detonated over the Hollywood sign an amazing 49 times, and City Hall has crumbled during the Big One, mother of all earthquakes, another 28 times, then sandstorms, comets, Japanese invaders, and Bermuda grass have all had their moments as well. A reasonably comprehensive list of these means of destruction and their frequency would include:

Nukes	49
Earthquakes	28
Hordes (invasion)	10
Monsters	10
Pollution	7
Gangs/terrorism	6
Floods	6
Plagues	6
Comets/tsunami	5
Cults	3
Volcanoes	2
Firestorms	2
Drought	1
Blizzard	1
Devil	1
Freeway	1
Riot	1
Fog	1
Slide	1
Bermuda grass	1
Global warming	1
Sandstorm	1
"Everything"	1

Third, the abiding hysteria of Los Angeles disaster fiction, and perhaps of all disaster fiction—the urge to strike out and destroy, to wipe out an entire city and untold thousands of its inhabitants—is rooted in racial anxiety. From the earliest nineteenth-century examples of the literary destruction of London and New York to the latest survivalist fantasies about Los Angeles, white fear of the dark races lies at the heart of such visions (with the sardonic critique of cults and fringe culture coming in a distant second). And it is this obsession, far more than anxieties about earthquakes or nuclear weapons, that leads us back to the real Los Angeles as well as to the deepest animating fears of our culture. It is this constellation of fears—and their attendant pleasures—that makes the taxonomy of disaster fiction something more than a purely academic (and perhaps amusing) exercise.

If race ultimately unlocks the secret meaning of Los Angeles disaster fiction, its apparitions have changed over time. In novels written before 1970, when Los Angeles was still the most WASPish of large American cities, racial hysteria was typically expressed as fear of invading hordes (variously yellow, brown, black, red, or their extraterrestrial metonyms). After 1970, with the rise of a non-Anglo majority in Los Angeles County, the city turns from an endangered home into the Alien itself; and its destruction affords an illicit pleasure not always visible in previous annihilations. But let us begin more or less at historical ground zero, tracing the genealogy of Los Angeles disaster fiction back to its origins in the modern fascination with dead cities. By late Victorian times, this was an ancestry already dominated by implacable race wars and imagined genocides.

2. URBAN ESCHATOLOGY

Lo! Death has reared himself a throne
In a strange city lying alone
Far down within the dim West
　　　　　　　Edgar Allan Poe, "The City in the Sea"

A starting point: Lisbon was the Hiroshima of the age of reason. Goethe, six at the time of the destruction of the Portuguese capital by earthquake, tsunami, and fire in 1755, later recalled how Lisbon's "Demon of Fright" undermined belief in the rational deity of the *philosophes*. "God, said to be omniscient and merciful, had shown himself to be a very poor sort of father, for he had struck down equally the just and the unjust."[5]

The Lisbon catastrophe, together with the rediscovery of Pompeii and Herculaneum only a few years earlier, were profound shocks to the philosophical "optimism" (a word coined in 1737) that had infused the early Enlightenment under the influence of Newton, Leibnitz, and Pope. The "best of all possible worlds," it seemed, was subject to inexplicable and horrifying disasters that challenged the very foundations of reason. Following Voltaire's famous lampoon of Leibnitz as Dr. Pangloss in his skeptical masterpiece *Candide,* Lisbon and Pompeii—and, later, the French revolutionary Terror of 1791— became the touchstones of a fundamentally modern "pessimism" (a word first used by Coleridge in 1795) that found its inspiration in historical cataclysm rather than the Book of Revelation.[6]

One influential literary template for this anti-utopian sensibility was Jean-Baptiste Cousin de Grainville's *Le Dernier Homme.* Written in 1805 at the apogee of Napoleonic power, this strange novel by a bitter enemy of the *philosophes* depicted mankind's disappearance as the result of soil exhaustion, human sterility, and a slowly dying sun. Although Grainville had been a cleric under the ancien régime and religious motifs are present, his book is likely the first in any language to sketch a realistic scenario of human extinction. Moreover, it inspired Mary Shelley's three-volume epic of despair, *The Last Man* (1826), which chronicles how a late-twenty-first-century utopian age of peace and prosperity is transformed, by plague and religious fundamentalism, into a terrifying End Time whose sole survivor—the Englishman Lionel Verney—is left at book's end in the howling ruins of the Roman Coliseum. *The Last Man,* although a bad novel, was an intellectual watershed, the first truly secular apocalypse.[7]

From the dandified fringe of Shelley's circle also came the most popular urban disaster novel of all time, Edward Bulwer-Lytton's *Last Days of Pompeii* (1834). Bulwer-Lytton, who began his political life as a Godwin radical and ended it as secretary for the colonies, eulogized the cultured and cosmopolitan decadence of the doomed Roman summer resort in the shadow of Vesuvius. Written during the turbulent days after the passage of the first Reform Bill and the rise of Chartism, the novel can also be read as a premature elegy for the equally decadent British upper classes, whom Bulwer-Lytton saw as threatened by their own (sociopolitical) catastrophe: the coming of universal suffrage. In the century-long run of its popularity, however, the novel offered its readers the typically Victorian titillations of orientalized sensual splendor followed by sublime, all-consuming disaster. *The Last Days of Pompeii* would become the most filmed novel of the early years of cinema, with at least four movie versions made between 1903 and 1913 alone.[8]

In American literature, the city of doom is a potent image in such early novels as Charles Brockden Brown's *Arthur Mervyn* (1799) and a "Lady of Philadelphia"'s *Laura* (1809), both of which portray the horror of the "yellow plague" (yellow fever) in Philadelphia. In succeeding decades, the great city, with its teeming masses of immigrants and "papists," was routinely demonized as the infernal antipode to the republican homestead and small town. This nativist anti-urbanism reaches a hallucinatory crescendo in George Lippard's gothic tale of oligarchy and corruption, *The Quaker City* (1844). Philadelphia is again depicted as a nocturnal labyrinth of temptation and crime—its evil center the mysterious Monk Hall guarded by the monstrous "Devil Bug." As literary historian Janis Stout points out, Lippard may have been the first to paint a fictional portrait of the American city by invoking something beyond simple terror of place: the full fury of metaphysical catastrophe. "At the end of the book, in an apocalypse which the reader scarcely knows how to accept, 'Death-Angels,' 'forms of mist and shadow,' hover over the city."[9]

Edgar Allan Poe and his amazing glosses on the Last Days excepted, fictions of secular doom virtually disappeared between 1850 and 1880, that long sunny afternoon of mid-Victorian expansion. In their different ways, the Crystal Palace and Jules Verne's novels exemplified the bourgeois optimism of the age of capital. Even the carnage of the Civil War, in which Richmond and Atlanta became the first American cities reduced to charred brick, failed to cast a pall over the civilization of the steam engine. After the Paris Commune and the Depression of 1876, however, the spell was broken. An explosion of copycat novels were soon speculating on the possibilities of a future mechanized world war between the great powers. Most of these culminated in a German or French invasion of England and the sacking of London. Other writers, traumatized by events as distinct as the Paris Commune, the Fenian conspiracy, and Chinese emigration to North America, began to question the survival of Victorian civilization in the face of imagined revolt by the numerically superior "lower classes" and "lower races."

The first of these racial cataclysms, published in 1880, was written not by a European but by a California populist. Pierton Dooner's *Last Days of the Republic* describes the conquest and destruction of the United States by a "human ant-colony" of Chinese coolies. The novel begins in San Francisco, where selfish plutocrats have encouraged unrestricted Chinese immigration to depress wages. Desperate white workingmen attempt to massacre the Chinese but are ambushed and slaughtered by militia under the command of the oligarchs. The Chinese are then granted the vote, which they use to enlarge their political and economic beachhead. Ultimately, there is a savage civil war which the coolies win by virtue of their superior numbers and insect-like capacity for self-sacrifice. The banner of the Celestial Empire is finally raised over the smoking ruins of Washington, D.C.

> The very name of the United States of America was thus blotted from the record of nations. . . . The Temple of Liberty had crumbled; and above its ruins was reared the colossal fabric of barbaric splendor known as the Western Empire of His August Majesty, the Emperor of China and Ruler of All Lands.[10]

A contemporary sensation, Dooner's novel introduced a plot idea—alien infiltration/yellow hordes—that, like Shelley's "last man" narrative, has flourished to the present day. It was punctually followed the next year by four more archetypes of future disaster. In Benjamin Park's satirical short story, "The End of New York," strategic bombing makes its first appearance in fiction as an invading Spanish armada uses balloon-borne nitroglycerine canisters to destroy Manhattan from the air. Total American capitulation is only prevented by the fortuitous appearance of a friendly Chilean fleet(!), a useful if far-fetched foil for Park's denunciation of "the weakness of our navy and the unprotected position of our seaports."[11]

Mary Lane's *Mizora: A Prophecy* describes an elite, subterranean society of women living in a lush paradise under the North Pole. As critic Naomi Jacobs has pointed out, this parthenogenic utopia is the realization of a single-minded eugenic philosophy typical of the period: "At the very foundation of Mizoran perfection," she writes, "is the racial purity of its inhabitants, who are all blond-haired and fair-skinned." Just as men were biologically eliminated some 3,000 years before, so too were all women of dark complexion. Since the "elements of evil belong to the dark race," its extinction has been the precondition for the moral and mental perfection of Lane's blond goddesses.[12]

Meanwhile, the popular English writer and advocate of Anglo-Saxon union W. Delisle Hay published back-to-back novels—*The Doom of the Great City* and *Three Hundred Years Hence*—portraying alternative futures. In the first, London is choked to death by its poisonous fogs and toxic wastes. In the second, white civilization is on the verge of transforming the world into a superindustrial utopia that includes greenbelts in the Sahara, flying machines, and television. The major obstacle to progress is the continued existence of "worthless Inferior Races but a step above beasts." The air fleets of the "Teutons" solve this problem by unleashing "a rain of death to every breathing thing, a rain that exterminates the hopeless race." As I. F. Clarke has emphasized in his pathbreaking study of nineteenth-century futurism, one of the chapters in *Three Hundred Years Hence*—"The Fate of the Inferior Races" ("a billion human beings will die")—seems now an eerie anticipation of *Mein Kampf* (or the more recent *Turner Diaries*).[13]

These tales opened the gates to a flood of apocalyptic fiction. Overwhelmingly a literature written for and consumed by the urban middle classes, it depicted the nightmare side—chaos and violence as the necessary expression of "survival of the fittest"—of the crude social Darwinism that was the pitiless ethos of the age of the robber barons. In such stories, growing fears of violent social revolution and of the "rising tide of color" accompanied increasing anxieties over the inevitability of future world wars between the imperialist powers. New means of mass destruction—microbes, radioactivity, poison gases, and flying machines—conquered the pulp press years, sometimes decades, before they were added to the arsenals of the major powers. At the same time, the purported discovery of "canals" on Mars by several eminent astronomers gave plausibility to fears that the earth was menaced by malevolent extraterrestrials. The result was a proliferation of doom fiction that established virtually all the conventions of the genre still in use today.[14] As historian W. Warren Wagar has written, "Between 1890 and 1914 alone,

> almost every sort of world's end story that one finds in later years was written, published, and accepted by a wide reading public. Great world wars that devastated civilization were fought in the skies and on imaginary battlefields dwarfing those of Verdun and Stalingrad. Fascist dictatorships led to a new Dark Age, class and race struggles plunged civilization into Neolithic savagery, terrorists armed with superweapons menaced global peace. Floods, volcanic eruptions, plagues, epochs of ice, colliding comets, exploding or cooling suns, and alien invaders laid waste to the world.[15]

In the United States, more than in Europe, the disaster novel remained fixated on the specter of subversive immigrants and non-whites. The Irish-led Manhattan "draft riots" of 1863, suppressed with great difficulty by regular army units sent from Gettysburg, gave shape and color to nativist fears. Thus, in John Ames Mitchell's *Last American* (1889), the alien hordes actually turn green and destroy New York after massacring its Protestant bourgeoisie. A Persian expedition, reconnoitering the wasteland of Manhattan in the year 2951, excavates numismatic evidence of this Irish-led insurrection: a

1937 half-dollar (illustrated in the book) with the bulldog image of "Dennis Murphy Imperator"—"the last of the Hy-Burnyan dictators." The explorers also discover the rusting hulk of the Statue of Liberty, Delmonico's, Astor House, and a thousand-year-old blonde moldering in her bed. During a side trip to Washington, D.C., they encounter the "last American" of the title skulking in the ruins. He is slain in a brief scuffle and his skull taken back to Persia to be displayed in a museum.[16]

Late-twentieth-century New York is consumed by an equally terrible revolutionary disaster in Ignatius Donnelly's *Caesar's Column: A Story of the Twentieth Century* (1890). Minnesota populist leader Donnelly uses a gory brush to portray the final conflict between a debased, immigrant proletariat and a Jewish-dominated financial oligarchy. With the aid of the "Demons," a band of mercenary airmen who drop poison gas on New York's wealthy neighborhoods, the slum hordes, led by Caesar Lomellini, an ogrelike Italian giant, exterminate bourgeois society. A quarter-million well-dressed corpses form the pedestal of the grotesque column Lomellini builds to commemorate "the Death and Burial of Modern Civilization."[17]

Racial as well as class cataclysm—in Donnelly the difference almost collapses—remained popular fare in the gilded age. With the annihilation of native Americans almost universally accepted as a necessary cost of progress, some writers began to experiment with other genocides. In *The Last Days of the Republic,* for instance, Dooner disposed of the entire ex-slave population in a single, enigmatic line. "Blacks," he wrote, "rapidly and noiselessly disappeared—perished, it seemed, by the very act of contact" with their Chinese conquerors.[18] A decade later, in his Jim Crow novel *The Next War* (1892), King Wallace openly exulted at the biological extinction of black America.[19] Northern and Southern whites, finally overcoming their Civil War animosities, unite in a war of extermination against a rebellious black population. After a failed attempt to poison all whites on the first day of the twentieth century, 30 million blacks flee into the Southern mountains where, completely surrounded by the white armies, they die of exposure and starvation. With cold matter-of-factness, Wallace

The Brooklyn Bridge, A.D. 2951 (*The Last American*)

describes a "continuous and unbroken line of dead infants, none of whom were older than six or seven."*

The yellow hordes, introduced by Dooner and Hay, meanwhile, returned in a bloodthirsty trilogy by English writer M. P. Shiel—*The Yellow Danger* (1899), *The Yellow Wave* (1905), and *The Dragon* (1913)—in which hundreds of millions of fiendish Chinese are slaughtered by naval heroes who, when firepower alone fails, resort to the bubonic plague. Shiel was then widely imitated by other writers,

---

* Wallace claimed that the absurd black conspiracy in his novel was "based on facts already firmly established" and that "the very day fixed for exterminating the white race, December 31, 1900, as given in the story of *The Next War,* is the identical date fixed upon by the [actual] conspirators."[20]

including Jack London, whose 1906 short story, "The Unparalleled Invasion," solves the "Chinese problem" with all-out germ warfare followed by a massacre of any survivors. As the white races recolonize China "according to the democratic American program," an odd peace sets in as "all nations solemnly pledge themselves never to use against one another the laboratory methods of warfare they had employed in the invasion of China."[21]

Only two English-language novels broke ranks with the xenophobic obsessions of late-nineteenth-century futurism. One was naturalist Richard Jefferies's influential *After London, or Wild England*, published in 1885, which foretold the environmental collapse of the unsustainable industrial metropolis. The only major writer of British catastrophe fiction before H. G. Wells "to spring from the working people," in his case the rural yeomanry, Jefferies, like Donnelly, despised the urban financial oligarchy that had starved the countryside of credit and ruined the small farmer. His images of London transformed into a vast miasmatic swamp, according to critic Darko Suvin, convey a "loathing of upper-class pride and prejudice based on money power." Although Jefferies helped prepare the way for the gothic socialist vision of William Morris (whose *News from Nowhere*, 1891, is a utopian reworking of *After London*, where ruined industrialism becomes the seedbed for a craft and cottage renaissance), the sheer ferocity of his anti-urbanism puts him in a category apart, a kind of Victorian Edward Abbey.[22]

The other novel, of course, was Wells's great anti-imperialist allegory *The War of the Worlds*, which stood white supremacy on its head by depicting the English as helpless natives being colonized and slaughtered by technologically invincible Martians. The novel grew out of a conversation between Wells and his brother about the then-recent extinction of native Tasmanians by English settlers. His precise, almost block-by-block description of the Martian destruction of London ("It was the beginning of the rout of civilization, of the massacre of mankind") stunned British readers, who in 1898 were forced to confront, for the first time, what it might be like to be on the receiving end of imperial conquest. Within a year of its trans-Atlantic

serialization in *Cosmopolitan,* American newspapers had already pla-
giarized the story and printed terrifying accounts of Martian attacks
on New York and Boston.* (Los Angeles, thanks to Paramount
Films, would follow in 1953.)

Yet even Wells, who ended the book with a powerful call for a "com-
monweal of mankind," was obsessed with race. In his earlier novel *The
Time Machine* (1895), he forecast the evolutionary divergence of the
human race into antagonistic species represented by the pale, gentle
Eloi and the hideous, troglodytic Morlocks who eat the Eloi. In *The
Island of Dr. Moreau* (1896) he horrified readers with the image of animals transformed by vivisection into humanoid monsters—analogues
for mutant, inferior races. Years later, the Yellow Peril makes a melo-
dramatic appearance in *The War in the Air* (1907), Wells's saga of a
world conflagration ignited by Wilhelmine Germany's sneak attack on
New York City.[24]

Prefiguring the Martian attack in *Independence Day,* a German
zeppelin armada, emblazoned with the Iron Cross, turns Manhattan's
Broadway into a "hideous red scar of flames"—slaughtering American civilians "as though they had been no more than Moors, or Zulus,
or Chinese." This atrocity, however, is only the prelude to the "Asiatic
Armada" that brings modern civilization to an end in the skies over
Buffalo, New York. While the Americans and their European allies
are preoccupied with a counterattack against the German "aerial
Gibraltar" at Niagara Falls, thousands of Japanese and Chinese air-
ships suddenly darken the sky.

> The Japanese and Chinese have joined in. That's the supreme
> fact. They've pounced into our little quarrels. . . . The Yellow
> Peril was a peril after all![25]

---

* *New York Journal* writer Garret Serviss serialized a pro-imperialist sequel, *Edison's
Conquest of Mars* (1898), which depicted the great inventor invading the Red Planet and
eliminating all of its inhabitants. In a climax of vulgar Darwinism, "it was the evolution of
earth against the evolution of Mars. It was a planet [Earth] in the heyday of its strength
matched against an aged and decrepit world [Mars]."[23]

Holocaust on Broadway (*The War in the Air*)

The plots of *After London, The Time Machine,* and *The War in the Air* were freely combined in the most popular American end-of-the-city novel from the Edwardian era: George England's *Darkness and Dawn,* first serialized in *Cavalier* magazine in 1912.[26] Readers were particularly thrilled by the story's opening pages which, like *War in the Air,* depict the destruction of New York's newly built skyscrapers. Allan and Beatrice (a handsome engineer and his beautiful secretary) awake from a century of suspended animation on the forty-eighth floor of the ruined Metropolitan Tower overlooking Union Square.

From their high perch, they survey a scene of utter devastation. The great Flatiron Building is a "hideous wreck," while the Brooklyn Bridge has collapsed and the Statue of Liberty is just "a black misshapen mass protruding through the tree-tops." Manhattan has become the first skyscraper ghost town. They quickly leave this "city of death" (meaning, of course, dead immigrants) to search for other Anglo-Saxon survivors of the unexplained catastrophe.

George England, like Jack London, was both a socialist and an Aryanist. Inevitably, on the road to rebuilding civilization, his "white barbarians" must fight a pitiless war of extermination against "the Horde," a species of cannibal ape-men—reminiscent of Wells's Morlocks—whom the reader is led to assume are the devolved offspring of inferior races. Once the ape-men are annihilated, progress is rapid because "labor reaps its full reward" in the cooperative commonwealth established by the survivors. In the last scene, Allan points to a swift-moving light in the sky: "Look Beatrice! The West Coast Mail!"[27] It is a biplane from Southern California bearing the hope of a new age.

3. THE COMING HORDES

Shortly after dark last Saturday night, a large force of Jap paratroopers was dropped from carrier-based aircraft into Santa Monica, a coastal suburb of the City of Los Angeles.
"President Roosevelt," in Invasion! *(1943)*

Given this sinister genealogy, it is hardly surprising that Los Angeles disaster fiction was inaugurated, not by earthquake, flood, or firestorm, but by a Japanese invasion of Southern California in Homer Lea's lurid 1909 account, *The Valor of Ignorance.*[28] Lea was one of the strangest creatures of California's Progressive era. In defiance of his twisted spine and sickly physique, he was driven by the belief that he was the reincarnation of a mythic Chinese warrior destined to lead vast armies into battle. During his student days at Occidental College and then Stanford his napoleonic fantasies were the butt of ridicule. He nonetheless managed while still in his twenties to wrangle a Chinese military commission during the Boxer Rebellion with the wild claim that he was Robert E. Lee's grandson.

Although his ragtag regiment disintegrated after a few skirmishes, Lea skillfully wove his exploits into an elaborate legend that persuaded the exiled Chinese nationalist Sun Yat-sen (whose military judgment was notoriously poor) to appoint him his "chief of staff" based in Los Angeles. With a gruff regular army veteran named O'Banion as drill-sergeant, Lea attempted to turn a motley but enthusiastic mob of Chinese students and busboys into a revolutionary army. For several years they were a colorful sight, marching and target shooting in the hills of Griffith Park and the Pacific Palisades.

Lea's patronizing sinophilia was only exceeded by his obsession with the Japanese military threat to the West Coast. In *The Valor of Ignorance,* he argued that, without a great Pacific fleet to protect its coastal cities, the United States was impotent to resist the "inevitable invasion." Lea surmised that a Japanese force would strike first at Hawaii and Alaska, then occupy the Puget Sound, before steaming toward Los Angeles.

Lea later claimed that he had spent seven months—usually on a burro, but sometimes carried in the arms of O'Banion—in a painstaking reconnaissance of possible invasion routes and battlefields throughout Southern California. Los Angeles, he argued, was utterly defenseless on its seaboard side: "One regiment [could] occupy the city with impunity." Moreover, the mountain-ringed region, while so easily assailed from its sea, was virtually impregnable from the desert side. In *The Valor of Ignorance,* the Japanese feint at the "worthless" fortifications at San Pedro then land unopposed (for the first but hardly the last time in disaster fiction) at Santa Monica. The next day at their leisure they occupy Los Angeles, essentially completing "the conquest of southern California." From this superb base of operations, invulnerable to American counterattack, the Imperial Army is able to move vast numbers of troops northward to surround and besiege San Francisco. Bombarded by Japanese artillery emplaced in

Oakland and Marin, San Francisco's hysterical business leaders force its small garrison to surrender, and the ensuing national political crisis, amplified by "class and sectional insurrections," leads to the imposition of a military monarchy in the eastern states.

With the Hearst press, which immediately championed Lea's book, acting as bellows, *The Valor of Ignorance* ignited an anti-Japanese frenzy that consumed white California in the years immediately before the First World War and, again, in the early 1920s. Even if Lea was only following in the footsteps of Dooner, he was later credited by authorities as diverse as Clare Booth Luce and Carey McWilliams with being the creator of the modern "Yellow Peril": the demagogue "who first combined the phrase with the doctrine and applied the argument specifically to the West Coast."[29]

Lea was followed, in turn, by J. U. Giesy, whose xenophobic 1915 potboiler, *All for His Country,* was an example of an irresistible American genre, the "Edisonade." In this popular story type, modeled on Serviss's *Edison's Conquest of Mars,* a brilliant young inventor is initially spurned until his invention—in Giesy's case, a huge radium-powered airship—proves necessary to save the day.[30] In a narrative clearly inspired by Pancho Villa's famous 1915 cross-border raid on Columbus, New Mexico, Mexican troops (this time *federales*) invade the Southwest. They are quickly driven back, and the pursuing American army, including all the garrison troops from California, is lured deep into Mexico—exactly the diversion that Mexico's secret ally Japan has been waiting for.

With clocklike precision a clandestine Japanese army, previously disguised as humble laborers, house servants, and immigrant farmers, attacks California's major cities. San Francisco quickly surrenders to the "slant-eyed hordes." In Southern California, however, there is more resistance and thus greater carnage. For the first time in fiction, Los Angeles burns.

> It was a night of alarms; of the trooping of armed men; of sudden assault and a desperate defense in some quarters; of slaughter and burning, and rapine beyond description. Half of the

city of Los Angeles alone was destroyed by fire, and while it burned the conquerors patroled its streets and shot down those who fled the flames.[31]

Despite valiantly improvised resistance by Los Angeles's amateur aviators, the city is overwhelmed in a single day. The rest of California quickly falls, and in the following months the Japanese unveil a terrifying new weapon, "a winged aerial torpedo" (something like a modern cruise missile), which they use to destroy America's Atlantic fleet. Left undefended, New York City is subjected to relentless aerial and naval bombardment. As in *Darkness and Dawn,* the world's tallest skyscraper, the newly built Metropolitan Tower, is "toppled like a great tree." A stunned President Gilson is on the verge of accepting the terms of a Japanese ultimatum, when "as a climax," the Japanese demand a special act of Congress "recognizing the Japanese claims to descent from Aryan rather than Mongol stock, which should establish them as a Caucasian people, and recognizing the full rights of intermarriage between themselves and all persons of both sexes in the United States."[32]

Rather than accept biological "Orientalization"—"Myself I had rather slay my daughters," proclaims Gilson—the government abandons Washington and retreats toward Chicago leaving scorched earth behind. In an Armageddon-like battle, the Americans are on the verge of annihilation, when the long-awaited "miracle ships" finally arrive. Stillman, the inventor, had been pouting in Utah. With a handful of superhero aviators, he destroys the formerly invincible hordes and saves white womanhood from the ultimate nightmare of yellow sperm.*

---

* The Giesy novel was coordinated with a ferocious broadside of Hearst propaganda that included Sunday supplement spreads on Nippo-Mexican invasion plans (fall 1915) followed by a sensationalized Hearst-produced film, *Patria,* in which the Japanese invaders of California—later changed to Mexicans by wartime censors—attempt to rape popular heroine Irene Castle. In 1920 the Hearst newspapers again stirred fears of an imminent Japanese sneak attack. Naval intelligence investigated the absurd rumor, which caused widespread panic in Los Angeles, that alien submarines had been landing munitions and poison gas near San Pedro "for the use of Japanese troops in the invasion of California."[33]

Although a Japanese sneak attack on West Coast cities (this time from the air) also figures in two 1927 novels—Charles Downing's *The Reckoning* and W. D. Gann's *The Tunnel Thru the Air**—the most popular Yellow Peril story of the Harding-Coolidge years was Peter Kyne's best-selling *Pride of Palomar* (1921), originally serialized in *Cosmopolitan*.[34] Its publication coincided with a wave of pogroms against Japanese farmers in the rural areas of California. The "pride" in the title refers to "pride of race," and white civilization in Southern California is depicted as besieged by "locust-like" swarms of Japanese farmers and laborers. Don Mike Farrel returns from battling the Bolshevik menace in Siberia only to discover that his own beloved "San Gregoria Valley" at the foot of Mount Palomar is about to be sold to the diabolical potato baron Okada, who has used white proxies to circumvent laws restricting Asian landownership.

Don Mike, descended from "blond Spaniards and an Irish grandfather," is a grand seigneur who speaks to his "mongrelized" peons in bizarre Tudor meter: " 'My good Pablo,' he queried, 'what has come over thee of late? Thou art of a mien as sorrowful as that of a sick deer.' " (Pablo, in turn, says things like "Never no woman that boy kees since hees mother die twenty year before.") He is an idealized image of the contemporary ranchers and citrus growers who were the mainstay of Southern California's Progressive movement and its core values of reform, efficiency, and white supremacy.

He is also the mouthpiece for their racial fears. A fanatical social Darwinist, he worries that Anglo-Saxons lack the "fitness" to survive all-out economic competition with the thrifty, hardworking Japanese; an imperialist in a conquered land, he is terrified that the tables are about to be turned on him.

> They will dominate us, because they are a dominant people;
> they will shoulder us aside, control us, dictate to us, and we

---

* "The battle waged thruout the night and when the sun rose the next morning, the beautiful city of Los Angeles was in ruins. Thousands of people had been killed and most of the important buildings had been destroyed. The people of Los Angeles were more excited than they had ever been during an earthquake" (*The Tunnel Thru the Air*).[34]

shall disappear from this beautiful land as surely and as swiftly as did the Mission Indians. While the South has its negro problem—and a sorry problem that is—we Californians have had an infinitely more dangerous problem thrust upon us. We've got to shake them off. We've got to.[36]

Kyne's Japanese immigrants, in other words, are analogues to the Martians in *War of the Worlds*: invincible invaders, even if armed with garden hoes instead of death rays. In its own perverse way, the novel is a backhanded tribute to the indefatigible industry and sacrifice of the Issei generation. Its underlying racial hysteria—the fear that whites cannot successfully compete under conditions of equality—remains alive today in white panic about Asian achievements in California's public schools.* In the end, lamely enough, Kyne can only furnish Don Mike with two fists and the admonition to Okada:

> Now listen, O child of Nippon, to the white man's words of wisdom. You're going to depart from El Toro in a general northerly direction and you're going to do it immediately if not sooner. And you're never coming back.[37]

Come back, however, the Japanese do, with terrible vengeance, in Whitman Chambers's 1943 novel *Invasion!* Chambers fills in the grisly details that *The Valor of Ignorance* (reissued in 1942 with an introduction by Clare Booth Luce) and *All for His Country* left out. Santa Monica is again the open door to invasion, although this time from the air as the Japanese drop paratroopers, accompanied by incendiary and poison gas bombardments that reduce much of Los Angeles to stucco rubble.

A small group of civilian and military survivors, hiding in a MacArthur Park storm drain, are transformed into guerrilla warriors by Happy McGonigle, a brawny Irish-American who exults in killing

---

* That this is hardly a new fear is attested by a 1905 headline in the rabidly anti-Oriental *San Francisco Chronicle:* "Brown Asiatics Steal Brains of Whites!"

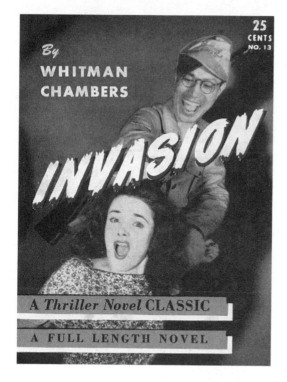

The Japanese return (1943)

the Japanese, depicted as apes or insects, with his bare hands. Mc-
Gonigle's band finds revenge at the bloody corner of Alvarado and
Glendale in Echo Park ("littered with wrecked cars and a blackened
tank and smashed trucks") when they surprise a platoon of Japanese
soldiers eating oranges (a particularly obscene image to Chambers).
McGonigle delegates the execution of the prisoners to a sadistic Jewish GI named Abe.

> Abe came into sight at the end of the short hallway beyond the
> open door. His grimy uniform was spattered with bright arte-
> rial blood. There was fresh blood on the butt of his gun. His
> eyes were feverish.
>
> "Two down," he announced grimly, "and two to go. Bring
> the bastards into the slaughter house, sergeant."[38]

When they are not murdering prisoners or dodging Japanese
patrols in the bombed-out industrial district near the river, McGonigle's guerrillas are arguing over politics. Chambers, like Dooner, was

a racist populist who ranted against upper-class defeatism in the face of the Yellow Peril. As the mortally wounded Hap' McGonigle sets off on a suicide mission against the Japanese, he enumerates the domestic enemies of total race war and the more egalitarian (white) society which unconditional victory will ensure:

> "You tell'em chum," he started again to crawl toward the cellar. "... the Tory papers with their stinking little punks preaching treason. . . . Dutchess county sluts that sent Ham Fisher back to Congress . . . the Palm Beach Tories . . . Bertie and Willie . . . all the mucking bastards—that're trying to make us lose this war—because they're afraid of the brave new world our dying men are building."[39]

4. ROMANTIC DISASTER FICTION

I hold the lives of millions at my mercy!
Roger Seaton in The Secret Power *(1921)*

When the Japanese were not overrunning early-twentieth-century California, courageous matrons were saving it. The most popular story type to emerge from the 1906 San Francisco earthquake and fire was the woman-centered romance-in-the-ruins. In more than a score of novels, including Elizabeth Worthington's *Twenty Eight Seconds and After* (1906), Sara Dean's *Travers: A Story of the Earthquake* (1907), Evelyn Green's *The City of the Golden Gate* (1909), Emma Allen's *The Awakening of the Harwells* (1913), and Charlotte Canty's *The Whimsey Girl* (1913), women assume heroic roles—generally as motherly angels—in the moral reconstruction of a once lewd and frivolous city.

The 1920s queen of angelic catastrophe fiction, Marie Corelli, created just such a heroine for her popular 1921 novel, *The Secret Power: A Romance of the Time.* In it Los Angeles for the first time is destroyed by earthquake *and* atomic explosion—nothing, as it turns out, that a good woman couldn't handle. Corelli, now forgotten, was once an incredibly popular author of women's fiction. Her style, in those pre-bodice-ripping days, was unparalleled for its neurasthenic desperation and romantic breathlessness. ("Oh, big moon of California, why? Oh, pagan gods and goddesses and fauns and fairies, tell me why?")[40] In this incomparably strange story, she hijacks the Edisonade plot for her own protofeminist purposes.

Roger Seaton is the world's foremost nuclear physicist as well as a self-proclaimed Nietzschean superman. A recluse, he lives in a cabin in the San Gabriel Mountains above Pasadena, tinkering with his homemade atomic bomb, which Corelli describes presciently as "equal to millions of bombs of the same size and energy as used in the trenches."[41] His maid, Manella Soriso, is a naive but ravishing "daughter of Spanish California" who yearns to become his "love slave," despite the fact that he brutally ignores her. His heart, it seems, was broken in a previous tryst with Morgana Royal, a "modern Cleopatra" who is the richest woman in the world and, as chance would have it, the second most "brilliant theorist of the future development of radio-activity." When not engaged in telepathic conversations with the inhabitants of a mysterious city in the Sahara, she tools around the world in her great airship, the "White Eagle," a flying boudoir powered by "throbbing atomic disks . . . resembling the suckers on the tentacles of a giant octopus."[42] On one of these jaunts, she visits Roger and immediately develops a sapphic solidarity with Manella, whose unrequited passion for Roger she instantly recognizes. A few weeks later, Manella startles Roger while he is playing with his atomic toys in his cave-laboratory, and he accidentally drops his bomb. The ensuing explosion sets off a gigantic earthquake that devastates the Los Angeles area, killing most of its inhabitants.

> All the sunny plains and undulating hills of the beautiful stretch of land in Southern California, in the centre of which the "Plaza" hotel and sanatorium had stood, were now unrecognizable—the earth was torn asunder and thrown into vast heaps—great rocks and boulders were tumbled over each other

pell-mell in appalling heights of confusion, and, for miles around, camps and houses were in ruins. The scene was one of absolute horror.[43]

The Secret Power here suddenly rejoins the eugenical and genocidal preoccupations of mainstream disaster fiction. Morgana, an implacable Nietzschean, is unmoved when she learns of the mass tragedy. "The human race in its present condition," she coldly observes, "is an unweeded garden and it wants clearing." She is, however, loyal to her friends and immediately flies over from Sicily (where—don't ask why—she shares a castle with a flirtatious priest) to retrieve the bodies of Roger and Manella. Her miraculous radium treatments restore the beautiful Manella to full health but leave Roger a helpless infant, confined to bed where he mutters incessantly, "I am the master of the world."[44]

Both Manella and Morgana are delighted with the scope that Roger's invalidism affords their maternal instincts. Manella marries Roger, while Morgana flies off to her "Brazen City" in the Sahara. In her last telepathic message to Manella, Morgana relishes their matriarchal triumph: " 'Masters of the world' are poor creatures at best . . . but the secret Makers of the New Race are the gods of the Future."[45]

The heroic role of maternal instinct in the face of catastrophe also figures centrally in Beulah Marie Dix's altogether more modern novel *Pity of God,* published in 1932.[46] Dix was the first writer to incorporate a real Los Angeles disaster into her plot—the 1928 collapse of the newly built St. Francis Dam (vaguely disguised by Dix as the "San Vincente Dam"), which killed 385 people.

Pity of God is an acid portrait—prefiguring later stories by Faulkner and Cain—of an old-stock American family morally decomposing in the Southern California sunshine. The novel chronicles the last day in the lives of the Vickerys, who have just moved into a monstrous Spanish-Colonial home in the posh new suburb of "San Andreas," north of the San Fernando Valley.

The mother, Ethel Vickery, is a grotesque figure, the embodiment of every middle-class fad and prejudice, whose family wealth has

Ruins of St. Francis Dam

given her despotic power over her unsuccessful husband, Joe. He, in turn, is infatuated with his secretary, but they cannot afford to run away together until Joe makes a killing (in a deal that Ethel will casually derail in the course of the day). Ethel's father, a contrite and beaten old man living in the empty shell of betrayed memories, silently observes their vicious warfare.

Scheming and remorseless, the teenage Vickery sons, Jed and Robbie, meanwhile, might have been early models for Eric and Lyle Mcnendez. Jed has knocked up the German maid (who is also being stalked by the family's sinister chauffeur), while Robbie thinks he is losing his eyesight from moonshine. To complete this cancerous family portrait, Dix adds Jed's fiancée, Babby Marsh, the quintessential spoiled Valley Girl of the 1920s. Only the Vickerys' two younger daughters—still oblivious to the mayhem in the household—retain their innocence.

The two girls are eventually saved by a redeeming maternal figure, their widowed aunt Cornelia, whose own husband and daughter died during the great influenza epidemic at the end of the First World War. The Vickery family is fast asleep when Cornelia is awakened by an image of her dead daughter and a strange moaning in the earth farther up San Andreas Canyon. San Vincente Dam is collapsing. Grabbing the two little girls, she sprints desperately for the top of a nearby hill.

> Cornelia gave a glance up the canyon. Nightmare. Never to be forgotten. A solid wall rolling down the canyon. Towering wall that reached from ridge to ridge. Black marble wall marching. Starlight caught upon its demoniac surface. Like a black mirror. Incredible, gigantic mirror. The sky was splitting with the thunder of its coming.[47]

At dawn Cornelia and the girls are horrified to discover that the Vickery mansion has vanished without a trace. The deluge has stripped the soil to bedrock, leaving nothing behind "but banks of mud, and, sullen, yellowish, steadily flowing water." San Andreas—a Sodom with red-tiled roofs—has been obliterated by the angry fist of a Calvinist god.*

5. CULT-CATASTROPHE

Take any boulevard and in the fourth bungalow on the right they'll be busy raising the dead or talking things over with Dante and Shakespeare.

The Doomsday Men *(1938)*

Kooky religious cults and (un)natural disaster—often with racist or anti-Semitic undertones—became pea and pod in Los Angeles fiction after 1930. The initial coupling of the two had, however, been made nearly a century earlier, when, according to the Reverend William Money, Jesus Christ accosted him on a New York street corner and

---

* Floodwaters administer a further moral cleansing, though without the saving grace of an angelic heroine, to Los Angeles's nouveaux riches in Rupert Hughes's *City of Angels* (1941), based upon the actual hundred-year storm of February–March 1938.

ordered him to go west, to Los Angeles. Arriving in 1840, when the city was just a dusty hamlet, Money immediately cornered the market on faith-healing, utopianism, and astrology. A self-proclaimed "astronomer and weather prophet," he predicted earthquakes, storms, and comets. He also authored a popular chiliastic tract, *Reform of the New Testament Church* (reputed to be the first English-language book published in the city), while brawling with the local Catholic clergy and, later, U.S. occupation authorities.[48]

Despite the enmity of the region's leaders, Money succeeded in founding the Southland's first commune—based on common property and total obedience to himself—around a weird octagonal house in San Gabriel known as the Moneyan Institute. From sect headquarters, he periodically issued revelations and prophecies. Shortly before he died in 1880, "the pioneer cultist drew a strange map entitled 'Wm. Money's Discovery of the Ocean,' which showed the city of San Francisco toppling into the Pacific. When local newspapers refused to publish it, Money invoked a curse on Los Angeles, damning it to the same fate."[49]

Money's curse, needless to say, has never been lifted. Indeed, after the First World War, "God's coming destruction of Los Angeles" became a staple of Sunday morning sermons in the huge gray granite churches built to accommodate a million new immigrants from the Midwest. Corn-belt fundamentalism, with its traditional yeoman antipathy toward the "evil city," collided head-on with the libertine culture of the Hollywood movie colony in an urban *kulturkampf.* Each side would resort to doomsday imagery to damn and excoriate the other.

The victory of Iowa-born auto-parts dealer John Porter in the 1929 mayoral election was the high-water mark of fundamentalist power in Los Angeles. Porter, a secret member of the Ku Klux Klan, according to his enemies, had pledged to maintain the city as "the last stand of native-born Protestant Americans." His leading supporter was "Fighting" Bob Shuler, the powerful pastor of Trinity Methodist Church, whom historian Kevin Starr has called the "Savonarola of the Southland." Shuler invoked God's wrath almost weekly against the predominantly Jewish film industry. "There are poisons here that shall destroy the home, besmirch the virtue of womanhood and sully every whitened principle of social intercourse unless a mighty cleansing be wrought." In preaching his "Gospel of Fear," he interpreted every disaster— whether man-made (like the collapse of the St. Francis Dam in 1928) or natural (like the 1933 earthquake and the 1934 floods)—as merely a down payment on Los Angeles's well-earned final judgment.[50]

On the other side, the local literati, adopting the sarcastic style of H. L. Mencken, fought back with articles and pamphlets that increasingly depicted the Midwesterners as a geriatric army of doom. In a famous jibe, Edmund Wilson, on a 1930 swing through Southern California, took up the cudgels for the Hollywood intelligentsia, describing Shuler's American Gothic congregation as "those dowdy and dry-faced women, those dowdy and pasty girls, those old men with thin necks and sparse hairs, drooping forward their small bald foreheads, drawing in their recessive chins."[51] In San Diego, he parodied the death wish of these "doom people" as they discover that Southern California is no panacea for their ennui and despair:

> They stuff up the cracks of their doors and quietly turn on the gas; they go into their back sheds or back kitchens and eat antpaste or swallow Lysol; they drive their cars into dark alleys, get into the back seat and shoot themselves; they hang themselves in hotel bedrooms, take overdoses of sulfonal or barbital; they slip off to the municipal golf links and there stab themselves with carving-knives; or they throw themselves into the bay, blue and placid, where gray battleships and cruisers guard the limits of the broad-belting nation.[52]

It was left to Montana novelist Myron Brinig to first mate Los Angeles evangelicalism and bohemia in a savage satirical novel that ended in mock apocalypse. Brinig's *Flutter of an Eyelid* (1933) is actually a roman à clef based on a Palos Verdes swimming club that included photographer Edward Weston, impresario Merle Armitrage, and other well-known avant-gardists of the time.[53] Brinig, equally repelled by all of Southern California's fringe cultures, skewers both the club and its fundamentalist enemies in a surreal plot that moves at blitzkrieg speed toward the fulfillment of Money's curse.

Caslon Roanoke, Harvard man and esteemed historical novelist, is suffering from an acute case of Puritan gloom, when his doctor orders him out to Los Angeles for sunshine and recreation. He is instantly seduced by the fluttering eyelids of stunning Sylvia Prowse, whom he meets at a cocktail party in the bohemian beach colony of Alta Vista.

> "And you?" he dared to address her at last. "What do you do?"
> "I give and receive pain," she said.
> "Ah, that's interesting," said Caslon, already in pain.[54]

After this typically L.A. introduction, and a skinny-dip in the Pacific with Sylvia (where he marvels at his unexpected erection), Caslon becomes a full-fledged member of a libidinous clique that includes Angela Flower (a thinly disguised version of revivalist Aimee Semple McPherson).[55] When Angela is not healing the lame and blind at her Ten Million Dollar Heavenly Temple, she is prowling Alta Vista for "love meat" to feed her voracious sexual appetite.

On one of Angela's forays, she beds a handsome but dim-witted sailor who is a dead-ringer for a blond Jesus. After secretly grooming him for resurrection, she goes on radio to announce the Second Coming in downtown Los Angeles.[56] For a while, "Jesus" (who becomes a fervent city booster and movie fan) is more popular than Valentino or Lindbergh, but gradually the novelty fades, and many listeners begin to "turn the dial to a different station, a dance orchestra, a comedy sketch, a talk on beauty preparations."

Desperate, Angela promises that Jesus will walk on the waves at Venice Beach; and indeed he does defy gravity for a few moments—until, that is, he sees Sylvia swimming in the nude. Her fluttering eyelids break his trance and he sinks like a stone. Thousands of his disconsolate followers—Wilson's doom people—then cast themselves into the sea "in a final, conclusive baptism of death. . . . Heads bobbed up and down like cocoanuts cast off from a sinking ship, and stomachs that resembled fat pink islands, floated for a time before they dropped

Sister Aimee (1933)

from view." Inferring from Jesus' death and other occult signs that the end is nigh, Caslon wisely retreats to Boston on the eve of a cataclysmic earthquake. For the first time in pulp fiction, all of the Southland "slides swiftly, relentlessly, into the Pacific Ocean."[57]

> Los Angeles tobogganed with almost one continuous movement into the water, the shore cities going first, followed by the inland communities; the business streets, the buildings, the motion picture studios in Hollywood where actors became stark and pallid under their mustard-colored makeup.[58]

By one of those strange coincidences that Brinig evidently relished, his manuscript was at the printer on 10 March 1933 when an earthquake devastated Long Beach and Los Angeles's southern suburbs. (During the brief disruption of communications with the outside world, a rumor spread eastward that the entire metropolis had been obliterated.) This coincidence underscores the uncertain boundary between irony and tragedy when it comes to the destruction of Los Angeles. *The Flutter of an Eyelid* was one of those novels pregnant with the whole potentiality of a new genre. Indeed, Brinig virtually invented the Los Angeles disaster novel as a distinctive form by fusing regionally specific themes (cults, beach culture, Hollywood) with catastrophe in a ruthless Swiftian vision that repels any sympathy for the outlandish city and its even more bizarre inhabitants.*

In *The Flutter of an Eyelid* can be found many of the ingredients that would make Nathanael West's 1939 novel *Day of the Locust* famous, including zombielike Midwesterners, bizarre churches, a caricature of Aimee Semple McPherson, and an apocalyptic mob scene comparable to a great natural disaster. Yet, while West's novel has attained immortality—a staple of college survey courses in American literature—*The Flutter of an Eyelid* is totally forgotten. Certainly, West is the tauter, more indelibly "modernist" writer, but Brinig has the greater claim to thematic originality. The decisive factor in the failure of Brinig's otherwise darkly humorous and imaginative novel may well have been his unpardonable descent into ethnic caricature. Many readers, and eventually his own editors, interpreted Brinig's treatment of one character's obsessive, self-hating "Jewishness" as overt anti-Semitism. Despite Brinig's explicit denunciation of anti-Semites in a later Los Angeles novel, *The Flutter of an Eyelid*—never reprinted or issued in paperback—sank into obscurity under the weight of its unsavory reputation. As a result, West received the patent for literary invention that properly belonged to Brinig, while Edgar Cayce collected residuals for superquake clairvoyance.

In fact, West was not even the next in line to exploit the fruits of Brinig's imagination. A year before *Day of the Locust* was published, the well-known British playwright and novelist J. B. Priestley penned *The Doomsday Men,* which implicated the Los Angeles cult scene in a plot to blow up the world with an atomic bomb. Priestley's mad cult leader Father John and his two equally delusional brothers (a famous physicist and a wealthy banker) decide "to end the world's pain" and

---

* Brinig may also be the spirit with whom the famous clairvoyant Edgar Cayce communicated in 1936 when, supposedly in a deep trance, he saw Southern California sink into the Pacific during a great earthquake. This prediction, subsequently attributed to Nostradamus as well, would be repeated by six prominent psychics in the 1970s, although there was disagreement about whether Los Angeles would be totally submerged or continue to exist as an island (as in the 1997 film *Escape from L.A.*).[59]

give mankind "a good night's sleep" by detonating their secret super-weapon from a white tower in the Mojave Desert. John's grim follow-ers—"they were nearly all middle-aged or elderly, and a hard-faced lot, many of them with a strong weather-beaten look, not like city folks"—gather on the hillsides around the tower to sing death psalms. At the last moment, the world is saved by a drunken Hollywood stunt pilot who crashes his biplane into one of the power pylons supplying energy to the white tower.[60]

Priestley later disowned *The Doomsday Men,* written with an eye to quick movie adaptation, as "a mistake."[61] But its popularity, like that enjoyed by *Day of the Locust,* confirmed the continuing allure of Brinig's cult-catastrophe formula, as did another Los Angeles novel, *The Devil Is a Lonely Man,* published posthumously in 1946 (its author, Morrison Wood, had perished on the Bataan death march). Racial hysteria erupts from every page of this bizarre novel, which reads like a seriously psychotic version of *Gone with the Wind.* Sena-tor Anthony Wayne—a Southern grandee transplanted to Southern California—manipulates a nihilistic religious sect, the Church of Love, to make himself master of Los Angeles. At the height of his power, however, Wayne discovers to his horror that his beautiful wife "under her blond coloring . . . is a Negress." With a raging flood in the background as a symbol of racial chaos, Wayne flings his wife out of an airplane and then kills himself.[62]

In his 1954 novel *Messiah,* Gore Vidal gave the Brinig subgenre a high gloss polish without descending into the racial inferno. He tells the story of the hypnotic mortician John Cave—a combination of L. Ron Hubbard, Rasputin, and Dr. Jack Kevorkian—who incarnates the death wish in an age of nuclear pessimism. With the help of Hol-lywood's top publicist, a kitchen cabinet of rich Southern Californi-ans, and the new mesmerism of television, Cave transforms himself from an obscure Los Angeles cult leader into a modern god whose stunningly simple message is "Death is Good." When his own con-tinued existence suggests a contradiction in terms, he is summarily murdered by his fanatical disciples, each of whom nurtures his or her own messianic ambition.

With their irresistible franchise on Thanatos, the doom people begin to take over the entire world, fighting bitter civil wars with Catholics and orthodox Jews. The novel itself is recounted from a hiding place in the ancient (still Moslem) city of Luxor by Gene Luther, a sexually impotent classicist who has elaborated Cave's simplistic utterances into a baroque theology of Cavesword. As agents of mother goddess Iris Mortimer (his former girlfriend) close in all around him, Luther—who has become Cavesway's Trotsky in exile—recalls driving across Los Angeles with Iris to hear Cave speak for the first time. His last free thought before falling under Cave's hypnotic influence was a startling vision of inevitable (atomic?) devastation.

> As we drove down the empty streets, I saw ruins and dust where houses were and, among the powdery debris of stucco all in mounds, the rusted antennae of television sets like the bones of awful beasts whose vague but terrible proportions will alone survive to attract the unborn stranger's eye.[63]

6. GROUND ZERO

There will be those who say that the end came, I mean the END, with an avenging God and the whole shebang. . . . But I say there was a race of hardy laughers, mystics, crazies, who knew their real homes, or who had been drawn to this gold coast for years, and they lived through the destroying light, and on, into Light ages.

Golden Days (1987)

Was the first nuclear weapon tested off the coast of San Diego during the administration of Grover Cleveland? Or was the atomic bomb invented in 1907 by Pasadena's most famous resident, Upton Sinclair? A tongue-in-cheek case can be made for each of these astounding propositions.

Thus, at the climax of Thomas and Anna Fitch's 1891 potboiler *Better Days: Or, Millionaire of To-morrow,* the millionaire hero, in an effort to persuade the representatives of the world powers assembled at the Hotel Coronado in San Diego to abandon war, stages an early Bikini test by blowing up the nearby Coronado Islands with an explosive called "potentite."[64] This is one of the earliest appearances in fiction of a nonbiological doomsday weapon with the capacity to destroy cities and even entire civilizations. Together with a few other novels of the later 1890s, it directly prefigured the apocalyptic powers of atomic energy.[65]

Although H. G. Wells—tutored by his eminent physicist friend Frederick Soddy—usually receives credit for inventing both the term and the concept of the "atomic bomb" in his prophetic 1914 novel *The World Set Free,* Upton Sinclair claimed to hold an earlier patent. In 1907, while living in New Jersey, he wrote a "little farce comedy of the future" based on a story idea that he had purchased from a fellow socialist named Fred Warren. It was never produced as a play but was finally published by the author in Pasadena as a novel, *The Millennium (A Comedy of the Year 2000)* in 1924.

The story opens at a Neronian party in the half-mile-high Manhattan "Pleasure Palace" of Lumley-Gotham, the emperor of America's financial aristocracy. His chief scientist has just discovered a new radioactive element, "X-radiumite," which he hopes will power communication with the inhabitants of Mars. Unfortunately, the vial of pure radiumite is also incredibly dangerous. "The Professor declared that if the jar were dropped, the result would be the annihilation of all animal life upon the surface of the globe." Naturally, the professor drops the jar.[66]

The only survivors are 11 passengers on a new intercontinental superplane. Sinclair then uses the conventions of the "last man" story to satirize the bourgeoisie's inability to survive in a world without servants or employees. The pilot and butler become the heroes of the new society, while one of the plutocrats starves to death amid his hoarded wealth.

If Sinclair's chronological claims are correct, then his comic atomic explosion predated *The World Set Free,* although it was Wells's horrifying vision of aerial atomic warfare in the "world war of 1958" that became the template for future nuclear catastrophe fiction.[67] The awkward atomic devices in Corelli and Priestley were both spin-offs of Wells, although the plots of both novels were too comic opera to inspire fear. The first truly convincing account of the horror of nuclear warfare was Philip Wylie's astonishing 1943 short story, "The Paradise Crater," with Los Angeles again nominated as ground zero. According to literary historians Bruce Franklin and Paul Brians, the pioneer West Coast sci-fi writer was put under house arrest, "even threatened with death," for compromising the security of the Manhattan Project with this tale of a former Olympic hero who battles a terrorist network of Nazi refugees in Southern California in the year 1965.[68] Sneaking into the Nazis' secret cavern, the hero (unwisely) sabotages their cache of atomic weapons. As the ensuing explosion obliterates Los Angeles and shoots flames 40 thousand feet into the sky, Wylie anticipates the terrifying scenes that 18 months later would come true in Hiroshima and Nagasaki.[69]

The authorities did not allow this chilling premonition of nuclear destruction to be published until the war was over. Then, with the beginning of the Cold War, the nukes began to fall like fiery rain on Los Angeles.

In the 1953 Paramount version of *The War of the Worlds,* for example, the air force sends the Flying Wing to drop an H-bomb—to no effect—on the Martian invaders gathered in the Puente Hills. The angry Martians retaliate by blowing the ziggurat off the top of Los Angeles's City Hall.* Robert Aldrich, in his 1955 film adaptation of Mickey Spillane's *Kiss Me Deadly,* punishes the evil Lily Carver (and most of Malibu) with a personal nuclear holocaust when she foolishly

---

* As local yokels unwisely advance toward the white-hot Martian capsule, one nervously asks, "What shall we say to them?" The other furrows his brow in deep thought. "Welcome to California?" he suggests.

opens a Pandora's box containing stolen plutonium.[70] The rebellious supercomputer in charge of the U.S. nuclear arsenal in Dennis Jones's *Colossus* (1966) punishes tampering by exploding a few megatons over downtown Los Angeles.[71] (The City of Angels, however, gets its revenge in Dennis Palumbo's 1979 satire *City Wars* by teaming with San Francisco to nuke obnoxious Sunbelt rival Dallas.)[72]

Ground zero books and movies, like the alien airship fantasies of the 1890s, accommodated a full spectrum of racial and biological phobias. Thus, while writers were struggling to destroy Los Angeles in new and ever more preposterous ways, B-moviemakers were rearming the screaming yellow hordes with nuclear weapons. In *Port of Hell* (1954), a freighter enters Los Angeles Harbor containing a Chinese A-bomb set to explode in 12 hours. Square-jawed Dane Clark, playing a port inspector, races against time to drag the bomb out to sea. A decade later, wily Chinese agents, in *Dimension Five* (1966), hide an even bigger bomb in a Los Angeles–bound rice ship. This time Jeff Hunter and his Asian sidekick, France Nuyen, use time travel belts to foil the conspiracy. Really pissed off now, the Red Chinese decide to tunnel under the Pacific using a superlaser in *Battle Beneath the Earth* (1967). Mao is stopped before he reaches Malibu by "Sinbad" actor Kerwin Mathews.

In Robert Moore Williams's 1961 novel, *The Day They H-Bombed Los Angeles,* stunned survivors of the mushroom cloud over the harbor emerge from a San Pedro bomb shelter to discover that Los Angeles was nuked, not by the "dirty commies," but by the Pentagon. The reason: to destroy the giant mutant protein molecules—nightmare by-products of American H-bomb testing in the South Pacific—that have invaded Southern California. Arriving as a scum on the surface of waves, the molecules, like monster versions of Richard Dawkins's selfish genes with "no morals of any kind," have been turning the population into crazed, flesh-eating zombies led by howling wolf women. The patriotic survivalists, led by an FBI agent and a tough ex-marine, exterminate vast multitudes of the living dead in heroic hand-to-hand combat. In the novel's most emotional scene,

Red hordes under Malibu (*Battle Beneath the Earth*)

---

a "bullet knocks a molecule out of control" (?), allowing a dying zombie to briefly regain his humanity.

> "This is the human part of me talking," Eric Bloor's whisper came again. "This is the kid you once knew; the kid who was scared of a pet poodle, the kid who had to whistle to find the courage to pass a cemetery at night."[73]

Steve De Jarnett's 1988 film *Miracle Mile* finds black humor as well as true love at ground zero. Until the ICBMs come arcing over the Hollywood sign, it is not clear whether nuclear war is really imminent or Los Angeles has simply been unhinged by rumor. The city—riven by crime and racial conflict—is so close to meltdown that the H-bombs are almost superfluous. Yet, even on the last shopping day in the history of the world, romance manages to brighten the face of extinction. As doomed lovers Harry and Julie slowly sink into the La

The Pentagon nukes L.A.

Brea Tar Pits, they find consolation in the prospect that "we will metamorphosize together."

The culmination of the Los Angeles nuke novel is undoubtedly Carolyn See's much praised *Golden Days* (1987), a "survivor's tale" with a feminist twist. Edith Langley and Lorna Villanelle are best friends who have bootstrapped their way through 30 years of broken marriages, unreliable lovers, and single parenthood to finally achieve power and comfort as independent women. In the face of sudden nuclear devastation, the true measure of their strength emerges. Lorna becomes a new age prophetess while Edith saves her extended family.

Investing her two "ladies of the canyons" with mythic, Gaian powers of survival and regeneration, See picks up the threads of the classic genre, sketched earlier, of women's romantic disaster fiction. But her critique of the male gender is considerably more radical. In Edith's view, humanity has been literally "led by the dick" to the edge of extinction. In order to explain the final descent into nuclear war, she tells the story of one day in the life of an average middle-class man—"just a man, you know?"—as he is driven by his fear of death and the imperatives of his penis to betray his wife, mistresses, and children. Whether he realizes it or not, he is a shareholder in the same missile-wielding phallocracy—"the great on-going dick-waving contest of the centuries"—that ultimately betrays life itself.

> In the last minutes, women turned on their husbands: "You, you did this!" speaking in tones, the tones they had used before only when giving birth, so that some men, even in the midst of their great fear were blown off the planet looking sheepish. By you, the women meant men, males: Caspar Weinberger, Alexander Haig, Ronald Reagan, but afterwards they couldn't remember those names, only the shape of the missiles and the bragging and bullying that had preceded these times. For a while a few women went to the few intact male corpses they could find, castrated them, pinned the bloody, dried penises to walls and tree trunks, with the scrawled word peacekeeper, but soon it didn't seem worth the trouble.[74]

Edith's (and See's) feminist righteousness is laced with extraordinary snobbery. Topanga Canyon, where Edith has built her nest, is a redoubt of special people ("our friends, our family") who had the courageous good taste to spend the last days before the holocaust enjoying dinner at Spago or making love on the beach. Meanwhile, "the stupid ones, the really stupid ones, who lived in the goatish eastern suburbs of L.A.—Pomona, Covina, Alhambra, Upland—took their impulse to flee but took it east. Can you believe it?" Edith gloats over the destruction of the blue-collar plains and ticky-tacky suburban valleys. When desperate refugees from the flatlands (should we assume minorities?) seek refuge in the canyons and hillsides they are speared by her "loving neighbors."

Indeed, the "golden days" of the novel's ironic title glow because only the most spiritually sensitive and ecologically in-tune people— a new age mistress race—have endured to enjoy the matriarchal utopia that women like Edith and Lorna are building on the ruins of the old phallocentric world. Without bad or "stupid" people around, Southern California again becomes lushly Edenic, and the new Topangans can live off seeds and wildflowers. That is why there is no mourning in Edith's tale, only an increasingly creepy celebration of gourmet survivalism.

7. GREEN GATES OF HELL

"I have made an unusual discovery," said Doctor Grimsby.
"What is that?" asked Doctor Maxwell.
"Los Angeles is alive."
Doctor Maxwell blinked.
"I beg your pardon," he said.

"The Creeping Terror" (1961)

Since Richard Jefferies first imagined London dying in its own sewage and pollution in the mid-1880s, ecological self-destruction has been a minor, but persistent, theme in urban disaster fiction. The emergence of the modern environmental movement in the late 1960s opened a larger niche for the "ecocatastrophe novel" as a subgenre in its own right. Like the inevitability of nuclear war, the biological unsustainability of the giant city is now firmly lodged in contemporary doom consciousness.

Los Angeles, of course, is perfectly cast in the role of environmental suicide. Only Mexico City has more completely toxified its natural setting, and no other metropolis in the industrialized Northern Hemisphere continues to grow at such breakneck speed. It is not surprising, then, that the climax of the postwar boom in the mid-1960s saw the parallel emergence of fictional and nonfictional accounts of imminent ecological collapse, frequently in tandem with Malthusian fears about too many poor people of color.

Yet nothing written in the past 30 years comes close to the mordancy of Ward Moore's 1947 comic novel, *Greener Than You Think*.[75] Moore was the first writer to convincingly turn the tables on Los Angeles: the city that had for decades consumed nature in voracious bulldozer bites is itself bitten back and consumed. His novel is about the lawn that ate Hollywood. It is, by turns, the funniest and the most frightening Los Angeles disaster book ever written.

Albert Weener is a huckster down on his luck but convinced that he possesses messianic sales potential. An obscure want ad introduces him to Josephine Spencer Francis, the inventor of Metamorphizer, a superfertilizer that allows plants to metabolize virtually anything. Francis wants to end world hunger by increasing grain production, but Weener is only interested in his commission. Ignoring her complaints about "imbeciles [who] grow grass in a desert," he peddles her formula door-to-door as a miracle treatment for tired lawns: "One shot of Meta—one shot of Francis' Amazing Discovery and your lawn springs to new life."[76]

His first and only customers, in a dowdy section of Hollywood, are the Dinkmans. Their lawn is the most miserable in the neighborhood; an embarrassing toupee of yellowing Bermuda grass, the color of "moldy straw." But once Meta stimulates its insatiable appetite, Los Angeles, and eventually the world, is doomed. In the futile war against the Dinkmans' lawn, mowers are replaced by sickles, then by flamethrowers, tanks, and B-29s, and, finally, by atomic bombs. All the explosive energy expended against the devil grass merely increases the fervor with which its green tentacles clutch the city.

> Out through Cahuenga Pass it flowed, toward fertile San Fernando Valley. Steadily it climbed to the hilltops, masticating sage, greasewood, oak, sycamore and manzanita with the same ease it bolted down houses and pavements. Into Griffith Park it swaggered, mumbling the planetarium, Mount Hollywood, and Fern Dell in successive mouthfuls and swarmed down to the concrete-bed of the Los Angeles River. Here ineffectual shallow pools had preserved illusion and given tourists something at which to laugh in the dry season; the weed licked them up like a thirsty cow at wallow.[77]

After the failure of an air force incendiary attack, the seat of government is hurriedly evacuated to the refugee mecca of Pomona. Religious sects proclaim the divinity of the grass. Real estate speculators commit suicide. Politicians suggest emigration to Mars. And refugees' mouths gape as they look back, toward the west, at the towering green mountain of hungry grass where City Hall once stood. It is left to *Time* magazine to pronounce the official obituary: "Death, as it must to all, came last week to Los Angeles. The metropolis of the Southwest died gracelessly, undignifiedly . . . swallowed up, Jonahwise, by the advance of the terrifying Bermuda grass."[78]

While the grass pauses to digest Southern California, the government builds an enormous Maginot Line of salt across the desert. The green juggernaut resumes its advance, but as Weener watches from a balloon, it is stopped in its tracks by the band of salt. There is national thanksgiving. ("In frantic joy women were raped in the streets, dozens of banks were looted, thousands of plate-glass windows were smashed, while millions of celebrants wept tears of 86 proof ecstasy.")[79] As business returns to normal, the United States and the USSR decide to go to war.

The commie hordes, with a delightful taste for Ansel Adams scenery, land on the California coast at Big Sur, Cambria, and San Simeon. San Francisco is eventually captured and Market Street is renamed "Krassny Prospekt." All this, however, is a mere warm-up for the major Red Army offensive (on snowshoes) across the Grass. It is *War and Peace* gone mad.

> Long after their brave start the crazed and starving survivors began trickling into the American lines where they surrendered. They were dull and listless except for one strange manifestation: they shied away fearfully from every living plant or growth, but did they see a bare patch of soil, a boulder or stretch of sand, they clutched, kissed, mumbled and wept over it in a very frenzy.[80]

Soon the Grass resumes its terrible advance, over the Rockies and down into the amber fields of wheat, crossing the Mississippi at Dubuque. Weener, whose fortunes are serendipitously synchronized to those of Mrs. Dinkman's lawn, has meanwhile become America's corporate master through shrewd war profiteering. With other members of his ruling elite, he decamps for Europe as total panic breaks out in the shrinking circle of American cities. . . . (With respect for the pleasure of Moore's future readers in mind, I will not divulge the last half of this astounding novel.)

In his 1961 short story, "The Creeping Terror," Richard Matheson spoofed both Moore and Los Angeles's out-of-control suburban growth. Following freakish deluges in the summer of 1972, Los Angeles itself suddenly jolts to life as a single asphalt-and-citrus megafungus. Its spores, in the form of erratic orange trees, suddenly appear in the middle of Nebraska wheat fields, while delusional Midwesterners in bathing suits "wander helplessly across the plains and prairies searching for the Pacific Ocean." Within a year only New England is still resisting the mindless blob. As the Los Angeles city limits inexorably encircle the Puritans' "city on the hill," proud Bostonians choose mass suicide rather than surrender to bermuda shorts and drive-in theaters. Shortly afterward the nation's capital is moved to Beverly Hills and a new anthem is adopted: "Sing out O land, with flag unfurled! Los Angeles! Tomorrow's World!"[81]

Ecogigantism—as with Moore's globe-choking lawn or Matheson's fungal suburban sprawl—soon became the dominant allegorical device in environmental science fiction. The giant mutant ants in Gordon Douglas's 1954 film *Them!* may be the products of nuclear testing in the desert, but when they move into the Los Angeles River—now entombed in concrete and steel—they become potent symbols of the city's destruction of nature as well. Other icky mutants—covered with slime and oozing toxic juices—attempt to turn Los Angeles into a friendly environment for fungi in Robert Hutton's independent film *The Slime People* (1963). Ecocrud again rises to the surface in Stephen Traxler's *Slithis* (1978), gobbling up aging hippies and Porsche-set yuppies alike in Venice Beach.

"One giant slurb," stretching from Santa Barbara to the Mexican border, is the dystopian vision in Curt Gentry's *Last Days of the Late, Great State of California* (1968). Although Gentry disposes of Southern

Nature's revenge (*Them!*)

California (and part of the Bay Area) with one of Reverend Money's long slides into the Pacific—"Oh, my God! Los Angeles has vanished!!"—the San Andreas event is strictly window dressing in an only semifictional polemic. "The greatest irony of all," Gentry explains, "is that no earthquake or act of God was necessary to destroy California. Man, with his ingenuity, was managing to do it all by himself."[82]

Gentry's book, written a few years after the Watts riot, is memorable for its conjugation of environmental crisis and that familiar creature of the catastrophe genre—race war. On the one hand, Gentry argues that suburbanization, like Moore's Bermuda grass, is devouring natural resources and open space at rates that will soon force residents to depend on their own reclaimed sewage as the primary water supply. On the other hand, he speculates that "in time the major claims to distinction of San Francisco, Oakland, Los Angeles, San Diego" may well be that "they were the battlegrounds where the great war between whites and blacks was fought." The confluence of environmental breakdown and race war, he feared, would result in not just "destruction, but something in many ways worse, living death."[83]

Race and ecology are also combined, along with wall-to-wall sex, in Philip Wylie's 1971 soft-core potboiler, *Los Angeles: A.D. 2017.* Publishing magnate Glen Howard awakens from a 47-year sleep to discover that Los Angeles has been destroyed by an omnibus environmental catastrophe that features toxic algal blooms, arctic frosts, and a final exterminating smog. Anticipating the worst, big corporations and their executives have clandestinely built underground pleasure domes for survival. New Los Angeles, Howard discovers, is a subterranean version of the Playboy mansion, where a few thousand select inhabitants (like the golden people in See's novel) grope and orgy while waiting for the surface to become habitable again. In order to enhance "executive-quality genes" in the surviving population, however, reproduction is organized on strict eugenic principles. As Howard's girlfriend explains, the environmental collapse (nature's "final solution") was really a providential deliverance from rampant overpopulation, mongrelization, and "race decay." "Runts, culls. The feeble-minded!" she rants. "The more your 'humane' values held, and the more your medical arts advanced, the more of these genetic nothings were allowed to live, even to breed."[84]

8. THE CINEMATIC DISASTER NOVEL

With incredible speed, the city of Los Angeles virtually disintegrates. The earth tilts and is torn apart, creating crevasses that swallow hundreds of screaming men and women. High buildings crumble into rubble and dust. Elevated freeways collapse, dropping cars and trucks to destruction below.

Earthquake *(1974)*

If there is an iron law of disaster in Southern California, it is simply that bad news for the region is usually good news for "the industry." Like one of the indestructible parasites of disaster fiction, Hollywood fattens on the spectacle of natural catastrophe and racial turmoil, exploiting the free "production values" provided by Los Angeles's periodic upheavals. The classic example was the San Fernando earthquake of February 1971, which killed 64 people and damaged 23,000 structures. Its aftershocks were still rattling windows in Universal City when MCA commissioned Mario Puzo, the best-selling author of *The Godfather*, to craft a screenplay about the city's destruction by the Big One.

Detente had already thrown the nuclear doomsday genre into recession, and Universal was looking for a new disaster film to replicate the box office success of *Airport*. According to George Fox, the (comedy) writer who was later imported to finish Puzo's script, the San Fernando earthquake had led one of MCA's top executives to a stunning epiphany:

> It occurred to me that in just about every disaster movie you had a bunch of people getting on a boat or a plane. *Airport, Poseidon Adventure, High and the Mighty,* damned near all of them. But millions of men and women hardly ever get on boats or planes. What about a picture where the common disaster comes to them, instead of the other way around? Let's get that audience![85]

The audience was "got," of course, with the most expensive special effects budget in history. Director Mark Robson (a veteran of Val Lewton's famous low-budget horror unit at RKO) conscripted an extraordinary production team that included two Academy Award–winning art directors, John Ford's former film editor, and the industry's top model builders, special-effects cinematographers, matte artists, and stunt people. After convincingly leveling half the city and killing off thousands of extras, their master touch was the collapse of the Hollywood Reservoir during one of the aftershocks. Audience anxiety was raised by Sensurround, a gimmicky system of hidden speakers whose low-frequency vibrations emulated the rumble of a real earthquake. With unusual toughmindedness, the screen-

Earthquake (1974)

play let Charlton Heston and Ava Gardner drown and refused a heroic resolution. The screenplay's final line was: "Distant sirens wail, and National Guard gunfire crackles, as Los Angeles burns on."[86]

The huge success of the film (advertised by Universal as the first "super-spectacular") spurred others to emulate its combination of tense characterizations (all the figures in *Earthquake* are portrayed at the edge of personal abysses) and a Cecil B. DeMille approach to disaster scenes. Indeed, in the decade following the film's premiere in 1974, more than a dozen novels—all aspiring to be made into successor films—diligently copied this underlying formula while diversifying the agencies of doom to include comet impacts, tsunamis, landslides, firestorms, blizzards, and even giant alligators.[87] In every case the novel's treatment was fundamentally cinematic, with emphasis on a climactic disaster scene equivalent to the bursting of the Hollywood Reservoir.

Unlike the screenplay for *Earthquake,* however, which downplayed Los Angeles's racial tensions, subsequent disaster fictions openly exploited white anxiety and xenophobia. The 1970s were a period of transition in Los Angeles, as the WASP stronghold became a cosmopolitan metropolis with an emergent non-Anglo majority. Mexican immigrants were displacing Midwesterners as the largest single "ethnic" group, and the city was bitterly dividing over issues of school busing, tax reform, crime, and police abuse. Whites were bolting from the public school system in growing numbers, and the first gated and walled subdivisions had started to appear. Surfing and beach blanket bingo were giving way to a hyperviolent gang culture. And there was growing apprehension that natural disaster might destroy the increasingly precarious firewall that separated the suburban "us" from the inner city "them."

The Manson Family's satanic fantasy of "Helter-Skelter"—an anarchic race war unleashed by a giant earthquake or its equivalent—proved an irresistible lure to disaster writers of the 1970s. While Puzo was still struggling with the intricacies of the first draft of *Earthquake,* Rudolph Wurlitzer had already ejaculated the Burroughsian, methamphetamine-propelled stream of consciousness known as *Quake* (1972). An M 7.6 earthquake wrecks the Tropicana Motel on Santa Monica Boulevard in the first paragraph, and like an insect colony suddenly exposed to the light, the crazed survivors either fuck or kill each other in the ruins of Hollywood, while organized gangs undertake more systematic action. After escaping a mass execution in a high school football stadium, Wurlitzer's unnamed protagonist is captured by some delirious sadists (shades of Alex and his droogs in *Clockwork Orange*) who drip hot marshmallows into his eyes and place a severed head on his catsup-smeared chest. His last words: "Oooooooooooh!"[88]

The first novel inspired by the San Fernando quake that had big-screen ambitions, however, was Alistair MacLean's *Goodbye California* (1977). In it the king of cold war macho pulp (*Guns of Navarone, Ice Station Zebra,* etc.) attempts to conjugate the Big One with a far-fetched yellow hordes conspiracy. Islamic guerrillas from Mindanao kidnap leading nuclear physicists and force them (with the help of an infamous Argentine torturer) to build a dozen hydrogen bombs, using plutonium stolen from California nuclear power plants. To demonstrate their malevolence, the terrorists detonate one of the devices under Santa Monica Bay. The resulting tsunami "was not a wave in the true sense, just an enormously smooth and unbroken swell, completely silent in its approach, a silence that served only to intensify the impression that here was an alien monster . . . bent upon a mindless destruction."[89]

The breathtaking image of a mile-high tsunami slamming into Santa Monica was simultaneously the pièce de résistance of *Lucifer's Hammer,* a potboiler by Larry Niven and Jerry Pournelle. As horrified Soviet and American astronauts watch from their orbiting space station, the dozen mountain-sized fragments constituting the nucleus of Comet Hammer-Brown (aka the Hammer) devastate the Northern Hemisphere. A huge impact in the eastern Pacific sends a Himalayan wall of water toward poor old Santa Monica Beach, where some terminally "stoked" surfers are waiting. On the precipice of the towering curl, one after another loses balance and catapults down the face of the "green wall" until only "Gil" is left.

> Death. Inevitable. If death was inevitable, what was left? Style, only style. . . . The wave's frothing peak was far, far above him; the churning base was much too close. His legs shrieked in the agony of exhaustion. One board left ahead of him, ahead and below. Who? It didn't matter; he saw it dip into chaos, gone. Gil risked a quick look back: nobody there. He was alone on the ultimate wave.[90]

Yet even at this supreme existential moment, Gil's attention (like the authors') is diverted by the fantasy of movie rights:

> Oh, God, if he lived to tell this tale, what a movie it would make! Bigger than *The Endless Summer,* bigger than *The Towering Inferno:* a surfing movie with ten million in special effects! If only his legs would hold! He already had a world record, he must be at least a mile inland, no one had ever ridden a wave for a mile! But the frothing, purling peak was miles overhead

and the Barrington Apartments, thirty stories tall, was coming
at him like a flyswatter.[91]

With Los Angeles a drowned Atlantis, the second half of the novel
abruptly shifts to the foothills of the Sierra, where the surviving "haves"
regroup to battle invading "have-nots." The war of extermination that
follows is essentially the same one the Aryan survivors waged against
the cannibal ape-men in George England's *Darkness and Dawn*. On
one side is Republican Senator Arthur Jellison's Stronghold, dominated by local farm owners and refugee capitalists from Beverly Hills.
Admission to this fortified country club is restricted to conservative
property owners, beautiful women, and a handful of scientists and
craftsmen selected for their unique expertise.

On the other side is the New Brotherhood, a kind of nomadic Jones-
town led by Henry Armitage, a mad preacher who proposes to complete the work of the Hammer by leveling every vestige of technology,
social rank, or race distinction. His followers include a band of can-
nibalistic "street brothers" from South Central, a few organizers for
the farmworkers' union, some fanatical white environmentalists
obsessed with destroying California's last remaining nuclear power
plant, and all the outcast survivors refused admission to the Stronghold. They are united as "living Angels" by their sacramental consumption of human meat.

The Stronghold's defenders use mustard gas and homemade napalm
to annihilate the savage invaders who crawl "like snails . . . leaving trails
of red slime" to the river to die. The few wounded Angels left alive on
the battlefield are summarily executed by the novel's hero, a former
Hollywood television producer named Harvey Randall, who cheerfully
notes that their bodies "make good fertilizer." The rest of the captured
Brotherhood are put to work as slaves on Senator Jellison's plantations,
while the San Joaquin Nuclear Plant, saved from Armitage's Luddite
fury, powers the Stronghold's rapid expansion.[92]

As only British reviewers seemed to have noticed, "the new America
begins to emerge as a white nuclear state that has gassed its enemies
and reintroduced slavery."[93] Nonwhites, with the exception of the

Stronghold's "Tule Indian" allies, are all but extinct. Only 10 blacks are left alive in California (not including the token black astronaut befriended by Senator Jellison), and the citizenry of the Stronghold rejoice when they find out that China, wiped out by a joint USA-USSR nuclear strike, is being recolonized by European Russian refugees. *Lucifer's Hammer*—a best-seller published by Playboy Press—resonates with the exterminationist fury of a nineteenth-century racial polemic.

Although comets, blizzards, firestorms, and even volcanoes expanded the creative range of disaster fiction over these years, the great earthquake remained the central image of doomsday Los Angeles. Like the San Fernando quake 22 years before, the January 1994 Northridge earthquake was immediately followed by literary and cinematic aftershocks. Within two weeks, the famed sci-fi writer Arthur Clarke had produced a movie treatment, later turned into *Richter 10* (1996) by his collaborator, Mike McQuay. The novel, which begins by recounting how Lewis Crane, the world's greatest seismologist, lost his family in the Northridge quake 30 years before, is an interesting benchmark for the genre's evolution since *Earthquake*.

Race war and natural disaster, intricately entangled with one another, are now coequal themes. Crane, who believes he can use hydrogen bombs to weld tectonic plates together and stop future earthquakes, plays a complicated game of geopolitics with the giant Chinese corporations that now control America and the rest of the word. His brilliant African-American assistant, Dan Newcombe, is gradually sucked into a jihad being waged by the Nation of Islam in the "War Zone" of South Central Los Angeles. Later a devastating earthquake (a repeat of the 1812 New Madrid catastrophe) changes the course of the Mississippi River and gives secessionist blacks an independent foothold on reclaimed river bottoms. Following a series of bloody ghetto rebellions in Los Angeles and elsewhere, hundreds of thousands of blacks emigrate to "New Cairo," which becomes an independent nation with Newcombe—now called "Talib"—as its Nelson Mandela.

Crane, meanwhile, predicts the ultimate Los Angeles temblor, the Richter 10 of the book's title, for 3 June 2058. The Elysian Park fault will fissure the whole city, "dropping entire blocks miles down into the ground, never to be seen again . . . a conflagration the likes of which hasn't been seen on this planet in millions of years." Crane invites his old friend Talib to join him at ground zero, as most of the city's hysterical population flees toward refugee camps in Oregon and Arizona, leaving only the gangs and cult groups behind. The two old comrades walk "into the guts of the city, destruction and anarchy reigning all around them. So much had changed in Crane's time on Earth; so much had stayed the same. There were the looters, the Rockers, who were now called the Seismos, the suicides, and the Cosmies dressed in white robes with the Third Eye emblazoned in red on their chests."[94]

Crane and Talib await the Moneyan apocalypse in the rooftop restaurant of a Wilshire skyscraper with a spectacular view of the Los Angeles Basin. As the city is shaken apart, they download the contents of their brains into a computer and instantly reincarnate themselves as grandfatherly virtual spirits, watching over the utopian colony that Crane has providentially founded on the dark side of the moon. Helter-Skelter unexpectedly gives way to an old-fashioned romantic ending reminiscent of Morgana Royal's triumphant flight to the Brazen City in Corelli's *Secret Power.*

9. FINAL SOLUTIONS

What a miracle it is to walk streets which only a few weeks ago were filled with non-Whites lounging at every street corner and in every doorway and to see only White faces— clean, happy, enthusiastic White faces, determined and hopeful for the future! No sacrifice is too great to successfully complete our revolution and secure that future for them— and for the girls of the 128th Los Angeles Food Brigade.

The Turner Diaries *(1978)*

From the late 1970s, the Los Angeles disaster novel was fundamentally reconfigured. The preceding decade's focus on the disaster event in all its cinematic glory was superceded by a renewed interest in the "survivor's tale" of life among the ruins.[95] But two very different kinds of postcatastrophe fiction emerged: what might be called the "magical dystopian" and the "armageddonist." As we shall see shortly, many of the city's best writers—all of whom fall into the liberal or radical dystopian camp—have exploited catastrophe to fashion alternative Los Angeleses with surreal topographies, genders, and futures. Cataclysm, usually without racial subtitles, allows them to shape fantastic physical and psychic landscapes out of old clichés. In effect, they have become the local franchise of magical realism.

The other road to the apocalypse, however, leads back to the racial infernos of Dooner, Hay, Wallace, and Shiel. The key figure here is the wild Aryan warrior slugging it out with evil aliens or mutants in the urban wasteland. The seminal text for contemporary armageddonists is unquestionably Philip Francis Nowlan's Buck Rogers saga, composed of two novellas, "Armageddon 2419 A.D." and "The Airlords of Han," serialized in *Amazing Stories* in 1928 and 1929.[96] Although not specifically about Los Angeles, the extraordinarily popular Nowlan stories have influenced all subsequent survivalist fiction cast in the Aryan-versus-Alien mode.

Nowlan begins where Dooner ended, with a "Mongolian Blight" in control of the former United States. Buck Rogers is a latter-day Rip Van Winkle who has been asleep for five hundred years in an abandoned Pennsylvania coal mine, kept alive by radioactive gas. He awakens to discover that white Americans have been reduced to a handful of wild tribes living in the forests and wastelands outside the 15 skyscraper cities of their Manchurian conquerors, the Han Airlords. The technologically superior Hans (truly alien since they have inbred with extraterrestrials) had used "disintegrator rays" to conquer the world early in the twenty-second century.

For generations the scattered American "gangs" have been waging futile guerrilla warfare against the invincible Hans. Doughboy hero Rogers, however, unites them into a powerful army wielding a secret weapon, a synthetic element called "Inertron" that is "dense in molecular structure" but has no weight, heat, or kinetic energy. Under

Rogers's leadership, they eventually besiege and destroy the great Han cities—Nu-Yok, Si-kaga, Sa-Lus, etc.—in terrible hand-to-hand combat. Although when briefly captured Rogers is treated as an "honored guest" by the "decadently civilized" Airlords, the ferocious American tribesmen show no mercy to any Han unlucky enough to fall into their hands. Every single Manchurian is eventually hunted down and butchered in a joyous "reclamation of America."

> Hans who reached the ground alive were never taken prisoner. Not even the splendid discipline of the Americans could curb the wild hate developed through centuries of oppression, and the Hans were mercilessly slaughtered when they did not save us the trouble by committing suicide.... Thrust! Cut! Crunch! Slice! Thrust! Up and down with vicious, tireless, flashing speed swung the bayonets and axe-bladed butts of the American gunners.[97]

Four aspects of the Buck Rogers story, read today, are particularly striking. First is the ironic inversion of the hordes plot: the alien Han are now urban and sophisticated, while the Americans have reverted to the primitive values—a warrior ethos, leadership by heroes, communal property, and so on—supposedly characteristic of their Germanic ancestors. Second, the Americans are organized into local tribes or fighting gangs that eerily prefigure the "militia movement" of the 1990s. Third, the city is now the physical and cultural incarnation of the aliens and their values, and so its destruction has become a sacred obligation. Fourth, the Aryans struggle not just for supremacy but for racial purification. Victory means the biological eradication of the aliens, including children (like Airlord San-Lan's charming nine-year-old daughter, Lu-Yan).*

---

* Later editions of the Buck Rogers stories have expurgated racist locutions ("inhuman yellow blight," "yellow incubus," etc.) and changed the uniformly Anglo-Saxon surnames of the Americans to reflect a multiethnic cast.[98]

In 1978 the American Nazi Andrew Macdonald recycled Buck Rogers's war against the Hans, element by element, as a nauseating fantasy about the ethnic cleansing of Los Angeles by revolutionary white supremacists. *The Turner Diaries* (supposedly kept by the "white martyr" Earl Turner) has become justly infamous as the "bible" of Timothy McVeigh and other neonazi terrorists. It is far less appreciated, however, that the central drama of the *Diaries* is a pornographically detailed description of the Los Angeles Holocaust. It is intended to be an instruction manual.

After a federal crackdown on gun owners, the "Organization" and its internal "Order" of Aryan warriors (presumably a fusion of formerly separate militia groups) launch a guerrilla war to rid the earth of Jews and nonwhites. The FBI building in Washington, D.C., is blown up, as is the federal office complex in Houston (four thousand dead). A grenade attack kills half the Los Angeles City Council, and hundreds of Jewish and black leaders are assassinated. Taking advantage of the national chaos created by these bombings and the ensuing race riots, about a thousand Order fighters, coordinated by a secret field command post in the San Fernando Valley, attack Los Angeles— the corrupt citadel of alien races and white race traitors—on the Fourth of July 1993.

Concentrating on the city's vulnerable infrastructure, they cripple LAX, blow up freeway overpasses, set the harbor ablaze, and cut the aqueduct. White liberals are shot on the spot, as are blacks caught outside a half-dozen holding areas. White supremacists are inflamed by the discovery of grisly evidence that blacks have reverted to cannibalism. ("The unfortunate whites were dragged from their cars, taken into a nearby Black restaurant, butchered, cooked, and eaten.") A Pentagon counterattack is blunted by mutinous white troops, and the guerrillas use captured tanks to crush last-ditch LAPD resistance at Parker Center downtown. A week later, all of Southern California (including the ICBM silos at Vandenberg Air Force Base) has fallen under the control of the Organization, becoming the core of the emergent Aryan Nation.[99]

"The Day of the Rope" (skinhead graffiti)

The first act of the new regime is the brutal expulsion of seven million blacks and Latinos from the Los Angeles region. This exodus is designed to destabilize the Southwest ("a new form of demographic warfare") and undermine any residual support for the "System" among whites. Meanwhile, hundreds of thousands of Jews and people of mixed ethnicity ("mongrels") are marched into the mountains north of Los Angeles, where they are slaughtered with machine guns and hand grenades. Finally, on 1 August—the terrible "Day of the Rope"—the Organization turns to the white race traitors. Sixty thousand are hung "from tens of thousands of lampposts, power poles, and trees."

Even the street lights at intersections have been pressed into service, and at practically every street corner I passed this evening on my way to HQ there was a dangling corpse, four at every intersection. Hanging from a single overpass only about a mile from here is a group of about 30, each with an identical placard around its neck bearing the printed legend, "I betrayed my race." Two or three of that group had been decked out in academic robes before they were strung up, and the whole batch are apparently faculty members from the nearby UCLA campus.[100]

After the purification of Southern California, the Organization nukes the "contaminated cities" of Miami, Toronto, and New York, killing at least 60 million people. ("Fortunately, the heaviest death toll in this country has been in the largest cities, which are substantially non-white.") Later, after all nonwhites have been exterminated in North America, Aryan revolutions in Britain and Germany complete the construction of a European Fourth Reich. "The blood flowed ankle-deep in the streets of many of Europe's great cities . . . as the race traitors, the offspring of generations of dysgenic breeding, and hordes of Gastarbeiter met a common fate."[101]

Mimicking the ancient plots of W. Delisle Hay's *Three Hundred Years Hence* (1881), M. P. Shiel's *Yellow Danger* (1889), and Jack London's "Unparalleled Invasion" (1906), the Organization then resorts "to a combination of chemical, biological and radiological means, on an enormous scale, to deal with the problem [of Asia]. . . . Over a period of four years some 16 million square miles of the earth's surface, from the Ural Mountains to the Pacific and from the Arctic Ocean to the Indian Ocean, were effectively sterilized." With non-whites extinct, "the great dawn of the New Era broke over the Western world."[102]

After reading *The Turner Diaries* it is impossible to have a benign attitude toward the survivalist novels—all isomorphs of Nowlan's original mise-en-scène—that proliferate like noxious weeds after 1978. Clute and Nicholls, editors of *The Encyclopedia of Science Fiction,* denounce this ultraviolent, male action genre as "the nightmare

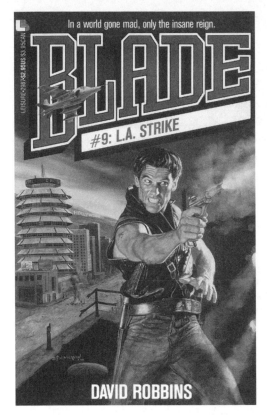

In a world gone mad, only the insane reign.

BLADE

#9: L.A. STRIKE

DAVID ROBBINS

The sons of Buck Rogers

at the bottom of the barrel of SF. Sadistic, sexist, racist, pornographic, gloating and void, survivalist fiction is an obscene parody . . . a grotesquely decayed form of Heinleinian relish at the defeat of 'civilian' values when the 'real' world bares its teeth."[103]

The post-Vietnam right-wing backlash provided the impetus for most of the serial survivalist novels, published as paperback originals and comprising up to a hundred installments. In various episodes of Ryder Stacy's *Doomsday Warrior,* Jerry Ahern's *The Survivalist,* William Johnson's *Ashes,* and David Robbins's *Blade,* the sons of Buck Rogers battle Russian invaders in the half-sunken, irradiated ruins of Los Angeles. Jason Frost's *Warlord* meanwhile uses his deadly crossbow against Zulu KGB agents, Vietnamese assassins, and a Soviet submarine crew under the toxic dome of the "Long Beach Halo," which isolates postapocalyptic Southern California from the rest of the world. The commies are replaced by their equally detestable surrogates—ecol-

THE LITERARY DESTRUCTION OF LOS ANGELES | 337

ogists and vegetarians—in a vicious 1982 installment of Robert
Adams's *Horse Clans* saga.*

By the mid-1980s, however, demonized caricatures of Los Angeles's
nonwhite majority à la Turner had begun to supplant the Red Menace
as survivalist fiction's significant Other. Ridley Scott's 1982 film *Blade
Runner* had already popularized the image of twenty-first-century Los
Angeles as a sinister entrepôt of alien cultures and races. Thus, in
Steven Barnes's *Streetlethal* (a 1983 episode in the *Aubry Knight*
series), the "Great Quake and Firestorm" had shifted remaining white
affluence to Santa Monica while the ruined slums of central Los Angeles became "The Maze." Here, under the thumb of the evil Ortega car-
tel, the degenerate population is addicted to the hallucinogenic moth
grubs that have replaced nickel rocks of crack cocaine. Many are
infected with the horrible "Thai-IV" syndrome, a nightmare successor
to AIDS that turns its victims into repulsive "Spiders":

> A huge Black woman with most of her upper teeth rotted away
> pressed her face against the window. The glistening wet rings of
> advanced Thai-IV left circular slicks when she pulled away. She
> noticed Promise's shiver of disgust and laughed, a hollow
> sound as the Spiders continued on their way.[104]

Nicolas Cain's repulsive *Little Saigon* series dispenses with the arti-
fice of a ruined future; instead, like Peter Kyne in *Pride of Palomar,*
Cain crudely depicts the racial catastrophe here and now. Nam-vet
Luke Abel and his Metro Asian Gang Taskforce shoot it out with a
"Vietcong" of 2,500 Asian gang-bangers on the mean streets of Orange
County's Vietnamese enclave. When Abel is not seething against
"ACLU maggots and sleazeballs" who are trying to spoil his private

---

* Perhaps the most phallically hysterical specimen in this subgenre is Lionel Derrick's
Penetrator series, which features action hero Mark Hardin, who battles the hordes from his
stronghold near Barstow in the Mojave Desert. Psychoanalysts will rejoice over such typical
cover copy as "the Penetrator tangles with the PLO in the tightest knot of his career!"

Vietnam War, he is ordering his men to "fill that gang-banger Chevy with hot lead!" or advising local women that "every discriminating girl in Little Saigon knows the gwai-loh cops working the Bolsa beat got peckers long and thick as Bangkok gourds." When a despondent scion of an old Orange County family commits suicide, Abel finds the following note: "Can't take it anymore. Gooks everywhere, fucking up the entire country. Gooks and spicks and niggers."[105]

The perception of a Southern California "overrun by gooks" is not confined to hard-core survivalist writers in combat fatigues and Doc Martens. Whitley Strieber and James Kunetka's 1986 novel *Nature's End,* like Niven and Pournelle's *Lucifer's Hammer,* voices the same preoccupations in the guise of "quality fiction." "The huge population of the L.A. Metroplex—Indo-Chinese, Vietnamese, Mexican, African—is not unlike that of Calcutta in the way it acts and looks." Helpless middle-class whites are caught between the anvil of natural disaster (the catastrophic wildfires that sweep the flanks of the afflu-ent Hollywood Hills) and the hammer of urban violence (the dread Asian "dragon" gangs that prowl the light-rail system and dip their headbands in the blood of their victims).[106]

Asians-as-killer-robots are also a strident cliché in James Cameron's 1995 screenplay for *Strange Days,* Kathryn Bigelow's film about the Helter-Skelterish last day of the twentieth century in Los Angeles. Vita Minh is "a slit-eyed stone fox, very tough," while her boyfriend, Tran, the leader of a homicidal Vietnamese street gang, is simply feral. "His parents squatted in rice-paddies and got napalmed. He went to high school in Huntington Beach and watched MTV. He has no discernible value system except personal survival."[107] But, for all this, *Strange Days* is restrained compared to John Carpenter's delirious *Escape from L.A.* (1997), which manages to sample (in the hip-hop sense) every mean image and racist undertone of survivalist fiction in the service of an ostensibly liberal plot about Los Angeles as the reverse Ellis Island of a Christian fascist America. The result is a cinematic nervous breakdown.

The ultimate armageddonist fiction—and final solution to the "gook" problem—however, comes from the eschatological pen of

Christian Coalition founder Pat Robertson. In his 1995 novel, *The End of the Age,* God himself decides to flush Los Angeles down the toilet with a "giant meteor" and a mile-high tsunami shamelessly purloined from *Lucifer's Hammer.* The sole survivors are some Orange County conservatives who have providentially evacuated to Colorado and a family of Chicano fundamentalists hiding in trenches on the top of Mount Wilson.

Divine genocide against Southern California neatly disposes of a disagreeable population and allows Robertson to clear the decks for the real action: righteous Texas Protestants battling Satan (now president of the United States) and his minions (a billion demonic Indians, Pakistanis, Persians, and Arabs). Ultimately, one of Robertson's square-jawed Christian heroes, former defense secretary Al Augustus, gets to dis Beelzebub in person:

> "Listen to me, you snake-headed freak," he shouted. . . .
> "You've been a loser from the very beginning. Jesus Christ is
> the winner, and I'm on His team. And just for the record, I have
> eighteen Poseidon missiles aimed at the heart of Babylon at this
> minute."[108]

10. ALIEN AFFINITIES

*The city burning down, armies of looters and killers roaming
the streets, still the turistas. Hell, the riot was a better draw
than the Universal Studios tour and Rat Town combined.*
"Slag Like Me" (1994)

The overtly fascist apocalyptics of survivalist fiction were complemented throughout the 1980s by a growing obsession with a clandestine and eroticized extraterrestrial presence. Hollywood likewise was experimenting with the concept of shipwrecked aliens as Los Angeles's next ethnic minority. In the shadowlands of white anxiety, the distinction between the images of space alien and illegal alien was subjected to repeated elision. Immigration and invasion, in a paranoid register, became synonyms.

Although "hordes" had been a fundamental element in the social imaginary of Southern California, extraterrestrials were relatively rare before the 1980s. The region may have been the Cold War heartland of UFO subculture, but monstrous aliens usually took their vacations elsewhere—preferably in Tokyo or New York. Apart from the impressive Martian armada in the 1953 film version of *War of the Worlds,* most of Los Angeles's space invaders were low-budget campers like the aliens who raised Dracula and Vampira from the dead in Ed Wood's gloriously awful *Plan Nine from Outer Space* (1956), the immense mutant mollusks from the Salton Sea in *The Monster That Challenged the World* (1957), or the invisible Martians who terrorized Hollywood starlets in *The Day Mars Invaded Earth* (1962). Even Karkong, the giant invader from planet Ionus who wiped out San Diego in a 1957 novel, bypassed the fleshpots of Los Angeles in order to follow the desert power lines to Boulder Dam and a final high-voltage meal.[109]

In the 1980s, however, "the secret alien invasion," in the classic mold of *Invasion of the Body Snatchers* (1956) and *The Invaders* (1967–68), suddenly became the theme of more than a score of Los Angeles–based novels, films, and television thrillers. Thus extraterrestrials hijacked bodies (*The Hidden,* 1987), conducted trophy hunts among the homeless (*Predator 2,* 1990), jumped out of black holes (*Peacemaker,* 1990), and infiltrated the local power structure (*They Live!* 1988, and *V: Prisoners and Pawns,* 1985). They were aided in their depredations, moreover, by zombies (*Dead Heat,* 1988), warlocks (*Warlocks,* 1989), clones (*Nemesis,* 1992), androids (*Blade Runner,* 1982), 35-foot-long alligators (*Alligators,* 1981), and the Devil (*Prince of Darkness,* 1987). In their most disturbing incarnation (*The Rapture,* 1991), aliens appeared as exterminating Angels of the Apocalypse, ordering a born-again Christian mother to redeem her earlier sexual promiscuity by slaying her own child.

With their insistence that "aliens are already among us," these tales echoed highly publicized claims that "real" extraterrestrials were on a sexual crime spree in the Los Angeles suburbs. *The Tujunga Canyon Contacts* (1980), a lurid tale of alien seductions and kidnappings, established the San Fernando Valley as the unchallenged capital of otherworldly lust.[110] Likewise the 1983 film *The Entity*—"based on a true incident"—recounted how a Los Angeles widow supposedly had been raped and terrorized by an invisible demon. Other "survivors" mesmerized local television audiences with claims that bug-eyed molesters in flying saucers had already commenced the "genetic colonization of Los Angeles." By 1990, a thriving regional network of support groups provided counseling to hundreds of self-proclaimed victims of alien or supernatural sexual predation.

Such classic sexual hysteria—with aliens playing the role that in Freud's time had usually been attributed to fathers and doctors—is typically the iceberg tip of more widespread social anxieties. In this case, the post-1980 boom in imagined aliens coincided with the increasing visibility of immigrants from Mexico, Central America, and East Asia in the daily life of the Los Angeles region. Like the Aryan survivalist novel, the fantasy of alien impregnation played off white fear and disorientation in the face of irreversible demographic change.

Indeed, this underlying equation between alien invaders and illegal immigrants became the manifest theme of the popular film (1988) and short-lived television series (1989–90) *Alien Nation*. The original screenplay was written by Rockne O'Bannion (borrowing heavily from John Sayles's 1984 film *Brother from Another Planet*), while more than a dozen veteran fantasy and sci-fi writers contributed to the television episodes and their novelizations.

The Tenctonese, or "Newcomers" as they are called in official jargon (just "slags" to ordinary racists), arrive one day over the Mojave Desert in a six-mile-long, interstellar version of an eighteenth-century slave ship. The ship's cargo is a portable proletariat of 260,000 humanoids genetically engineered for hard labor on dismal space colonies. Like the Africans on board the *Amistad,* they have rebelled against their slave masters. After an initial quarantine in camps, they are resettled in a downtown Los Angeles neighborhood that closely resembles the Cen-

tral American MacArthur Park district. Ideally suited for work in toxic industries like oil refining and smelting, they are immediately socialized to the poverty, alienation, and addiction of the urban underclass. A handful are allowed to become aspirant professionals (like LAPD detective George Francisco) or ambitious ethnic entrepreneurs. In successive paperback and television installments, the Tenctonese become magnets for every familiar cliché about ghetto life.

A typical dive in "Slagtown," for example, uncannily evokes the hostile ambience of Florian's "dine and dice emporium" on Central Avenue in the famous opening scene of Raymond Chandler's *Farewell My Lovely*—except that all the customers are now as big as Moose Malloy:

> Few humans ventured beyond the outskirts of Slagtown at all save for government workers, and even the police preferred to avoid this end of the alien ghetto. Only the X-Bar seemed at home, a brightly hued carrion feeder set down among the dark

storefronts and boarded-up apartment buildings. . . . The menial laborers lounging in front of the bar looked like rejects from the Raiders' offensive line, big and battered. They glared with undisguised antagonism at the two detectives.[111]

Alien Nation, however, did more than simply recycle racial clichés. Some episodes displayed a paternalistic multiculturalism leavened by occasional bursts of more radical rhetoric. Thus, in one installment, Micky Cass, a *Los Angeles Times* journalist emulating John Howard Griffith's famous impersonation in *Black Like Me,* goes undercover as a Newcomer in Slagtown. His shocking exposés of routine prejudice and police brutality eventually lead to his grisly torture-murder in a vat of hydrochloric acid. Meanwhile, all of Los Angeles's warring ethnic gangs have united to torment the vulnerable Newcomers. When Danny Mikubeh, the charismatic leader of the Tenctonese Nightshade gang, begins to drive the predatory *fehn* ("hair": their slang term for humans) out of the neighborhood, he is beaten to death by the LAPD. This Rodney King–like atrocity sparks a week-long street uprising comparable to the 1992 riots.[112]

The real theme of "Slag Like Me," however, is miscegenation. Sexual hysteria about alien impregnation is tackled headlong. All the major figures in the novelization are involved in interracial or interspecies relationships. Although the fundamental inequalities of the city are portrayed as virtually unreformable (Los Angeles is "wall-to-wall shit" according to the "good" LAPD protagonist, George Francisco), there is real hope for more personal tolerance, with intermarriage regarded as a positive goal. This "melting pot" view of alien-human relations, even if compromised by the failure to imagine constructive social change, is worlds apart from the genocidal preoccupations of most survivalist fiction.

Some liberal writers have even tried to infiltrate the Alien-versus-Aryan story—the most reactionary of disaster genres. Although the parallel novel and television series *V,* for example, followed the standard Buck Rogers plot of alien invaders and American resisters, it assumed no Manichaean division between good and evil. Both sides share the burdens of ordinary morality. While individual members of the reptilian horde defect to the human side out of genuine conscience, some earthlings are only too happy to become quislings for the diabolic Commander Diana. In *Prisoners and Pawns,* the Los Angeles segment of *V,* there is even a sympathetic account of how "alien and repulsive" humans first appear from the standpoint of the frightened saurians.[113]

No one, however, has been more outrageous in his persistent attempts to dress liberal or radical messages in right-wing clothing than director John Carpenter. His 1989 film, *They Live!* is probably the ultimate example of political transvestism. It opens with a rainbow army of unemployed camped out in wastelands (the MacArthur Park district again) under the shadow of downtown Los Angeles's towering skyscrapers. The middle class, thanks to Ronald Reagan and his successors, has become extinct, and as in *Caesar's Column,* society is now strictly divided between millionaires and tramps. Special eyeglasses, however, reveal that the yuppies in Porsches are really invading space aliens. This is the pretext for a gruesome guerrilla uprising (shades of Caesar Lomellini and Earl Turner) that eventually extirpates the Armani aliens—perhaps the first example of "liberal genocide."

11. MAGICAL DESTRUCTIONS

Palm trees rise through the crown of the Brown Derby, pumas prowl the corner of Hollywood and Vine, waiting for unwary tourists, hyenas and jackasses have left their footprints in the silt outside Mann's Chinese Theatre.

Hello America *(1981)*

The Dystopian City—disassembled by disaster and rebuilt by imagination—is our final genre. Los Angeles new wave fiction emerged in the 1980s, bearing the imprint of such diverse influences as J. G. Ballard, Toni Morrison, William S. Burroughs, Marge Piercy, and Ursula LeGuin, but its roots go back to the first and greatest of the many "survivor's tales" situated in Southern California: Aldous Huxley's *Ape and Essence* (1949).

Conceived, according to a biographer, "at the end of a long, dark corridor" in Huxley's life, marked by his growing nausea with Hollywood, a violent studio strike, the assassination of his hero Gandhi, and the inception of the nuclear dark age, this short novel rages with Swiftian spleen. Huxley caricatures himself as a once idealistic, now jaded screenwriter who becomes obsessed with a rejected script that falls off the back of a studio trash truck.

The mysterious screenplay opens in February 2108, several generations after World War III has scourged and poisoned the Northern Hemisphere. Scientists from the New Zealand Re-Discovery Expedition to North America make landfall at a desolate beach formerly known as Santa Monica. Los Angeles (once "more brassieres than Buffalo, more deodorants than Denver, more oranges than anywhere")[114] is a sprawling concrete ruin scoured by desert winds and shifting sand dunes. The few thousand survivors of all-out atomic and bacteriological Armageddon face slow but inevitable extinction from genetic damage and the consequent birth defects. Rather logically, they have accepted that history is fundamentally evil and now worship Belial, the Lord of the Flies.

One of the New Zealanders, a shy but handsome botanist named Poole, is captured and brought to the Hollywood Cemetery, where survivors are preoccupied with looting graves for jewels and clothes. ("Except for a greenish discoloration around the toes, the stockings are in perfect condition.") Eventually he is granted an audience with "His Eminence, the Arch-Vicar of Belial, Lord of the Earth, Primate of California, Servant of the Proletariat and Bishop of Hollywood," who reigns in Pershing Square—"still the hub and centre of the city's cultural life."[115]

Women draw water from a well in front of the Philharmonic Auditorium, while small boys stagger under heavy loads of fuel—books from the old library. A butcher, standing in a cloud of flies, is merrily slaughtering an ox strung between two rusty lampposts. (" 'That looks good,' says the Chief genially. The butcher grins and, with bloody fingers, makes the sign of the horns.")[116] The Biltmore Hotel's coffeeshops and bars have become busy workshops where women weave on primitive looms while men craft human bones into drinking cups and flutes. Pitiful mothers with monster babies wait in the main lobby. On Belial Day, the babies will be sacrificed in the Coliseum as prologue to the annual two-week-long public mating season. For the rest of the year, women wear NO!s sewn across their breasts and thighs.

As the Bishop of Hollywood explains to the good Anglican Poole, none of this is deliberate cruelty, only the desperate eugenics of a biologically doomed society. Impressed by Poole's botanical expertise and, especially, by his knowledge of irrigation (the Los Angeles Aqueduct was blown up during the war), the Bishop offers him the supreme honor of castration and admission to the ruling priesthood. Poole, of course, abdicates his larger social responsibilities and instead absconds with a beautiful girl, one of the small minority whose hormones still operate 365 days a year. On a clear moonlit night they leave behind the "cosy bourgeois ruins" of Los Angeles and begin the long trek over the rugged San Gabriel Mountains, stopping only to peel a hardboiled egg over the grave of William Tallis, the mysterious author of "Ape and Essence." They are the first of many to escape from Los Angeles.

If, as biographer David King Dunaway claims, *Ape and Essence* represents a vanguard critique of "postwar optimism," expressed through Huxley's "savage attack on the land he had adopted, Southern California," then the Los Angeles fiction of the 1980s may bear a similar relationship to the optimism of the 1960s and 1970s.[117] What truly unifies the diverse novels and short stories of the 1980s into a single subgenre of postcatastrophe Los Angeles fiction, however, is not so much their dystopian dispositions as the way they use the Dream-to-Nightmare metastasis to evoke fantastic geographies. Like *Ape and Essence,* these fictions favor hyperbolic landscapes and detailed mappings of new ecologies to old locations. To borrow a term from science, new wave

Los Angeles fiction is fundamentally *ergodic:* it substitutes space for time, phantasmagoric topographies for linear narrative.*

J. G. Ballard, of course, is the unchallenged master of such literally "sur-real" topographies—the foremost travel writer in the land of the apocalyptic. His preference for the urban disaster mode, as critic Colin Greenland has emphasized, arises from the wish shared by the surrealists "to destroy the manifest form of the external world and release the deep desires latent in it. . . . Whatever the exact nature of catastrophe, it has disrupted the continuity of history and left a world of arbitrary fragments from which the survivors must piece together their own realities."[118] One of Ballard's favorite tricks is to transpose alien climates, vegetations, and zoologies to familiar urban landscapes.

A spectacular instance is his 1981 novel, *Hello America,* which borrows Huxley's pretense of a voyage of rediscovery (this time from Europe) to depict the United States a century after environmental cataclysm beginning in the 1990s has transformed the land. Desertified New York, with sand dunes creeping up the necks of its skyscrapers, is contrasted with tropicalized Los Angeles, with "tapestries of Spanish moss a thousand yards long" hanging from the concrete skeletons of its ancient freeways. The Los Angeles River, along with its Hollywood and Bel Air tributaries, has become a jungle torrent through a vast rain forest that has swallowed a million tract houses. Spider monkeys have taken over the Hollywood Bowl, while alligators sun themselves next to Beverly Hills swimming pools. Like a second Chichén Itzá, the shadowy forms of abandoned shopping centers and movie studios can be glimpsed through openings in the forest canopy. Agents of President Charles Manson excavate the old Lockheed plant in Burbank in a frenzied scavenger hunt for nuclear weapons that the raving mad Manson eventually launches against his own capital in Las Vegas.[119]

---

* More precisely, *ergodicity* as formulated by Ludwig Boltzmann, the father of probabilistic mechanics, implies the statistical equivalence of measurements in time and space. "The mean of observations of an individual over time is equal to the mean of observations of many individuals at a single moment over an area."

A graceful and elegiac narrative, occasionally interrupted by bolts of surrealist lightning, Kim Stanley Robinson's 1984 debut novel, *The Wild Shore* (the first of his *Orange County* trilogy), is shrewdly frugal in its deployment of such Ballardian imagery. This "diary" of 17-year-old Henry, with its affecting account of pioneer families struggling against nature in rustic San Onofre Valley, reads like a classic coming-of-age tale. The difference, of course, is that San Onofre, once the site of Nixon's "Western White House," is now a human refugium between the ruins of suburban Orange County, with its bedouin-like scavenger bands, and the radioactive hills of Camp Pendleton. A surprise nuclear war half a century earlier has shattered California into innumerable survivalist shards, analogous to pre-mission Indian cultures. Old-timers recite trembling tales of a long-lost Magic Kingdom in Anaheim. Japanese patrol boats, meanwhile, enforce a mysterious UN embargo on contact with the outside world.[120]

If Robinson offers an intricate exploration of a single locality (elaborated in two further novels), Tim Powers provides a hallucinatory road map to the entire Southern California region a century after its destruction. *Dinner at Deviant's Palace* (1985) is Chaucerian in its colorful delineation of a medievalized "Ellay," under siege from a "San Berdoo" army and separated from the white-walled "Holy City of Irvine" by the poisoned desert of the "Inglewood Desolate." Powers's futuristic geography is also richly loric in the Celtic sense: formerly anomic freeway suburbs are now magical ruins invested with legends and place spirits. The darkest spot in this reenchanted landscape is a "terrible nightclub of the damned"—Deviant's Palace in the "savage carnival town" of Venice. It is described by Powers's picaresque minstrel Rivas:

> The place was supposed to be more a nightclub than anything else, and Rivas remembered one young lady who, after he'd impatiently broken off their romance even more quickly than he'd instigated it, had tearfully told him that she was going to get a waitress job at Deviant's Palace. He had never permitted himself to believe that she might really have done it, in spite of

A hallucinatory road map

the evening when a walruslike thing that a gang of fishermen had netted and dragged to shore and were butchering by torchlight rolled its eyes at him and with its expiring breath pronounced the pet name she'd always called him.[121]

This unsettling conjugation of eerie geography with unspeakable acts, the marvelous with the monstrous, has a proper technical name—the *uncanny*—and its leading practitioner in recent Los Angeles fiction is Steve Erickson. In his acclaimed 1986 novel, *Rubicon Beach,* the narrator Cale repeatedly witnesses a darkly beautiful woman—"her mouth the color of blood"—beheading a kneeling man along one of Los Angeles's innumerable canals. Later Cale will discover that the victim is probably himself and that his corpse is cropping up all over town. This enigma is hardly addressed before Cale fades away and Erickson introduces Catherine: Cale's likely executioner and the second of three protagonists who may be alternative embodiments of the same complex character.[122]

Each of Erickson's poetic but opaque novels takes off from a familiar Ballardian premise. *Days Between Stations* (1985) portrays Los

Angeles, like New York in *Hello America,* besieged by the desert sands that will inevitably bury it; while in *Rubicon Beach,* Los Angeles has, like London in Ballard's *The Drowned World* (1962), been partially engulfed by the sea. In *Leap Year* (1989), on the other hand, Erickson returns to the canonical image of Los Angeles after the quake when "residents will live a quasiprehistoric existence, travelling by foot on undriveable roads, bartering goods . . . fleeing the fires that roar from the earth and then returning to hover around them on cold unsheltered nights."[123]

But Erickson is Ballard supercharged and fractalized. His landscapes and characters, nestled within one another like Russian dolls, churn in constant metamorphosis. As in a Bosch painting, there is a troubling excess of meaning. Torrents of surreal metaphor form dense eddies around each character until sudden, sometimes inexplicable, ontological leaps carry the story forward into a new dreamscape. Erickson's ruined cities, moreover, are not merely enchanted: they are supernatural life-forms with occult powers of their own. The city-as-alien has become a living monstrosity.

The drowned corpse of Los Angeles in *Rubicon Beach,* for example, has learned to sing. "It came out of the buildings, a distinct and different melody out of each one." Cale listens to the "gurgling and howling" of the storefronts in Chinatown, while elsewhere dead office towers are "shrieking" and abandoned restaurants are "hissing." Sleepless and disoriented, he can only find relief near the Los Angeles River, "the flat roar of which was a lull after days of screaming cities." In this confusion between sound and place, in this Los Angeles "where music is the topographical map," radios have become subversive "compasses of anarchy." As the unfortunate Cale soon discovers, however, it is also a capital offense to own one.[124]

Veteran sci-fi writer Robert Silverberg's meat-and-potatoes prose could not be less like Erickson's highly styled, nonlinear fabulations. Yet his 1995 novella, "Hot Times in Magma City," may trump the genre for the sheer originality of its imagined geography. An M 7.6 earthquake on the previously unsuspected Yucaipa fault unroofs a large magma dome underneath Pomona. Strange hissing is soon followed by blasts of noxious gas and showers of red-hot rock. A large blister in the freeway suddenly becomes a baby volcano 40 feet high, and Mount Pomona is born. Unable to stop the lava flows erupting in backyards and minimalls across the eastern San Gabriel Valley, desperate authorities at "Volcano Central" beg help from Iceland: "frosty-eyed men with names like Svein Steingrimsson and Steingrim Sviensson who look upon fighting volcanoes as some kind of Olympic sport."[125]

Silverberg's story focuses on a day in the life of one of the crews that the Icelanders have trained. At first sight, Cal Mattison's motley gang of halfway house inmates—"miscellaneous boozers, druggies, crank-gobblers, and other sad substance-muddled fuckupniks"—are most unlikely heroes. But when these casualties of the drug wars climb inside their Melnar suits, they are transformed into elite lava-fighters, willing to face 2,000-degree lava outbreaks at close hand. Working in clouds of scalding steam, they use their water hoses "like sculptors" to cool and form basalt dams at the head of the flow. Their small victories, however, are inevitably compromised by new eruptions.

Crew chief Mattison, a former studio carpenter with a "boozing jones," occasionally wonders what the future will be like as "the whole eastern half of the Los Angeles Basin is littered with new little mountains in the middle of what used to be busy neighborhoods." Upon reflection, however, Mattison decides that "somebody else will have to figure out how to repair Los Angeles"; his responsibility is to keep the crew in action, one day at a time, while relishing lifetime employment in a job he loves. He could not be more grateful for the way things have worked out: "As if God has sent the volcanoes to Los Angeles as a personal gift to him, part of the recovery program of Calvin Thomas Mattison, Jr."[126]

In the end, Silverberg's simple story is a clever variant of the old plot in which alien or natural menace (asteroid, Martian invasion, or volcano) unifies a warring and divided humanity. Mount Pomona, now 2,000 feet high and still growing, has become the perfect moral equivalent of war—the Keynesian reemployment surrogate for the scores of closed-down defense plants. Although fighting the lava may be Sisyphean labor, the camaraderie of battle restores social dignity to Los Angeles's lost souls. The angel of disaster has paradoxically become their friend.

12. WRATH OF GOD?

Who needs a reason to destroy L.A.?
Pauline Kael, "The Current Cinema: Decadence" (1974)

Another boiling hot day, 8 August 1996. More than a hundred nervous cops, including local police, sheriff's deputies, FBI, and ATF agents ("the same cast as Waco"), surround Muhammad Mosque No. 27 in the black-majority city of Inglewood, just east of LAX. The building has been the object of a bitter court battle between the Nation of Islam and the legal owner. After a tense confrontation, which has included much pushing and shoving as well as the macing of a leading Fruit of Islam official, the police finally manage to evict the Muslims. A week later in Chicago, a spokesperson for the Nation of Islam's angry leader pronounces the curse of Allah upon Southern California.

> The Honorable Louis Farrakhan told me to announce to the media that not 30 days will pass before an earthquake will strike the state. . . . The wrath of God will show itself in a major earthquake for this attempt to uproot upstanding citizens from their community. California has been the site of many wicked incidents and this earthquake will destroy this part of the state.[127]

By recruiting God to his personal jihad, Minister Farrakhan joins the armageddonist army of Reverends Schuler and Robertson. He also holds hands with Newt Gingrich's friend, Republican Congresswoman Andrea Seastrand from Santa Barbara, who believes just as fervently as Farrakhan that Southern California deserves the same fate as Sodom and Gomorrah. Pointing out that "we probably have the most adulterers living here in California, child pornographers and

The fire next time (1992)

molesters . . . and divorce, family breakups, all of that evil," Seastrand cites the Second Chronicles as biblical authority for collective punishment. "California has been given so many signs," she said in 1996, "floods, drought, fires, earthquakes lifting mountains two feet high in Northridge. Yet people turn from His ways."[128]

But who, exactly, will be punished? Farrakhan's blanket condemnation of Southern California fails to consider which communities are most likely to suffer the appalling consequences of a giant earthquake. In fact, nature will discriminate along the geological contours of local housing segregation. The blue-collar flatlands of the Los Angeles Basin, home to a Latino, Asian, and black majority, will almost certainly sustain the greatest damage. Indeed, the African-American community sits astride the lethal Newport-Inglewood fault, whose last slippage in 1933 devastated downtown Long Beach and Compton. Congresswoman Seastrand, safe in her Montecito mansion, might not care if the Crenshaw district is swallowed whole by the earth, but it would certainly grieve the local Nation of Islam.

Of course, the minister's careless threat may simply be an expression of a generally eccentric personality. Farrakhan devoutly believes that Mars is inhabited by skinny, seven-foot-tall black people and claims that he was personally beamed aboard a "mother ship" UFO in 1975 for a reunion with the spirit of Elijah Muhammad. In this respect, of course, he is as quintessentially American as apple pie or Joseph Smith or Mary Baker Eddy. But crank or not, his declarations carry significant weight, and the casualness with which this self-proclaimed champion of the oppressed writes off Los Angeles—the largest nonwhite-majority city in the nation—is disturbing.

Perhaps it also fits into a larger pattern. Historians of British culture have had little difficulty arguing a connection between the popularity of the death-of-London novel in the 1885–1950 epoch and national anxieties about the decline of empire. It is tempting to assert an analogous relationship between the literary destruction of Los Angeles and the nervous breakdown of American exceptionalism.

The dazzling growth of suburban Southern California was, after all, the incontestable symbol of national prosperity in the decades between Lend-Lease and Watergate. A well-paid job in an aerospace plant and a ranch-style home in a sunny subdivision, only minutes away from the beaches and Disneyland, was the lifestyle against which other Americans measured the modernity of their towns and regions. Millions of Americans, especially the young, envied those lucky enough to live in the Land of Endless Summer.

Now the tables have turned and metropolitan Los Angeles—with its estimated 500 gated subdivisions, 2,000 street gangs, 4,000 mini-malls, 20,000 sweatshops, and 100,000 homeless residents—is a dystopian symbol of Dickensian inequalities and intractable racial contradictions. The deepest anxieties of a postliberal era—above all, the collapse of American belief in a utopian national destiny—are translated into a demonic image of a region where the future has already turned rancid. "California Here I Come" has been replaced by bumperstickers vowing "Not Yet L.A." and "Californians Go Home."

If Los Angeles's fictional disasters, then, in some sense track national discontents as well as local histories, they also mobilize deep-rooted cultural predispositions. It is probably no accident that the first

American best-seller, way back in 1662, was Michael Wigglesworth's poem *The Day of Doom.* Literary historians have long asserted the constitutive role of the "apocalyptic temper" in the American imagination. Perhaps this temper is now focused on the city whose environmental and social crises form a giant lightning rod for disaster.

Similarly, in its postwar migration from countryside to suburb, millenarian Christianity has preserved its fierce allegiance to the image of Satan's metropolis engulfed in righteous flames.[129] Although New York City was originally the seat of the Antichrist, his capital has moved to Los Angeles, where contemporary fundamentalists expect the world will begin to unravel during the approaching countdown to the millennium. As we have seen, the Hollywood film industry happily agrees.

But if some of the deep structures of our culture are ganging up on Los Angeles, making it the scapegoat for the collapse of the American century, race remains the crucial category. From Dooner's white populists to Buck Rogers, from Homer Lea to Pat Robertson, Armageddon has been imagined as a war of extermination between the white and colored worlds. Gangster rap is routinely condemned on every major editorial page in the nation, but novels like Niven and Pournelle's *Lucifer's Hammer,* with its smug genocide of Latinos and blacks ("good fertilizer"), pass unremarked in the literary mainstream. ("Massively entertaining," croaked the *Cleveland Plain-Dealer.*) Indeed, what statistic is more depressing than the 28 million copies sold since 1970 of Hal Lindsay's raving fundamentalist apocalypse, *The Late, Great Planet Earth,* with its casual incineration of Los Angeles and an entire chapter devoted to the extermination of the Yellow Peril?[130]

As we have seen, disaster fiction encompasses diverse subgenres with strikingly different literary and political itineraries. "Cult-catastrophe" and "new wave dystopias," in particular, have been powerful imaginative strategies, frequently yielding writing of an exceptional standard. But there should be no doubt that the ritual sacrifice of Los Angeles, as rehearsed incessantly in pulp fiction and film, is part of a malign syndrome, whose celebrants include the darkest forces in American history.

BEYOND

BLADE RUNNER

Every American city boasts an official insignia and slogan. Some have municipal mascots, colors, songs, birds, trees, even rocks. But Los Angeles alone has adopted an official nightmare.

In 1988, after three years of debate, a galaxy of corporate and civic celebrities submitted to Mayor Bradley a detailed strategic plan for Southern California's future. Although most of *L.A. 2000: A City for the Future* is devoted to hyperbolic rhetoric about Los Angeles's irresistible rise as a "world crossroads" comparable to imperial Rome or LaGuardian New York, a section in the epilogue, written by historian Kevin Starr, considered what might happen if the city failed to create a new "dominant establishment" to manage its extraordinary ethnic diversity. "There is, of course, the *Blade Runner* scenario: the fusion of individual cultures into a demotic polyglotism ominous with unresolved hostilities."[1]

Blade Runner—Los Angeles's dystopic alter ego. Take the Grayline tour in 2019: the mile-high neo-Mayan pyramid of the Tyrell Corporation drips acid rain on the mongrel masses in the teeming ginza far below. Enormous neon images float like clouds above fetid, hyperviolent streets, while a voice intones advertisements for extraterrestrial suburban living in "Off World." Deckard, a postapocalypse Philip Marlowe, struggles to save his conscience and his woman in an urban labyrinth ruled by malevolent biotech corporations.

With Warner Brothers' release of the more hardboiled "director's cut" a few months after the Rodney King riots, Ridley Scott's 1982 film version of Philip K. Dick's novel (*Do Androids Dream of Electric*

L.A.'s "official nightmare"

Sheep?) reasserted its sway over our increasingly troubled sleep. Ruminations about the future of Los Angeles now take for granted the dark imagery of *Blade Runner* as a possible, if not inevitable, terminal point for the former Land of Sunshine.

Yet for all of *Blade Runner*'s glamor as the reigning star of sci-fi dystopias, its vision of the future is strangely anachronistic and surprisingly unprescient. Scott, in collaboration with "visual futurist" Syd Mead, offered a pastiche of imaginary landscapes that Scott himself has conceded to be "overkill."[2] Peel away the overlays of Yellow Peril (Scott is notoriously addicted, as in his subsequent film *Black Rain,* to urban Japan as the face of Hell) and noir (all those polished black marble interiors), peel away the high-tech plumbing retrofitted to street-level urban decay—what remains is the same vista of urban gigantism and human mutation that Fritz Lang depicted in *Metropolis.*

The sinister man-made Everest of the Tyrell Corporation as well as all the souped-up rocket-squad cars darting around the air space are obviously the progeny—albeit now swaddled in darkness—of the famous city of the bourgeoisie in that 1931 Weimar film. But Lang himself was only plagiarizing from contemporary American futurists: above all, architectural artist Hugh Ferriss, who, together with Chrysler Building designer Raymond Hood and Mexican architect-archaeologist Francisco Mujica (visionary of urban pyramids like the Tyrell tower), popularized the coming "Titan City" of hundred-story skyscrapers with suspended bridge highways and rooftop airports. Ferriss and company, in their turn, largely reworked already existing fantasies—common in Sunday supplements since 1900—of what Manhattan might look like at the end of the century.[3]

Blade Runner, in other words, remains yet another edition of the core modernist fantasy of the future metropolis—alternately utopia or dystopia, *ville radieuse* or Gotham City—as monster Manhattan.* Such imagery might best be called "Wellsian" since as early as 1906, in his *Future in America,* H. G. Wells was trying to envision the late twentieth century by "enlarging the present"—represented by New York—to create "a sort of gigantesque caricature of the existing world, everything swollen up to vast proportions and massive beyond measure."[5]

Ridley Scott's caricature may have captured ethnocentric anxieties about multiculturalism run amok, but it failed to engage the real Los Angeles—especially the great unbroken plains of aging bungalows, stucco apartments, and ranch-style homes—as it erodes socially and physically into the twenty-first century. In fact, his hypertrophied Art Deco Downtown seems little more than a romantic conceit when compared to the savage slums actually being born in the city's inner belt of decaying postwar suburbs. *Blade Runner* is not so much the future of the city as the ghost of past imaginations.

In my 1990 book, *City of Quartz,* I explored various tendencies toward the militarization of the Southern California landscape. Events since the 1992 riots—including a four-year-long recession, a sharp decline in factory jobs, deep cuts in welfare and public employment, a backlash against immigrant workers, the failure of police reform, and

---

* Scott actually had planned to shoot *Blade Runner* in New York but was forced to change locations after Warner Brothers' front office complained about the extra costs.[4]

an unprecedented exodus of middle-class families—have only reinforced spatial apartheid in greater Los Angeles. As the endless summer
comes to an end, it seems that L.A. 2019 might well stand in a dystopian
relationship to most traditional ideals of a democratic metropolis.

But what kind of dystopian cityscape, if not *Blade Runner*'s, might
the unchecked evolution of inequality, crime, and social despair ultimately produce? Instead of following the grain of traditional clichés
and seeing the future merely as a grotesque, Wellsian magnification of
technology and architecture, would it not be more fruitful to project
existing trends along their current downward-sloping trajectories?
Octavia Butler, who despite her renown as a science-fiction novelist
still lives in her old neighborhood in black and Latino northwest
Pasadena, adopts precisely this strategy in her 1993 novel *Parable of
the Sower*. Like William Gibson, the author of *Neuromancer,* and
other "cyberpunk" writers, she uses disciplined extrapolation to
explore the dark possibilities of the near future.

Butler simply takes existing helter-skelter and turns up the volume
a few notches: the Big One has left parts of the city in ruins, riots happen every weekend, drought has killed all the lawns, the middle class
has withdrawn to walled suburbs, and the working poor have been left
to fend for themselves. Los Angeles, in sum, has become "a carcass
covered with too many maggots." Lauren Olamina and her proud
family in the multiracial suburb of "Robledo" are slowly engulfed by
chaos as the street poor—now gaunt, famished shadows of human
beings—wait like jackals to devour the neighborhood. After the massacre of her family and her neighbors, Lauren flees northward, away
from Los Angeles, with thousands of other refugees. There are no
invasions from outer space or technological Frankensteins in *Parable
of the Sower*. "Instead, things are unraveling, disintegrating bit by bit."

> We rode our bikes to the top of River Street past the last neigh-
> borhood walls, past the last ragged, unwalled houses, past the
> last stretch of broken asphalt and rag and stick shacks of squat-
> ters and street poor who stare at us in their horrible empty way,
> and then higher into the hills along a dirt road. At last we dis-

mounted and walked our bikes down the narrow trail into one of the canyons that we and others use for target practice. . . . If we find corpses in one, we stay away from it for a while.[6]

In what follows, I offer an extrapolative map of a future Los Angeles that is already half-born. Since the 1992 riots, premonitions of Butler's low-rise dystopia, with urban decay metastasizing in the heart of suburbia, have become commonplace. But the map itself—although inspired by the writings of Butler and Gibson—most closely resembles a diagram that Ernest W. Burgess, a sociologist at the University of Chicago, popularized during the 1920s.[7] As one historian has described it: "There is no more famous diagram in social science than that combination of half-moon and dartboard depicting the five concentric urban zones which appear during the rapid expansion of a modern American city such as Chicago."[8]

For those unfamiliar with the Chicago school of sociology's canonical study of the "North American city" (actually, 1920s Chicago generalized as archetype), Burgess's dartboard represents the spatial hierarchy into which the struggle for the survival of the urban fittest supposedly sorts social classes and their respective housing types. As imagined by academic social Darwinism, it portrays a "human ecology" organized by the "biological" forces of concentration, centralization, segregation, invasion, and succession. My remapping takes Burgess back to the future. It preserves such "ecological" determinants as income, land value, class, and race but adds a decisive new factor: fear.

1. SCANSCAPE

You can't commit crimes if you know that Big Brother is watching you.

Hollywood landowner (1994)

Is there any need to explain *why* fear eats the soul of Los Angeles? Only the middle-class dread of progressive taxation exceeds the cur-

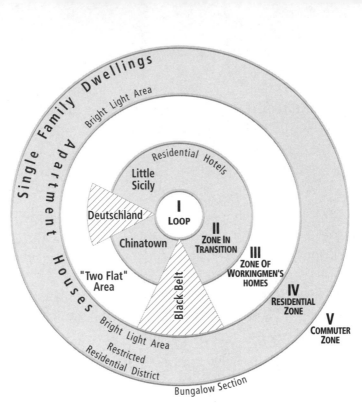

"The most famous diagram in social science"

rent obsession with personal safety and social insulation. In the face of intractable urban poverty and homelessness, and despite one of the greatest expansions in American business history, a bipartisan consensus insists that any and all budgets must be balanced and entitlements reduced. With no hope for further public investment in the remediation of underlying social conditions, we are forced instead to make increasing public and private investments in physical security. The rhetoric of urban reform persists, but the substance is extinct. "Rebuilding L.A." simply means padding the bunker.

As city life grows more feral, the various social milieux adopt security strategies and technologies according to their means. As with Burgess's dartboard, the pattern resolves itself into a series of concentric zones with a bull's eye in Downtown. To the extent that these security measures are reactions to urban unrest, it is possible to speak about a "riot tectonics" that episodically convulses and reshapes urban space. After the 1965 Watts rebellion, for instance, downtown

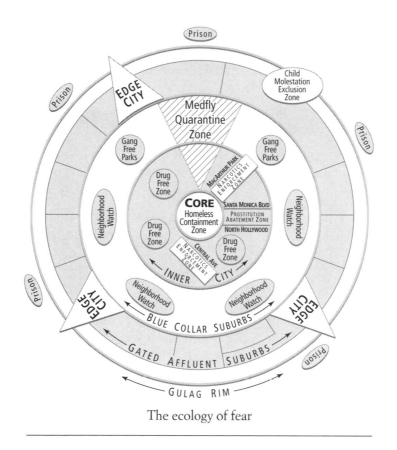

The ecology of fear

Los Angeles's leading landowners organized a secretive "Committee of 25" to deal with perceived threats to redevelopment efforts.[9] Warned by the LAPD that a black "inundation" of the central city was imminent, the committee abandoned efforts to revitalize the city's aging financial and retail core. Instead, it persuaded city hall to subsidize the transplanting of banks and corporate front offices to a new financial district atop Bunker Hill, a few blocks to the west. The city's redevelopment agency, acting as a private planner, bailed out the committee's lost investments in the old business district by offering discounts far below real market value on parcels of land within the new core.

The key to the success of this strategy, celebrated as Downtown's "renaissance," was the physical segregation of the new core and its land values behind a rampart of regraded palisades, concrete pillars, and freeway walls. Traditional pedestrian connections between

Bunker Hill and the old core were removed, and foot traffic was elevated above the street on "pedways"—as in Hugh Ferriss's imaginary Titan City—access to which was controlled by the security systems of individual skyscrapers. This radical privatization of Downtown public space, with its ominous racial overtones, occurred without significant public debate.

The 1992 riots vindicated the foresight of Fortress Downtown's designers. While windows were being smashed throughout the old business district, Bunker Hill lived up to its name. By flicking a few switches on their command consoles, the security staffs of the great bank towers were able to cut off all access to their expensive real estate. Bullet-proof steel doors rolled down over street-level entrances, escalators instantly froze, and electronic locks sealed off pedestrian passageways. As the *Los Angeles Business Journal* pointed out, the riot-tested success of corporate Downtown's defenses has only stimulated demand for new and higher levels of physical security.[10]

One consequence of this demand has been the continuing erosion of the boundary between architecture and law enforcement. The LAPD have become central players in the Downtown design process. No major project now breaks ground without their participation. Police representatives have exerted effective pressure against the provision of public toilets ("crime scenes" in their opinion) and the toleration of street vending ("lookouts for drug dealers"). The riots also provided suburban police departments with a pretext for enhancing their involvement in planning and design issues. In affluent Thousand Oaks, for example, the sheriff's liaison to the planning commission persuaded the city to outlaw alleys as a "crime prevention priority."[11]

Video monitoring of Downtown's redeveloped zones, meanwhile, has been extended to parking structures, private sidewalks, and plazas. This comprehensive surveillance constitutes a virtual *scanscape*—a space of protective visibility that increasingly defines where white-collar office workers and middle-class tourists feel safe downtown. Here Los Angeles, however, has no monopoly on Orwellian technology. Nearly one hundred British town centers, thanks to an initiative of the former Tory government, are now enclosed within the panoptic gaze of closed-circuit television monitors mostly operated by private contractors.[12]*

These "City Watch" programs, zealously promoted by surveillance technology industry leader ADT, may soon become the international norm. Hollywood, for example, has just established California's first official "Videotape Surveillance Zone" in the drug-ridden Yucca Street neighborhood just west of the famed Capital Records building.[14] The legendary Hollywood sign, meanwhile, is guarded against vandals and hikers by state-of-the-art motion detectors and infrared cameras with radar-activated zoom lenses. "Intruders' pictures are recorded on a computer disk as evidence and city park rangers are alerted. Then loudspeakers warn trespassers that they are being watched and that authorities are on their way."[15]

Inevitably, video monitoring will sooner or later be linked with home security systems in a seamless continuity of surveillance over daily routine. Indeed, up-market lifestyles may soon be defined by the ability to afford "electronic guardian angels" to watch over the owner and all significant others in her or his life. A Beverly Hills security expert, who retails clandestine video systems that allow affluent working parents to monitor their low-paid nannies and maids, compared the boom in sales following the 1997 trial of Louise Woodward (the British nanny accused of murdering a Boston-area infant) to the middle-class run on local gunstores after the 1992 riots.[16] Science and technology journals, for their part, have recently heralded the advent

---

* British leadership in the surveillance of urban space derives in part from the British army's several decades of experimentation with electronic counterinsurgency and antiterrorist city planning in Belfast. However, the cost-effectiveness of such technology in peacetime is questionable. In King's Lynn, the first mainland British town to adopt total surveillance, "the cameras' most frequent success is catching people dropping litter or urinating in public."[13]

of "digital super-surveillance" based on gadgets like pocket radars, millimeter-wave video cameras, infrared automatic tracking, code grabbers and rotaters, retinal scanners, voice keys, finger mappers, and thermal facial imagers. "Brave New World," according to the *New Scientist,* is now off the shelf:

> It is a world where there will be nowhere to hide, nor anywhere to hide anything. There are already devices under development that will see through walls and strip-search suspects from a distance, looking under their clothes and inside their bodies. Individuals may be identified by their unique smells and tracked down, or "recognised" electronically, even before they have had time to complete a crime. And thanks to cheap digital video cameras and powerful new search algorithms, individuals will be tracked by computers. There will be no anonymity even in the once welcoming crowds.[17]

A premier platform for the new surveillance technology will be that anachronism of the nineteenth century: the skyscraper. Tall buildings are becoming increasingly sentient and packed with deadly firepower. The skyscraper with a mainframe brain in *Die Hard* (actually F. Scott Johnson's Fox-Pereira Tower in Century City) anticipates a new generation of architectural antiheroes as intelligent buildings alternately battle evil or become its pawns. The sensory systems of many of Los Angeles's new office towers already include panopticon vision, smell, sensitivity to temperature and humidity, motion detection, and, in a few cases, hearing. Some architects now predict that the day is coming when a building's own artificially intelligent computers will be able to automatically screen and identify its human population, and even respond to their emotional states, especially fear or panic. Without dispatching security personnel, the building itself will be able to manage crises both minor (like ordering street people out of the building or preventing them from using toilets) and major (like trapping burglars in an elevator).

2. THE INVISIBLE RIOT

If, as some contend, the Los Angeles riots were a class rebellion, then this neighborhood is rebel-held territory.

Los Angeles Times *(1992)*

Friday, 5 May 1992. The armored personnel carrier squats on the corner like *un gran sapo feo*—a "big ugly toad"—according to nine-year-old Emerio. His parents talk anxiously, almost in a whisper, about the *desparecidos:* Raul from Tepic, big Mario, the younger Flores girl, and the cousin from Ahuachapan. Like all Salvadorans, they know about those who "disappear"; they remember the headless corpses and the man whose tongue had been pulled through the hole in his throat like a necktie. That is why they came here—to zip code 90057, Los Angeles, California.[18]

Their neighborhood, on the edge of MacArthur Park, is part of the large halo of older, high-density housing surrounding the scanscape of the fortified core. These tenement districts perform the classic functions of Burgess's "zone in transition": providing urban ports of entry for the city's poorest and most recent immigrants in this case from Mexico, Guatemala, and El Salvador rather than Ireland and Bohemia—who work in Downtown hotels and garment factories. But the normally bustling streets are now eerily quiet. Emerio's parents are counting their friends and neighbors, Salvadoran and Mexican, who are suddenly gone.

Some are in the county jail on Bauchet Street, little more than brown grains of sand lost among the 17,000 other alleged *saqueadores* (looters) and *incendarios* (arsonists) detained after the most violent American civil disturbance since enraged Irish immigrants burned Manhattan in 1863. Those without papers are probably already back in Tijuana, broke and disconsolate, cut off from their families and new lives. Violating city policy, the police fed hundreds of hapless undocumented *saqueadores* to the INS for deportation before the ACLU or immigrant rights groups had even realized that they had been arrested.

Mid-City Los Angeles

For many days the television talked only of the "South Central riot," "Black rage," and the "Crips and Bloods." Truly, the Rodney King case was a watershed in national race relations, a test of the very meaning of the citizenship for which African-Americans have struggled for four hundred years. It was also the fuse on an explosive accumulation of local grievances among young blacks, ranging from Chief Gates's infamous mass detentions ("Operation Hammer") to the murder of 15-year-old Latasha Harlins by a Korean grocer in 1991. But the 1992 upheaval was far more complex than the 1965 Watts rebellion, although some issues, especially police abuse, remained the same. While most of the news media remained trapped in the black-and-white world of 1965, the second Los Angeles riot burst emphatically into technicolor.

Emerio's parents know that thousands of their neighbors from the MacArthur Park district, as well as from the adjoining Mid-Wilshire area and the Hollywood flatlands—together constituting Los Angeles's Mid-City district—also looted, burned, violated curfew, and went to jail. Despite the tabloid media's obsession with black violence, only 36 percent of the riot arrestees were African-American, while 52 percent had Spanish surnames and 10 percent were white. Moreover, the greatest density of riot-related "incidents" occurred north of the Santa Monica Freeway in predominantly Latino and Asian areas. Indeed, nearly as many suspects were booked by the LAPD's Ramparts station, which polices Emerio's neighborhood, as by all four stations which make up the department's South Bureau in South Central Los Angeles. Even the Hollywood station made twice as many arrests as the 77th Street station, which patrolled the supposed riot epicenter— where truck driver Reginald Denny was nearly beaten to death—at the intersection of Florence and Normandie Avenues.[19]

This invisible Mid-City riot, conflated by most news reports with events in majority-black areas,* was driven primarily by empty bellies

---

* The "independent" press was as fixated as the mainstream on exclusively black-and-white images of the riots. The Institute for Alternative Journalism's *Inside the L.A. Riots,* for example, contains 70 dramatic photographs, only one of which clearly depicts a Latino (a small boy).[20]

and broken dreams, not by outrage over the acquittal of the cops who beat Rodney King. It was the culmination of a decade of declining economic opportunity and rising poverty followed by two years of recession that tripled unemployment in Los Angeles's immigrant neighborhoods. Academic studies since the riot have shown that Mexican and Central American immigrants arriving after 1980 had less hope than their predecessors of finding stable, entry-level positions in a regional economy that had become supersaturated with unskilled labor. "Massively growing numbers of Mexican immigrants," according to UCLA sociologist Vilma Ortiz, "have been packed into a relatively narrow tier of occupations."[21] Already by 1980, starting wages for new arrivals had fallen by 13 percent compared to 1970, and in the decade that followed, the portion of the Los Angeles population falling below the poverty line grew by a full percentage point or more each year.[22]

Then, 1990: cutbacks in defense spending and the bursting of the Japanese financial bubble (source of massive "super-yen" investments in Los Angeles real estate during the 1980s) converged to plunge the Southern California economy into its worst recession since 1938. An incredible 27 percent of national job loss was concentrated in the Los Angeles metropolitan region. In Los Angeles County this translated into a catastrophic 30 percent decline in manufacturing employment that savaged light industry, where Mexican immigrants make up the majority of workers, as well as aerospace and military electronics.[23] The impact of the recession, moreover, was intensified by simultaneous cutbacks in AFDC and MediCal benefits as well as deep slashes in local school budgets. Tens of thousands of families lost their tenuous economic footholds, while the number of children living in poverty increased by a third during the course of the recession.[24]

For anyone who cared to pay attention there were dramatic social storm warnings in the months before the spring 1992 riots. Indeed, no image revealed the mixed origins of the upheaval more clearly than the photograph published in the *Los Angeles Times* three days before Christmas 1991. It showed part of the throng of 20,000 women and children, predominantly recent Latino immigrants, waiting outside skid row's Fred Jordan Mission for the handout of a chicken, a dozen corn tortillas, three small toys, and a blanket. According to the *Times,* "Eight blocks were cordoned off around 5th Street and Towne Avenue to accommodate the crush of people. Some in the five-hour line said they were willing to brave the gritty streets for what one woman described as her 'only possibility' for a Christmas dinner."[25] Human distress on so broad a scale had not been photographed in California since the famous depression-era documentaries of Margaret Bourke-White and Dorothea Lange.

Nineteen-thirties-type misery was no surprise, however, to food bank volunteers, who had been warning city officials about the ominous decline in emergency food resources, or to public health workers, who were reporting classic symptoms of malnutrition—anemia and stunted growth—in nearly a quarter of the poor children passing through a county screening program.[26] Other visible barometers of the crisis included the rapidly growing colonies of unemployed busboys, gardeners, and construction laborers living on the desolate flanks of Crown Hill across from Downtown or in the concrete bed of the Los Angeles River, where the homeless are forced to use sewage outflow for bathing and cooking.

Emerio's parents and their neighbors spoke of a gathering sense of desperation in early 1992, a perception of a future already looted of opportunity. The riot arrived like a magic dispensation. In Mid-City neighborhoods people were initially shocked by the violence, then mesmerized by the televised images of black and Latino crowds in South Central Los Angeles helping themselves to mountains of desirable goods without interference from the police. On the second day of unrest, 30 April, the authorities blundered twice: first by suspending school and releasing the kids into the street, second by announcing that the National Guard was on the way to help enforce a dusk-to-dawn curfew.

Thousands immediately interpreted this as a last call to participate in the general redistribution of wealth in progress. Looting exploded through the majority-immigrant neighborhoods of Mid-City, as well as

Christmas food line, 1991

Echo Park, Van Nuys, and Huntington Park. Although arsonists struck wantonly and almost at random, the looting crowds were governed by a visible moral economy. As one middle-aged lady explained to me, "Stealing is a sin, but this is more like a television game show where everyone wins." In contrast to the looters on Hollywood Boulevard who stole Madonna's underwear from Frederick's, the masses of Mid-City concentrated on the prosaic necessities of life like cockroach spray and Pampers.

A veteran fifth-grade teacher in the area explained to me the attitudes of the hardworking and otherwise law-abiding families who were swept up in the looting.

> I teach at a new school which is a block west of Olympic and Hoover. My students and I watched from our classroom window as a video store burned. Later, my wife, who teaches at Hoover Street School, and I watched on television as stores near our schools were looted by parents and students whom we recognized.

Since most of the liquor stores and markets in this area greatly overcharge the customers for poor quality merchandise, there is great resentment. My students told me that when some of them saw Viva Market, on Hoover and Olympic, being looted as they watched television, their parents immediately left the apartment only to return an hour later with food and other items. They didn't see this as a "riot," just an opportunity to get even with the "exploiters."

There was no coordination or planning by the people north of the Santa Monica Freeway, other than that provided by the roadmap shown on television. . . . I do not think that Korean stores were attacked for exclusively ethnic reasons. If Korean-owned liquor stores were burned, Korean travel agencies and beauty-shops were not touched. The uprising was directed against the police and rip-off merchants in general. It was driven by economic desperation and class resentment, not race.[27]

The official reaction to this postmodern bread riot was the biggest multiagency law enforcement operation in history. For weeks afterward, elite LAPD Metro Squad units, supported by the National Guard, swept through the tenements in search of stolen goods, while Border Patrolmen from as far away as Texas trawled the streets for undocumented residents. Meanwhile, thousands of *saqueadores,* many of them pathetic scavengers captured in the charred ruins the day after the looting, languished for weeks in the county jail, unable to meet absurdly high bails. One man, apprehended with a packet of sunflower seeds and two cartons of milk, was held on $15,000 bond. Some curfew violaters received 30-day jail sentences, despite the fact that they were either homeless or spoke no English. Angry suburban politicians, meanwhile, outbid one another with demands to deport immigrants and strip their U.S.-born children of citizenship.

The riot also accelerated the flight of capital and jobs from the Wilshire corridor, just west of MacArthur Park, that forms the high-rise commercial spine of the Mid-City area. Known as "Los Angeles's

High-rise ghost town

Champs Elysées," this two-mile segment of Wilshire Boulevard once boasted such icons as the Ambassador Hotel, I. Magnin, Perino's, the Brown Derby, and Bullock's Wilshire. Insurance companies, corporate law offices, and county agencies formerly consumed millions of square feet of circa 1950s modernist office space. The economic decline of the area began in the mid-1970s when leading tenants began to relocate to newer properties on the booming west side. Office workers and professionals who lived in apartment complexes north and south of Wilshire soon followed, as did restaurants, department stores, and hotels. The residential vacuum was filled by thousands of Mexican and El Salvadoran immigrants, while Korean small businesses brought back retail vitality. But the hemorrhage of white-collar jobs and sales taxes was permanent.

During the riots, looters did $10 million damage to Bullock's, the last of the Wilshire landmarks to remain open—it promptly closed its doors for good. In less than a year, home prices in the nearby exclusive enclave

of Hancock Park had fallen by a staggering $200,000. As remaining cor-
porate tenants bolted for the west side, desperate landlords tried to give
away premium office space at $1 per square foot but found few takers.
In the year before the riot, there had been much speculation in the business press that large Korean investors might be induced to resurrect
what was already being called colloquially the "Wilshire ruins." However, the destruction or looting of nearly two thousand Korean family
businesses during the riot scotched that possibility for the foreseeable
future.[28] As a result, Los Angeles has added a unique category to
Burgess's urban ecology: the modern high-rise ghost town.

3. FREE-FIRE ZONE

We have to reclaim this area street by street, alley by alley.
LAPD Ramparts Division spokesperson (1990)

By mid-May 1992, the National Guard, together with the army and
the marines, had withdrawn from the inner city neighborhoods of
Los Angeles. Flags folded and rifles stacked, thousands of citizen-
soldiers returned to their ordinary suburban lives. As the humvees
and trucks moved out, another army, the Eighteenth Street gang,
immediately resumed its occupation of Los Angeles's Mid-City area.
Some members taunted departing guardsmen with the boastful chant
that weary neighbors had been hearing for years: "Soy Eighteen with
a bullet / I got my finger on the trigger / I'm gonna pull it."

Back in 1927, Burgess's student Frederic Thrasher had shocked
readers of his classic study *The Gang* with the claim that Chicago's
1,313 street gangs had a total membership of 25,000 boys and young
men.* A half-century later, *veteranos* with "Diez-y-Ocho" tattoos

---

* As a "human ecologist," Thrasher studied gangs in the same way that a wildlife biologist might study predators or a plant ecologist a prairie. Gangs, he emphasized, "develop in
definite and predictable ways, in accordance with a form or entelechy that is predetermined
by characteristic internal processes and mechanisms, and have, in short, a nature and natural history."[29]

emblazoned across their chests boast that their gang alone has that many members in hundreds of cliques spread across Southern California, as well as in rapidly growing franchises in Las Vegas, Mexico City, and San Salvador. According to Los Angeles district attorney Gil Garcetti, Eighteenth Street is "the largest criminal street gang in the country." Born on the edge of Downtown in the early 1960s, it has become the General Motors of Los Angeles street culture.[30]

The first Latino gang to break into the lucrative rock cocaine market otherwise dominated by black street gangs, the Eighteenth Street "nation" controls a wide swath of crack-saturated turf in the Mid-City area. Sixty other Latino and Asian gangs fight over the dregs of this business, occasionally with local cliques of Eighteenth Street. As a result, the LAPD's Ramparts Division (home to the hard cops celebrated in several of Joseph Wambaugh's gritty police novels) frequently holds the unenviable record of investigating more homicides than any other neighborhood police jurisdiction in the country. Nearby MacArthur Park, once the jewel in the crown of the city's park system, is now a free-fire zone where crack dealers and street gangs settle their scores with shotguns and uzis. In a single bad year, 30 or more corpses were found crumpled on the grass, stuffed in park trash cans, or half-buried in the muck at the bottom of the lake. Indeed, when the lake was drained a few years ago for subway construction, a local artist constructed a huge collage out of the several dozen rusted handguns he recovered from the lake bed.

By their own admission, the overwhelmed inner city detachments of the LAPD have been unable to keep track of all the bodies on the street, much less deal with common burglaries, car thefts, and gang-organized protection rackets.[31] Like Octavia Butler's Pasadena residents in 2024, the present-day occupants of the transition zone are left to fend for themselves. Lacking the resources or political clout of more affluent neighborhoods, they have turned to Mr. Smith and Mr. Wesson, whose names follow "protected by . . ." on handmade signs decorating humble homes all over South Central and Mid-City Los Angeles.

Slumlords, meanwhile, are conducting their own private reign of terror against drug dealers, petty criminals, and deadbeat tenants.

"The free-fire zone"

Faced with "zero tolerance" laws authorizing the seizure or destruction of properties used for drug sales, they are hiring their own goon squads and armed mercenaries to "exterminate" crime on their premises. Shortly after the 1992 riots, *Times* reporter Richard Colvin accompanied one of these crews on a swashbuckling rampage through the Westlake, Venice, and Panorama City districts.

Led by a six-foot-three, 280-pound "soldier of fortune" named David Roybal, this security squad was renowned among landlords for its efficient brutality. Suspected drug dealers and their customers, along with rent-in-arrears tenants and other landlord irritants, were physically driven from buildings at gunpoint. Those who resisted or even complained were beaten without mercy. In a Panorama City raid a few years earlier, "Roybal and his crew collared so many residents and squatters for drugs that they converted a recreation room into a holding tank and handcuffed arrestees to a blood-spattered wall." The LAPD knew about this private jail but ignored residents' protests. An envious police officer told Colvin, "If we could do what these security guards do, we'd get rid of the crime problem, just like that."[32]

Roybal and his gang resemble the so-called *matadors,* or hired gun-slingers, who patrol Brazilian middle-class neighborhoods and fre-quently, while the police deliberately turn their backs, execute persistent criminals, even street urchins. Their common refrain is that "they get the job done when all else has failed." As one of Roybal's most aggressive competitors boasted:

> Somebody's got to rule and when we're there, we rule. When somebody says something smart, we bodyslam him, right on the floor with all of his friends looking. We handcuff them and kick them and when the paramedics come and they're on the stretcher, we say: "Hey, sue me."[33]

In addition to these rent-a-thugs, the inner ring has also spawned a vast cottage industry manufacturing wrought-iron bars and grates for home protection. An estimated 100,000 inner city homes, like cages in a human zoo, have "burglar bars" bolted over all their doors and win-dows. As in a George Romero movie, working-class families now lock themselves in every night from the zombified city outside. As one res-ident told the *Los Angeles Times,* "The bars remind me of being in prison in my own house. But sometimes you do things you don't like in the interest of security." Yet such security may be a cruel illusion. The Los Angeles Fire Department estimates that at least half of the city's barred homes lack the legally required quick-release mechanisms that allow residents to escape in an emergency. The result has been a recent epidemic of horrific fires in which entire trapped families have been immolated in their bungalows or apartments.[34]

The prison cell finds many other architectural resonances in the postriot inner city. Even before the Rodney King uprising, most liquor and convenience stores, taking the lead from pawnshops, had com-pletely caged in their cash register counters, sometimes with lifesize cardboard cutouts of policemen placed near the window. Even local greasy spoons had begun to exchange hamburgers for money through bulletproof acrylic turnstiles. Now the same design—call it the "Brinks" aesthetic—has been extended to social service offices and hospitals. In light of recent cutbacks in welfare programs and medical services, along with all-day waits in welfare lines or for emergency medical treatment,[35] the county has sought to protect employees from public rage through the comprehensive installation of metal detectors, video monitors, convex surveillance mirrors, panic buttons, chairs bolted to the floor, and "interview booths divided by thick, shatter-proof glass partitions." Not surprisingly, advocates for the poor have denounced this paranoid environment in which welfare mothers are treated like dangerous inmates in a high-security prison.[36]

Schools also have become more like prisons. Even as per capita education spending has plummeted in many local school districts, scarce resources are being absorbed in fortifying school grounds and hiring more armed security police. Teenagers complain bitterly about overcrowded classrooms and demoralized teachers, about decaying campuses that have become little more than daytime detention centers for an abandoned generation. Many students are literally locked in during school hours, while new daytime curfew laws—the violation of which carries stiff penalties for parents—allow police to treat truancy as a criminal offense. In some Southern California communities, the police have direct access to computerized school records. In the Los Angeles Unified School District kids who become informers on fellow students' drug habits are rewarded with concert tickets, CDs, and new clothes, and if Mayor Riordan gets his way, the LAPD may even gain its very own high school: a "junior police academy" magnet school that would be a national first.[37]

The school yard, meanwhile, has become a killing field. Scores of students since 1985 have been wounded or killed during school hours. As a result, high school students in Los Angeles are now checked for weapons by metal detectors as they enter school each morning. At Long Beach's Lindbergh Junior High School, frequently raked by gunfire, administrators built a 900-foot-long, 10-foot-high wall "to deflect bullets" fired from a neighboring public housing project. At a Santa Monica elementary school, little kids regularly practice "drive-by drills." Just as their parents once learned to cower under desks in case of a nuclear attack, so are today's students "taught to drop at a teacher's signal in case of another drive-by shoot-ing—and stay there until they receive an all-clear signal."[38]

Federally subsidized housing and public housing projects, for their part, are coming to resemble the "strategic hamlets" that were used to incarcerate the rural population of Vietnam. Although no Los Ange-les housing project is yet as militarized as those in San Juan, Puerto Rico, where the National Guard was sent in by the governor, or as technologically sophisticated as Chicago's Cabrini-Green, where reti-nal scans (as in the opening sequence of *Blade Runner*) are used to check IDs, the housing authority police exercise absolute control over residents' freedom of movement.[39]

In a city with the nation's worst housing shortage, project tenants, fearful of eviction, are reluctant to claim any constitutional protection against unlawful search or seizure. Like peasants in a rebel country-side, they are routinely stopped and searched without probable cause, while their homes are broken into without court warrants. In several projects, public access is restricted by guard posts, and residents must submit lists of frequent visitors. And, as in other big cities, federal "one strike and you're out" regulations allow managers to evict other-wise innocent tenants of federally subsidized housing for crimes com-mitted by their relatives or guests: a policy of collective punishment similar to that long practiced by Israelis on the West Bank.*

4. HALF-MOONS OF REPRESSION

Zoning can stifle crime problems that police could never stamp out before.

LAPD vice cop (1993)

In the original Burgess diagram, "pie slices" or "half-moons" repre-senting ethnic enclaves ("Deutschland," "Little Sicily," or "the Black

---

* In November 1997, three mothers from a housing project in Venice, aided by the ACLU, challenged the constitutionality of the "one strike" policy in a major lawsuit against the federal government.[40]

Belt") and specialized architectural ecologies ("residential hotels" or "the two-flat area") are wedged into the city's concentric socioeconomic structure. In contemporary metropolitan Los Angeles, new species of enclaves are emerging in sympathy with the militarization of the landscape. For want of any generally accepted name, we might call them "social control districts." They merge the sanctions of the criminal or civil code with landuse planning to create what Michel Foucault would undoubtedly have recognized as a yet higher stage in the evolution of the "disciplinary order" of the modern city. Growing like weeds in a constitutional no man's land, Southern California's social control districts can be distinguished according to their specific juridical modes of imposing spatial "discipline."

"SOCIAL CONTROL DISTRICTS"

Juridical Mode	Examples of "Crime"
Abatement	Graffiti, prostitution
Enhancement	Drugs, guns
Containment	Homeless, medflies
Exclusion	Homeless, drugs, gangs, child molestors

Abatement districts, currently enforced against graffiti and prostitution in signposted neighborhoods of Los Angeles and West Hollywood, extend the traditional police power over nuisance (the legal fount of all zoning) from noxious industry to noxious behavior. Financed by fines collected (on prostitution offenses) or special sales taxes levied (on spray paints, for example), they devote additional law enforcement resources to specific social problems. Going a step further, business leaders in Little Tokyo and Hollywood have proposed the establishment of self-taxing "improvement districts" which would be able to hire private security guards to supplement the police. Needless to say, this would further erode the already fuzzy boundary between public and private policing in Los Angeles.

Since the 1992 riots, moreover, the LAPD has buttressed abatement programs by interventions in the zoning process. Using computer software to identify hot spots of prostitution, petty crime, and drug use, the police now routinely veto building and operating permits for "crime magnet" businesses. "Most commanding officers don't want new bars in their area, or new liquor locations or new dance halls," a police spokesperson explained to the *Los Angeles Times*. "What you have is an increased police interest in using zoning laws as vehicles to stop these businesses when they have problems." The LAPD considers this a logical extension of "community-based policing," but some Latino community leaders have complained that it really constitutes discrimination against Spanish-speaking mom-and-pop businesses like meat markets and *tiendas* (corner grocery stores) that need liquor sales to break even. Drinkers simply shop at supermarkets instead.[41]

Enhancement districts, represented all over Southern California by the "drug-free zones" and "gun-free zones" surrounding public schools, add extra federal or state penalties ("enhancements") to crimes committed within a specified radius of public institutions. In other cases, new laws, targeted at specific groups and locations, criminalize otherwise legal behavior. As a condition of probation, for example, prostitutes are now given maps demarcating areas, including parts of Hollywood, South Central, and the San Fernando Valley, where they can be arrested simply for walking down the street. In Costa Mesa (Orange County) prostitutes are further humiliated by having their clothes confiscated after arrest. They are released from jail wearing flimsy white paper jumpsuits.[42]

From the circumscription of a group's otherwise legal behavior, it is a short step to *containment* districts designed to quarantine potentially epidemic social problems or, more usually, social types. In Southern California these undesirables run the gamut from that insect illegal immigrant, the Mediterranean fruit fly, to homeless people. Since the early 1980s, the city of Los Angeles has tried to prevent the spillover of cardboard "condos" into surrounding council districts or into the more upscale precincts of Downtown by keeping homeless people "contained" (the official term) within the 50-square-block area of skid row. In 1996, the city council formalized the status quo by declaring a portion of skid row's sidewalks an official "sleep-

"Homeless containment district"

ing zone." As soup kitchens and skid row missions brace themselves for a new wave of homelessness in the wake of recent state and federal welfare reforms, the LAPD maintains its traditional policy of keeping street people herded within the boundaries of the nation's largest outdoor poorhouse.

Obverse to containment is the formal *exclusion* of pariah groups from public space or even the city limits. The tactics are sometimes ingenious. In Anaheim, for instance, a city-supported citizens' group ("Operation Steer Clear") dumped tons of steer manure in local parks in the hope that the stench would drive away drug dealers and gang members. "Anticamping" ordinances, likewise, have been passed by a spate of Southland cities, including the "Peoples' Republic" of Santa Monica, with the goal of banishing the homeless from sight. Since such exclusion ordinances merely sweep a stigmatized social group onto the next community's doorstep, each city, in a chain reaction, adopts comparable legislation in order to avoid becoming the regional equivalent of a human landfill.

Similarly, Los Angeles and a score of smaller cities have used sweeping civil injunctions—whose constitutionality was upheld by the California Supreme Court in January 1997—to prevent gangs from congregating in parks or on street corners. Although one high-ranking LAPD official has complained that these "gang-free zones" merely push gang activity into adjoining neighborhoods, they are highly popular with vote-conscious district attorneys and city council members who love the image that the injunctions broadcast of decisive action and comprehensive deterrence.[43] In a typical example, a Los Angeles judge banned Eighteenth Street homeboys in one neighborhood from "associating in public view" in groups larger than two, even in their own front yards. He also imposed an 8 P.M. curfew on juvenile gang members and banned the use of cellular phones and pagers. In addition, his injunction prohibited Eighteenth Street members from whistling in public—a form of signaling, the city attorney alleged, used by lookouts for drug dealers.[44]

As civil libertarians have pointed out, the social control district strategy penalizes individuals, even in the absence of a criminal act, merely for group membership. "Status criminalization," moreover, feeds off middle-class fantasies about the nature of the dangerous classes. And fearful fantasies have been growing in hothouse fashion. In the mid-1980s, for example, the ghost of Cotton Mather suddenly appeared in suburban Southern California. Allegations that local daycare centers were actually covens of satanic perversion wrenched courtrooms back to the seventeenth century. In the course of the McMartin Preschool molestation trial—the longest and most expensive such ordeal in American history—children testified about molester-teachers who flew around on broomsticks and other manifestations of the Evil One.

The creation by the little city of San Dimas of the nation's first "child-molestation exclusion zone" was one legacy of the accompanying collective hysteria, which undoubtedly mined huge veins of displaced parental guilt. This Twin Peaks–like suburb in the eastern San Gabriel Valley was signposted from stem to stern with the warning:

"Hands Off Our Kids! We I.D. and Fingerprint Our Kids for Safety."
It is unclear whether the armies of lurking pedophiles in the mountains above San Dimas were deterred by these warnings, but any post-
Burgess mapping of urban space must acknowledge the power that
bad dreams now wield over the public landscape.

5. THE NEIGHBORS ARE WATCHING

*What we should be doing is trying to restore an equilibrium
of arms to the streets, not chasing the delusion that with
tighter restrictions we can get bad guys to give up their arms.*
Pro-vigilante law professor (1993)

A few years ago an anxious delegation of police officials from the
former East Germany contacted the Los Angeles Police Department. Faced with a massive upsurge in crime and ethnic violence following unification, they were eager to meet the department's most
celebrated personality. They were not inquiring about Chief Willie
Williams or his predecessor Daryl Gates, but about "Bruno the Burglar," the felonious 'toon in a mask, who appears on countless signs
that proclaim the borders of "Neighborhood Watch" communities.[45]
The Neighborhood Watch program—comprising more than 5,500
crime surveillance block clubs—is the LAPD's most important con-
tribution to urban policing. Throughout what Burgess called the
"Zone of Workingmen's Houses," which in Los Angeles includes the
owner-occupied neighborhoods of the central city as well as older
blue-collar suburbs in the San Fernando and San Gabriel Valleys, a
huge network of watchful neighbors provides a security system midway between the besieged, gun-toting homeowners of the transition
zone and the private police forces of more affluent, gated suburbs.
The brainchild of former police chief Ed Davis, the Neighborhood
Watch concept has been emulated in hundreds of North American

San Dimas child molestors

and European cities from Seattle to London. In the aftermath of the 1965–71 cycle of unrest in South Central and East Los Angeles, Davis envisaged the program as the anchor for a "basic car" policing strategy designed to rebuild community support for the LAPD. He wanted to reestablish a strong territorial identity between patrol units and individual neighborhoods. Although his successor Daryl Gates preferred the commando bravado of SWAT units to the public-relations-oriented basic car patrols, Neighborhood Watch continued to flourish throughout the 1980s.

According to LAPD spokesperson Sgt. Christopher West, "Neighborhood Watch clubs are intended to increase local solidarity and self-confidence in the face of crime. Spurred by their block captains, residents become vigilant in the protection of each other's property and well-being. Suspicious behavior is immediately reported and homeowners regularly meet with patrol officers to plan crime-prevention tactics." An off-duty cop in a Winchell's Donut Shop in Silver Lake was more picturesque. "Neighborhood Watch is like the wagon train in an old-fashioned cowboy movie. The neighbors are the settlers and the

Circling the wagons

goal is to teach them to circle their wagons and fight off the Indians until the cavalry—the LAPD—can ride to their rescue."[46]

Needless to say, this Wild West analogy has its sinister side. Who, after all, gets to decide what behavior is "suspicious" or who looks like an "Indian"? The obvious danger in any program that conscripts thousands of citizens as police informers under the official slogan "Be on the Look Out for Strangers" is that it inevitably stigmatizes innocent groups. Inner city teenagers are especially vulnerable to flagrant stereotyping and harassment.

At one Neighborhood Watch meeting I attended in Echo Park, an elderly white woman asked a young policeman how to identify hardcore gang members. His answer was stupefyingly succinct: "Gangbangers wear expensive athletic shoes and clean, starched tee-shirts." The woman nodded her appreciation of this "expert" advice, while others in the audience squirmed in their seats at the thought of the youth in the neighborhood who would eventually be stopped and searched simply because they were well groomed.

Critics also worry that Neighborhood Watch does double duty as a captive constituency for police interests. As Sgt. West acknowledged, "Block captains are appointed by patrol officers and the program does obviously tend to attract the most law-and-order conscious members of the community." These pro-police residents, moreover, tend to be unrepresentative of their neighborhoods. In poor, youthful Latino areas, Watch captains are frequently elderly, residual Anglos. In areas where renters are a majority, the Watch activists are typically homeowners or landlords. Although official regulations are supposed to keep the program apolitical, block captains have long been regarded as the LAPD's precinct workers. In a bitter 1986 election, for example, the police union routinely used Neighborhood Watch meetings to campaign for the recall of the liberal majority, led by Rose Bird, on the California Supreme Court.

The "community policing advisory boards" established in the wake of the Rodney King beating have been hardly more independent. Although a reform commission headed by Warren Christopher criticized the LAPD's refusal to respond to citizen complaints, it failed to provide for elected advisory boards. As with Watch groups, board members serve strictly at the pleasure of local police commanders. When the Venice advisory board endorsed a spring 1992 ballot measure crafted by the Christopher Commission but opposed by the police union, they were summarily fired by the captain in charge of the Pacific Division.[47]

Since the 1992 riots some Neighborhood Watch groups have, with police encouragement, engaged in forms of surveillance that verge on vigilantism. In the San Fernando Valley, for example, volunteers from the white, upper-income neighborhoods of Porter Ranch and Granada Hills have been informally deputized as stealth auxiliaries in the police war against black and Latino gang youth. Clad in black ninja gear, they "perch in the dark on rooftops or crouch in vacant apartments, peering through shrouded windows," in hopes of photographing or videotaping graffiti taggers and drug peddlers. In a twist on the Rodney King affair, the videos are then used by the police as evidence in court.[48]

Several law-and-order pundits believe that Los Angeles needs to go even further and like Israel "flood the streets . . . every bus, shop and public space" with armed auxiliaries trained at police firing ranges and recruited from the respectable classes ("over forty and with a clean criminal record").[49] As a first approximation to this ideal "vigilantopolis," the LAPD has turned a blind eye on openly armed and menacing groups of homeowners and businessmen. In the Mid-City area, the ethnic enclave of "Koreatown" bristles with automatic weapons and informal militias composed of veterans of the Korean military who promise "punishment in kind" in the event of another attack on their businesses. Similarly in Hollywood, a member of the county Republican Central Committee claims that she has organized a gun-toting posse—"old West style"—to render summary justice to looters in the next riot:

> Civilians can deal with crime more easily because we are not hampered by constitutional restrictions like the police. We can slam and jam. People were nice in the last riot. Next time we will shoot looters first and ask questions later. A lot of blood will be spilled.[50]

Some already has. In January 1995, self-appointed vigilante William Masters II shot two young men—he described them as "skinhead Mexicans"—whom he discovered painting graffiti on a Hollywood Freeway overpass in the San Fernando Valley. Eighteen-year-old Rene Arce died at the scene; David Hilo, 20, was wounded in the buttocks. The *Los Angeles Times* reported that police "were overwhelmed by dozens of calls from graffiti-haters supporting Masters. Attorneys volunteered to represent him; other residents offered money for a possible defense fund; and one man showed up at the jail, saying that he wanted to take Masters to dinner for performing a 'profound service to the community.' " Outraged Latino leaders demanded his indictment for manslaughter, but the district attorney let him go and arrested Hilo instead. As Masters snarled after his release: "Where are you going to find twelve citizens to convict me?"[51]

6. PARALLEL UNIVERSES

Hollywood . . . exists only as a state of mind, not as a geographical entity.

Regional historian Carey McWilliams (1946)

Burgess and his students, who took 1920s and 1930s Chicago as a vast sociological laboratory, never had doubts about the raw "reality" of the phenomena that they were systematically surveying. Empirical method was matched to empirical reality. The mythography of the city played no part in the research program of the Chicago School. Although the 1892 and 1933 Chicago world's fairs were theme parks *avant la lettre,* urban sociology had not yet made conceptual space for the city as simulation.

Today there is no way around the issue. The contemporary American metropolis simulates or hallucinates itself in at least two senses. First, in the age of electronic culture and economy, the city creates its own virtual double through the complex architecture of its information and media networks. Perhaps, as William Gibson has suggested, three-dimensional computer interfaces will someday allow postmodern flaneurs to stroll through the luminous geometry of the mnemonic city where databases have metamorphosed into "blue pyramids" and "cold spiral arms." If so, urban cyberspace, as the simulation of the city's information order, will be experienced as even more segregated than traditional urban space. South Central Los Angeles, for example, is a data and media black hole, without local cable programming or links to major data systems. Just as it became a housing-and-jobs ghetto in the postwar period, it is now evolving into an off-net electronic ghetto.

Second, social fantasy is now embodied in "tourist bubbles"—historical districts, entertainment precincts, malls, and other variations on theme parks—that are partitioned off from the rest of the city. As all the postmodern philosopher kings (Baudrillard, Eco, Jameson) constantly remind us, Los Angeles is the world capital of such "hyperreality." This distinction has deep historical roots. Southern California's pioneering theme parks of the 1930s and 1940s were primarily architectural simulations of the movies and later of television shows. At the old Selig Zoo in Lincoln Heights, for example, you could enter the jungle set for Tarzan and Sheena, while at Knotts Berry Farm or its spin-off Calico ghost town in the Mojave Desert, you could participate in a typical Western. Disneyland, of course, opened the gates to the Magic Kingdom of cartoon creatures familiar from both the movie screen and television set.

Today Los Angeles itself, or rather its idealization, has become the subject of simulation and caricature. With the recent downsizing of the aerospace industry in Southern California, the tourism/hotel/entertainment sector—now treated as a single superindustry by most regional economists—has emerged as the area's largest employer. But tourists are increasingly reluctant to venture into the imagined dangers of Los Angeles's "urban jungle." As one MCA/Universal official complained: "There's somebody on every street corner with a 'Work for Food' sign, [and the city] is not fun anymore."[52]

Yet there is a growing hunger among younger members of the middle class for pedestrian-scale public space. The accelerating privatization of experience associated with life in gilded ghettos and gated suburbs has created a craving for crowds, street life, and spectacle. Entertainment megacorporations like MCA and Disney—whose film and record subsidiaries tirelessly disseminate dark images of city life—think they can capitalize on this demand for urban sensation by recreating vital bits of city life within the secure confines of their theme parks. The consumers of this junk-food version of urbanity are generally homogeneous crowds of upscale shoppers and tourists, and there is little of the real "promiscuity" (that "intimacy of strangers of all classes") that Burgess claimed animated Chicago and New York in the 1920s. Moreover, a largely invisible army of low-wage service workers, who themselves live in Bantustans like Santa Ana barrio (Disneyland) or the Hollywood flatlands (Universal City), keep the machinery of unreality running smoothly.

Because these created landscapes often exploit real or perceived historical places while competing with one another over authenticity, some complex dialectics ensue. Simulations tend to copy not an original (where that even exists) but one another. Consider the multiple or exponentialized hyperrealities involved in current corporate battles to monopolize the stardust known as "Hollywood."

HOLLYWOOD(S): POWERS OF SIMULATION

Hollywood[1]	Social reality (slum)
HOLLYWOOD[2]	Movie-made spectacle
HOLLYWOOD[3a]	Disney-MGM (Florida)
HOLLYWOOD[3b]	Universal (Florida)
HOLLYWOOD[4]	CityWalk (L.A.)
(Hollywood)[5]	Redevelopment project

For the past 75 years there has been an uneasy fit between the movie-made HOLLYWOOD! image and the actual Hollywood district. Indeed, at any level, "Hollywood" is a difficult concept to come to grips with, elusive and elastic at the same time. First of all, there is maximum official disagreement about where Hollywood is even located. Each Los Angeles city and county agency has a service unit called "Hollywood," yet no two share the same boundaries and only one is identical to the city limits of the short-lived City of Hollywood (1903–10). The police, in other words, arrest suspects in one Hollywood, while the sanitation department picks up trash in another. Only the overlap between competing official Hollywoods remains uncontroversial.

Second, identification with Hollywood has waxed and waned over time. In the 1930s and 1940s, the Hollywood name was sprinkled like gold dust over subdivisions and stores far outside the most notional boundaries of Babylon. Two of the most famous "Hollywood" businesses, for example, were not located in Hollywood at all. The original Frederick's of Hollywood sold its fantasy lingerie in downtown Los Angeles (it later moved to Hollywood Boulevard), while Dolphins of Hollywood, the city's premier R&B record store, was in South Central Los Angeles. A suburb in the San Fernando Valley, meanwhile, was christened "North Hollywood," as if a post office address alone could confer instant glamor on rows of humble bungalows.

By 1960, however, as the Hollywood flatlands rapidly decayed, the once magical name turned into a stigma. Neighborhoods that had previously basked in the reflected glory of Hollywood now rushed for the symbolic exits. "East Hollywood" disintegrated into Los Feliz and Silverlake. "West Hollywood," on the other hand, kept the name but incorporated itself as a separate designer city-state. Universal Studios, Hollywood, became Universal Studios, Universal City (a "county island" of unincorporated land totally controlled by MCA). Even dowdy Burbank, once the butt of Rowan and Martin jokes, became a preferred address for renegade Hollywood firms.

Movie stars, of course, had never lived in the Hollywood tenement district, and by 1930 most of the big studios had relocated to the suburbs. The actual Hollywood of the golden age (according to Carey McWilliams) was "lonely, insecure, full of marginal personalities, people just barely able to make ends meet; a place of opportunists and confidence men, petty chiselers and racketeers, bookies and race-track touts; of people desperately on the make."[53]

The HOLLYWOOD! in the imagination of the world's movie public was kept tenuously anchored to its namesake location by a calendar of ritual (premieres, the Academy Awards, footprint ceremonies) and the magical investment of a dozen or so locations (the Bowl, Graumann's Chinese and Egyptian Theaters, Musso and Franks, the corner of Hollywood and Vine) as tourist shrines. This celluloid Lourdes was a thin beauty strip between the inaccessible splendor of the hills and the crushed hopes of the flats.

But over the past generation, as the real Hollywood has gone from picturesque dilapidation to hyperviolent slum, even the rituals have ceased and the facade has crumbled. The socioeconomic decline of Hollywood is vividly illustrated by census snapshots of one of its core neighborhoods: the area east of Vine and north of Sunset that contains such landmarks as Capitol Records, CBS, Pantages Theatre, and the Hollywood Palladium. In 1940 the population was 84 percent native-born white, and the median income just slightly below that of Los

Angeles County as a whole. For the next 20 years, the area maintained the same general character, although the median income slipped to 82 percent of the county median by 1960. Today, after three decades of further change, the population largely consists of recent Mexican and El Salvadoran immigrants, and family income is a bare 47 percent of the median—poorer than most parts of South Central Los Angeles.[54]

A watershed was crossed in 1992 when the "flea people" of Nathanael West's nightmare actually rioted in the wake of the Rodney King decision. While the poor in the rest of the city were looting shoe stores and supermarkets, however, Hollywood's underclass—inspired by a perverse cult of celebrity—broke into Frederick's naughty lingerie museum and stole Madonna's knickers. (Despite a massive reward, the purloined undergarment is still at large.) As one local council candidate moaned, "Hollywood is supposed to be a dream machine, not the nightmare it has become."[55]

As Hollywood's immiseration eroded the historic linkage between signifier and signified, it gradually became possible to imagine the resurrection of HOLLYWOOD! in a more affluent, more secure neighborhood. Thus, in Orlando, Disney created a stunning Art Deco mirage of MGM's golden age, and arch-competitor MCA countered with its own idealized versions of Hollywood Boulevard and Rodeo Drive at Universal Studios Florida. (Matsushita, meanwhile, bought the MGM film library that contains some of the most sacred incarnations of mythical HOLLYWOOD!)

The elopement of Disney and HOLLYWOOD! to Florida, of course, further depressed real estate values back in real-time Hollywood. After bitter battles with local homeowners and small businessmen unable to bear any added tax burden, the major Hollywood Boulevard landowners won approval from the city council for a $1 billion face-lift. In their plan for the "Hollywoodization of Hollywood," the boulevard would be transformed into a gated theme park, anchored by entertainment megacomplexes at each end. Poor surrounding neighborhoods would be kept at arm's length from the boulevard until they were gentrified or torn down. But while the redevelopers were still negotiating with potential investors (like the billionaire Bass brothers of Fort Worth), MCA pulled the rug from under Hollywood redux with the announcement that its nearby tax-dodge enclave Universal City would construct a parallel urban reality called "CityWalk."

Designed by master illusionist Jon Jerde, CityWalk is an "idealized reality": the iconic features of Hollywood, along with Olvera Street and Mid-Wilshire, synthesized in "easy, bite-sized pieces" for consumption by tourists and residents who "don't need the excitement of dodging bullets . . . in the Third World country" that Los Angeles has become. CityWalk incorporates examples of Mission Revival, Deco, streamlined Moderne, and L.A. Vernacular (the Brown Derby restaurant), as well as 3-D billboards, "a huge blue King Kong hanging from a 70-foot neon totem pole," and a sheriff's substation for security. To alleviate the sense of artificiality in this melange, Jerde proposed to add a "patina of age" and a "dash of grit":

> Using decorative sleight of hand, the designers plan to wrap the brand new street in a cloak of instant history—on opening day, some buildings will be painted to suggest that they have been occupied before. Candy wrappers will be embedded in the terrazzo flooring, as if discarded by previous visitors.[56]

Since the opening of CityWalk in 1993, plans for Hollywood redevelopment have been more or less shipwrecked. Even spruced up and Disneyfied there is no way that the real boulevard can compete with the Platonic ideal-type on Universal's private hill.* As MCA has taken pains to emphasize, CityWalk is "not a mall" but a "revolution in urban design," a monumental exercise in sociological hygiene. But critics have wondered if it isn't, instead, the architectural equivalent of the neutron bomb: the city emptied of all lived experience. "Have we so

---

* The latest, post-CityWalk scheme for Hollywood Boulevard, sponsored by the TrizacHahn Corporation, envisions a Biosphere-like entertainment mall next to the Chinese Theater. *Los Angeles Times* architecture critic Nicolai Ouroussoff describes the one-million-square-foot design as "a gigantic, multilevel version of Via Rodeo—the themed, upscale shopping haven in Beverly Hills."[57]

lost L.A. as a real city," asked historian Kevin Starr, "that we need this level of social control for anything resembling the urban experience?"[58]

7. OZZIE AND HARRIET IN HELL

The golden days in the canyon had ended badly.
  Ken Nunn, Pomona Queen *(1992)*

Once upon a time a placid town, celebrated in millions of picture post-cards, basked in the golden glow of its orchards. Its official slogan was "The Place of Wealth, Health and Plenty." In the 1920s it was renowned as the Queen of the Citrus Belt, with one of the highest per capita incomes in the nation. In the 1940s it was so modally middle class—the real-life counterpart of Andy Hardy's hometown—that Hollywood used it as a preview laboratory to test typical audience reactions to new films. In the 1950s it became a commuter suburb for thousands of Fathers-Know-Best in their starched white shirts.

Now its nearly abandoned downtown is surrounded by acres of vacant lots and derelict homes. ("Eventually the only shoppers in sight were the winos lined up in the early morning liquor line in front of Thrifty's drugstore.")[59] Its major employer, an aerospace corporation, pulled up stakes and moved to Tucson. The 4H Club has been replaced by local franchises of the Crips and Bloods. Since 1970 nearly 1 percent of its population has been murdered. Indeed, six people—including four teenagers—were murdered in a single 36-hour period in January 1997.[60]

"It" is Pomona, Los Angeles County's fourth largest city (population 134,000). Although Pomona, according to Burgess's old-fashioned cartography, is a "bungalow suburb" in the "commuter zone," it displays most of the pathologies typically associated with a battered inner city. As in Butler's fictional Robledo, so in Pomona paradise has morphed into hell. "There [are] iron bars on the windows of the Cinderella tract," and what "plays in Pomona" now is mayhem and despair.[61]

What plays now is mayhem

Pomona's incidence of poverty exceeds Los Angeles's, and its homicide rate, in bad years, approaches Oakland's or Baltimore's. Its density of gang membership, as a percentage of the teenage male population, rates among the highest in the country. A 1993 survey of 828 communities ranked Pomona as the eleventh worst in the nation for the welfare and health of children. In some of its schools, 80 percent of the students are poor enough to qualify for free school lunches. Each year one-third of Pomona Unified School District's seniors fail to graduate, 10 times the dropout rate of the neighboring college community of Claremont.[62]

Years of urban renewal, meanwhile, have left its downtown as desolate as a miniature Detroit, while its proudest achievement—the tax-subsidized development of a walled, upper-income neighborhood known as Philips Ranch—has only exacerbated the sense of disenfranchisement in poorer areas like the "Island," "Sin Town," and the "Flats." Although a recent mayor was a Latino (as well as a Mormon and Republican), real power in this 65 percent Latino and black community is still firmly monopolized by the Anglo business elite—the grandchildren of those long-gone orchard owners—who still live in the big houses "on the hill" in Ganesha Heights.

Pomona is not a unique case. Across the nation, hundreds of aging suburbs are trapped in the same downward spiral from garden city to crabgrass slum. This silent but pervasive malaise dominates the political middle landscape. Needless to say, the arrival of this *second* urban crisis—potentially comparable in magnitude to the seemingly endless ordeal of the inner cities—does not fit comfortably into either political party's current agenda.* Although urbanists and local government researchers have been screaming at the top of their lungs for several years about the rising distress in older suburbs, most politicos have kept their heads buried deep in the sand.[63]

The failure of politicians to address, or even grasp, the acuteness of the suburban malaise explains much of the populist rage that currently threatens the two-party status quo. America seems to be unraveling in its traditional moral center: the urban periphery. Indeed, the 1990 census confirmed that 35 percent of suburban cities had experienced significant declines in median household income since 1980. This downward income trend reflected the loss of several million jobs, amplified by corresponding declines in home values and tax resources.[64]

As a result, formerly bedrock "family value" towns like Lakewood, Ohio (outside Cleveland), Upper Darby, Pennsylvania (outside Philadelphia), Brockton, Massachusetts (outside Boston), and University City, Missouri (outside St. Louis), are now experiencing the social destabilization that comes in the wake of the erosion of traditional job and tax bases.[65] As the *National Journal* tried to warn largely inattentive policymakers several years ago, "Older working-class suburbs are starting to fall into the same abyss of disinvestment that their center cities did years ago."[66] The playing field between the inner city and the older suburb has been leveled—both are below sea level now.

In Southern California, such suburban decline has sometimes been anything but a slow bleed. Recent aerospace and defense closures—

---

* These older or "first ring" suburbs overlap Burgess's "residential" and "commuter" zones. They include older "street-car" suburbs as well as first-generation automobile suburbs.

like Hughes Missile Division's abrupt departure from Pomona or Lockheed's abandonment of its huge Burbank complex—have had the social impact of unforeseen natural disasters. Following the Lockheed shutdown, welfare case loads in the eastern San Fernando Valley soared by 80,000 in an 18-month period. In the Valley as a whole (population 1.2 million), one in six residents now lives below the poverty line, and one in ten collected an unemployment check in 1995. Gang violence has relentlessly kept pace with the new immiseration. The "most dangerous street in Los Angeles," according to the LAPD, is not in South Central or East Los Angeles; it is Blythe Street in the Valley, a few blocks from the corpse of a GM assembly plant shut down in 1993.[67]

But older suburbs' losses are usually someone else's gain. Just as post–World War II subdivisions once stole jobs and tax revenues from central cities, so now their pockets are being picked in turn by new urban centers further out on the spiral arms of the metropolitan galaxy (and unanticipated by the Chicago school) that Joel Garreau has named "edge cities." It has been estimated, for example, that the older suburbs of Minneapolis–St. Paul lost 38 percent of their jobs during the 1980s to the "Fertile Crescent" of edge cities on the metro region's southwest flank.[68] Schaumburg and central DuPage County—west of O'Hare International Airport—have had similarly adverse impacts on the older suburban communities of Cook County, as have the young edge cities of Contra Costa County on the east San Francisco Bay's traditional blue-collar suburbs.[69]

In Los Angeles County, the 18-mile-long, tapeworm-shaped City of Industry puts a bizarre spin on the idea of the edge city. It won incorporation in 1958 through the gimmick of counting mental patients in a nearby asylum as permanent residents and had the same mayor (answering to the same small elite) for 40 years until he was succeeded by his son. Although tiny in population (just 680 residents), it is an economic superpredator, monopolizing most of the tax assets of the southern San Gabriel Valley, including 2,100 factories, warehouses, and discount outlets as well as a world-class golf course and resort hotel. In its malign influence on surrounding tax-starved, mainly Latino suburbs like La Puente and South El Monte (which play the role of dormitories for City of Industry laborers) it has been compared to an "economic atom bomb."[70]

The edge cities, moreover, have rapidly translated their rising populations and economic power into political hegemony. Consider the composition of the post-1994 Republican leadership in the House of Representatives. At the time of the Republican "revolution," even veteran political commentators asked, "Who are these guys?" The answer is that they were the gang from the edge cities. Speaker Gingrich and his top lieutenants represented, with few exceptions, the affluent and self-contained outer suburbs. The younger generation of Republicans from Southern California's booming edge cities constituted one of the most notable contingents.[71]

TEAM GINGRICH

Congressman	Edge City
Bill Archer	Route 290 (Houston)
Dick Armey	Irving/Las Colinas (Dallas)
Phil Crane	Schaumburg (Chicago)
Chris Cox	Irvine (Orange Co., Calif.)
Randy Cunningham	Del Mar (San Diego)
Dave Drier	Arcadia (Los Angeles)
Elton Gallegly	Simi Valley (Ventura Co.)
Newt Gingrich	Buckhead Co. (Atlanta)
Henry Hyde	DuPage Co. (Chicago)
John Kasich	Suburban Columbus (Ohio)
Bill McCollum	Orange Co. (Florida)
Ron Packard	Mission Viejo (Orange Co., Calif.)
James Talent	U.S. 40 corridor (St. Louis)
Curt Weldon	King of Prussia (Penn.)

Source: *Almanac of American Politics* (New York, 1996).

Residents of older suburbs are finally coming to understand what inner city people have known for decades: their own tax dollars finance their own inevitable decline. The federal interstate highway system, together with state-funded water projects like the California Aqueduct and Arizona's Salt River Project, provide massive subsidies for the proliferation of otherwise uneconomic edge suburbs. A recent

Chicago study, for example, has shown that it costs $60,000 to hook up a new house in an outer suburb to the utility infrastructure as against $5,000 for the same house in an existing suburb. "Who foots the bill? Taxpayers in the established suburbs."[72]

This one-sided competition between old and new suburbs is bringing latent class divisions in the historic commuter belts to the surface. As HUD Secretary Andrew Cuomo recently conceded, "There is no monolith anymore called 'suburbs.' "[73] Intersuburban tensions are particularly conspicuous in Los Angeles's vast tract-house hinterlands. Widening socioeconomic and ethnic chasms divide northern and southern Orange County, the upper and lower tiers of the San Gabriel Valley, northwestern Riverside County and the I-15 corridor, and the east and west sides of the San Fernando Valley. Landscape amenities help shape this new metropolitan hierarchy. As a rule of thumb, Los Angeles County's affluent white suburbanites have retreated to choice foothill and beachfront communities, while the white working class has moved to new commuter suburbs on the edge of the desert in northern Los Angeles and western San Bernardino and Riverside Counties. The older "burbs" have become majority black, Latino, and Asian. As in the San Francisco Bay region, there is a permanent cold war over tax revenue and allocation of public services between the poorer flats and the tonier hills.

The have-not suburbs have, moreover, accelerated their own decline by squandering scarce tax resources in zero-sum competitions for new investment. Too many poor communities have tried to upscale themselves through draconian social engineering (restriction or even removal of low-income residents) and desperate bids to beef up the tax base. If a decade ago, every aging suburb from Compton to Pomona had to have its own auto mall, now the magic bullet is believed to be a card casino (and both Compton and Pomona have been thrown into upheaval over schemes to build one). Redevelopment programs, which in California devour 10 to 15 percent of local tax revenue, have become little more than cargo cults, praying for miraculous investments that never come.

In addition to the dramatic hemorrhage of jobs and capital over the last decade, aging suburbia also suffers from premature physical obsolescence. Much of what was built in the postwar period (and continues to be built today) is throwaway architecture, with a functional lifespan of 30 years or less. California "dingbats" (as the two-story apartment blocks with palm trees are colloquially known) and other light-frame Sunbelt apartment types are especially unsuited to support the intergenerational continuity of community and property. At best, this stucco junk was designed to be promptly recycled in perennially dynamic housing markets, but such markets have stagnated or died in much of the old suburban fringe.

Now millions of units of what design critic Reyner Banham famously caricatured as "Tacoburger Aztec" and "Polynesian Gabled" are fast eroding into the slum housing of the year 2000.[74] Our ur-suburb, the San Fernando Valley, is a telling example. The colossal $42 billion damage inflicted by the 1992 Northridge earthquake clearly exposed this building quality crisis as residents were literally killed by shoddy construction. Although no one has yet attempted the calculation, there is little reason to suppose that this suburban housing deficit—the inability to finance the replacement costs of obsolete and unrestorable building stock—will be any smaller than Clinton's once famous but now forgotten national "infrastructure deficit." Nor is it likely, as declining suburbs become the new pariahs, that the financial market's invisible hand will linger longer than it takes to draw a fatal red line around their prospects for housing reinvestment. The same grim calculations apply to the neglected social infrastructure, the schools, parks, libraries, and the like of 1920–60 suburbia.

All of this, of course, is especially bad news for poor, inner city residents who are being urged by every pundit in the land to find their salvation in the suburbs. Indeed, confronted with virtually paleolithic conditions of life in collapsing city neighborhoods, hundreds of thousands of blacks and Latinos are finally finding it possible to move into the subdivisions where Beaver Cleaver and Ricky Nelson used to live. The once monochromatic San Fernando Valley now has a slight non-Anglo majority of Latino, black, Middle Eastern, and Asian residents, including more than 500,000 recent immigrants. There are more people of Mexican descent in Ozzie-and-Harriet land than in East L.A.

But their experiences too often repeat the heartbreak and disillusionment of the original migrations to the central cities. What seemed from afar a promised land is, at closer sight, a low-rise version of the same old ghetto or barrio. Like a maddening mirage, good jobs and good schools are still a horizon away, in the new edge cities. The "good ole boy" regimes that hold power in the interregnum between white flight and the slow accession of new black or Latino electoral majorities usually loot every last cent in the town treasury before making their ungraceful exits. As a result, minorities typically inherit municipal scorched earth—crushing redevelopment debts, demoralized workforces, neglected schools, and deserted business districts—as their principal legacy from the old order.

In the meantime, the stranded and forgotten white populations of these transitional communities are too easily tempted to confuse structural decay with the sudden presence of neighbors of color. The vampirish role of the edge cities in sucking resources from older or poorer suburbs is less evident than the desperate needs of growing populations dependent on the dole. Political discourse, moreover, constantly valorizes resentments against the poor and people of color, while remaining discreetly silent about the real structures of urban inequality. As a consequence, in the older suburban fringe of Southern California, where little else is flourishing, hate crime is booming.

8. LOW-INTENSITY RACE WAR

You have been Judged GUILTY by the Orange County chapter of WAR, White Aryan Resistance. . . . We look forward to meeting you in persons [sic].

Skinhead warning (1993)

Before the skinheads shot Mike Bunche Robinson, they pulverized his face with karate kicks and punches. The beating was so sadistic that his body had to be identified through fingerprints. The coroner warned his girlfriend not to view the disfigured corpse. Robinson, a well-liked VW mechanic from the blue-collar San Bernardino suburb of Highland (60 miles east of Los Angeles), was killed on 22 August 1995. He was the fifth African-American to be murdered by skinheads in Southern California in two years. In another era his death would have been called a lynching. Now he was just part of the body count in a low-intensity race war that the criminal justice establishment and the mainstream press have largely ignored.[75]

The current wave of racial killings began in September 1993, just two months after the sensational FBI arrest of eight "Fourth Reich" skinheads for plotting to blow up black churches in South Central Los Angeles. A young African-American woman, Tina Roxanne Rodriguez, was beaten to death in front of her young daughter by two skinhead women screaming racial slurs in the parking lot of a La Habra (Orange County) shopping center. An estimated 20 to 30 white bystanders made no effort to rescue Rodriguez as her brains were literally pounded out on the pavement.[76]

Then, in August 1994, a black sophomore at Santa Margarita High in southern Orange County was lured into an ambush in the Portola Hills. Encircled by a mob of 30 young whites shouting "Get the nigger!" 15-year-old Ruben Vaughan, a stellar athlete and scholar, was viciously beaten and stabbed with a screwdriver. He was hospitalized in critical condition with a shattered jaw, broken nose, and seven stab wounds. Two weeks later, another young black man from southern Orange County, 20-year-old Jody Robinson, was kidnapped, tortured, and murdered by what sheriffs described as another skinhead gang.

In September, black longshoreman Vernon Flournoy, who had moved from Hollywood after the 1992 riots "to get away from urban troubles," was gunned down outside a McDonald's restaurant in Huntington Beach by two skinheads. This popular beach town, the center of South Coast surfing culture, was also the home of the Fourth Reich skins arrested the previous year. For years the strip of cafés and surf shops along Main Street had been terrorized by gangs of skinheads from the Long Beach and Orange County areas.[77] Thus police were not surprised that the older of Flournoy's killers, 19-year-old Jonathan Kinsey, was carrying Hitler quotations in his wallet when arrested. In addition to the slaying of Flournoy, Kinsey was also charged with (and eventually convicted of) the attempted murder of two Latinos a month earlier, also in Huntington Beach.[78]

The next murder took place in Riverside shortly before Christmas 1994. Rodd Jackson was simply backing out of his driveway when 26-year-old Michael Brown screamed, "Fuck you, nigger!" and blasted him with a sawed-off shotgun. Brown had just been released from state prison and, according to Riverside homicide investigators, had boasted to friends of belonging to a "Nazi supremacist" group, presumably the prison-based Aryan Brotherhood.[79]

A few months later, three skinheads opened fire on a group of African-Americans near Antelope Valley High School in Lancaster (Los Angeles County). Four people, including an 11-month-old baby, were seriously wounded. In the following weeks, a black woman was beaten by racists after she and her husband refused to move out of a Palmdale trailer park, and a black teenager was stabbed by three white youth, again in front of Antelope Valley High. The FBI later confirmed that three skinhead gangs—the Nazi Lowriders, the Palmdale Peckerwoods, and the Metal Minds—were active in Los Angeles's high desert suburbs where rapid growth in the minority population has coincided with a steep downturn in local employment.[80]

In March 1995, it was Mike Robinson's turn. The killers—four skinhead men in their early twenties—were burglarizing the home of a white friend of Robinson's, unaware that the African-American youth was asleep in a bedroom. When they discovered 20-year-old Robinson, they tied him up, then savaged and shot him. His friend was beaten but allowed to live. While San Bernardino County sheriffs were searching for Robinson's killers, several black and Latino homes in Highland were paint-bombed and covered with skinhead graffiti. The NAACP, exasperated with official inaction, urged the federal Justice Department to undertake an investigation of the local hate crime wave.[81]

Skinheads were also on the rampage in Orange County through the summer and fall of 1995. In the city of Orange, skins screaming Nazi slogans attacked a local punk rock club, roughing up a black guitarist, before turning on a young Asian-Indian customer whom they beat unconscious with metal pipes. Six months later, on 28 January 1996, Thien Minh Ly, the former president of the Vietnamese American Student Association at UCLA, was practicing in-line skating at a high school in Tustin when he was stabbed to death by two skinheads. The shock wave that rocked Orange County's large Vietnamese community was intensified when sheriffs revealed a letter that one of the murderers, 21-year-old Gunner Lindberg, had written to a prison friend in New Mexico.

I stabbed him in the side about 7 or 8 times he rolled over a little so I stabbed his back out 18 or 19 times then he layed flat and I slit one side of his throught on his jugular vain. Oh, the sounds the guy was making were like Uhhh. Then Dominic said "do it again" and I said "I already Did. Dude." "Ya, Do it again" so I cut his other juggular vain, and Dominic said "Kill him do it again" and I said "he's already Dead" Dominic Said "Stab him in the heart" So I stabbed him about 20 or 21 times in the heart.

Then I wanted go back and look, so we Did and he was deing just then taking in some bloody gasps of air so I nidged his face with my shoe a few times, then I told Dominic to kick him, so he kicked the fuck out of his face and he still has blood on his Shoes.[82]

In February, more of the neonazis who infest Huntington Beach accosted a 20-year-old native American near a lifeguard tower. Confronted with the usual skinhead challenge ("Do you believe in white power?"), George Mondragon attempted to run away but was tackled to the ground and stabbed 27 times in the chest, liver, back, neck, colon, and hands. Miraculously, he survived.[83] A month later, 59-year-old native American Jerry Jordan ended up on life support with multiple skull fractures and several broken ribs after an encounter with local skinheads in the Riverside County town of Redlands. During the previous year, Redlands had been terrorized by several cross burnings and a number of racist assaults. Police claimed that the local skinheads "target people they believe are a burden to society, such as homeless people and welfare recipients."[84]

Over the next few months, racial violence returned to the Antelope Valley, where randomly selected African-Americans were attacked with baseball bats and machetes by the Nazi Lowriders. In searching for the ringleader, 22-year-old Danny Williams, sheriffs described him as having "swastikas tattooed on his right hand and a hooded Ku Klux Klan figure on his left shoulder."[85] (Williams was eventually arrested, but he escaped from jail and had to be tracked down again.)[86]

According to the Los Angeles County Commission on Human Relations, attacks on blacks increased 50 percent from 1995 to 1996. With 995 hate crimes reported countywide in 1995, metropolitan Los Angeles became the nation's capital of racial (539 crimes) and sexual orientation (338 crimes) violence. (The remaining 118 attacks were motivated by religious hatred.) The commission's annual report also noted that racially motivated crimes had been clearly clustered in older suburban areas like Long Beach, Westchester, Harbor Gateway, and Van Nuys, as well as in the economically troubled Antelope Valley. Although the human relations commissioners cautioned that the report "does not say it has become open season on African Americans," the dramatic surge in attacks on blacks suggested otherwise.[87]

Obvious questions remain unanswered. What are the links between these atrocities? Has racial murder become an initiation rite into the Aryan Brotherhood? Although the FBI and the Justice Department finally intervened in the Antelope Valley cases in 1996, following desultory efforts by Los Angeles County sheriffs, there has been no investigation of the overall pattern of white supremacist violence throughout the Los Angeles metropolitan periphery. As civil rights lawyers have frequently pointed out, hate crimes are grossly underreported by local police and sheriffs, while state-level statistics have only become available since 1995.[88] Law enforcement agencies, by any measure, have been strangely reluctant to acknowledge the extent of the racist violence or to probe into the deeper recesses of Southern California's white supremacist subcultures.

Indeed, official attitudes are a serious part of the problem. In Orange County, where according to the father of one victim "hate crime is becoming a popular sport," minority activists have complained for years about an official double standard. Although District Attorney Michael Capizzi has routinely fed anti-Latino and anti-Vietnamese hysteria with high-profile mass arrests (often for little more than parking tickets) in the Santa Ana barrio and Little Saigon, he has refused to acknowledge the plague of white violence sweeping his county, despite 105 skinhead attacks in 1995 alone (as reported by the Orange County Human Relations Commission).[89]

Similar criticisms have been made in the Antelope Valley. "Local officialdom," according to Mike Kirkland, a prominent leader in the African-American community, "keeps its head buried in the sand. Despite dramatic evidence, including burning crosses and the fire-bombing of a Latino family, they kept downplaying the skinhead phenomena. Now our kids have been shot in front of their own schoolhouse, yet the board of education is more concerned with getting rid of affirmative action than confronting racism."[90] As if to confirm Kirkland's point, city officials and sheriff's deputies were still insisting two years later—after a dozen more incidents and the arrival of the FBI—that "we just aren't getting very many hate-crime reports."[91]

Joe Hicks, the outspoken director of the Los Angeles Multicultural Collaborative, believes that such official complacency has contributed to the relegitimation of public racism. "We are seeing the rebirth of white supremacism as a material force, where racism of the word quickly becomes racism of the deed." Hicks suggests the metaphor of Russian dolls. "The largest doll, of course, is Pete Wilson, but inside is Rush Limbaugh. Open a few dolls more and find Mark Fuhrman. And inside him is a smirking Timothy McVeigh."[92] The chilling McVeigh reference may be apt. In late fall 1995 the LAPD busted four young whites in the San Fernando Valley who were allegedly negotiating to sell a staggering quantity of high explosives, which they had stolen from a rock quarry, to a local skinhead group. Who knows what terrifying recipes from the *Turner Diaries* may yet be concocted in Los Angeles's suburban badlands?

9. THE GULAG RIM

You touch the fence and you die.
Official at Calipatria State Prison (1994)

The road from Mecca follows the Southern Pacific tracks past Bombay Beach to Niland, then turns due south through a green maze of marshes and irrigated fields. The bad future of Southern California rises, with little melodrama, in the middle distance between the skeleton of last year's cotton crop and the aerial bombing range in the Chocolate Mountains. From a mile away, the slate-gray structures resemble warehouses or perhaps a factory. An unassuming road sign announces "Calipatria State Prison." This is the outer rim of Los Angeles's ecology of fear, and it has no equivalent on Burgess's chart.[93]

Calipatria, which opened in 1993, is a "level 4," maximum security prison that currently houses 10 percent of California's convicted murderers, 1,200 men. Yet the guard booth at the main gate is unmanned, as are 10 of its 12 perimeter gun towers. If the startling absence of traditional surveillance looks negligent, it is deliberate policy. As Daniel Paramo, the prison's energetic public relations officer, explains, "The warden doesn't trust the human-error factor in the gun towers; he puts his faith, instead, in Southern California Edison."[94]

Paramo is standing in front of an ominous 13-foot electric fence, sandwiched between two ordinary chain-link fences. Each of the 15 individual strands of wire bristles with 5,000 volts of Parker Dam power—about 10 times the recognized lethal dosage. The electrical contractors guarantee instantaneous death. (An admiring guard in the background mutters: "Yeah, toast. . . .")

A bad future: Calipatria prison

The original bill authorizing the high-voltage "escape-proof" fence sailed through the legislature with barely a murmur. Cost-conscious politicians had few scruples about an electric bill that saved $2 million in labor costs each year. And when the warden quietly threw the main switch in November 1993, there was general satisfaction that the corrections system was moving ahead, with little controversy, toward its high-tech future. "But," Paramo adds ruefully, "we had neglected to factor the animal-rights people into the equation."

The prison is just east of the Salton Sea—a major wintering habitat for waterfowl—and the gently purring high-voltage fence immediately became an erotic beacon to passing birds. Local bird-watchers soon found out about the body count ("a gull, two owls, a finch and a scissor-tailed flycatcher") and alerted the Audubon Society. By January, Calipatria's "death fence" was an international environmental scandal. When a CNN crew pulled into the prison parking lot, the Department of Corrections threw in the towel and hired an ornithologist to help them redesign the fence.

The result is the world's only birdproof, ecologically responsible death fence. Paramo has some difficulty maintaining a straight face as he points out $150,000 in innovations: "a warning wire for curious rodents, anti-perching deflectors for wildfowl, and tiny passageways for burrowing owls." Calipatria has also built an attractive pond for visiting geese and ducks.

Although the prison system is now at peace with bird lovers, the imbroglio roused the powerful California Correctional Peace Officers' Association (CCPOA) to question management's right to "automate" the jobs of the 30 sharpshooters (three shifts per tower) replaced by the fence. To proceed with his plan to lethally electrify all the state's medium and maximum security prisons (23 of 29 facilities) in the coming years, Director of Corrections Joe Gomez may have to negotiate a compromise with the CCPOA that preserves more of the "featherbed" gun tower jobs.

Calipatria's four thousand inmates, most of them from the tough ghettos and barrios of Los Angeles County, shed few tears for either the ducks or the guards. Their lives are entirely absorbed in the daily struggle to survive soul-destroying claustrophobia and ever threatening racial violence. Like the rest of the system, Calipatria operates at almost double its design capacity. In the state's medium security facilities, squalid tiers of bunk beds have been crowded into converted auditoriums and day rooms much as in overflowing county jails. In "upscale" level-4 institutions like Calipatria, on the other hand, a second inmate has simply been shoehorned into each of the tiny, six-by-ten-foot one-man cells.

When "double celling" was first introduced into the system a decade ago, it helped fuel a wave of inmate violence and suicide. Civil liberties advocates denounced the practice as "cruel and unusual punishment," but a federal judge upheld its constitutionality. Now inmates can routinely expect to spend decades or even lifetimes (40 percent of Calipatria's population are lifers) locked in unnatural, and often unbearable, intimacy with another person. The psychological stress is amplified by a shortage of prison jobs that condemns nearly half the inmate population to serve their sentences idly in their cells watching infinities of television. As behavioral psychologists have testified in court, rats confined in such circumstances invariably go berserk and eat each other.

The abolition of privacy, together with the suppression of inmate counterculture, are explicit objectives of "new generation" prisons like Calipatria. Each of its 20 housing units is designed like a two-story horseshoe with a guard station opposite. Yet another variation on Jeremy Bentham's celebrated eighteenth-century panopticon prison, this "270 plan" (referring to the guards' field of vision) is intended to ensure continuous surveillance of all inmate behavior. Official blurbs boast of a "more safe and humane incarceration" and an end to the "fear-hate syndrome" associated with prisons that tolerate zones of unsupervised inmate interaction.

In practice, however, panopticonism has been compromised by construction shortcuts and chronic understaffing. Although toilets sit nakedly in the middle of the recreational yards as symbols of institutional omniscience, there are still plenty of blind spots—behind tier stairs or in unsurveilled kitchen areas—where inmates can take revenge on staff or one another. As Paramo warns visitors when they sign the grim waiver acknowledging California's policy of refusing to negotiate for hostages, "The war is on."

For a quarter of a century, California prisons have institutionalized episodic violence between inmate guerrilla armies. The original order of battle, after the death of Black Panther leader George Jackson in 1971, allied the Black Guerrilla Family and La Nuestra Familia (mainly Northern California Latinos) against the Aryan Brotherhood and the East L.A.–based Mexican Mafia (or EME). Today there are also rising Asian and Central American gangs, but the carnage has been centralized into a merciless struggle for power between blacks and the EME.

In part, this race war reflects dramatic recent shifts in California's population. In 1988, new prison admissions were 35 percent black and 30 percent Latino; by 1993, however, the proportions were 41 percent Latino and 25 percent black. As a result, the system now has a slight Latino plurality (although blacks remain the largest group in Calipatria). EME reportedly has used this new clout—both inside and outside the walls—to attack the black monopoly on the sale of crack cocaine. Calipatria's gang intelligence officer claims that the recent death of Joe Morgan—the EME's legendary founder and sometime prison statesman—cleared the way for a younger, more ruthless leadership.

In Calipatria's case, the last riot between blacks and Latinos occurred in July 1995, when 13 inmates were stabbed. One guard described the melee, which apparently started in the central kitchen and spread to the housing units, as "the EME blindsiding the Crips." As a result, the prison was locked down for four months, and the day rooms have been abandoned as too dangerous for mixed use. Paramo keeps a display of some of the captured weapons in his office, including what looks like an obsidian dagger but is actually a shank made from melted black garbage bags.

To deal with such explosions, California's higher level prisons have introduced new and extreme sanctions. Each institution, for example, now has its own internal SWAT unit—or Special Emergency Response Team—capable of countering outbreaks with staggering amounts of firepower and paramilitary expertise. These elite units have been widely praised for preventing inmate-upon-inmate slaughters like that in the New Mexico State Penitentiary in 1984. The price of such prevention, however, seems to be an extraordinary toleration of official violence. Over the last decade, trigger-happy guards have killed 38 inmates in California institutions (including three in Calipatria)—more than triple the *total* of the six other leading prison population states and the federal penitentiary system combined.[95]

Staff at Calipatria speak with measured awe of CCPOA president Don Novey, a former Folsom prison guard, who has made the Correctional Officers the most powerful union in the state. Under his leadership, the CCPOA has been transformed from a small, reactive craft union into the major player shaping criminal justice legislation and, thereby, the future of the California penal system. Part of the secret of Novey's success has been his willingness to pay the highest price for political allies. In 1990, for example, Novey contributed nearly $1 million to Pete Wilson's gubernatorial campaign, and CCPOA now operates the second most generous PAC in Sacramento.[96]

Novey has also leveraged CCPOA's influence through his sponsorship of the so-called victims' rights movement. Crime Victims United, for example, is a satellite PAC receiving 95 percent of its funding from CCPOA. Through such high-profile front groups, and in alliance with other law enforcement lobbies, Novey has been able to keep Sacramento in a permanent state of law-and-order hysteria. Legislators of both parties trample each other in the rush to put their names at the top of new, tougher anticrime measures, while ignoring the progressive imbalance between the number of felons sentenced to prison and the existing capacity of Department of Corrections facilities.[97]

This cynical competition has had staggering consequences. Rand Corporation researcher Joan Petersilia found that "more than 1,000 bills changing felony and misdemeanor statutes" had been enacted by the legislature between 1984 and 1992. Taken together, they are utterly incoherent as criminal justice policy, but wonderful as a stimulus to the kind of carceral Keynesianism that has tripled both the membership and the average salary of the CCPOA since 1980. While California's colleges and universities were shedding 8,000 jobs, the Department of Corrections hired 26,000 new employees to guard 112,000 new inmates. As a result, California is now the proud owner of the third largest penal system in the world (after China and the United States as a whole).[98]

A host of critics, including an official blue ribbon commission, have tried to wean the legislature from its reckless gulagism. They have produced study after study showing that superincarceration has had a negligible impact on the overall crime rate, and that a majority of new inmates are either nonviolent drug offenders (including parolees flunking mandatory urinalysis) or the mentally ill (28,000 inmates by official estimate). They have also repeatedly warned that a day of reckoning will come when the state will have to trade higher education, literally brick by brick, to continue to build prisons.[99]

Politicians do not dispute that this day is now close at hand. When one education leader in testimony before the legislature pointed to the inverse relationship between the college and prison budgets, state senator Frank Hill (R-Whittier) acidly retorted: "If push came to shove, the average voter is going to be more supportive of prisons than of the University of California."[100] Although it costs taxpayers more than twice as much to send an 18-year-old to prison as to university, politicians reap greater rewards from lobbyists and conservative voters for building cells than for building classrooms.

It was not surprising, therefore, that the legislature instead of hitting the brakes went full throttle in 1994 with a "three strikes" law (subsequently enshrined in the state constitution by a referendum in 1994) which doubles sentences for second felonies and mandates 25 years to life for three-time losers.[101] As a direct result, Department of Corrections planners predict a 262 percent increase in the penal population (to 341,420) by 2005 (as contrasted to 22,500 inmates in 1980). Commenting on these projections, a spokesman for Governor Wilson simply shrugged his shoulders: "If these additional costs have to be absorbed, I guess we'll have to reduce other services. We'll have to change our priorities."[102]

It is sobering to recall that the Department of Corrections with 29 major "campuses" is already more expensive than the University of California system, and that young black men in Los Angeles and Oakland are twice as likely to end up in prison as in college. The three strikes law, moreover, is widening racial disparities in sentencing. According to data from Los Angeles County public defenders, African-Americans made up 57 percent of the early three strikes filings, although they are only 10 percent of the population. This is 17 times the rate of whites, although other studies have shown that white men commit at least 60 percent of rapes, robberies, and assaults.[103] The majority-suburban legislature, however, has been unfazed by studies demonstrating the profound racial inequities of recent criminal legislation.

Initial hopes that Cruz Bustamante—the Fresno Democrat who in 1997 became the first modern Latino Assembly Speaker—would restore some sanity to crime-and-punishment debates were quickly dashed when Bustamante tried to outflank Governor Wilson on the subject of capital punishment for minors. When Wilson suggested death sentences for criminals as young as 14 (the current minimum age is 18), Bustamante responded that he might "with a tear in my eye, cast a vote to execute 'hardened criminals' as young as 13." (Thanks to bipartisan legislation in 1996, 14-year-olds in California can already be tried as adults and receive life imprisonment for serious felonies.)[104]

To Tom Hayden—one of the few members of the legislature to publicly denounce the three strikes legislation—such bravado about executing children is more proof that California is sinking into a "moral quagmire . . . reminiscent of Vietnam." "State politics has been handcuffed by the law enforcement lobby. Voters have no real idea of what they are getting into. They have not been told the truth about the trade-off between schools and prisons, or the economic disaster that will inevitably result. We dehumanize criminals and the poor in exactly the same way we did with so-called gooks in Vietnam. We just put them in hell and turn up the heat."[105]

10. THE MARS FLEET

He took a torch and moved into the plastic city and with the flame touched the walls here or there. The city bloomed up in great tosses of heat and light. It was a square mile of illumination, big enough to be seen out in space.
Ray Bradbury, The Martian Chronicles (1950)

Once upon a time—in the rocket summers of my childhood—it was widely believed that Los Angeles's ultimate suburb would be the planet Mars, not a maximum-security prison in the desert. The outer edge of the "commuter belt" in Burgess's diagram would become extraterrestrial. If this now seems preposterous, it is only because our imagined futures have worn poorly over the ensuing years. The 1990s in particular have been a funeral decade, interring many of the hopes and fantasies of the earlier twentieth century. If today Eisenhower-era images of the suburbanization of the solar system seem more than wacky, it would have seemed equally absurd 40 years ago to have predicted that nearly two million Americans would greet the next century from the insides of jails and prisons.

In 1954 when I was as enthralled as any other eight-year-old by rocket science and the imminent exploration of space, *Collier's* magazine published a tantalizing article by recycled Nazi rocket scientist Wernher von Braun and magazine editor Cornelius Ryan. "Can We Get to Mars?" prophesied that new Lewises and Clarks in space suits would plant Old Glory on the 16-mile-high summit of Olympus Mons by 1996.[106] The article was superbly illustrated by Chesley Bonestell, whose prolific images of space travel in Sunday supplements and popular magazines fired the American imagination during the 1950s.* Bonestell, a trained architect who had worked as a special effects artist on Orson Welles's *Citizen Kane,* later painted a magnificent landscape of the 1990s Mars fleet assembling in near space above the Pacific coastline. Far below the rocket armada is a vast nocturnal metropolis—a thousand diamond points of light—rendered by Bonestell in exquisite detail. The metropolis, of course, is Los Angeles.[108]

After a century of boosterism and self-aggrandizement, this was the city's most triumphant image. The *Los Angeles 2000* report's immodest boasting about becoming the "global crossroads city" and "a modern Alexandria" is decidedly second fiddle to the overreaching hyperbole of "Los Angeles—Portal to the Solar System." Like his contemporary, Ray Bradbury, whose *Martian Chronicles* depicted American subdivisions on the red planet, Bonestell dramatized the 1950s moral and imaginative equivalence between the utopia of space conquest and the utopia of suburbia. In his painting, the counterpoint to the ballet of soaring rocket planes is the perfect euclidean geometry of Los Angeles's future suburbs as they probe the desert along the routes of new freeways.

In the mid-1950s, of course, the freeways were still applauded as technological wonders, and suburbia was a dream only half unfolded.

---

* According to historian Howard McCurdy, "Bonestell did for space what Albert Bierstadt and Thomas Moran accomplished for the American western frontier." In addition to his famous illustrations for the *Collier's* series on space exploration, he worked on the art design for the 1953 film version of *War of the Worlds* (Mars attacks downtown Los Angeles), and his images help inspire the famous "Mission to Mars" ride at Disneyland.[107]

The Mars fleet assembles

Developers could not tear down orange groves fast enough to meet the demand for tract houses for the burgeoning workforce of the aerospace industry. Although what was being built in those huge sheds in Burbank, Long Beach, Downey, Canoga Park, and Pomona was usually an official secret, eight-year-olds imagined that they must include prototype rocketships to the moon and eventually Mars. Kids in the San Fernando Valley, luckier than most, could actually hear the giant rocket engines being tested by the air force at Rocketdyne's sprawling test range in the Santa Susana Mountains. A whole generation raised on the bold promises of von Braun and the futuristic

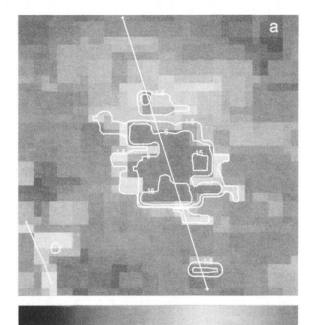

The L.A. riot from space

images of Bonestell was awaiting with great expectation that epochal view of Los Angeles from space.

History, however, has given us a stranger vista. Fast forward to 30 April 1992, just a few years before the predicted departure of von Braun's Mars fleet. A multisensor, polar-orbiting satellite operated by the National Oceanic and Atmospheric Administration makes its normal pass over the Pacific coast of North America. At exactly 03:47 the satellite's onboard Advanced Very High Resolution Radiometer (AVHRR) images "an exceptionally large thermal anomaly, extending over more than 85 square kilometers." The infrared picture is received in San Diego and transmitted to the University of Hawaii's Satellite Oceanography Laboratory where it is analyzed by a team of geophysicists. They are pleased by the "astounding sensitivity" with which the radiometer has resolved individual hot spots even of sub-pixel size.[109]

When researchers compare this image with a 1985 infrared image of the same place taken by the French satellite SPOT (Système Pro-batoire pour l'Observation de la Terre), they easily distinguish two kinds of thermal fingerprints. Both satellites have photographed the same urban "heat islands"—downtown, the international airport, and a large oil refinery—but only AVHRR has imaged the large, much hotter anomaly southwest of downtown and similar but smaller anomalies in the north and south. SPOT's infrared remote sensing in 1985 had registered these areas as "cool." Seven years later, they are suddenly molten.

AVHRR, of course, has taken the temperature of a social explosion. The large anomaly, researchers explain, "corresponds to south central Los Angeles, where an average of three new fires were started each minute during the three hours preceding the image." The temperature maximum is located along Manchester Avenue near the intersection where Reginald Denny was beaten on the previous day. A second anomaly, north of the Santa Monica Freeway, coincides with a cluster of arson fires near the corner of Venice Boulevard and Western Avenue in Mid-City, while "the isolated but intense hot spot to the south of the image is the Compton Center Mall, where a department store was burning."[110]

In this fashion, the Rodney King riot, although composed of tens of thousands of individual acts of anger and desperation, was perceived from orbit as a unitary geophysical phenomenon, comparable to the eruption of Mount Pinatubo in the Philippines in 1991 or the huge fires (also a form of arson) that consumed Indonesian forests in 1997. Indeed, had alien voyeurs really been watching the earth from a secret observatory on the moon or suburbs on Mars, they would have been mesmerized by Los Angeles's extraordinary combustibility. No other urban area on the planet so frequently produces large "thermal anomalies." Seen from space, the city that once hallucinated itself as an endless future without natural limits or social constraints now dazzles observers with the eerie beauty of an erupting volcano.

NOTES

Chapter 1. The Dialectic of Ordinary Disaster

1. According to Leszek Starkel, Opid's Camp in Los Angeles County's San Gabriel Mountains holds the world record for maximum rainfall in one minute (0.64 inches). Another San Gabriel Mountains rain gauge, Hoegee's Camp in Big Santa Anita Canyon, held for decades the world record for one day (26.08 inches). (See Starkel, "The Role of Extreme [Catastrophic] Meteorological Events in Contemporary Evolution of Slopes," in Edward Derbyshire [ed.], *Geomorphology and Climate* [London, 1976], p. 210; and *Los Angeles Times* [henceforth *LAT*] 28 May 1950.)

2. Trinda Bedrossian, "1995 Storm Events," *California Geology,* September/October 1996, pp. 111–19.

3. Peter King, "The Latest 100-Year Disaster," *LAT* 15 March 1995.

4. See table in *New York Times* 15 May 1995.

5. See quotation in editorial, *LAT* 19 July 1994. In March 1997, the governor's Office of Emergency Services updated Northridge earthquake damage to $42 billion, including business losses, unemployment, and worker's compensation payments (*LAT* 13 March 1997).

6. California, Seismic Safety Commission, *Northridge Earthquake: Turning Loss to Gain* (Sacramento, 1995), p. 2.

7. *LAT* 15 March 1995.

8. *LAT* 2 September 1994.

9. U.S. Bureau of the Census, *Geographic Mobility: March 1993 to March 1994,* cited in *LAT* 11 October 1995. The net migration (moved-in minus moved-out) from the Los Angeles area was –351,000. Income decline data are from University of Southern California's Southern California Studies Center as reported in *LAT* 9 February 1998.

10. See Benoit Mandelbrot, *The Fractal Geometry of Nature* (New York, 1977), p. 248 passim.

11. Boyle Workman, *The City That Grew* (Los Angeles, 1935), p. 31

12. Cf. Herbert Bolton, *Fray Juan Crespi: Missionary Explorer on the Pacific Coast, 1769–1774* (Berkeley, 1927), pp. 132, 136, 139–143, 152–55; Herbert Bolton (ed.), *Historical Memoirs of New California by Fray Francisco Palou* (Berkeley, 1926), p. 135; and Herbert Bolton, *Font's Complete Diary: A Chronicle of the Founding of San Francisco* (Berkeley, 1931), pp. 237–38, 244–45.

13. See Kenneth Thompson, "Negative Perceptions of Early California," *California Geographer* 18 (1978).

14. Richard Slatta, *Comparing Cowboys and Frontiers* (Norman, 1997), pp. 10–15.

15. See, e.g., Charles Nordhoff, *California for Health, Pleasure and Residence* (New York, 1873).

16. Charles Dudley Warner, *Our Italy* (New York, 1896), p. 18. See also Peter Remondino, *Mediterranean Shores of America* (New York, 1902).

17. Andreas Schimper, *Plant-Geography upon a Physiological Basis,* trans. P. Groom (Oxford, [1892] 1909), p. 122. For a critical discussion of IBP and its legacies, see chapters 5 and 6 in Frank Golley, *A History of the Ecosystem Concept in Ecology* (New Haven, Conn., 1993).

18. See chapter 5 in J. R. McNeill's magisterial environmental history: *The Mountains of the Mediterranean World* (Cambridge, 1992).

19. Thanks to IBP grants, an international network for comparative Mediterranean ecological research was established. A preliminary synthesis, concentrating on the structural characteristics of Mediterranean vegetation, was presented at the First International Conference on Mediterranean-Type Ecosystems (MEDECOS) in Valdivia, Chile, in 1973. Subsequent MEDECOS conferences have been organized around themes of fire ecology, biological invasions, role of nutrients, biotic resilience, and landscape management. Cf. F. di Castri and H. Mooney, *Mediterranean-Type Ecosystems: Origins and Structure* (New York, 1973); H. Mooney and C. Conrad (eds.), *Proceedings of the Symposium on the Environmental Consequences of Fire and Fuel Management in Mediterranean Ecosystems,* U.S. Forest Service General Technical Report WO-3 (Washington, D.C., 1977); H. Mooney (ed.), *Convergent Evolution in Chile and California: Mediterranean Climate Ecosystems* (Stroudsburg, Pa., 1977); M. Cody and H. Mooney, "Convergence versus Nonconvergence in Mediterranean-Climate Ecosystems," *Annual Review of Ecological Systems* 9 (1978); F. di Castri, A. Goodal, and R. Specht (eds.), *Mediterranean-Type Shrublands* (Amsterdam, 1981); C. Conrad and Walter Oechel (eds.), *Proceedings of the Symposium on Dynamics and Management of Mediterranean-Type Ecosystems,* U.S. Forest Service Research Paper PSW-58 (Washington, D.C., 1982); F. Kruger, D. Mitchell, and J. Jarvis (eds.), *Mediterranean-Type Ecosystems: The Role of Nutrients* (Berlin, 1983); B. Dell, A. Hopkins, and B. Lamont (eds.), *Resilience in Mediterranean-Type Ecosystems* (Dordrecht, 1986); R. Groves and F. di Castri (eds.), *Biogeography of Mediterranean Invasions* (Cambridge, 1991); and Mary Kalin, Paul Zedler, and Marilyn Fox (eds.), *Ecology and Biogeography of Mediterranean Ecosystems in Chile, California and Australia* (New York, 1995).

20. Cf. di Castri (1973); and Mooney, *Convergent Evolution.* Mediterranean plants also exemplify "parallel evolution": tracking in similar ways the changes over time in their environment. See Cody and Mooney, "Convergence versus Nonconvergence," pp. 271–77.

21. Cf. Thomas Blackburn and Kat Anderson (eds.), *Before the Wilderness: Environmental Management by Native Californians* (Menlo Park, 1993); Mooney and Conrad, *Proceedings;* and Stephen Pyne, *Burning Bush: A Fire History of Australia* (New York, 1991).

22. "The landforms of the Mediterranean lands can be considered a distinct, polygenetic group . . . comparable in geologic history, structure, lithology and ground cover" (David Bradbury, "The Physical Geography of the Mediterranean Lands," in di Castri, Goodal, and Specht, *Mediterranean-Type Shrublands.* See also N. Thrower and D. Bradbury, "The Physiography of the Mediterranean Lands," in di Castri [1973]).

23. Cf. Bolton, *Crespi,* pp. 146–49; and Bolton, *Palou,* pp. 134–35.

24. *LAT* 15 December 1997. See also C. Miller et al., "Potential Hazards from Future Volcanic Eruptions in the Long Valley–Mono Lake Area," USGS Circular 887 (Washington, D.C., 1982); and David Hill et al., "Response Plans for Volcanic Hazards in the Long Valley Caldera and Mono Craters Area," USGS Open File Report 91-270 (Washington, D.C., 1992).

25. Thus Robert Howard contrasts the different outlooks, conditioned by their natural milieux, of eastern and western geographers. See his "Physiographic Region in Physical Geography and Geomorphology: Historical Appraisal and Reevaluation," *California Geographer* 24 (1984), p. 78.

26. Carl Sauer, "The Settlement of the Humid East," *Climate and Man: Yearbook of Agriculture, 1941* (Washington, D.C., 1941), p. 18.

27. For the eastern United States, see the discussion of the relative geomorphic importance of seasonal rainfall versus rare hurricanes in Douglas Johnson, *Land Degradation* (Cambridge, Mass., 1995), pp. 111–13.

28. Quoted in Donald Worster, *Nature's Economy* (Cambridge, 1977), pp. 14–15.

29. Stephen Jay Gould, *Time's Arrow, Time's Cycle: Myth and Metaphor in the Discovery of Geological Time* (Cambridge, Mass., 1987). Gould declines to make the (too?) obvious connection between traditional English landscape ideology and a gradualistic theory of the earth.

30. Charles Pyke, *Some Meteorological Aspects of the Seasonal Distribution of Precipitation in the Western United States and Baja California,* University of California, Water Resources Center Paper 139 (Los Angeles, October 1972), p. 64; and *LAT* 6 March 1938 (review of local storm history).

31. Cf. William Graf, "The Arroyo Problem," in K. Gregory (ed.), *Background to Paleohydrology* (New York, 1983); and Moshe Inbar, "Effects of a High Magnitude Flood in a Mediterranean Climate," in L. Mayer and D. Nash (eds.), *Catastrophic Flooding* (Boston, 1987).

32. The classic study of humid regions is M. Wolman and J. Miller, "Magnitude and Frequency of Forces in Geomorphic Processes," *Journal of Geology* 68 (1960). For recent case studies from Spain, Israel, and Southern California on the dominant role of extreme events in Mediterranean environments, see John Thornes, "Catchment and Channel Hydrology," in Athol Abrahams and Anthony Parsons (eds.), *Geomorphology of Desert Environments* (London, 1994); Inbar Zev Naveh, "The Role of Fire in the Mediterranean Landscape of Israel," in Mooney and Conrad, *Proceedings;* and R. Cooke, *Geomorphological Hazards in Los Angeles* (London, 1984).

33. National Research Council, *Material Fluxes on the Surface of the Earth* (Washington, D.C., 1994), p. 8.

34. N. Lifton and C. Chase, "Tectonic, Climatic and Lithologic Influences on Landscape Fractal Dimension," *Geomorphology* 5 (May 1992), p. 81.

35. D. Gorsline and R. Douglas, "Analysis of Sedimentary Systems in Active-Margin Basins: California Continental Borderland," in Raymond Ingersoll and W. Ernst (eds.), *Cenozoic Basin Development of Coastal California,* Rubey Volume 6 (Englewood Cliffs, N.J., 1987), p. 70.

36. Cf. Schimper, *Plant-Geography;* and Kenneth Hewitt, *Regions of Risk* (Harlow, 1997), p. 229.

37. To illustrate the strength of this causal linkage: as much as "70% of all sediment production in California's chaparral is triggered by fire" (Walter Wells, "Hydrology of Mediterranean-Type Ecosystems: A Summary and Synthesis," in Conrad and Oechel, *Proceedings,* p. 429).

38. See Jonathan Phillips, "Deterministic Uncertainty in Landscapes," *Earth Surface Processes and Landforms* 19 (1994): 391.

39. Lifton and Chase, "Tectonic," p. 81.

40. Ibid., pp. 78–80. Using sophisticated computer models of the San Gabriel Mountains, these authors are attempting to untangle the respective roles of climate ("short wavelength roughness") and tectonics ("long wavelength roughness") in creating topography—a project impossible to conceive before the advent of Mandelbrot's fractal geometry.

41. Pyne, *Burning Bush,* p. 62.

42. Deborah Jensen, Margaret Torn, and John Harte, *In Our Own Hands: A Strategy for Conserving California's Biological Diversity* (Berkeley, 1993), p. 45.

43. Naveh, "Role of Fire," pp. 151–56. Naveh contrasts the "homeostatic self-stabilization" of temperate biomes with "perturbation dependent" Mediterranean ecosystems.

44. Robert Yeats, Kerry Sieh, and Clarence Allen, *The Geology of Earthquakes* (Oxford, 1997), p. 16. Also Y. Bentor, "Geological Events in the Bible," *Terra Nova* 1 (1989), pp. 326–38.

45. Campsite interview with Scott Stine, 1996 (Mike Davis, "When the Rivers Ran Dry," *Los Angeles Weekly* 20 September 1996). See also *Global Environmental Change Report* (24 June 1994), p. 2.

46. Scott Stine, "Extreme and Persistent Drought in California and Patagonia during Mediaeval Time," *Nature* 369 (16 June 1994), pp. 546–49.

47. Ibid., p. 549.

48. Interview with Stine (1996); Jeff Hecht, "California's Climate Poised on a Knife Edge," *New Scientist* (25 June 1994), p. 10 (Graumlich); and Blake Edwards, "Endless Summers," *Pacific Discovery* (spring 1995), p. 5 (Ingram).

49. D. Larson and J. Michaelsen, "Climatic Variability: A Compounding Factor Causing Culture Change among Prehistoric Coastal Populations," unpublished manuscript, 1989 (on file, Department of Anthropology, California State University, Long Beach); Owen Davis, "Rapid Climate Change in Coastal Southern California Inferred from Pollen Analysis of San Joaquin Marsh," *Quaternary Research* 37 (1992), pp. 89–100; K. Cole and R. Webb, "Late Holocene Vegetation Changes in Greenwater Valley, Mojave Desert, California," *Quaternary Research* 23 (1985), pp. 227–35; and presentation by Matthew Boxt, Owen Davis, and Kevin Pope at "Southern California Before 1900," conference held at California State University, Northridge, September 1996.

50. Cf. P. Martz, *Social Dimensions of Chumash Mortuary Populations in the Santa Monica Mountains Region,* Ph.D. thesis, Department of Anthropology, University of California, Riverside, 1984; and P. Walker et al., "The Effects of European Contact on the Health of Alta California Indians," in David Thomas (ed.), *Columbian Consequences,* vol. 1 (Washington, D.C., 1989), p. 210.

51. L. Mark Raab, "The Dead at Calleguas Creek: Climatic Stress, Punctuated Cultural Evolution and the Emergence of Chumash Chiefdoms," unpublished manuscript.

52. For a survey of synchronous drought crises and their cultural impacts in California, the Colorado Plateau, and the Great Plains, see Terry Jones et al., "The Medieval Climatic Anomaly in Western North American Prehistory," *Current Anthropology,* submitted July 1996. For the Maya, see David Hodell, "Possible Role of Climate in the Collapse of Classic Maya Civilization," *Nature* 375 (1 June 1995), pp. 391–94. For further bibliography, see F. Alayne Street-Perrott, "Drowned Trees Record Dry Spells," *Nature* 369 (16 June 1994), p. 518.

53. Interview with Stine (1996). See also Scott Stine, "A Medieval Climatic Anomaly in the Americas," *Proceedings of the Conference on Water, Environment, and Society in Times of Climate Change, Ben-Gurion University (July 1996)* (Tel Aviv, 1998).

54. Interview with Scott Stine, 1998.

55. Gerard Bond et al., "A Pervasive Millennial-Scale Cycle in North Atlantic Holocene and Glacial Climates," *Science* 278 (14 November 1997), pp. 1257–66.

56. *Global Environmental Change Report,* p. 2.

57. Charles Rosenfeld, "The Geomorphological Dimensions of Natural Disasters," *Geomorphology* 10 (1994), p. 28.

58. See Bernice Wuethrich, "El Niño Goes Critical," *New Scientist,* 4 February 1995.

59. David Hill, "Pacific Warming Unsettles Ecosystems," *Science* 267 (31 March 1995), pp. 1911–12.

60. Cf. R. Baker, "Large-Scale Fluvial Palaeohydrology," in K. Gregory (ed.), *Background to Paleohydrology* (New York, 1983), p. 474; Laura Haston and Joel Michaelsen, "Long-Term Central Coastal California Precipitation Variability and Relationships to El Niño–Southern Oscillation," *Journal of Climate* (September 1994), pp. 1373–88, quote on p. 1386; Malcolm Hughes and Peter Brown, "Drought Frequency in Central California since 101 BC Recorded in Giant Sequoia Tree Rings," *Climate Dynamics* 6 (1992), pp. 161–67; and Stine, "Extreme and Persistent Drought," p. 549.

61. Scott Stine, "Climate, 1650–1850," *Sierra Nevada Ecosystem Project: Final Report to Congress,* vol. 2, *Assessments and Scientific Basis for Management Options* (Davis, 1996), p. 29; and Lisa Graumlich, "A 1000-Year Record of Temperature and Precipitation in the Sierra Nevada," *Quaternary Research* 39 (1993), pp. 249–55.

62. Michael Rymer and William Ellsworth (eds.), *The Coalinga, California, Earthquake of May 2, 1983,* USGS Professional Paper 1487 (Washington, D.C., 1990), pp. 1–2.

63. Yeats, Sieh, and Allen, *Geology of Earthquakes,* p. 335. The theoretical possibility of blind thrust faults, however, had been the subject of speculation as far back as 1934, when a geologist working in the Appalachian fold-and-thrust belt had proposed that the folds were caused by ramps in the thrust sheets.

64. Technically, thrust faults (with a dip less than 45 degrees) are a subset of reverse faults (with a dip less than 90 degrees, where the hangingwall block has moved up with respect to the footwall block). For an up-to-date exposition, see chapter 10, "Reverse Faults and Folds," in Yeats, Sieh, and Allen, pp. 301–68.

65. Jian Lin and Ross Stein, "Coseismic Folding, Earthquake Recurrence, and the 1987 Source Mechanism at Whittier Narrows, Los Angeles Basin, California," *Journal of Geophysical Research* 94 (10 July 1989), p. 9621.

66. R. Yerkes, "The Tectonic Setting of the Northridge Earthquake," *Earthquakes and Volcanoes* 25, no. 2 (1996), pp. 12–17.

67. Lin and Stein, "Coseismic Folding," p. 9614.

68. Quoted in Kealy Davidson, "Learning from Los Angeles," *Earth* (September 1994), p. 46.

69. For an engaging portrait of Davis and Namson, as well as other leading characters in this story, see T. Heppenheimer, *The Coming Quake* (New York, 1990), esp. pp. 212–24.

70. James Dolan and Kerry Sieh, "Structural Style and Geomorphology of the Santa Monica–Hollywood Fault System," *Eos* 72 (1991), pp. 319–20; and Association of Engineering Geologists, "Tectonic Geomorphology of the Northern Los Angeles Basin," *Field Trip Guide: Engineering Geology of the Los Angeles Basin* (Los Angeles, 1992).

71. Dolan and Sieh, "Structural Style"; Thomas McNeilan et al., "Style and Rate of Holocene Slip, Palos Verdes Fault, Southern California," *Journal of Geophysical Research*

101 (10 April 1996), pp. 8317–34; and *Orange County Register* 27 October 1995 (on Whittier fault).

72. Dr. Paul Reasenberg quoted in Richard Monastersky, "Seismic Sunday," *Science News* 142 (1993), p. 74.

73. See Cinna Lomnitz, *Fundamentals of Earthquake Prediction* (New York, 1994), pp. 35–54. Despite its title, this is the most comprehensive presentation of the new, "earthquakes as organized chaos" paradigm in seismology.

74. Wayne Thatcher, "Order and Diversity in the Modes of Circum-Pacific Earthquake Recurrence," *Journal of Geophysical Research* 95 (1990), pp. 2609–24. For overviews of the debate, see Max Wyss, "Seismic Cycle Not So Simple," *Nature* 345 (24 May 1990), pp. 290; and Christopher Scholz, "Earthquakes as Chaos," *Nature* 348 (15 November 1990), pp. 197.

75. Cf. on injuries, Anshel Schiff, "Hospitals with Emphasis on Lifelines," in Anshel Schiff (ed.), *Northridge Earthquake: Lifeline Performance and Post-Earthquake Response* (Sacramento, 1995), p. 288; and on damage, Mary Comerio et al., *Residential Earthquake Recovery* (Berkeley, 1996), p. xvii.

76. Paul Somerville, "Implications of the Northridge and Kobe Earthquakes for the National Earthquake Hazard Reduction Program," *Seismological Research Letters* 68 (September/October 1997), p. 711 ("lucky near miss"); and Richard Kerr, "Bigger Jolts Are on the Way for Southern California," *Science* 267 (13 January 1995), p. 176.

77. Davidson, "Learning from Los Angeles," p. 45.

78. James Dolan et al., "Prospects for Larger or More Frequent Earthquakes in the Los Angeles Metropolitan Region," *Science* 267 (13 January 1995), pp. 199–205.

79. Consulting geologists Thomas Davis and Jay Namson had been warning about this possibility since the Whittier Narrows quake. See (with Robert Yeats) "A Cross Section of the Los Angeles Area: Seismically Active Fold and Thrust Belt, the 1987 Whittier Narrows Earthquake, and Earthquake Hazard," *Journal of Geophysical Research* 94 (10 July 1989), pp. 9644–64.

80. Quoted in R. Monastersky, "Los Angeles Faces a Dangerous Quake Debt," *Science News* (21 January 1995), p. 37.

81. Dolan et al., "Prospects," p. 200.

82. Ibid., p. 203.

83. Hough quoted in Monastersky, "Los Angeles," p. 37; and Working Group on California Earthquake Probabilities, "Seismic Hazards in Southern California: Probability of Earthquakes, 1994 to 2024," *Bulletin of the Seismological Society of America* 85 (April 1995), pp. 388, 394, 420.

84. Sieh quoted in Davidson, "Learning from Los Angeles," p. 47. Dolan et al. ("Prospects," p. 199) identified six fault systems as candidates for a possible catastrophic quake cascade: (1) the Sierra Madre at the foot of the San Gabriels; (2) the Elysian Park and Compton blind thrust system under the Los Angeles Basin; (3) the Hollywood–Santa Monica–Malibu zone; (4) the Oak Ridge fault system in the Santa Susanas; (5) the San Cayetano system in Ventura County; and (6) the Palos Verdes fault. David Jackson, "The Case for Huge Earthquakes," *Seismological Research Letters* 67 (January–February 1996), p. 3.

85. See "Waiting for the 'Big One'?" *Geotimes,* November 1996, pp. 8–10.

86. David Jackson quoted in Richard Kerr's overview of the shift toward a "communications model" of fault interaction, "Seismologists Learn Language of Quakes," *Science* 271 (16 February 1996), pp. 910–11.

87. Ruth Harris and Robert Simpson, "In the Shadow of 1857–The Effect of the Great Ft. Tejon Earthquake on Subsequent Earthquakes in Southern California," *Geophysical Research Letters* 23 (1 February 1996), pp. 229–32.

88. L. Knopoff et al., "Increased Long-Range Intermediate-Magnitude Earthquake Activity prior to Strong Earthquakes in California," *Journal of Geophysical Research* 101 (10 March 1996), pp. 5779–96.

89. Frank Press and Clarence Allen, "Patterns of Seismic Release in the Southern California Region," *Journal of Geophysical Research* 100 (10 April 1995), pp. 6421–30. Also Kerr, "Seismologists Learn Language," p. 910.

90. Cf. *LAT*, 18 March 1998; E. Field, D. Jackson, and J. Dolan, "An Integrated Seismic-Hazard Source Model for Southern California," SSA 1998 *Abstracts;* T. Hanks and R. Stein, "Seismicity in Southern California Since 1903," AGU 1997 Fall Meeting *Abstracts;* and K. Mueller, L. Grant, and E. Gath, "Late Quaternary Growth of the San Joaquin Hills Anticline—A New Source of Blind Thrust Earthquakes in the Los Angeles Basin," SSA 1998 *Abstracts.*

91. Barbara Brown, "Climate Variability and the Colorado River Compact," in Michael Glantz (ed.), *Societal Responses to Regional Climatic Change* (Boulder, Colo., 1988), pp. 289–94. See also R. Baker, "Large-Scale Fluvial Palaeohydrology," in Gregory, *Background to Paleohydrology,* p. 474.

92. See FEMA director James Lee Witt's announcement in *LAT* 25 October 1997.

93. Stanford University study, led by Haresh Shah, quoted in *LAT* 16 August 1994.

94. Earthquake Engineering Research Center, *Preliminary Report on the Seismological and Engineering Aspects of the January 17, 1994 Northridge Earthquake* (Berkeley, 1994), pp. 1-1, 3-1.

95. J. Rial, "A Note on the Relationship between a Sedimentary Basin's Basement Topography and the Damage Pattern of Earthquakes: Chaos and Order," *Seismological Research Letters* 68 (May–June 1997), p. 451. Forecasting of basement resonance is complicated by reflections from basin sides that generate chaotic effects.

96. Long-period motions, which are least attenuated by distance from epicenter, primarily threaten large rigid structures like high-rises, freeway interchanges, and bridges (like the Vincent Thomas bridge in San Pedro). See T. Teng and J. Qu, "Long-Period Ground Motions and Dynamic Strain Field of Los Angeles Basin during Large Earthquakes," *Bulletin of the Seismological Society of America* 86 (October 1996), pp. 1417–33.

97. Cf. Kim Olsen et al., "Three-Dimensional Simulation of a Magnitude 7.75 Earthquake on the San Andreas Fault," *Science* 270 (8 December 1995), p. 1628; and C. Saikia and N. Smith, "Influence of Los Angeles Basin Structure on Ground Motions from a M 7.9 Earthquake Using a 2-D Relative Site Transfer Function Technique," *Seismological Research Letters* 68 (March–April 1997), p. 314 (civic center).

98. Cf. *LAT* 20 July, 8 August, and 24 August 1984 and 30 December 1996.

99. *LAT* 20 July and 10 November 1994 and 17 January 1995. City building officials, incredibly, let owners of damaged buildings repair the fractured welds with the same alloy and technique that failed in the first place. See *LAT* 23 November 1994.

100. Heaton quoted in *LAT* 22 December 1996.

101. Quoted in Richard Monastersky, "The Fatal Fling," *Science News* 145 (25 June 1994), p. 409.

102. Thomas Heaton et al., "Response of High-Rise and Base-Isolated Buildings to a Hypothetical M 7 Blind Thrust Earthquake," *Science* 267 (13 January 1995), pp. 206–11.

See also Thomas Heaton, "Opinion," *Seismological Research Letters* 66 (March–April 1995), p. 5.

103. Mark Kluver, "Building Code Trends and the Danger of Earthquake-Induced Fires," in International Conference of Building Officials, *Proceedings of the Pacific Rim Conference of Building Officials, 9–13 April 1989* (Honolulu, 1989), pp. 114, 199.

104. Robert Canfield, emergency preparedness coordinator for Los Angeles, interviewed in Richard Monastersky, "Can Los Angeles Ride Out a Stronger Quake?" *Science News* 145 (16 April 1994), p. 245.

105. Tousson Toppozada et al., "Earthquake Planning Scenario for a Major Earthquake on the Newport-Inglewood Fault Zone," *California Geology,* April 1989, pp. 75–83; and interview with seismic survey geologist Glen Borchardt, Oakland, September 1993. Department of Mines earthquake simulations—essentially reruns of historic temblors under modern conditions of development—are baseline disaster planning scenarios for emergency agencies. The project was initiated in 1981 after FEMA advised Governor Brown that California would not be able to cope with a major earthquake emergency.

106. C. Scawthorn et al., "Fire-Related Aspects of the January 17, 1994, Northridge Earthquake," in Michael O'Rourke (ed.), *Lifeline Earthquake Engineering: Proceedings of the Fourth U.S. Conference* (San Francisco, 1995), p. 685.

107. For official evaluations of lifeline performance during the Northridge quake, cf. Schiff, *Northridge Earthquake;* and O'Rourke, *Lifeline Earthquake Engineering.*

108. California, Seismic Safety Commission, *Northridge Earthquake,* p. 3.

109. Carl Sepponen, "Fire Department Emergency Response," in Schiff, *Northridge Earthquake,* pp. 323–25.

110. At the time, hospital lobbyists contended that it would cost more than $21 billion to retrofit all the hospitals in the state. See *LAT* 29 January 1994.

111. The two big university-run hospitals have competed strenuously for federal funds: when USC tripled its damage estimate (including a quotient of "upgrade") from $400 million to $1.3 billion, UCLA immediately raised its cost of repair from $630 million to $1 billion. At time of writing, about $1 billion in total aid to both institutions has been promised by the Clinton administration (cf. *LAT* 21 October 1994 and 22 March 1997).

112. *LAT* 18 January 1995.

113. *LAT* 18 August 1994 and ("Special Quake Report: One Year Later") 15 January 1995.

114. Interview in *LAT* 4 February 1994; see also *Los Angeles Daily News* 28 January 1994.

115. *LAT* 4 February 1994; building inventory from Hope Seligson et al., "Seismic Vulnerability Assessment for Southern California," paper presented at Fifth U.S. National Conference on Earthquake Engineering, Chicago, July 1994, table one.

116. Comerio et al., *Residential Earthquake Recovery,* p. xviii.

117. *LAT* 10 June 1994.

118. Jon Healey, "Critics Call for Better Way to Deal with Catastrophes," *Congressional Quarterly* (29 January 1994), p. 169.

119. For comparison of disaster costs and federal impacts on Miami and Los Angeles, see Nancy Bolton and Larry Kimbell, "The Economic and Demographic Impact of the Northridge Earthquake," working paper, UCLA Business Forecasting Project University of California (Los Angeles, 1996).

120. Northridge figures from California Office of Emergency Services (*LAT* 13 March 1997); Hurricane Andrew, from Insurance Information Institute (*New York*

Times 15 May 1995) and "Losses Due to Natural Hazards," *Natural Hazards Observer,* (September 1996), p. 17.

121. David Lauter in *LAT* 21 January 1994.

122. Were major physical improvements dressed up as repair of earthquake damage? It is curious that over the course of 1994 the city and county of Los Angeles, together with the universities, doubled their initial damage claims without challenge from FEMA. Cf. *LAT* 16 December 1994 and 8 January 1995.

123. Comerio et al., *Residential Earthquake Recovery,* p. 4.

124. Ibid.

125. Ibid.

126. Healey, "Critics Call," p. 169; "Disaster Aid vs. the Deficit," *Congressional Quarterly* (29 January 1994), p. 168; press briefing from the office of Congressman Obey, 1994; and *LAT* 4 February 1995. If FEMA were abolished, Obey's constituents would still have the federal flood insurance program to rebuild their homesteads after deluges.

127. Clinton quoted in *LAT* 28 July 1995. See also George Hager, "Senate Clears Recision Bill after Months of Wrangling," *Congressional Quarterly* (22 July 1995), p. 2157.

128. Senator Leroy Greene (majority whip), *Budget Briefing 13* (27 April 1995); and Federal Funds Information for States, *Budget Brief 95* (1 August 1995).

129. See the special report "Disaster Response," *Congressional Quarterly Research* (15 October 1993).

130. *LAT* 9 October 1995.

131. See "Briefing," *Geology Today* (January–February 1997), p. 2.

132. John McPhee, *The Control of Nature* (New York, 1989), pp. 196–97.

Chapter 2. How Eden Lost Its Garden

1. Yi-Fu Tuan, "Thought and Landscape: The Eye and the Mind's Eye," in D. Meinig (ed.), *The Interpretation of Ordinary Landscapes* (New York, 1979), p. 92. For a superb discussion of the social dialectics of the "constructed" citrus landscape, see the essays by Douglas Sackman, Anthea Hartig, and Michael Steiner in the spring 1995 issue of *California History.*

2. Olmsted Brothers and Bartholomew and Associates, *Parks, Playgrounds and Beaches for the Los Angeles Region* (Los Angeles, 1930), p. xiv.

3. Ibid., p. 23.

4. Ibid., pp. xiii, 1–3.

5. Charles Fletcher Lummis, *Los Angeles and Her Makers* (Los Angeles, 1909), pp. 244–45.

6. Dana Bartlett, *The Better City* (Los Angeles, 1907), pp. 33–35.

7. Testimony of Mrs. Noel of the National Women's Trade Union League to the Commission on Industrial Relations, Los Angeles, 1914 (*Final Report and Testimony Submitted to Congress by the Commission on Industrial Relations,* 64th Cong., 1st sess., 1916, S. Doc. 415, vol. 6, p. 5735).

8. Judge Silent quoted in the *Los Angeles Herald* 1 March 1910.

9. Robinson's proposal for weaving the city's parks into a continuous greenbelt system was later amplified by Park Commissioner J. B. Lippincott, who envisaged magnifi-

cent, intersecting park corridors from Westlake (today's MacArthur Park) to Silverlake, and from Elysian Park to Griffith Park. See *Los Angeles Express* 27 May 1911.

10. Charles Mulford Robinson, *The City Beautiful: Report to the Municipal Art Commission* (Los Angeles, 1909), p. 32.

11. Ibid., p. 3.

12. Testimony of Frederick Law Olmsted, Jr., to Citizens' Committee on Parks, Playgrounds and Beaches, *LAT* 22 February 1928; and Los Angeles County, Regional Planning Commission, *Preliminary Report on Existing County Parks* (Los Angeles, 1928), p. iv. The commission pointed out that "most neglected are neighborhood parks and playgrounds within walking distance of the masses" (p. iii).

13. Olmsted and Bartholomew, *Parks,* p. 5.

14. Ibid., p. 11.

15. Ibid., p. 10.

16. Ibid., pp. 14–16.

17. Ibid.

18. Regional Planning Conference, *Minutes of the 1924 Session* (Los Angeles, 1924).

19. Olmsted and Bartholomew, *Parks,* pp. 14–16. The multiple-use strategy for riparian corridors was an Olmsted design trademark. For an earlier example, see Olmsted Brothers, *Report upon the Development of Public Grounds for Greater Baltimore* (Baltimore, 1904).

20. Olmsted and Bartholomew, *Parks,* p. 22.

21. Ibid.

22. Cf. Frederick Law Olmsted, Jr., Harlan Bartholomew, and Charles Cheney, *A Major Traffic Street Plan for Los Angeles* (Los Angeles, 1924); Olmsted Brothers and Ansel Hall, *Proposed Park Reservations for East Bay Cities* (Oakland, 1930); and Frederick Law Olmsted, Jr., "Palos Verdes Estates," *Landscape Architecture* 17 (July 1927).

23. *LAT* 12 and 14 March 1929.

24. *Los Angeles and San Gabriel Rivers and Their Tributaries, and Ballona Creek, Calif.,* 76th Cong., 3rd sess., 1940, Doc. 426, serial 10599, pp. 11–26.

25. Olmsted and Bartholomew, *Parks,* p. 16.

26. See "Land Index Map of Railroad and Utility Property," in California, Railroad Commission, Engineering Department, *Report on Railroad Grade Crossing Elimination and Passengers and Freight Terminals in Los Angeles* (Sacramento, 1920).

27. *Flood Control Advocate*—a four-page tabloid distributed by the Flood Control Committee before the 20 February 1917 election. The major issue in the election was whether flood control works would be financed by a special assessment of floodplain landowners (the position of opponents, including the Progressives and Socialists) or by general revenue bonds (the self-serving position of proponents like Shoup and the committee). The heavily promoted bond measure passed.

28. See Elmer Belt, president of the California State Board of Health, "Sanitary Survey of Sewage Pollution of Santa Monica Bay," *Western City,* June 1943, pp. 17–22.

29. A strikingly similar conjunction of environmental disasters reoccurred in *annus horribilis* 1987–88. See my *City of Quartz* (London, 1990), pp. 196–203.

30. Richard Neutra, "Homes and Housing," in George Robbins and L. Deming Tilton (eds.), *Los Angeles: Preface to a Masterplan* (Los Angeles, 1941), pp. 189, 194–95.

31. Theodore Pratt, *The Valley Boy* (New York, 1946), p. 8.

32. Robert E. Alexander, "The San Fernando Valley," unpublished manuscript, 1990, p. 80. Cf. Charles Bennett, "Planning for the San Fernando Valley," an address intended for the war-canceled convention of the Urban Land Institute, November 1944

(in John Randolph Haynes archives, UCLA Special Collections); and Los Angeles City Planning Commission, *Accomplishments—1944* (Los Angeles, 1945), pp. 5–12.

33. Shortly before his death in 1992, I had an opportunity to talk with Alexander at some length about the social and environmental implications of his 1945 San Fernando Valley zoning plan.

34. Alexander, "San Fernando Valley," p. 82.

35. Ibid.

36. Ibid.

37. William Whyte, "Urban Sprawl," *Fortune* 57 (January 1958), p. 302.

38. Los Angeles County, Regional Planning Commission, *Master Plan of Land Use* (Los Angeles, 1941); and Los Angeles County, Regional Planning Commission, *East San Gabriel Valley* (Los Angeles, 1956).

39. See Mark Northcross, "Los Angeles County: Biting the Land That Feeds Us," *California Tomorrow* 36; and Raymond Dassmann, *California's Changing Environment* (San Francisco, 1981), p. 81.

40. County Citizens' Committee, op. cit.; and Richard Jahns, "Seventeen Years of Response by the City of Los Angeles to Geologic Hazards," *Geologic Hazards and Public Problems: Conference Proceedings* (Santa Rosa, 1970), p. 266.

41. Donald Coates, *Environmental Geomorphology and Landscape Conservation, vol. 2, Urban Areas* (Stroudsburg, Pa., 1974), p. 273.

42. Calculated by architect Christopher Wegscheid (Southern California Institute of Architecture, 1994) using data that I supplied on historical aggregate (sand and gravel) production in Los Angeles County.

43. Garrett Eckbo, *Landscape for Living* (New York, 1949), pp. 27, 245.

44. Ibid., pp. 45, 111–12.

45. EDAW (Eckbo, Dean, Austin, and Williams), *Open Space, the Choices before California: The Urban Metropolitan Open Space Study* (San Francisco, 1969), pp. 22–23. See also EDAW, *State Open Space and Resource Conservation Program for California* (Sacramento, 1972).

46. Ibid., pp. 15, 24.

47. Ibid., p. 41.

48. Ibid., p. 42.

49. Ibid., p. 45.

50. Garrett Eckbo, "Parklands in the Urban Desert" (originally published in *Cry California,* 1966), reprinted in John Hart (ed.), *The New Book of California Tomorrow: Reflections and Projections from the Golden State* (Los Altos, 1984), pp. 150–53.

51. Ventura–Los Angeles Mountain and Coastal Study Commission, *Final Report to the Legislature,* prepared by Eckbo, Dean, Austin, and Williams (6 March 1972), pp. [6.1], [12B15.1].

52. Ibid., pp. [9.2], [12B3.1].

53. Thomas Kent, Jr., *Open Space for the San Francisco Bay Area: Organizing to Guide Metropolitan Growth* (Berkeley, 1970); and Alfred Heller (ed.), *The California Tomorrow Plan* (Los Altos, 1972).

54. League of Women Voters of Los Angeles County, *Open Space in Los Angeles County* (Los Angeles, 1972), p. 33. The League also emphasized that the county supervisors and planning commissioners contemptuously ignored their own recreation and open space plans, making no effort to restrict development in targeted areas (p. 22).

55. For a concise account, see W. David Conn, *Environmental Management in the Malibu Watershed: Institutional Framework* (Washington, D.C., 1975).

56. See *Coalition for Los Angeles County Planning in the Public Interest v Board of Supervisors, Los Angeles County,* Superior Court: C-63218 (12 March 1975).

57. *LAT* 3 April, 16 May, and 9 July 1979.

58. For bleak assessments, cf. *LAT* 2 December 1990; and Betsey Landis, "Significant Ecological Areas: The Skeleton in Los Angeles County's Closet?" in J. E. Keeley, *Interface between Ecology and Land Use in California* (Los Angeles, 1993), pp. 112–13, 116.

59. Data from Southern California Association of Governments (1996).

60. What follows is largely based on Jim Churchill's detailed critique of the Newhall Ranch Environmental Impact Report in 1996 and subsequent interviews with Barbara Wample of the Friends of the Santa Clara River in fall 1997.

61. *Newhall Land Fact Sheet.*

62. *LAT* 3 and 24 November 1996. Newhall Land and Farming Company's campaign contributions, 1992–96, furnished by Jim Churchill.

63. *LAT* 24 November 1996; and Newhall Ranch brochures.

64. Newhall Ranch brochures.

Chapter 3. The Case for Letting Malibu Burn

1. Data provided by office of Los Angeles City Council member Michael Hernandez, whose First District includes the Westlake community.

2. David Weide, "The Geography of Fire in the Santa Monica Mountains," M.A. thesis, Department of Geography, California State University, Los Angeles, 1968, pp. 1–2, 87, 91; Klaus Radtke, Arthur Arndt, and Ronald Wakimoto, "Fire History of the Santa Monica Mountains," in *Symposium on the Dynamics and Management of the Mediterranean-Type Ecosystems* (Berkeley, 1982), pp. 440–441; and Jerry Meehan, "Avoiding Déjà Vu: The Historic Wildfire Corridor," *American Fire Journal,* May 1991, pp. 14–15.

3. For a recent overview of aboriginal "fire farming," see Thomas Blackburn and Kat Anderson (eds.), *Before the Wilderness: Environmental Management by Native Californians* (Menlo Park, 1993).

4. W. W. Robinson, *Rancho Topanga Malibu Sequit: An Historical Approach* (Los Angeles, 1958); and Frederick Hastings Rindge, *Happy Days in Southern California* (Cambridge, Mass., 1898).

5. The Santa Ana–driven pattern of October through December conflagrations in the Santa Monicas contrasts with the interior ranges where the fire season reaches its climax in July (Weide, "Geography of Fire," pp. 34–35).

6. Environmental Protection Agency (Region IX), *Final EIS/EIR: Las Virgenes-Triunfo, Malibu-Topanga—Area Wide Facilities Plan* (San Francisco, 1977), pp. 2/112–2/115.

7. There is a vast literature, but see especially Sterling Keeley (ed.), *The California Chaparral: Paradigms Reexamined* (Los Angeles, 1989).

8. Quoted from a letter, 2 September 1994. See also his "Fire Behavior in Southern California Chaparral before Fire Control: The Mount Wilson Burns at the Turn of the Century," *Annals of the Association of American Geographers* 77, no. 4 (1987); and "Fuel-Driven Fire Regimes of the California Chaparral," in press.

9. Michael Rogers, "Fire Management in Southern California," in *Symposium,* pp. 496–98.

10. For the history of fire suppression in the mountains of Southern California, cf. Ronald Lockmann, *Guarding the Forests of Southern California* (Glendale, 1981); and C. R. Clar, *California Government and Forestry* (Sacramento, 1959).

11. Richard Minnich, *The Biogeography of Fire in the San Bernardino Mountains of California,* University of California Publications in Geography, vol. 28 (Berkeley, 1988), pp. 5–6.

12. *Los Angeles Examiner* (henceforth *LAE*) 14 August 1928.

13. John Russell McCarthy, *These Waiting Hills: The Santa Monicas* (Los Angeles, 1925), p. xiii.

14. The area in question was Topanga Canyon. See testimony of M. Wolfe, editor of the *Western Comrade,* to the U.S. Commission on Industrial Relations, *Final Report,* 64th Cong., 1st sess., 1916, S. Doc. 415, vol. 6, p. 5849.

15. *LAE* 27 October 1929.

16. *LAT* 1–3 November 1930.

17. Olmsted made this proposal wearing two hats: first as director of the state park survey, then as chief consultant to a Los Angeles County citizens' commission. Cf. Olmsted quoted in *LAE* 3 January 1929; and Olmsted Brothers and Bartholomew and Associates, *Parks, Playgrounds and Beaches for the Los Angeles Region* (Los Angeles, 1930), pp. 97–114.

18. *LAE* 8 September 1936; and *LAT* 25–27 November 1938.

19. *LAE* 15 June 1938. One of the chief advocates of the proposed tax swap, UCLA provost E. R. Henrick, made an explicitly ecological argument for preserving "the rare . . . fauna and flora existing there" (Ibid.).

20. From *Rancho Malibu, An Historic Real Estate Offering,* quoted in Robinson, *Rancho,* p. 38.

21. Because of the 20-year threshold of chaparral combustibility, firestorms in the Santa Monicas tend to occur in alternate decades: 1910s, 1930s, 1950s, 1970s, and 1990s (see Radtke et al., "Fire History," p. 441).

22. Lawrence Clark Powell, "Personal Considerations," in W. Robinson and L. C. Powell, *The Malibu* (Los Angeles, 1958).

23. Quoted in Stephen Pyne, *Fire in America: A Cultural History of Wildland and Rural Fire* (Princeton, N.J., 1982), p. 404.

24. Ibid.

25. See the famous study by C. Countryman, *Mass Fires and Fire Behavior,* U.S. Forest Service Research Paper PSW-19 (Berkeley, 1964).

26. Pyne, *Fire in America,* pp. 404–15.

27. *LAE* 3 December 1958 (Malibu) and 2 January 1959 (Topanga Canyon). Weide also emphasizes the "exponential" increase in fire destructiveness. Eight major fires in the 1955–58 period consumed considerably more acreage than 19 previous fires in the 1936–54 period ("Geography of Fire," p. 18).

28. *LAT* 9 October 1982.

29. *LAE* 14 August 1960. A 1975 survey of all the planning and regulatory bodies responsible for the Malibu Creek watershed discovered that none used fire risk as a criterion for the regulation of development. See W. David Corn, *Environmental Management in the Malibu Watershed: Institutional Framework,* (Los Angeles, 1975).

30. One-third of the Santa Monica Mountains—70,000 out of a total of 220,000 acres—were already lost to development in some form by 1978. See Joseph Brown, "The Mountains and the Megalopolis," *Sierra,* May 1973, pp. 365–66.

31. Cf. Michael Heiman, *Coastal Recreation in California* (Berkeley, 1986), p. 51; and League of Women Voters of Los Angeles County, *Open Space in Los Angeles County,* (Los Angeles, 1972), p. 33.

32. Ivor Davis and Sally Ogle Davis, "Secrets of the 'Real' Malibu Colony," *Los Angeles Magazine,* October 1986, p. 153.

33. Thomas Mikkelson and Donald Neuwirth, *Public Beaches: An Owners' Manual* (Berkeley, 1987), p. 96.

34. Powell, "Personal Considerations," p. 60.

35. There were no less than 770 wildfires reported in California during the last half of September 1970 (*LAT* 27–29 September 1970).

36. *LAT* 29 September 1970.

37. Davis and Davis, "Secrets," p. 155.

38. Cf. *LAT* 23–27 October 1978, 9–10 October 1982, and 15–17 October 1985. As might have been predicted, the aftermath of the 1978 fire was another ratcheting-up of socioeconomic exclusivity.

39. The *Examiner* and the *Times* offered conflicting accounts of whether A. D. Bernhardt jumped from his third-story window or the roof. Cf. *LAE* and *LAT* 26 March 1952.

40. *LAT* 26–27 March 1952.

41. Ibid. Chief Alderson was later forced to retire because of his rabid opposition to the racial integration of the department.

42. The Del Rey tragedy (1 June 1924) captured local front pages for a week, but the only reference to the other beach fire, in a "three-story wooden hotel in Venice," that I have been able to discover comes from the California Commission on Immigration and Housing, *Eleventh Annual Report* (Sacramento, 1925), p. 19.

43. The study is described in a *LAT* clipping in Chamber of Commerce archives, box 36, Southern California Regional History Center, University of Southern California. Trade union allegations of false advertising to keep the local labor market overstocked are discussed in my "Sunshine and the Open Shop: Ford and Darwin in 1920s Los Angeles," *Antipode* 29 (October 1997).

44. See Los Angeles City Planning Department, "Final EIR on Earthquake Hazard Reduction in Existing Buildings before 1934 in the City of Los Angeles," EIR 583-78-CW (Los Angeles, 1980). Paul Groth has written a fascinating history of the residential hotel in the United States: *Living Downtown* (Berkeley, 1994).

45. *New York Times* 7–9 December 1946. The 1980 MGM Grand fire in Las Vegas took 84 lives.

46. *LAE* 26 March 1952.

47. See Donald Parsons, " 'This Modern Marvel': Bunker Hill, Chavez Ravine, and the Politics of Modernism in Los Angeles," *Southern California Quarterly* 75 (fall/winter 1993).

48. *LAT* 14–16 September 1970. Later, the arsonist, Castro Figueroa, was convicted on 19 counts of first-degree murder and sentenced to life in prison.

49. *LAT* 15–17 November 1973.

50. James Kinninger, letter to the editor, *LAT* 7 January 1977. Also see *LAT* 22 December 1976 for an account of the fire.

51. *LAT* 18 May 1979 and 6 November 1981.

52. *LAT* 22 December 1976.

53. See "Los Angeles' Slums: A Growth Industry" (a series), *LAT* 30 July 1989.

54. *LAT* 9–12 September 1982, 18 February 1984, 31 July 1985, and 23 December 1986.

55. *LAT* 14 and 21 May 1983.
56. Ibid.
57. *LAT* 5–6 May 1993.
58. Ibid.
59. *LAT* 31 October 1993.
60. *LAT* 7 November 1993.
61. *LAT* 3 November 1993. Also *Malibu Times* 11 November 1993.
62. The following streets were burned in 1956 and again in 1993: Carbon Canyon, Carbon Mesa, Rambla Pacifico, and Sumac Ridge.
63. *LAT* 6 November 1993.
64. *LAT* 3 November 1993.
65. *Malibu Times* 11 November 1993.
66. Ibid.; and *LAT* 30 October and 4–6 November 1993.
67. *LAT* 16 and 20 November 1993.
68. *LAT* 4 November 1993.
69. See *LAT* 5 November 1993 for a profile of the South Central Panthers, a professional firefighting unit made up of former gang members; for inmates, *LAT* 30 October 1993.
70. Ibid.
71. *Malibu Times* 11 November 1993; and *LAT* 18 November and 13 December 1993.
72. *LAT* 18 November and 13 December 1993.
73. *LAT* 5 November 1993.
74. "State officials" cited in *LAT* 13 December 1993.
75. See Rindge, *Happy Days,* pp. 122–23; C. R. Clar, *California Government and Foresty, Part 1: From the Spanish Days until the Creation of the Department of Natural Resources in 1927* (Sacramento, 1959), pp. 120–25, 377–79, 417–22; *LAE* 21 October 1942; and *LAT* 30 December 1956.
76. *LAT* 1 November 1993.
77. *LAT* 16 November 1993.
78. *LAT* 26–27 October 1978. The legislature then exempted homes destroyed by natural disaster from the requirements of the Coastal Act of 1976.
79. Mikkelson and Neuwirth, *Public Beaches,* p. 100.
80. *Malibu Times* 11 November 1993; and *LAT* 12 November 1993.
81. *Orange County Register* 2 October 1994.
82. *LAT* 20 October 1997.
83. For population density by community plan area and council district, see City Planning Department, *Population Estimate and Housing Inventory* (Los Angeles, 1993).
84. Hernandez interview, 14 June 1994.
85. Ibid.; and *LAT* 7 October 1993.
86. Ibid.
87. Ibid.
88. Hernandez interview.
89. Ibid.; and *LAT* 28 May 1994.
90. Quoted in *LAT* 19 April 1997.
91. *LAT* 29 July 1997.
92. Richard Lillard, "Mountain Men and Women in the New West of Los Angeles," *South Dakota Review* 19 (spring/summer 1981), pp. 29–40. Lillard's two most important books were *Desert Challenge: An Interpretation of Nevada* (1942) and *Eden in Jeopardy:*

Man's Prodigal Meddling with His Environment: The Southern California Experience (1966).

93. Ibid., p. 38.

94. Quoted from letter, 2 September 1994. His solution? "Privatize the fire disaster industry. In geographically definable disaster zones . . . get FEMA out of it. Red line these hazard zones and force people to pay insurance commensurate to the true danger they are living in. People living on the Fire Coast with their million-dollar homes will very likely be burned out within about twenty years. Therefore, their premiums should be about $50,000 annually. Such premiums just might result in more rational land use."

95. *Los Angeles Business Journal* 26 July 1993.

96. Cf. Larry Gordon, "Growing Migration to Fire-Prone Areas Fans Concern," *Los Angeles Daily News* 5 November 1993; and California, Department of Forestry and Fire Protection, *Fire Safety Guides for Residential Development in California* (Sacramento, 1993), p. 1.

97. A summary of the report appeared in *LAT* 21 March 1997.

98. Gordon, "Growing Migration."

99. Cf. *LAT* 5 November 1993; and *Los Angeles Daily News* 14 November 1993.

100. Interviewed in *LAT* 4 November 1993.

101. Cf. Federation of Hillside and Canyon Associations, Inc., "President's Message," *News,* October 1991; and *LAT* editorials, 4 November 1993.

Chapter 4. Our Secret Kansas

1. The account that follows is gleaned from the *Pasadena Star* 26 and 28 January 1918; and Ford Carpenter, "Whirlwind of January 26, 1918, at Pasadena, Cal." *Monthly Weather Review* 46 (April 1918), pp. 178–79.

2. American Meteorology Society, *Glossary of Meteorology* (Boston, 1990); and Charles Doswell, "What Is a Tornado?" Internet, 13 April 1996.

3. Joseph Moran et al., *Meteorology,* 5th ed. (Upper Saddle River, N.J., 1997), p. 340.

4. The twister ended its life in the five-thousand-foot-high San Gabriel Mountains that form Pasadena's northern rampart. Although fog and rain reduced visibility, a witness reported to the Los Angeles Weather Bureau that "he heard the crashing of the pine trees as [the tornado] plowed its way through the timber." Ford Carpenter, the meteorologist at the bureau, discovered abundant evidence of tree damage when he hiked in the area some weeks later (Carpenter, "Whirlwind," p. 179).

5. Editorial, *Pasadena Sun* 4 March 1898.

6. See Moran et al., *Meteorology,* pp. 299–301.

7. There is no coverage of the Pasadena disaster in the *Los Angeles Times,* the *Los Angeles Examiner,* or the *Los Angeles Evening Express* in the two-week period following 26 January. There are other instances where Los Angeles's media agreed to suppress news that was inimical to tourism. When a deadly bubonic plague epidemic broke out in Downtown in 1924, e.g., the major papers agreed to cover up the story. See W. Knox, "Los Angeles Campaign of Silence," *Nation* 121 (1925): 646–47.

8. Damaging Southern California Tornadoes, 1900–1997

Date	Location	Damage and Injuries		
		Major Structures	Homes/Businesses	Injured
1. 01.26.1918	Pasadena	2	12	1
2. 04.05.1926	La Crescenta	2		
3. 04.05.1926	San Diego	2		
4. 04.06.1926	National City	1	80	100
5. 04.06.1926	San Diego	2	50	
6. 04.07.1926	Santa Monica		5	
7. 03.15.1930	Hawthorne		160	1
8. 03.15.1930	Vernon	12	1	2
9. 03.15.1930	Carpenteria	1		
10. 02.12.1936	Alhambra	1	20	1
11. 02.12.1936	Long Beach	1	50	5
12. 02.12.1936	Torrance	1	1	
13. 01.12.1937	Downtown L.A.	2	1	12
14. 11.11.1944	Pomona		2	
15. 01.08.1950	South Central L.A.	1		
16. 01.12.1951	Torrance	1		
17. 05.11.1953	South Central L.A.	2		
18. 05.11.1953	El Monte		1	
19. 01.20.1954	Gardena		3	
20. 01.16.1955	Altadena		2	
21. 01.18.1955	Downtown L.A.	2	3	2
22. 05.03.1959	San Diego	1		2
23. 10.08.1961	Carlsbad/Oceanside	2	20	3
24. 05.14.1962	Gardena	3		
25. 11.09.1964	El Segundo	1	12	
26. 04.08.1965	Costa Mesa		1	
27. 11.25.1965	Pomona	1		
28. 11.07.1966	Lawndale	1	200	10
29. 11.07.1966	Costa Mesa		5	
30. 11.07.1966	Florence	1	1	
31. 11.07.1966	Newport Beach		2	
32. 04.18.1967	Santa Monica		1	
33. 12.20.1967	Santa Ana		6	
34. 07.23.1974	Hemet	1	12	
35. 03.16.1977	Fullerton	2	99	4
36. 03.16.1977	Buena Park		20	
37. 05.08.1977	Long Beach	1	45	
38. 02.10.1978	El Segundo		2	
39. 02.10.1978	Huntington Beach		45	6
40. 01.31.1979	Anaheim		5	
41. 01.31.1979	Santa Ana		12	
42. 01.31.1979	Universal City	1		
43. 02.20.1980	La Jolla		20	

		Damage and Injuries		
Date	Location	Major Structures	Homes/Businesses	Injured
44. 11.09.1982	Malibu		1	
45. 11.09.1982	Van Nuys	2	2	2
46. 11.09.1982	Lennox	1	2	
47. 11.09.1982	Long Beach		24	
48. 11.09.1982	Garden Grove	1	6	1
49. 11.09.1982	Mission Viejo	1		
50. 03.01.1983	Downtown L.A.	2	197	32
51. 03.01.1983	Pasadena	1		1
52. 03.01.1983	Santa Ana		21	
53. 09.30.1983	Hawthorne		68	3
54. 09.30.1983	Walnut Park		1	
55. 01.13.1984	Huntington Beach		2	
56. 05.30.1984	San Dimas	1		
57. 02.04.1985	Mission Gorge (San Diego)		10	
58. 03.16.1986	Anaheim	1	8	
59. 01.18.1988	El Toro		2	
60. 01.14.1990	San Diego	1		
61. 01.16.1990	Pico Rivera		1	
62. 02.15.1992	Camp Pendleton		1	
63. 03.20.1992	El Sereno	1	10	
64. 03.20.1992	Irvine	1		
65. 03.20.1992	Florence		2	
66. 12.07.1992	Moorpark		1	
67. 12.07.1992	Westminster		20	
68. 12.07.1992	Anaheim		1	
69. 12.07.1992	Carlsbad		3	
70. 12.29.1992	San Clemente		1	
71. 01.14.1993	Pomona		3	
72. 01.14.1993	Buena Park		110	
73. 01.17.1993	Lake Forest		31	
74. 01.17.1993	Downtown L.A.		1	
75. 01.18.1993	Huntington Beach		6	
76. 11.11.1993	Portola Hills		1	
77. 06.16.1995	Whittier		1	
Total		61	1,436	188

9. Carpenter, "Whirlwind"; Marion Dice, "Tornado at Vernon, Calif., March 15, 1930," *Monthly Weather Review* 58 (August 1930), pp. 324–25. Neither of these accounts is cited in the 1980s literature.

10. T. Smith and V. Mirabella, *Characteristics of California Tornadoes* (report to the University of California's Lawrence Livermore Laborary by Meteorology Research Inc., 1972); and J. Goodridge, H. Rhodes, and E. Bingham, *Windstorms in California* (Sacramento, 1979).

11. John Hales, "Synoptic Features Associated with Los Angeles Tornado Occurrences," *Bulletin American Meteorological Society* 66 (June 1985), pp. 657–62.

12. Warren Blier and Karen Batten, "On the Incidence of Tornadoes in California," *Weather and Forecasting* 9 (September 1994), pp. 301–15. The authors also benefited from the publication of Thomas Grazulis's epic work *Significant Tornadoes, 1680–1991* (St. Johnsbury, Vt., 1991), which catalogues every known North American tornado of F2 intensity or higher.

13. In the absence of usable indexes to the Los Angeles press before 1970, I examined thousands of "weather" photographs in the photo morgues of two major Los Angeles newspapers—the *Times* and the *Examiner*—to identify tornado events. (The 1918 Pasadena tornado, however, was discovered in the photo collection of the Huntington Library.) I also surveyed five daily newspapers (1900–1970) in the UCLA microfilm collection for peak tornado months, especially January and March. The mid-nineteenth century was checked through the index to the *Los Angeles Star* (UCLA Special Collections).

14. Relative frequences based on data from National Weather Service (1961–90, by state); and Blier and Batten, "On the Incidence," p. 307.

15. "The combination of the curvature of the coastline and the nearby mountains that are parallel to the coast appear to favor strong frictional convergence in onshore flow in the area of maximum coastal curvature near Los Angeles" (Hales, "Synoptic Features," p. 662). Blier and Batten propose three distinct (although interacting) modes of topographically influenced convergence: (1) convergence to the lee of, and vortex generation by, the mountain masses of Palos Verdes Peninsula and Santa Catalina Island; (2) convergence of air flows steered by the Transverse and Peninsular Ranges; and (3) differential surface friction created by the extreme curvature of the coastline ("On the Incidence," p. 309).

16. Blier and Batten, "On the Incidence," p. 307.

17. Oklahoma City figures from Moran et al., *Meteorology*, p. 338.

18. Blier and Batten, "On the Incidence," p. 307.

19. In the South, F1 tornadoes have a nasty reputation for killing people in mobile homes. Thus, on 20 February and 1 March 1997, two trailer dwellers died in "weak" tornadoes in Arkansas and Mississippi, respectively ("U.S. Killer Tornadoes of 1997," *Tornado Project Online,* Internet).

20. Damaging tornadoes (a small subset of the total incidence) have approached or crossed the present LAX boundaries in 1936, 1951, 1964, 1978, and 1983.

21. George Stewart, *Storm* (New York, 1941), p. 236.

22. *Evening Express* and *LAE* 5 April 1926.

23. *LAE* 6 April 1926.

24. *San Diego Union* 6 April 1926 (quote about "twister"); and *LAE* 9 April 1926.

25. Grazulis, *Significant Tornadoes*, p. 70; and Charles Doswell and Donald Burgess, "Tornadoes and Tornadic Storms: A Review of Conceptual Models," in C. Church et al., *The Tornado: Its Structure, Dynamics, Prediction, and Hazards,* AGU Geophysical Monograph 79 (Washington, D.C., 1993), p. 167.

26. *San Diego Union* 7 April 1926.

27. *LAT* 7 April 1926; and *LAE* 8 April 1926.

28. *San Diego Union* 6 and 7 April 1926 (quotes); *Los Angeles Record* 7 April 1926 ("50 homes").

29. *Evening Express* 7 April 1926; and *San Diego Union* 8 April 1926.

30. *LAE* and *San Diego Union* 8 April 1926.

31. *LAE* 9 April 1926.

32. *LAE* 10 April 1926. In December 1967, lightning ignited an underground storage tank at the Standard Oil refinery in El Segundo. Again, there was a "rain of ink." See *LAT* 20 December 1967.

33. J. Hissong, "Whirlwinds at Oil-Tank Fire, San Luis Obispo, Calif.," *Monthly Weather Review* (April 1926), pp. 161–63. See also *LAE* 9 April 1926.

34. *LAE, LAT,* and *Los Angeles Record* 16 March 1930.

35. *LAE* 16 March 1930.

36. *LAT* 16 March 1930 (first quote); and *LAE* 16 March 1930 (second quote).

37. *LAT* 16 March 1930 (Drew); and *Los Angeles Record* 15 March 1930 (quote).

38. *LAE* 16 March 1930.

39. *LAT* 16 March 1930 (damage estimate; saving kids); and *LAE* 16 March 1930 (*Lennox Tribune*).

40. Ibid.

41. Ibid.

42. *LAT* 16 March 1930 (first quote); and *LAE* 16 March 1930 (second quote).

43. Dice, "Tornado," p. 324.

44. *Pasadena Star-News* 15 March 1930; *LAT* 18 March 1930; and *LAE* 19 March 1930. A small tornado inflicted minor damage on Alhambra a few months later, on May Day (*Evening Express* 2 May 1930).

45. "It was in sight for about six minutes, and then ascended to the clouds. At the time of its appearance, a very heavy clap of thunder was heard in the direction of [illegible]" (*Los Angeles Star* 21 February 1852). This is the earliest published account that I have yet located of a Southern California tornado.

46. Harold Troxell and John Peterson, *Flood in La Cañada Valley, California, Jan. 1, 1934*, USGS Water Supply Paper 796C (Washington, D.C., 1937), p. 23.

47. *LAT* 13 February 1936.

48. *LAE* 13 February 1936 (first quote); and *LAT* 13 February 1936 (fallen derrick).

49. *LAE* 13 February 1936 (first quote); and *LAT* 13 February 1936 (second quote).

50. The latter is more likely, especially since the *LAT* described the "gale" responsible for the Torrance damage as "disappearing toward the east after approaching the city from the Palos Verdes Hills to the southwest" (13 February 1936).

51. Ibid.

52. *LAE* 13 January 1937.

53. Ibid. (quotes); and *LAT* 13 January 1937.

54. Arnold Court, *Tropical Cyclone Effects on California,* NWS Technical Memorandum WR-159 (Washington, D.C., 1980), pp. 16–18.

55. Harry Bailey, *The Weather of Southern California* (Berkeley, 1966), pp. 71–72.

56. *LAE* 23 December 1948. A short-lived waterspout, looking like "a huge black hose," was reported a mile off Playa del Rey on 26 December 1945 (*LAE* 27 December 1945).

57. *San Diego Union* and *LAT* 9 October 1961.

58. *San Diego Union, LAT* (end quote), and *Pasadena Star-News* (photos) 9 October 1961.

59. *Los Angeles Herald-Examiner* (henceforth *H-E*) and *LAT* 10 November 1964.

60. Ibid.

61. *LAT* 8 November 1966.

62. This is based on street addresses as well as on the map that appeared in the *LAT* (ibid.); the account in the *H-E* (November) is discrepant in reporting significant tornado damage in Lawndale and Hawthorne yet claiming that the twister began near 120th Street (in Hawthorne).

63. *H-E* 7 November 1966 (Lennox); and *LAT* 8 November (Ramona School; "exploded" quote).

64. *H-E* 8 November 1966; and *LAT* 9 November 1966.

65. G. Miller, "Oregon Tornadoes: More Fact Than Fiction," in Church et al., *The Tornado*, pp. 453–57 and discussion p. 477.

66. From caption accompanying photograph (Hal Schulz, 20 December 1967: no. 238243) in *Los Angeles Times* archive, UCLA Special Collections.

67. *LAT* 24 July 1974. This was a very weird summer day in Southern California: aside from the twister, erratic thunderstorms, a dust storm, and more than 20 wildfires, tens of thousands of jumbo squid, averaging more than two feet long, inexplicably "invaded" Southland beaches.

68. Howard Bluestein and Joseph Golden, "A Review of Tornado Observations," in Church et al., *The Tornado*, p. 320.

69. Doswell and Burgess, "Tornadoes," p. 170.

70. Ibid., p. 161.

71. *LAT* 17 March 1977.

72. *LAT* 18 March 1977 (Orange County edition).

73. Ibid.

74. *LAT* 19 May 1977.

75. For nonsupercell tornadoes, see Doswell and Burgess, "Tornadoes," pp. 167–70.

76. *LAT* 1 and 2 February 1979; and *H-E* 1 February 1979 (Oceanside).

77. *LAT* 1 February 1979.

78. Kealy Davidson, *Twister* (New York, 1996), p. 2.

79. J. Norton et al., "The 1982–83 El Niño Event off Baja and Alta California and Its Ocean Climate Context," in Warren Wooster and David Fluharty (eds.), *El Niño North: Niño Effects in the Eastern Subarctic Pacific Ocean*, Washington Sea Grant Program 85-3 (Seattle, 1985), pp. 44–72. See also J. Simpson, "El Niño–Induced Onshore Transport in the California Current during 1982–1983," *Geophysical Research Letters* 11 (1984), pp. 241–42; R. Reed and W. Blier, "A Further Study of Comma Cloud Development in the Eastern Pacific," *Monthly Weather Review* 114 (September 1986), pp. 1707–8; and T. Schonher and S. Nicholson, "The Relationship between California Rainfall and ENSO Events," *Journal of Climate* 2 (1989), pp. 1258–69.

80. See Mark Bove, "Impacts of ENSO on United States Tornadic Activity" (Tallahassee, Fla., 1996).

81. Norton et al., "1982–83 El Niño Event."

82. *LAT* 10 November 1982.

83. Ibid.; and *H-E* 10 November 1982.

84. *LAT* 10 November 1982.

85. *LAT* 11 November 1982.

86. See the discussion in Davidson, *Twister*, pp. 116–19.

87. *H-E* (bomb; Jones) and *LAT* 2 March 1983.

88. *LAT* 2 March 1983 (strange boat); *H-E* 2 March 1983 (camper truck; photo of trailer); and Hart et al., *The Los Angeles Tornado of March 1, 1983* (Washington D.C., 1985), p. 25 (photo of bent I-beams).

89. *LAT* 2 March 1983.
90. *LAT* 3 March 1983.
91. *H-E* 2 March 1983.
92. *Pasadena Star* 2 March 1983.
93. *LAT* 3 March 1983.
94. *H-E* and *LAT* (Bradley) 2 March 1983.
95. *LAT* 1 and 2 October 1983.
96. Hart et al., *Los Angeles Tornado,* pp. 38–39.
97. John Monteverdi and Steve Johnson, "A Supercell Thunderstorm with Hook Echo in the San Joaquin Valley, California," *Weather and Forecasting* 11 (1996), p. 246.
98. Ibid.
99. Grazulis, *Significant Tornadoes,* p. 198.
100. For an important discussion of the "synoptic controls" on the December tornado episodes in central and northern California, as well as further evidence for supercellular convection on the West Coast, see J. Monteverdi and J. Quadros, "Convective and Rotational Parameters Associated with Three Tornado Episodes in Northern and Southern California," *Weather and Forecasting* 9 (September 1994), pp. 285–300.
101. *LAT* 8 December 1992 and 15 January 1993.
102. *LAT* 18–19 January 1993; "Baghdad" quote from Roy Farmer, president of Lake Forest Keys Homeowner Association, in *LAT* 18 January 1993 (Orange County edition).
103. Long Beach *Press Telegraph,* 10–12 January 1998; and *LAT* 10 January 1998.

Chapter 5. Maneaters of the Sierra Madre

1. Interview with Steve Berman, May 1995.
2. *LAT* 9 March 1995.
3. See the fascinating discussion in William McCawley, *The First Angelinos: The Gabrielino Indians of Los Angeles* (Novato, 1996), pp. 146–47. Other animals considered *tsatsnitsam* included bears, spiders, centipedes, and stingrays.
4. See chapter 6 ("The Days of the Lions") and chapter 13 ("The Owl Woman"), in Leo Carrillo, *The California I Love* (Englewood Cliffs, N.J., 1961).
5. Interview with Scott Fike, July 1995.
6. *LAT* 3 April 1995.
7. Maurice Hornocker, "Learning to Live with Mountain Lions," *National Geographic,* July 1992, p. 60.
8. *New York Times* 2 August 1994.
9. This calculation is based on recent aerial photographs of the Southern California Association of Governments region (Ventura, Los Angeles, Orange, Riverside, and San Bernardino Counties) minus Imperial County, measured in half-mile segments.
10. Don Gill and Penelope Bonnett, *Nature in the Urban Landscape: A Study of City Ecosystems* (Baltimore, 1973), p. 38.
11. I am indebted to wildlife biologists Paul Beier and Cheryl Swift for information about cougar populations. For a typical account of coyote prosperity in the big city, see *LAT* 8 November 1996 (on La Mirada and the Coyote Hills).
12. Andrew Murr, "The Prime Evil Forest," *Newsweek,* 4 November 1996.

13. David Rothenberg, "Introduction," in David Rothenberg (ed.), *Wild Ideas* (Minneapolis, 1995), p. xiii.

14. Irene Klaver, "Silent Wolves: The Howl of the Implicit," in Rothenberg, *Wild Ideas,* p. 121.

15. Interview with Gary Snyder, April 1995.

16. Another is post-Soviet Vladivostok, where a Siberian tiger was recently seen in the streets.

17. David Klinger, quoted in *LAT* 10 December 1989; A. Dobson et al., "Geographic Distribution of Endangered Species in the United States," *Science* 275 (24 January 1997), pp. 550–53.

18. Charles Hogue, *Insects of the Los Angeles Basin,* 2nd ed. (Los Angeles, 1993), p. 45.

19. Anne Spirn, *The Granite Garden: Urban Nature and Human Design* (New York, 1984), p. 211.

20. Hornocker, "Learning," p. 60.

21. E.g., Lowell Adams, *Urban Wildlife Habitats: A Landscape Perspective* (Minneapolis, 1994), p. 65.

22. Joy Tivy, *Biogeography: A Study of Plants in the Ecosphere* (London, 1993), pp. 91–92. See also Marjorie Holland et al. (eds.), *Ecotones: The Role of Landscape Boundaries in the Management and Restoration of Changing Environments* (London, 1991).

23. Although the opossum, which has been migrating north from South America for thousands of years, undoubtedly would have made it to California by its own locomotion, the first immigrants seemed to have been imported by an incautious hunter looking for stimulation for his hounds. See Joseph Grinnell, "The Tennessee Possum Has Arrived in California," *California Fish and Game* (October 1914), pp. 114–16.

24. Thomas Blackburn and Kat Anderson, "Introduction: Managing the Domesticated Environment," in Thomas Blackburn and Kat Anderson (eds.), *Before the Wilderness: Environmental Management by Native Californians* (Menlo Park, 1993), pp. 18–19.

25. George Jefferson, "Late Pleistocene Large Mammalian Herbivores: Implications for Early Human Hunting Patterns in Southern California," *Bull. So. Cal. Acad. Sci.,* 1988, p. 99.

26. For the debate, cf. R. Lee Lyman, "On the Evolution of Marine Mammal Hunting on the West Coast of North America," *Journal of Anthropological Archaeology* 14 (1995); and Terry Jones and William Hildebrandt, "Reasserting a Prehistoric Tragedy of the Commons: Reply to Lyman," ibid.

27. Herbert Bolton, *Defensive Spanish Expansion as the Significance of the Borderlands* (Boulder, Colo., 1930).

28. Herbert Bolton (trans.), *Font's Complete Diary of the Second Anza Expedition* (Berkeley, 1930), p. 247; Harold Bryant, *Outdoor Heritage* (San Francisco, 1929), pp. 279, 389; Robert Cleland, *Cattle on a Thousand Hills* (San Marino, 1941), pp. 90–91; Charles Frederick Holder, "Fish and Game of the Forest Preserves," in Abbot Kinney, *Forest and Water* (Los Angeles, 1900), pp. 159–61; Richard Lillard, *Eden in Jeopardy* (New York, 1966), pp. 94–96; E. Nelson, "Status of the Pronghorned Antelope, 1922–24," USDA Bulletin 1345 (Washington, D.C., 1925), pp. 25–27; Douglas Peacock, "Once There Were Bears," *Pacific Discovery,* summer 1996, p. 8; H. Priestly (ed.), *A Historical, Political and Natural Description of California by Pedro Fages* (Berkeley, 1937); William Shaler, "First American Report" [1805], in John Caughy (ed.), *California Heritage* (Los Angeles, 1962), pp. 104–8; Edwin Starks, "A History of California Shore Whaling," *California Fish and Game* (7 October 1922), pp. 6–7; Robert Schmidt, "Gray Wolves in California: Their Presence and Absence," *California Fish and Game,* n.s. 77, no. 2 (1991), p. 80; and Stan-

ley Young and Edward Goodman, *The Puma: Mysterious American Cat* (Washington, D.C., 1946), p. 15 (on jaguars). I am unable to assess Charles Holder's claim (p. 160) that tule elk were once native to the Southern California grasslands.

29. Richard Dana, *Two Years Before the Mast* (Los Angeles, 1964), p. 140.

30. Victor Janssens, *The Life and Adventures in California of Don Augustin Janssens, 1834–1856* (San Marino, 1953), p. 25.

31. Horace Bell, *Reminiscences of a Ranger, or, Early Times in Southern California* (Los Angeles, 1881), p. 250.

32. Susanna Dakin, *A Scotch Paisano: Hugo Reid's Life in California, 1832–1852* (Berkeley, 1939), pp. 4–5; and Harris Newmark, *Sixty Years in Southern California,* 4th ed. (Los Angeles, 1984), p. 24.

33. Gen. James Rusling, *The Great West and the Pacific Coast* (New York, 1877), p. 333. See also Shaler, "First American Report," p. 105; and Ludwig Louis Salvator, *Los Angeles in the Sunny Seventies* (Los Angeles, 1929), p. 89.

34. T. Talbert, *My Sixty Years in California* (Huntington Beach, 1952), p. 40.

35. For a comparative evaluation of Southern California as cattle country, see Terry Jordan, *North American Cattle-Ranching Frontiers* (Albuquerque, 1993), pp. 159–60.

36. Harold Bryant, "California's Fur-Bearing Mammals," *California Fish and Game* (30 January 1915), pp. 96–107; and James Gibson, *Otter Skins, Boston Ships and China Goods* (Seattle, 1992), pp. 258–60. A few otter may have survived in the Channel Islands through the 1870s.

37. Richard Slatta, *Comparing Cowboys in the Americas,* pp. 20–24.

38. Elinor Melville, *A Plague of Sheep: Environmental Consequences of the Conquest of Mexico* (Cambridge, 1994). See also Andrew Sluyter, "The Ecological Origins and Consequences of Cattle Ranching in Sixteenth-Century New Spain," *Geographical Review* 86 (April 1986), pp. 161–78.

39. P. Mudie and R. Byran, "Pollen Evidence for Historic Sedimentation Rates in California Coastal Marshes," *Estuarine Coastal Mar. Sci.* 10 (1980): 305–16.

40. For hide shipments, see Marguerite Wilbur (trans.), *Duflot de Mofras' Travels on the Pacific Coast,* vol. 1 (Santa Ana, 1937), p. 190. On environmental damage, cf. Jordan, *North American Cattle-Ranching Frontiers,* p. 169; and Ronald Cooke and Richard Reeves, *Arroyos and Environmental Change in the American South-West* (Oxford, 1976), p. 169.

41. George Phillips, *Indians and Intruders* (Norman, Okla., 1993), p. 114. California mustangs later became the preferred mounts of the Pony Express as well as the cavalry regiments fighting the Apaches in Arizona. See Don Worcester, *The Spanish Mustang* (El Paso, Tex., 1986), p. 16.

42. Phillips, *Indians,* pp. 47, 103, 173. See also Hubert Bancroft, *History of California,* vol. 2, *1801–1824* (San Francisco, 1886), pp. 181–82.

43. Robert Gillingham, *The Rancho San Pedro* (Los Angeles, 1961), p. 82.

44. Walker was an interpreter with the American army during the Mexican War who became a friend and houseguest of Andres Pico, the gallant *Californio* leader whose superb horsemen had crushed Steven Kearney's U.S. dragoons at the battle of San Pasquel. His painting is reproduced in W. W. Robinson, *Panorama: A Picture History of Southern California* (Los Angeles, 1953).

45. Bell, *Reminiscences,* p. 138.

46. Woodrow Borah, "The California Mission," in Charles Wollenberg (ed.), *Ethnic Conflict in California* (Los Angeles, 1970), pp. 15–16. See also Brooke Arkush, "Yokuts Trade Networks and Native Cultural Change in Central and Eastern California," *Ethnohistory* 40 (Fall 1993), pp. 627–29.

47. L. Burcham, *California Range Land: An Historico-Ecological Study of the Range Resources of California* (Sacramento, 1957), p. 198

48. Based on Robert Schmidt's recent research (see n. 28), Stanley Young and Edward Goldman were unquestionably mistaken in not including Southern California in their well-known map of wolf distribution in pre-Columbian North America. (See Young and Goldman, *The Wolves of North America* [New York, 1944].)

49. Lillard, *Eden in Jeopardy*, p. 94. In other pastoral ecologies of Spanish America, packs of wild dogs were characteristic scavengers of the *matanzas* (see Melville, *Plague of Sheep*, p. 163), but I have found no reference to their existence in nineteenth-century Southern California. Grizzlies probably preempted the niche.

50. Cf. Sarah Bixby Smith, *Adobe Days*, 4th ed. (Fresno, 1974), pp. 55–56; and Walter Tompkins, *Goleta: The Good Land* (Goleta, 1966), p. 67 (locust).

51. For an estimate of damage, see Cooke and Reeves, *Arroyos*, pp. 3–4.

52. Quoted in Burcham, *California Range Land*, p. 193; see also the testimony of Smith, *Adobe Days*, p. 54. A few herds of longhorn survived on small ranches in the Southern California mountains and backcountry through the 1890s (John W. Robinson, *The San Bernardinos* [Arcadia, 1989], p. 12).

53. Jackson Graves, *My Seventy Years in California, 1857–1927* (Los Angeles, 1927), p. 117; and Cleland, *Cattle*, p. 131. On the El Niño origin of the droughts, crop failures, and epidemics of 1877–78, which killed more than 25 million people, see Neville Nichols, "Teleconnections and Health," in M. Glantz et al. (eds.), *Teleconnections Linking Worldwide Climate Anomalies* (Cambridge, 1991), p. 496.

54. Robinson, *San Bernardinos*, p. 12.

55. John W. Robinson, *The San Gabriels* (Arcadia, 1989), p. 82.

56. Tracy Storer and Lloyd Tevis, *California Grizzly* (Berkeley, 1955), pp. 187–91.

57. Robinson, *San Gabriels*, p. 212.

58. Storer and Tevis, *California Grizzly*, pp. 28–29, 249–57. There has been much debate about whether the grizzly shot in 1916 was an indigenous bear or an escapee from a zoo. John W. Robinson, historian emeritus of the local mountains, is sure that it was a wild animal. See *San Gabriels*, p. 20.

59. Testimony of Ernest Schaeffle, executive secretary of the Fish and Game Commission, in *California Fish and Game*, 30 January 1915, p. 2.

60. Bryant, *Outdoor Heritage*, p. 387.

61. Horace Annesley Vachell, *Life and Sport on the Pacific Slope* (New York, 1901), pp. 114–15.

62. Boyle Workman, *The City That Grew* (Los Angeles, 1935), pp. 45–46.

63. On market hunting, see Cleland, *Cattle*, pp. 23–31, 90–91, 230; condor quote in Lillard, *Eden in Jeopardy*, p. 95; for fishing with dynamite, see *Pasadena Weekly Star* 23 (July 1890).

64. For hunting rattlesnakes and coyotes (with dogs), as well as rooster pulling, see Dana, *Two Years*, pp. 156–58.

65. The best account is Thomas Dunlap, *Saving America's Wildlife* (Princeton, N.J., 1988); but also see James Trefethen, *Crusade for Wildlife* (Harrisburg, Pa., 1961).

66. Charles Frederick Holder, *Life in the Open: Sport with Rod, Gun, Horse, and Hound in Southern California* (New York, 1906), p. 195.

67. For a brief history, see Charles Frederick Holder, "Attempts to Protect the Sea Fisheries of Southern California," *California Fish and Game* (October 1914).

68. There is a directory of gun and tackle clubs in Holder, *Life in the Open*, pp. 393–95. See also Graves, *My Seventy Years*, pp. 191, 204.

69. Holder, *Life in the Open,* p. 19.

70. Workman, *City That Grew,* p. 131.

71. Holder, *Life in the Open,* pp. 28–31, 55–59, 86–92, 155–57.

72. Ibid., pp. 10, 115.

73. Ibid., pp. 41, 93.

74. Ibid., p. 31.

75. *Los Angeles Express* 16 and 19 February 1925; Kevin Hansen, *Cougar: The American Lion* (Flagstaff, Ariz., 1992), p. 67.

76. On the important role of the women's clubs movement, see *California Fish and Game* (10 April 1915), p. 123.

77. On Progressives' goals, see Harold Bryant, "A Brief History of the Non-Sale of Game in California," *California Fish and Game* (October 1914).

78. Dunlap, *Saving America's Wildlife,* p. 15.

79. Ibid., p. 12. For a typical attack on the Chinese, see Harold Bryant, "A Brief History of the California Fish and Game Commission," *California Fish and Game,* April 1921, pp. 74–75.

80. For the classic account of the "forest wars" in Hanoverian England and their bitter legacies, see Edward Thompson, *Whigs and Hunters: The Origin of the Black Act* (London, 1975). On the restriction of hunting as a cause of emigration to the United States, especially from the Celtic periphery, see Stuart Marks, *Southern Hunting in Black and White* (Princeton, N.J., 1993), p. 33.

81. Ernest Schaeffle, *California Fish and Game,* 1 October 1915, p. 2.

82. Quoted in Charles Vogelson, "The Equity of Game Laws," *Western Field,* (August 1902), p. 149.

83. Holder, *Life in the Open,* pp. 56, 262.

84. Midas Dekkers, *Dearest Pet: On Bestiality* (London, 1994), pp. 188–89.

85. Dunlap, *Saving America's Wildlife,* p. 15.

86. Stephen Budiansky, *Nature's Keepers: The New Science of Nature Management* (New York, 1995), p. 162.

87. Dunlap, *Saving America's Wildlife,* p. 51.

88. Cf. Charles Nordhoff, *California for Health, Pleasure and Residence* (New York, 1872), pp. 234–35; Robinson, *San Gabriels,* pp. 286, 291.

89. The citrus growers' "war against the mountains" is a major theme in C. Raymond Clar, *California Government and Forestry,* vol. 1 (Sacramento, 1959).

90. Holder, *Life in the Open,* pp. 116–18.

91. Harold Bryant, "Mountain Lion Hunting in California," *California Fish and Game* (October 1917), p. 160.

92. Jay Bruce, "The Problem of Mountain Lion Control in California," *California Fish and Game* 11 (January 1925), pp. 1–2.

93. Cf. J. Hunter, "The Control of the Mountain Lion in California," *California Fish and Game* 7 (April 1921); Earl Soto, "Lion—From Forest to Table," ibid. 17 (July 1931): 340–42; and D. McLean, "Mountain Lions in California," ibid. 40 (April 1952), pp. 151, 160.

94. Bruce, "Problem of Mountain Lion Control," pp. 3–4.

95. Los Angeles chief fire warden and forester Spence Turner quoted in *LAT* 5 October 1931. See also an earlier article about the elimination of cougars in the Santa Monica Mountains, "Career of Marauder Ended," *LAT* 8 October 1929.

96. Quoted in Tony Tanner, "Struggling into Fullness," *TLS,* 9 January 1998, p. 4.

97. Carl Hert quoted in Maurice Hornocker and Howard Quigley, "Mountain Lion: Pacific Coast Predator," in Harmon Kallman (ed.), *Restoring America's Wildlife: 1937–1987* (Washington, D.C., 1987), p. 179.

98. Gill and Bonnett, *Nature in the Urban Landscape,* pp. 98–99. For a short history of coyote persecution in the West, see Hope Ryden, *God's Dog: The North American Coyote* (New York, 1975), pp. 255–74.

99. James Trefethen, "The Terrible Lesson of the Kaibab," *National Wildlife* 5 (June–July 1967), pp. 4–9. The great die-off inspired Aldo Leopold's celebrated essay, "Thinking Like a Mountain," in *A Sand County Almanac* (New York, 1948).

100. William Rintoul, "How the West Side Boomed," in *Guidebook: Geology and Oil Fields, West Side Southern San Joaquin Valley,* 43rd annual meeting, Pacific Section, American Association of Petroleum Geologists (Bakersfield, 1968), p. 10.

101. Ibid.

102. Formally, Piper was head of the Biological Survey's Control Methods Laboratory in Denver, which developed, manufactured, and deployed predacides. See Rick McIntyre (ed.), *War against the Wolf* (Stillwater, Minn., 1995), pp. 18–19.

103. Rintoul, "How the West Side Boomed," p. 10.

104. Raymond Hall, "An Outbreak of House Mice in Kern County, California," *University of California Publications in Zoology* 30, no. 7 (1927), pp. 200–203. Hall estimated the numbers of mice "to be reckoned in tens, and possibly in hundreds, of millions" (p. 194).

105. Stanley Piper, "The Mouse Infestation of Buena Vista Lake Basin, Kern County, California, September 1926 to February 1927," in California, Department of Agriculture, *Monthly Bulletin* 17 (October 1928), pp. 538–60; A. Brazier Howell, "At the Cross-Roads," *Journal of Mammalogy* 11, no. 3 (1930), pp. 377–89.

106. Quote in McIntyre, *War against the Wolf,* pp. 307–9.

107. Quote in Dunlap, *Saving America's Wildlife,* pp. 55–56.

108. McLean, "Mountain Lions," p. 166.

109. Ryden, *God's Dog,* p. 151. See also p. 278 for reproductive response to persecution.

110. Cf. *LAT* 27 August 1981 and 21 January 1990 (magazine section). Pioneer longitudinal studies of coyote adaptation in urban Los Angeles are the subject of Don Gill's thesis summarized in Gill and Bonnett, *Nature in the Urban Landscape,* and the ongoing research of William Wirtz at Pomona College. Wirtz autopsied San Rafael Hill coyote carcasses and discovered that nearly 80 percent of their diet was garbage (*LAT* 20 June 1985).

111. *LAT* 25 March 1986 and 1 March 1992.

112. *LAT* 27 December 1989. Also *LAT* 9 September 1994. These population estimates have been recently challenged by the scrupulous research of Shawn Smallwood. ("Interpreting puma population estimates for theory and management," *Environmental Conservation,* 24:3 [1997].)

113. This characterization of the drought was based on new tree ring research; see Maurice Roos, "Is the California Drought Over?" in Kelly Redmond and Vera Tharp (eds.), *Proceedings of the Tenth Annual Pacific Climate (PACLIM) Workshop: April 4–7, 1993,* California Department of Water Resources Technical Report 36 (Sacramento, 1994), p. 123.

114. *LAT* 8 September 1990.

115. *LAT* 9 September 1994; and David Wicinas, *Sagebrush and Cappuccino: Confessions of an L.A. Naturalist* (San Francisco, 1995), p. 133.

116. Quoted in the *Pasadena Star-News* 1996.

117. *LAT* 5 August 1993 and 25 July 1994.

118. *LAT* 19 September 1993.

119. *LAT* 19 December 1994 and 3 April 1995.

120. California Wildlife Protection Coalition Web Page, 18 December 1995.

121. *LAT* 19 September 1993; and *San Diego Union-Tribune* 17 September 1995.

122. Ibid.

123. Ibid.

124. *San Francisco Chronicle* 13 February 1995.

125. California state voters' pamphlet, March 1996 general election; and Proposition 197 ads.

126. Paul Beier, "Cougar Attacks on Humans in the United States and Canada," *Wildlife Society Bulletin* 19 (1991), pp. 403–12.

127. California voters' pamphlet; and anti–Proposition 197 ads.

128. Ibid.

129. Cf. Carol McGraw and S. Sanger, "Big Cats, Big Trouble," *LAT* (magazine section) 1 March 1992, p. 26; and James Serpell, *In the Company of Animals* (Cambridge, 1986), p. 15.

130. Paul Beier, "Cougar Attacks on Humans: An Update and Some Further Reflections," in J. Borrecco and R. Marsh (eds.), *Proceedings of the 15th Vertebrate Pest Conference* (Davis, 1992), pp. 365–66.

131. Following the shooting of a cougar in a backyard in Valencia in February 1997, the *LAT* estimated that mountain lion sightings "appear to be multiplying." Since 1994 the paper has reported encounters "in Ventura, Conejo Valley, Tujunga, Arcadia, Thousand Oaks, Porter Ranch, Granada Hills and Irvine" (*LAT* 3 March 1997).

132. Bear incidents in Southern California increased from 13 in 1994 to 25 in 1995, prompting a summit conference between the Fish and Game Commission and representatives of nine animal rights groups (*Pasadena Star-News* 25 August 1995).

133. Paul Beier, "Determining Minimum Habitat Areas and Habitat Corridors for Cougars," *Conservation Biology* 7 (March 1993), p. 100.

134. *LAT* 26 May 1995.

135. Interview with Paul Beier, March 1995.

136. Budiansky, *Nature's Keepers,* p. 94.

137. For Griffith Park's coyotes through the 1960s, see Gill and Bonnett, *Nature in the Urban Landscape,* pp. 88–99; I interpolate my own observations for the 1970s–1990s.

138. Infected deer mice have been identified in Newport Beach, Malibu Creek, and Simi Valley (10 percent of all mice autopsied). There have been 10 deaths in California. On skunks and bats as rabies hosts, see California, Department of Health Services, Veterinary Public Health Section, *Guidelines for the Treatment, Investigation, and Control of Animal Bites* (Sacramento, 1992), pp. 29–32.

139. On opossums and typhus, see *Pasadena Star-News* 18 August 1995. For the controversy on Lyme disease in Malibu, see *LAT* 30 April 1997.

140. Allan Schoenherr, *A Natural History of California* (Berkeley, 1992), p. 106.

141. Other species of ground squirrels in Mediterranean environments also harbor the plague, most notably in South Africa. See F. K. Mitchell, "The Plague in Cape Town in 1901 and Its Subsequent Establishment as an Endemic Disease in South Africa," *South Africa Medical Journal* (29 June 1985), p. 19.

142. See Arno Kalen, *Man and Microbes* (New York, 1995), pp. 75–76. The French historian is Guy Bois.

143. For concise overviews of the third pandemic's origin, see *New York Times* 20 November 1910; L. Fabian Hirst, *The Conquest of Plague* (Oxford, 1953), pp. 101–4; and Vernon Link, *A History of Plague in the United States of America,* Public Health Service Monograph 26 (Washington, D.C., 1955), p. 1.

144. Cf. R. Pollitzer, *Plague* (Geneva, 1954), pp. 26–27; and Rajnarayan Chandavarkar, "Plague Panic and Epidemic Politics in India, 1896–1914," in Terance Ranger and Paul Slack (eds.), *Epidemics and Ideas: Essays on the Historical Perception of Pestilence* (Cambridge, 1992), pp. 203–40.

145. On the Honolulu pogrom, see Tin-Yuke Char, *The Sandalwood Mountains: Readings and Stories of the Early Chinese in Hawaii* (Honolulu, 1975), p. 101. London's odious tale, "The Unparalleled Invasion," can be found in Dale Walker, *Curious Fragments: Jack London's Tales of Fantasy Fiction* (Port Washington, N.Y., 1975). Written in 1906, it was first published in *McClure's Magazine* in 1910.

146. Link, *History of Plague,* p. 3; and Silvio Onesti, "Plague, Press, and Politics," *Stanford Medical Bulletin* 13 (February 1955), pp. 1–2.

147. Onesti, "Plague," pp. 4–7.

148. Ibid.; and *New York Times* 20 November 1910.

149. Cf. Link, *History of Plague,* p. 27; and California, State Board of Health, *Pneumonic Plague: Report of an Outbreak at Los Angeles, California, October–November 1924,* Special Bulletin 46 (Sacramento, 1925), pp. 30–31.

150. Quoted in *New York Times* 23 April 1910.

151. For a full account, see C. Eskey and V. Hass, Public Health Bulletin 254 (Washington, D.C., 1940).

152. Link, *History of Plague,* pp. 2–42.

153. California, State Board of Health, *Pneumonic Plague,* pp. 30–31.

154. Arthur Viseltear, "The Pneumonic Plague Epidemic of 1924 in Los Angeles," *Yale Journal of Biology and Medicine* 1 (1974), pp. 40–54.

155. I am grateful to William Deverell for letting me see his unpublished essay on the Los Angeles plague. See also California, State Board of Health, *Pneumonic Plague,* pp. 43–46.

156. California, State Board of Health, *Pneumonic Plague,* pp. 20, 36–37, 68, 106, and 124.

157. Interview with Kevin Pang, August 1995.

158. *LAT* 23 August 1995; and *Pasadena Star-News* 18 August 1995.

159. *San Bernardino Sun* 15 November 1995.

160. Ibid., 7 September 1996.

161. Alan Beck, *The Ecology of Stray Dogs* (Baltimore, 1973), pp. 24–55. The figure for Los Angeles dog feces is my calculation based on the assumption that the average dog produces 300 pounds per year.

162. Charles Gregg, *Plague!* (New York, 1978), pp. 236–38.

163. On the mystery of the Surat plague, see Christopher Wills, *Yellow Fever, Black Goddess: The Coevolution of People and Plagues* (Reading, Mass., 1996), pp. 90–102.

164. See interview with official in *Los Angeles Daily News* 3 January 1996.

165. Mark Winston, *Killer Bees: The Africanized Honey Bee in the Americas* (Cambridge, Mass., 1992), pp. 11–16, 40. This is a superb natural history by a world authority on bees.

166. Ibid., p. 126.

167. *Riverside Press-Telegraph* 25 October 1994. Nine years earlier, a swarm of Africanized bees was accidentally imported to Kern County in a shipment of oil-drilling

equipment from Venezuela. A heavy-equipment operator was attacked when he investigated the buzzing sound coming from the carcass of a fox. The swarm was eradicated.

168. *LAT* 24 March 1995.

169. *San Bernardino Sun* 3 January 1996.

170. Interview with Suzanne Goode, May 1997.

171. *Orange County Register* 25 April 1996.

172. Interview with Jack Hazelrigg, November 1995. See also T. Rinderer, "Africanized Bees: The Africanization Process and Potential Range in the United States," *Bull Entomol. Soc. Am.* 32 (1986), pp. 222–24.

173. Winston, *Killer Bees,* pp. 19–21, 51–54.

174. U.S. Army, Defense Pest Management Information Analysis Center, *Bee Resource Manual,* Technical Information Memorandum 34 (Washington, D.C., 1995).

175. Ibid.; and Winston, *Killer Bees,* pp. 51–52.

176. For an account of the infection and its local impact, see *Orange County Register* 1 July 1996.

177. A concise account of the district's history appears in its 1994 report.

178. What follows is based on my interview with Hazelrigg and tour of the district's headquarters in South Gate, November 1995.

179. Quote from "Bee Alert," U.C. Cooperative Extension; for the bees' habit of long-distance pursuit, see S. Schneider and L. McNally, "Colony Defense in the African Honey Bee in Africa," *Environmental Entomology* 21 (1992), pp. 1362–70.

180. Interview with Hazelrigg.

181. Winston, *Killer Bees,* pp. 52, 92. Also see O. Taylor, "African Bees: Potential Impact in the United States," *Bull. Entomol. Soc. of Amer.* 31 (1985), pp. 15–24.

182. John Muir, *The Mountains of California* (New York, 1961), p. 292.

183. McCawley, *First Angelinos,* pp. 51, 94–95, 175.

184. See Keith Thomas, *Man and the Natural World* (Oxford, 1985), pp. 79–80.

185. Cf. *Washington Post* 11 May 1996; and Raymundo Reynoso, "La fiebre del 'Chupacabras,' " *La Opinion* (Los Angeles) 26 May 1996.

186. Redaccion Noticiosa, *Chupacabras* (San Juan, 1996), p. 31.

187. Cf. Ibid.; *Washington Post* 11 May 1996; and *New York Times* 2 June 1996.

188. *La Opinion* 26 May and 14 June 1996.

189. For an engaging comparison of the Chupacabra as a political metaphor in Mexico and California, see Jose Prado, "El Chupacabras: From Mask of Oppression to Symbol of Resistance," paper presented at the National Association for Chicana/o Studies Conference, 1997.

190. *LAT* 16 February 1997.

191. This account based on the news coverage of KMEX (channel 34).

Chapter 6. The Literary Destruction of Los Angeles

1. Robert Heinlein, "The Year of the Jackpot" [1952], reprinted in Donald Wollheim (ed.), *The End of the World* (New York, 1956), p. 29.

2. For Dole's reaction to a screening of *Independence Day,* see *LAT* 30 July 1996.

3. Gunther Schuller, *The Swing Era: The Development of Jazz, 1930–1945* (New York, 1989), p. x.

4. Newton Baird and Robert Greenwood, *An Annotated Bibliography of California Fiction, 1664–1970* (Georgetown, 1971).

5. Quoted in T. Kendrick, *The Lisbon Earthquake* (Philadelphia, 1955), pp. 222–23.

6. Cf. chapter 7, "Optimism Attacked," in Kendrick, *Lisbon Earthquake;* and Otto Friedrich, *The End of the World: A History* (New York, 1982), pp. 179–212.

7. "The Last Man is an anti-Crusoe, conquered rather than conquering, cursed by his solitude, and sure of his defeat" (W. Warren Wagar, *Terminal Visions: The Literature of Last Things* [Bloomington, Ind., 1982], p. 13.)

8. On its film history, see Mick Broderick, *Nuclear Movies* (Jefferson, N.C., 1988), p. 2.

9. Janis Stout, *Sodoms in Eden: The City in American Fiction before 1860* (Westport, Conn., 1976), pp. 50–54.

10. Pierton Dooner, *The Last Days of the Republic* (San Francisco, 1880), p. 257.

11. Benjamin Park, "The End of New York," *Fiction Magazine,* 31 October 1881.

12. Quoted in Naomi Jacobs, "The Frozen Landscape," in Jane Donawerth and Carol Kolmerten (eds.), *Utopian and Science Fiction by Women: Worlds of Difference* (Ithaca, N.Y., 1992), pp. 194–95.

13. I. F. Clarke, *The Pattern of Expectation* (London, 1979), pp. 158–60.

14. The best, although by no means exhaustive, discussion of American futuristic novels from this period remains Thomas Clareson, "The Emergence of American Science Fiction: 1880–1915," Ph.D. thesis, University of Pennsylvania, Philadelphia, 1956. See also Roberta Scott and Jon Thiem, "Catastrophe Fiction, 1870–1914: An Annotated Bibliography of Selected Works in English," *Extrapolation* 24 (summer 1983).

15. Wagar, *Terminal Visions,* p. 20.

16. J. A. Mitchell, *The Last American: A Fragment from the Journal of Khan-Li, Prince of Dimph-Yoo-Chur and Admiral in the Persian Navy* (New York, 1889), pp. 32–33. The illustrations are spectacular.

17. Ignatius Donnelly, *Caesar's Column: A Story of the Twentieth Century* (Chicago, 1890). See also David Anderson, *Ignatius Donnelly* (Boston, 1980), pp. 67–80.

18. Dooner, *Last Days of the Republic,* p. 127.

19. King Wallace, *The Next War: A Prediction* (Washington, D.C., 1892), pp. 204–5.

20. Ibid., p. 15.

21. See London, "Unparalleled Invasion."

22. Darko Suvin, "Victorian Science Fiction, 1871–85: The Rise of the Alternative Sub-Genre," *Science-Fiction Studies* 10 (1983), pp. 164–65.

23. Garret Serviss, *Edison's Conquest of Mars* (New York, 1898; reissued in 1947), p. 35.

24. H. G. Wells, *The War in the Air, and Particularly How Mr Bert Smallways Fared while It Lasted* (New York, 1908; London 1907).

25. Ibid., p. 240.

26. George England, *Darkness and Dawn* (Boston, 1914).

27. Ibid., p. 670.

28. Homer Lea, *The Valor of Ignorance* (New York, 1909). A year earlier, Captain Pearson Hobson had warned magazine readers that a Japanese assault was "inevitable" on Los Angeles, San Francisco, and Seattle ("If War Should Come," *Cosmopolitan,* June–September 1908).

29. Quote from Carey McWilliams, *Prejudice: Japanese Americans—Symbol of Racial Intolerance* (Boston, 1944), p. 41.

30. J. Giesy, *All for His Country* (New York, 1915). On Edisonades, see John Clute and Peter Nicholls (eds.), *The Encyclopedia of Science Fiction* (New York, 1995), pp. 368–70.

31. Giesy, *All for His Country,* pp. 101–3.

32. Ibid., p. 197.

33. See Roger Daniels, *The Politics of Prejudice* (Berkeley, 1962), pp. 75–76, 83.

34. W. D. Gann, *The Tunnel Thru the Air* (New York, 1927), p. 280.

35. According to Carey McWilliams (*Prejudice,* p. 61), "The Kyne novel was largely based upon Mr. Montaville Flowers' *The Japanese Conquest of American Opinion* (1917)." Other contemporary portraits of the Japanese "menace" include Griffin Bancroft's *The Interlopers: A Novel* (New York, 1917), set in Southern California, and Wallace Irwin's *Seed of the Sun* (New York, 1921), set in the Sacramento Valley.

36. Peter Kyne, *The Pride of Palomar* (New York, 1921), p. 44.

37. Ibid., p. 269.

38. Whitman Chambers, *Invasion!* (New York, 1943), p. 90.

39. Ibid., p. 119.

40. Marie Corelli, *The Secret Power: A Romance of the Time* (New York, 1921), p. 20.

41. Ibid., p. 133.

42. Ibid., pp. 87–90.

43. Ibid., p. 275.

44. Ibid., p. 300.

45. Ibid., p. 332.

46. Beulah Marie Dix, *Pity of God* (New York, 1932). Another example of the genre, Samuel Hopkins Adams's tedious 1921 romance, *Success,* opens with a train wreck in the Mojave Desert, followed by a storm, dam collapse, and flash flood, which the hero and heroine use to surf across the desert in a small boat.

47. Dix, *Pity of God,* p. 353.

48. William Rice, *William Money: A Southern California Savant* (Los Angeles, 1943), pp. 47–51.

49. Curt Gentry, *The Last Days of the Late, Great State of California* (New York, 1968), p. 16.

50. Kevin Starr, *Material Dreams: Southern California through the 1920s* (New York, 1990), p. 137.

51. Edmund Wilson, "The City of Our Lady, The Queen of Angels" [1930], in *The American Earthquake* (New York, 1958), p. 388.

52. Ibid., p. 420. The distinctive Southern California way of death, of course, became the subject of Evelyn Waugh's famous postwar satire *The Loved One* (Boston, 1948).

53. Myron Brinig, *The Flutter of an Eyelid* (New York, 1933). Between 1929 and 1949, Brinig published 17 novels, including rich and moving portraits of immigrant life and class war in his hometown of Butte, Montana. (On the real people caricatured by Brinig in *Flutter of an Eyelid,* see Starr, *Material Dreams,* pp. 327–28.)

54. Brinig, *Flutter,* p. 27.

55. America's most famous woman evangelist was the frequent subject of satirical fiction. Cf. Ruth Mitchell, *Army with Banners* (New York, 1928); Dillwyn Parrish, *Praise the Lord!* (New York, 1932); Hector Chevigny, *Woman of the Rock* (New York, 1949); and Elsie Barber, *Jenny Angel* (New York, 1954).

56. Upton Sinclair, a notorious plagiarist of other people's plots, brought the Virgin Mary to contemporary Los Angeles in his 1938 novel, *Our Lady.*

57. Brinig, *Flutter,* pp. 151, 305.

58. Ibid., p. 305.

59. Cf. Alfred Webre and Philip Liss, *The Age of Cataclysm* (New York, 1974), p. 93; and Jeffrey Goodman, *We Are the Earthquake Generation* (New York, 1978), pp. 21, 23–24, 34, 40, 46. Cayce's still numerous followers overlook the Master's dramatic prediction of a catastrophic San Francisco earthquake to occur in 1936 (Webre and Liss, p. 98).

60. J. B. Priestley, *The Doomsday Men* (London, 1938), p. 51.

61. Vincent Brome, *J. B. Priestley* (London, 1988), p. 218.

62. Morrison Wood, *The Devil Is a Lonely Man* (New York, 1946).

63. Gore Vidal, *Messiah* (New York, 1954), p. 51.

64. Thomas and Anna Fitch, *Better Days: Or, Millionaire of To-morrow* (San Francisco, 1891).

65. Cf. R. Cromie, *The Crack of Doom* (London, 1895); and F. T. Jane, *The Violent Flame: A Story of Armageddon and After* (London, 1899).

66. Upton Sinclair, *The Millennium (A Comedy of the Year 2000)* (Pasadena, 1924), p. 49

67. See Mark Dowling, *Fictions of Nuclear Disaster* (Iowa City, 1987), pp. 2, 130.

68. Cf. H. Bruce Franklin, *Countdown to Midnight* (New York, 1984), p. 15; and Paul Brians, *Nuclear Holocausts: Atomic War in Fiction, 1945–1984* (Kent, Ohio, 1987), pp. 9–10.

69. Brians, *Nuclear Holocausts*, p. 10.

70. See the discussion of the movie version of *Kiss Me Deadly* in Broderick, *Nuclear Movies*, pp. 12–13.

71. Dennis Jones, *Colossus* (London, 1966); adapted as the film *The Forbin Project* (1970).

72. Denis Palumbo, *City Wars* (New York, 1979).

73. Robert Moore Williams, *The Day They H-Bombed Los Angeles* (New York, 1961), p. 100.

74. Carolyn See, *Golden Days* (New York, 1987), p. 172.

75. Ward Moore, *Greener Than You Think* (New York, 1947). Moore may have been influenced by the inverse plot of J. J. Connington's 1923 novel, *Nordenholt's Millions* (London), in which mutant denitrifying bacteria, accidently created when lightning strikes a petri dish, spreads across the globe, sterilizing topsoil and destroying plant life.

76. Ibid., p. 3.

77. Ibid., p. 53.

78. Ibid., p. 63.

79. Ibid., p. 74.

80. Ibid., p. 98.

81. Richard Matheson, "The Creeping Terror," in *Shock!* (New York, 1961), pp. 145, 147. (This was originally published in 1959 as "Touch of Grapefruits.")

82. Gentry, *Late, Great State of California*, p. 389.

83. Ibid., p. 370.

84. Philip Wylie, *Los Angeles: A.D. 2017* (New York, 1971), pp. 140–41.

85. George Fox, *Earthquake: The Story of a Movie* (New York, 1974), p. 71. (This contains the complete screenplay as well as a behind-the-scenes account of the film's production.) The executive quoted is producer Jennings Lang in conversation with MCA head Lew Wasserman.

86. Ibid., p. 64.

87. I regret that there is no room to discuss Raymond Hawkey and Roger Bingham's *Wild Card* (New York, 1974); Gerald Browne's *Slide* (New York, 1976); Thom Racina's

The Great Los Angeles Blizzard (New York, 1977); Chelsea Yabro's *False Dawn* (New York, 1978); Edward Stewart's *The Great Los Angeles Fire* (New York, 1980); and the 1981 film *Alligator* and its sequel.

88. Rudolph Wurlitzer, *Quake* (New York, 1972), p. 158.

89. Alistair MacLean, *Goodbye California* (London, 1977), p. 291.

90. Larry Niven and Jerry Pournelle, *Lucifer's Hammer* (New York, 1977), pp. 235–36. Los Angeles is also destroyed by extraterrestrial impact in radio astronomer Gerrit Verschurr's *Cosmic Catastrophes* (Reading, Pa., 1978); while San Bernardino and Tarzana are pulverized by asteroidal debris in Gregory Benford and William Rotsler's *Shiva Descending* (New York, 1980).

91. Niven and Pournelle, *Lucifer's Hammer*, p. 236.

92. Ibid., pp. 603, 615.

93. John Newsinger, "The Universe Is Full of Warriors: Masculinity, Hard Science and War in Some Novels by Larry Niven and Accomplices," *Foundation* 67 (Summer 1996), p. 52.

94. Arthur Clarke and Mike McQuay, *Richter 10* (New York, 1996), p. 361.

95. Survivalist fiction, of course, was already established, but it was not a dominant subgenre. Arch Oboler's independent film *Five* (1951), for example, portrayed the conflict between five people on a Malibu mountaintop after the bomb is dropped on Los Angeles. In a brutal scene, a compassionate black elevator operator, who has rescued an elderly white bank clerk, is murdered by a loudmouthed racist who also tries to abduct and rape the only woman survivor. Ward Moore's chilling 1953 short stories, "Lot" and "Lot's Daughter," also shifted the horror from the explosion of the bomb to the obscene aftermath: this time, an incestuous relationship between a Malibu accountant and his teenage daughter hiding out in the coastal range.

96. Reissued together in a "fix up" version as *Armageddon 2419 A.D.* (New York, 1962).

97. Ibid., pp. 98, 175.

98. For the definitive publishing history, see Alan Kalish et al., " 'For Our Balls Were Sheathed in Inertron': Textual Variations in 'The Seminal Novel of Buck Rogers,' " *Extrapolation* 29 (Winter 1988).

99. Andrew Macdonald, *The Turner Diaries*, Barricade Book edition (New York, 1996), p. 151. The original, privately published 1978 edition, circulated via mail order and gun shows, is reported to have sold more than 200,000 copies.

100. Ibid., pp. 160–61.

101. Ibid., pp. 191, 209.

102. Ibid., p. 209.

103. Clute and Nicholls, *Encyclopedia of Science Fiction*, p. 1188.

104. Steven Barnes, *Streetlethal* (New York, 1983), p. 75.

105. Nicolas Cain, *Little Saigon: #4 Off Limits* (New York, 1989), pp. 109–94.

106. Whitley Strieber and James Kunetka, *Nature's End* (New York, 1986).

107. James Cameron, *Strange Days: You Know You Want It* (New York, 1995), p. 80.

108. Pat Robertson, *The End of the Age* (New York, 1995), p. 237.

109. Allen Adler, *Mach 1* (New York, 1957).

110. Ann Drufell and D. Scott Rogo, *The Tujunga Canyon Contacts* (Englewood Cliffs, N.J., 1980).

111. Alan Dean Foster, *Alien Nation* (New York, 1988), p. 81. (This is the novelization of the original movie.)

112. Barry Longyear, *Slag Like Me: Alien Nation #5* (New York, 1994).

113. Howard Weinstein, *V: Prisoners and Pawns* (New York, 1985), pp. 148–49. The original *V* miniseries for NBC in 1983 was adapted by Kenneth Johnson from Sinclair Lewis's famous 1935 account of a fascist takeover of America, *It Can't Happen Here.*

114. Aldous Huxley, *Ape and Essence* (London, 1949), p. 43.

115. Ibid., pp. 66, 133.

116. Ibid., p. 66.

117. David King Dunaway, *Huxley in Hollywood* (New York, 1989), p. 214.

118. Colin Greenland, *The Entropy Exhibition: Michael Moorcock and the British "New Wave" in Science Fiction* (London, 1983), pp. 102, 108. "The Surrealists hoped eventually to draw from the juxtaposition of those dislocated fragments a new, super-reality, rather than a mere destruction of the old" (Lucy Lippard quoted in Jerome Ropthenberg and Pierre Joris [eds.], *Poems for the Millennium* vol. 1 [Berkeley, 1995], p. 466).

119. J. G. Ballard, *Hello America* (New York, 1981).

120. Kim Stanley Robinson, *The Wild Shore* (New York, 1984).

121. Tim Powers, *Dinner at Deviant's Palace* (New York, 1985), p. 58.

122. Steve Erickson, *Rubicon Beach* (New York, 1986).

123. Erickson, *Leap Year* (New York, 1989), p. 11.

124. Erickson, *Rubicon Beach,* pp. 13, 18, 27.

125. Robert Silverberg, "Hot Times in Magma City," in David Hartwell (ed.), *Year's Best SF* (New York, 1996), p. 65.

126. Ibid., p. 108.

127. Cf. Rosalind Muhammad, "Itching for Bloodshed," *Final Call,* 20 August 1996; and *LAT* 21 August 1996.

128. Quoted in George Skelton's "Capitol Journal," *LAT* 11 September 1996.

129. On the continuing popularity of "images of destroyed cities" in fundamentalist thought, see Paul Boyer, *When Time Shall Be No More: Prophecy Belief in Modern American Culture* (Cambridge, Mass., 1995), p. 259.

130. Ibid., pp. 5–6, 168–69.

Chapter 7. Beyond *Blade Runner*

1. *L.A. 2000: A City for the Future,* final report of the Los Angeles 2000 Committee (Los Angeles, 1988), p. 86.

2. Quoted in Paul Sammon, *Future Noir: The Making of* Blade Runner (New York, 1996), p. 75.

3. Cf. Hugh Ferriss, *The Metropolis of Tomorrow* (New York, 1929); and Francisco Mujica, *History of the Skyscraper* (New York, 1930).

4. Sammon, *Future Noir,* p. 76.

5. H. G. Wells, *The Future in America* (New York, 1906), pp. 11–12.

6. Octavia Butler, *Parable of the Sower* (New York, 1993), pp. 32, 110.

7. Ernest Burgess, "The Growth of the City: An Introduction to a Research Project," *Publications of the American Sociological Society* 18 (1924): 85–97; and Robert Park and Ernest Burgess, *The City* (Chicago, 1925). Urban ecology was resuscitated after

World War II with Amos Hawley's *Human Ecology: A Theory of Community Structure* (New York, 1950).

8. Dennis Smith, *The Chicago School: A Liberal Critique of Capitalism* (London, 1988), p. 28.

9. Mike Davis, "The Infinite Game: Redeveloping Downtown L.A.," in Diane Ghirardo (ed.), *Out of Site: A Social Criticism of Architecture* (Seattle, 1991).

10. Jim Hathcock, "Security Firms Overwhelmed by Sudden Demand for Riot Protection," *Los Angeles Business Journal* 27 July 1992.

11. *LAT* 6 August 1993 (Ventura County edition).

12. See Nicholas Fyfe, "City Watching: Closed Circuit Television Surveillance in Public Spaces," *Area* 28, no. 1 (1996).

13. Mark Ward, "Someone to Watch over Me," *New Scientist,* 20 January 1996, p. 13.

14. Ibid.

15. *New Scientist,* 24 August 1994, p. 18.

16. Interviewed by Warren Olney on "Which Way L.A." KCRW (FM), Santa Monica, 14 November 1997.

17. "Technospy: Nowhere to Hide," *New Scientist,* 4 November 1995, p. 4.

18. This is based on my first-hand reportage of the Los Angeles riot, "In L.A., Burning All Illusions," *Nation,* 1 June 1992. For an extended discussion of the riot's origins and immediate aftermath, see my "Who Killed Los Angeles?" *New Left Review* 197 (January–February 1993) and 199 (May–June 1993).

19. Riot incident and arrest figures from William Webster, special advisor to the Board of Police Commissioners, *The City in Crisis: Appendices* (Los Angeles, 21 October 1992).

20. Institute for Alternative Journalism, *Inside the L.A. Riots: What Really Happened—and Why It Will Happen Again,* ed. Don Hazen (New York, 1992).

21. Vilma Ortiz, "The Mexican-Origin Population: Permanent Working Class or Emerging Middle Class?," in Roger Waldinger and Mehdi Bozorgmehr (eds.), *Ethnic Los Angeles* (New York, 1996), p. 257.

22. The seminal study is Paul Ong, project director of the Research Group on the Los Angeles Economy, *The Widening Divide: Income Inequality and Poverty in Los Angeles,* report, Graduate School of Architecture and Urban Planning (UCLA 1989), p. 101 and passim.

23. Cf. Stephen Cohen, "L.A. Is the Hole in the Bucket," *LAT* 8 March 1993; Benjamin Cole, "Industrial Study Long on Problems, Short on Remedies," *Los Angeles Business Journal* 14 November 1994, p. 22; and DRI/McGraw Hill, *Gateway Cities Economic Strategy Initiative* (Downey, 1996), p. ii (executive summary).

24. Jennifer Wolch and Heidi Sommer, *Los Angeles in an Era of Welfare Reform: Implications for Poor People and Community Well-Being* (Los Angeles, 9 April 1997), pp. iv, 8, 11, 71.

25. Photograph by Jim Mendenhall, *LAT* 22 December 1991.

26. Wolch and Sommer, *Los Angeles,* p. 96.

27. Letter from Mike Dreebin, 28 March 1993.

28. Cf. *Los Angeles Business Journal* 26 July 1993, p. 24; and 22 July 1996, p. 18A.

29. Frederic Thrasher, *The Gang* (Chicago, 1927), pp. 4–5.

30. *LAT* 30 August 1997.

31. Repeated LAPD attempts "to take back the park," involving horse patrols, barricades, and 80-officer sweeps, usually end up trawling dozens of harmless but illegal street vendors. The gangs and crack dealers return as soon as the police leave.

32. *LAT* 19 October 1992.

33. Ibid.

34. *LAT* 20 July 1986.

35. In 1991, doctors at County-USC Medical Center told state officials that patients were dying because operating rooms were full and they were prematurely moved from ventilators. "We are being required to ration health care and at times to perform what amounts to passive euthanasia" (see *LAT* 18 December 1981).

36. *LAT* 27 January 1994.

37. *LAT* 9 February 1995.

38. Cf. Mary Jordan, "I Will Not Fire Guns in School. I Will Not Fire Guns in School," *Washington Post National Weekly Edition* 5–11 July 1993; and Kathleen Lund-Seeden, "Schools Step Up Security," *Outlook* (Santa Monica), 24 March 1992.

39. The Puerto Rican case—"the first time U.S. military units have been pressed into routine crime-fighting service with the police"—is an ominous precedent little appreciated on the mainland ("Puerto Rico Uses Troops to Occupy Housing Project," AP wire story, 2 October 1993).

40. *LAT* 22 November 1997.

41. *LAT* 26 September 1993.

42. *LAT* 4 May 1994 and 11 October 1995.

43. For the critical views of LAPD deputy chief Michael Bostic, see *LAT* 23 November 1997.

44. *LAT* 22 May 1997.

45. What follows is based on interviews with the LAPD used in my article, "Vigilancia Policial Comunitaria: Ventajas y Desventajas," *La Opinion* (Los Angeles) 17 May 1992.

46. Ibid.

47. *LAT* 15 April 1992.

48. *LAT* 17 March and 2 June 1993.

49. *LAT* 3 May 1993.

50. Interview with E. Michael, July 1992.

51. *LAT* 4–5 February 1995.

52. *LAT* 18 September 1993.

53. Carey McWilliams, *Southern California County* (New York, 1946), p. 334.

54. U.S. census figures, 1940, 1960, and 1990.

55. Michael Weinstein quoted in *LAT* 21 February 1993.

56. *LAT* 29 February 1992.

57. Nicolai Ouroussoff, "Could It Be Magic—Again?" *LAT* 23 November 1997.

58. Kevin Starr quoted in Anne Rackham and Brad Berton, "Three Projects' Woes Illustrate Saga of Hollywood Revival Gone Wrong," *Los Angeles Business Journal,* 29 November 1993.

59. Ken Nunn, *Pomona Queen* (New York, 1992), p. 177.

60. *LAT* 23 January 1997. Homicide statistics compiled from Pomona Police Department annual reports and California, Department of Justice, Bureau of Criminal Statistics, *Crimes and Arrests* (annual).

61. Nunn, p. 148.

62. Cf. *LAT* 25 May 1994.

63. The one politician who has not kept his head in the sand is Myron Orfield, the state representative from southwest Minneapolis. His book *Metropolitics: A Regional Agenda for Community and Stability* (Washington, D.C., 1997) is a brilliant case study of

how inner city neighborhoods and older blue-collar suburbs subsidize the edge city boom on the metropolitan periphery.

64. Rob Gurwitt, "Saving the Aging Suburb," *Governing,* May 1993, p. 38.

65. For a case study of Lockwood, Ohio, see Karen De Witt, "Older Suburbs Struggle to Compete with New," *New York Times* 26 February 1995.

66. "Suburbia's New Growing-Up Pains," *National Journal,* 6 November 1993, p. 2675.

67. For Hughes' shutdown in Pomona, see *Daily Bulletin* 26 and 30 March 1993; for the Valley, see *LAT* 16 September 1992 and 29 April 1994. Also Kathy Dixon et al., *Beyond Suburbia: The Changing Face of the San Fernando Valley,* report, Graduate School of Urban Planning (UCLA, June 1993).

68. "Mapping Out a Citistate's Future," *National Journal,* 23 October 1993, p. 2551.

69. See John McDonald and Paul Prather, "Suburban Employment Centres: The Case of Chicago," *Urban Studies* 31, no. 2 (1994).

70. Cf. *LAT* 14 November 1995; and City of Industry, *Factbook* (n.d.).

71. The other large batch of new Republicans come from the rapidly growing edge cities of Georgia, Florida (especially the I-4 corridor), and South Carolina. For an astute analysis of their rising power within national politics, see Ronald Brownstein, "Voters in Growing Southern Suburbs May Determine GOP's '96 Nominee," *LAT* 15 January 1996.

72. Scott Bernstein of Chicago's Center for Neighborhood Technology, quoted in Rochelle Stanfield, "Splitsville," *National Journal,* 3 April 1997, p. 864.

73. Ibid., p. 862.

74. Reyner Banham, *Los Angeles: The Architecture of the Four Ecologies* (New York, 1971), p. 177.

75. *San Bernardino Sun* 24, 29, 30, and 31 August 1995.

76. *LAT* 8 September 1993 (Orange County edition).

77. *LAT* 7 February 1996.

78. *Orange County Register* 17, 20, and 24 September 1994.

79. *Los Angeles Daily Journal* 6 March 1995.

80. *LAT* 16 February 1997.

81. *San Bernardino Sun* 6 September 1995.

82. Quoted in Mai Pham, "Another Senseless (Hate) Crime," *Turning the Tide,* (Summer 1996), pp. 41–42.

83. In this case one of the young attackers claimed to be a member of the Ku Klux Klan (*LAT* 7 February 1996).

84. *San Bernardino Sun* 15 March and 26 April 1996.

85. *LAT* 6 September 1996.

86. *LAT* 16 February 1997.

87. *LAT* 25 April 1997; see also column by Earl Hutchinson in *Los Angeles Daily News* 9 November 1997.

88. *San Bernardino Sun* 24 August 1996.

89. *LAT* 1 May 1996.

90. Interview with Mike Kirkland, September 1995.

91. *LAT* 16 February 1997.

92. Interview with Joe Hicks, September 1995.

93. What follows is based on formal interviews of prison staff at Calipatria State Prison in November 1994. In January 1995 I also spoke to several families of inmates, as well as one (anonymous) guard.

94. All statistics doubled-checked with Department of Corrections, "Institutional Population Characteristics" (Sacramento, August 1994).

95. *LAT* 27 October 1994.

96. Cf. *LAT* 6 February 1994; Joe Dominick, "Who's Guarding the Guards?" *Los Angeles Weekly* 2 September 1994; and Vincent Schiraldi, "The Undue Influence of California's Prison Guards' Union," *In Brief* (Center on Juvenile and Criminal Justice, San Francisco), October 1994.

97. Ibid.

98. Joan Petersilia, "Crime and Punishment in California," in James Steinberg et al. (eds.), *Urban America: Policy Choices for Los Angeles and the Nation* (Santa Monica, 1992).

99. Blue Ribbon Commission on Inmate Population Management, *Final Report* (Sacramento, January 1990).

100. *San Francisco Chronicle* 26 April 1993.

101. Cf. *LAT* 1 March 1994.

102. Cf. James Gomez, director of Department of Corrections, "Memorandum: Impact of 'Three Strikes' on Occupancy Level and Future Bed Needs," 4 March 1994; Department of Corrections, *Statewide Emergency Housing Information* (Sacramento, 6 January 1995); and Department of Corrections, *1996–2001 Five-year Facilities Master Plan* (Sacramento, June 1996).

103. Vincent Schiraldi and Michael Godfrey, "Racial Disparities in the Charging of Los Angeles County's Third 'Strike' Cases," *In Brief,* October 1994.

104. *LAT* 11 April 1997.

105. Interview with Tom Hayden, January 1995.

106. Wernher von Braun and Cornelius Ryan, "Can We Get to Mars?" *Collier's,* 30 April 1954.

107. Howard McCurdy, *Space and the American Imagination* (Washington, D.C., 1997), pp. 45–47.

108. "Assembling the Mars Fleet" was republished, with many of Bonestell's famous 1950s images, in Robert Richardson and Chesley Bonestell, *Mars* (New York, 1964), p. 88.

109. How the AVHRR can register fires smaller than pixels (the fundamental units of the image) requires a knowledge of Wien's law and Planck functions that might have fazed even von Braun. See Benedicte Dousset, Pierre Flamen, and Robert Bernstein, "Los Angeles Fires Seen from Space," *Eos* 74 (19 January 1993), pp. 33–38.

110. Ibid., p. 37.

ACKNOWLEDGMENTS

This book harvests the kindness and support of many wonderful people. I have particularly enjoyed talking to scientists and geographers whose ongoing research is transforming our understanding of Southern California's natural history: Paul Beier (mountain lions), Warren Blier (homegrown twisters), Suzanne Good (the Santa Monica Mountains), Ruth Harris (seismic gaps), Richard Minnich (fire ecology), Mark Raab (archaeology), Polly Schiffman (faunal history), Kerry Sieh (paleoseismology), and Scott Stine (epic droughts).

In all phases of this project I have received invaluable advice from David Reid, Mike Sprinker, and Dick Walker—three amazing minds who also buy the beer. Bill Deverell has shared generously from his incomparable knowledge of Los Angeles history, while Jim O'Connor has supplied a steady diet of challenging ideas about ecology and society. An early collaboration with Greg Goldin, the brilliant environmental writer for the *Los Angeles Weekly,* was crucial in defining the concept of the first chapter. State Senator Tom Hayden helped me see the deep social issues disguised in technical debates about earthquake safety and prison construction. Gary Snyder, wild America's poet laureate, gave me a remarkable interview.

I also owe much to helpful comments from Joe Day, Ruthie Gilmore, Kevin McMahon, Harvey Molotch, Catherine Mulholland, Victoria Nelson, Barry Sanders, Ted Steinberg, and Jon Weiner. This book was inspired in the first place by Stephen Pyne's extraordinary fire histories, and his work remains the unchallenged gold standard in the writing of environmental history.

Dace Taube, the curator of USC's wonderful Regional History Collection, is the guardian angel of Southern California historians. Alan Jutzi and Jennifer Watts at the Huntington Library likewise wear well-deserved halos. At the Getty Research Institute, Eulogio Guzman interrupted his own research project to help me search various special collections. In the quest for archival photographs, I received invaluable assistance from Alicia

Vogl-Saenz, Chief William Bamattre of the Los Angeles City Fire Department, Carolyn Cole of the Los Angeles Public Library, Michael Dawson of Dawson's Bookstore, and Tania Martinez-Lemke of the Los Angeles Center for Photographic Studies.

Brand Books in Glendale patiently helped me track down dozens of obscure Los Angeles "destruction" novels that could not be found in any library. David Deis contributed all the graphics. Kurt Meyer introduced me to the late Robert Alexander, and John Cloud first pointed out the astonishing Los Angeles paintings of Chesley Bonestell. In Dublin, Nick Spalding provided warmth and hospitality. Steve Berman and Lorna Fenenbock, sweethearts of the valley, have helped with everything.

Earlier chapter drafts were presented at the Center for Comparative History and Social Theory (UCLA), the Department of Geography (Berkeley), the Department of History (Irvine), the Getty Research Institute (Santa Monica), the Marxist Literary Group (1997 Corvallis meeting), and the Townsend Center for the Humanities (Berkeley). I am grateful for their financial and intellectual support.

Similarly, I thank the following editors for allowing me to reproduce material that originally appeared in their journals: Barbara Laurence and Roger Keil of *Capitalism, Nature, Socialism,* Hal Rothman of the *Environmental History Review,* Jean Stein and Deborah Triesman of *Grand Street,* Sue Horton of the *Los Angeles Weekly,* Katrina vanden Heuvel and JoAnn Wypijewski of *The Nation,* Robin Blackburn of the *New Left Review,* and Paul Rauber of *Sierra Magazine.*

Thanks to Margaret Crawford and Michael Rotundi. I have enjoyed the creative freedom of teaching for the last decade at the most exciting design school in the country: the Southern California Institute of Architecture. It has also been an honor to lecture regularly at UCLA's Cesar Chavez Center for Chicano Studies, as well as the Department of Geography at California State University, Northridge.

Sara Bershtel and Tom Engelhardt, my editors at Metropolitan Books, rescued this project from my confusion and self-doubt. Working with them has been an exhilarating intellectual experience that I will always cherish. I am also deeply grateful to Carly Berwick, Diana Gillooly, Elizabeth Shreve, and the rest of the hardworking staff at Metropolitan and Henry Holt.

Finally, the sweetest debt of all is owed to my wife, Alessandra Moctezuma, and her wonderful clan (especially the Duran family in Chula Vista). A busy artist, she still finds time to bring me magic.

ILLUSTRATION ACKNOWLEDGMENTS

American Geophysical Union (*Eos*): 421

Bancroft Library (University of California): 256

Berman, Steve: 60, 88

Bonestell Space Art: 420

Cardoso, Diego: 379, 385

California Historical Society (San Francisco): 219 (*Roping the Bear, Santa Margarita Rancho of Juan Foster,* oil on canvas by James Walker, gift of Mr. and Mrs. Reginald Walker); 235

Davis, Mike: 78, 133, 254, 289, 292, 299, 315, 316, 336, 342, 349, 376, 388, 389, 412

Del Mar Watson Photography: 43 (Del Mar Watson); 110 (Ray Graham); 118 (George Fry); 128 (Bill Beebe); 145 (Hal Schulz)

Dentzel Estate: 214

Dreamline Graphics (Dave Deis): 28, 89, 102, 116, 158, 203, 243, 364, 365, 370

Freeman, Andrew: 96

Frost, Nahvae: 142, 399

Huntington Library (San Marino): 13 (C. E. Watkins); 152

Los Angeles City Fire Department: 120, 121

Los Angeles Public Library: 189, 191 (*Los Angeles Herald-Examiner*)

Los Angeles Times Syndicate: 6 (Barrett Stinson); 9, 45 (Steve Dykes); 31 (Lacy Atkins); 55 (Julie Markes); 124 (J. Albert Diaz); 198 (Dave Gately); 374 (Jim Mendenhall)

Moctezuma, Alessandra: 270

Monthly Weather Review: 166, 170

Orange County Register: 263 (Jebb Harris)

Pasadena Historical Society: 224

Photofest: 278, 325, 360

Stine, Scott: 24

UCLA, Special Collections: 38, 181 (*Los Angeles Times*)
USC, Regional History Collection: 17, 106, 108, 113, 168, 232, 308 (*Los Angeles Examiner*); 64, 101, 303 (California Historical Society); 66, 70, 71, 75, 104 (Dick Wittington)
Wilson, Glen: 334, 353

INDEX

Entries in *italics* refer to illustrations and tables.